The Great Donkey Walk

By

Susan Chitty and Thomas Hinde

Copyright © 2005 Susan Chitty and Thomas Hinde

ISBN: 1-59048-215-8

The Long Riders' Guild Press 2005

First published in 1977

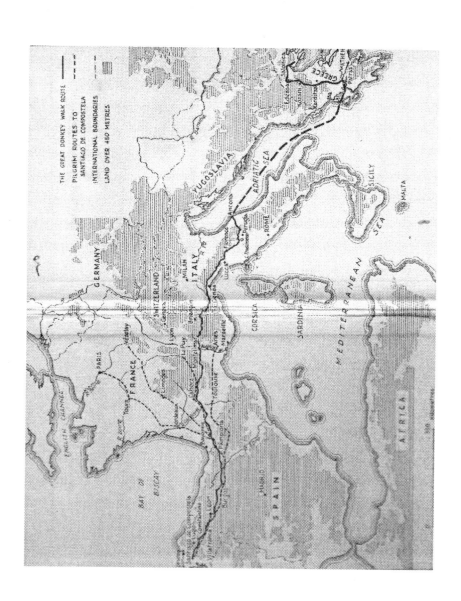

Also by Susan Chitty
Novels
    Diary of a Fashion Model
    White Huntress
    My Life and Horses
Biographies
    The Woman who wrote Black Beauty: a life of Anna Sewell
    The Beast and the Monk: a life of Charles Kingsley
    Gwen John
    Now to My Mother: a personal memoir of Antonia White
    That Singular Person Called Lear: a biography of Edward Lear
    Playing the Game: a biography of Sir Henry Newbolt
Other
    The Penguin Book of Horses (ed)
    On Next to Nothing (with Thomas Hinde)
    Charles Kingsley's Landscape

Also by Thomas Hinde
Novels
    Mr. Nicholas
    Happy as Larry
    For the Good of the Company
    A Place like Home
    The Cage
    Ninety Double Martinis
    The Day the Call Came
    Games of Chance
    The Village
    High
    Bird
    Generally a Virgin
    Agent
    Our Father
    Daymare
Biographies
    A Field Guide to the English Country Parson
    Capability Brown
    Courtiers
Other
    The Cottage Book
    Stately Gardens of Britain
    Forests of Britain
    Tales from the Pumproom: Nine hundred years of Bath

For
Andrew, Cordelia,
Miranda and Jessica

Contents

One

SPAIN

Two

FRANCE

Three

ITALY — THE NORTH

Four

ITALY — THE APENNINES

Five

GREECE

Maps

Illustrations

One

SPAIN

This health is one of the secrets of the amazing charm which seems inherent to this mode of travelling, in spite of all the apparent hardships with which it is surrounded in the abstract. Oh! the delight of this gipsy, Bedouin, nomade life, seasoned with un-fettered liberty! We pitch our tent wherever we please, and there we make our home — far from letters 'requiring an immediate answer', and distant dining-outs, visits, ladies' maids, band-boxes, butlers, bores, and button-holders.

Richard Ford, *Gatherings from Spain*

CHAPTER 1

Donkey hunting

My search for the donkeys began at six o'clock one May morning in a small café in Santiago de Compostela. An unshaven Spanish student, who had seen me alone, swayed drunkenly towards my table. He said his name was Angel and asked if he could be of service. I said I wanted *dos burros*.

"Two asses!" he said, in faltering English. "Alas, the only asses left in north-west Spain have joined the Civil Guard."

"But they told me Galicia was full of them," I said.

"There were many a few years ago," explained Angel, who had now been joined by a friend who was helping to hold him up. "Today all the farmers have tractors."

"How about the weekly horse fair?" I asked rather desperately. We had been assured that this existed and that donkeys could be bought cheaply there.

"There is no weekly horse fair," said Angel. "We have only two fairs in the year; Ascension and St. James. You might buy an ass at the *Feria de Ascensión*."

This was bad news. I was hunting for donkeys because my husband, Thomas, and I planned to walk from west to east across the whole breadth of southern Europe, starting from Santiago in Spain and ending at Smyrna in Turkey, using such famous routes as the pilgrim route to the shrine of St. James and following in such footsteps as Hannibal's across the Alps and the Crusaders' across Greece. To do this donkeys were essential as transport for our young children, Miranda and Jessica, and for the baggage. Ascension Day would not fall until May 8th and it was now May 2nd. The prospect of six days in our cavernous pension on the fourth floor was not appealing. We were sharing two rooms with the girls and our twenty-one-year-old son, Andrew, recently escaped from Oxford. Kit-bags of equipment filled the spaces between the beds and on the rare occasions when we could get into the evil-smelling bathroom the electric light switch (repaired with sticking plaster) gave us shocks.

If we were uncomfortable, poor Iago was more so. Iago was a small brown mongrel from an animal rescue centre at Haywards Heath. His duty would be to guard our camp. We had every intention of taking him back to England with us at the end of our journey and had already booked a place for him at the best quarantine kennel in Sussex. His mother had been a cairn and he had inherited her short legs and luminous brown eyes. The Spanish sailors on the ship that had brought us from Liverpool to Corunna had been most tolerant of him. So had the ticket inspector on the train from Corunna to Santiago. Not so Lolita, our heavily moustached landlady. Iago (although named after James, patron saint of the city and of Spain) had been banished to his travelling-kennel on the landing. It was to release him from this gloomy prison that I had gone out to a café so early that morning.

At eight o'clock Thomas and Andrew arrived with the children. When everyone was settled round a mound of *churros* (lengths of fried batter sprinkled with sugar) I broke the bad news about the donkeys.

"It's absurd!" said Thomas. "There must be donkeys in Galicia. It's the most primitive part of Spain."

"I don't fancy keeping the kids amused for six days in a *town*," said Andrew, whom we were employing as a tutor. We agreed that we would prove Angel wrong by finding two donkeys without waiting for the *Feria*. What did a drunken student know about donkeys?

The best method of donkey-hunting seemed to be to hire a taxi to take us round the villages. The driver could then act as a guide and interpreter. We calculated that although this would be expensive it might also be quick and save us money in the end. Our pension was costing us £4 a night and even one restaurant meal a day was expensive with five to feed. We set off up the hill towards the cathedral in search of a taxi.

The taxi drivers of Santiago are a proud body of men. They own large black Seats and decorate the dashboards with plastic statues of the Madonna, and the rear windows with gigantic wooden rosaries, decorations no doubt considered suitable in an ancient centre of pilgrimage. While waiting for fares the drivers of these sanctified vehicles stand in groups on the pavement quarrelling about football. We approached a battered version of Clark Gable, who flashed gold teeth as bright as the bumpers of his car, and put our proposition to him. After a lively discussion with his colleagues he informed us that, much though he would like to drive us round the villages, he would be wasting our money. There was only one place to buy a donkey in Galicia, and that was the *Feria de Ascensión*.

The time had obviously come to apply to superior authority. We had brought with us a letter from the cultural attaché at the Spanish embassy in London for just such an occasion. It explained our mission and requested help from *las autoridades competentes*. It was signed by Luis Villalba himself, and bore a fine crest embossed in blue with

the words *Embajada de España*. We carried it as the pilgrims carried
their scallop shells, and hoped that it, like them, would open doors
for us. We decided to take it to the Tourist Office, and demand to see
the *Jefe*.

The Tourist Office was opposite the cathedral and we were soon in
the maze of little streets that surround the world-famous shrine. Here
all was of granite. There were solid granite blocks under our feet and
fine granite arcades on either side of us, many carved with scallop
shells to mark pilgrim hospices. Jessica stopped and shouted with delight every time she saw one of these stone scallop shells. Although
she was only three, she recognised them because, at the farewell party
we had given before leaving England, the guests had come dressed as
pilgrims and had worn scallop shells. Thomas also was delayed, by
the temptation to photograph the old ladies in black who carried milk
churns on their heads and ladled the milk out in the doorways. In
Santiago the country pokes fingers into the town and there is a
glimpse of green hills at the end of every street.

The cathedral dominates the town. It rises like a yellow cliff in the
centre, demanding attention. It has two main façades, each facing a
square, but the finer façade faces the larger square, the famous Plaza
de Obbradaio. After the narrowness of the streets, the vast expanse of
the plaza comes as a shock. It dwarfs even the majestic palaces that
flank it. But it cannot dwarf the cathedral. This stands at the top of
a huge flight of steps, a baroque fantasy of pinnacles and curlicues
with pink valerian sprouting from them at dizzy heights. It is probably
the only cathedral in the world that has to be regularly weeded. The
causes of its fertility are the rain-bearing gales that come in from the
Atlantic.

The Tourist Office was housed in the Palacio de Rajoy, opposite the
cathedral. It filled a splendid stone hall with a long counter of padded
cowhide running down one side. There was no sign of human life, it
being out of season. Eventually a girl appeared who summoned a man
in uniform who, after some discussion, admitted us to an impressive
room behind the cowhide counter. In it a small man in a grey suit
sat behind a desk. His look of extreme suspicion melted somewhat after
he had read the ambassadorial letter, and he started hunting for
papers that he couldn't find and ordering his secretary to make phone
calls to people who were out. Finally, after explaining that he was the
Chief Public Relations Officer of Santiago, and showing us a printed
card to prove it, he embarked on an elaborate speech about how Galicia
was now mechanised and donkeys were therefore a rare if not dying
breed. He promised, however, to make further enquiries and suggested
that we return in three days' time, on Monday. We parted with many
handshakes, a gift of two hefty guide books, and, worse still, two china

statues of St. James lying dead in his boat, each weighing about a kilo.

The souvenir shops of Santiago are full of St. James in his boat. The legend is that the body of the apostle floated in a stone coffin from Rome, where he was martyred in A.D. 44, to Padrón which served Santiago as a port before the River Ulla silted up. For centuries the body lay in an unknown grave until in 813 a star led Bishop Theodomir to the spot, and the bishop caused a cathedral to be built there. It was for this reason that the town was called Compostela, from the Latin *campus stellae*, field of the star.

That evening we stumbled upon the trail of our first donkey. We were dining in a little restaurant hardly wider than a corridor, just behind the Plaza de Fonseca. Casimiro's restaurant is worthy of a mention. He offered a three-course meal with a great *olla* of stewed meats and chick peas as the main course, all for 100 pesetas (about 80p), and his señora was happy to leave her darning and heave the great cauldron of *caldo Gallego* (a vegetable soup) on to the range an hour early for the sake of the children. After a good meal, with an unlimited quantity of the vinegary purple wine known as *Ribero*, we told Casimiro about our proposed adventure, and he declared that it was *stupendo*. He went on to say that Pura, a thirteen-year-old girl who helped in the restaurant at weekends, actually owned a donkey, or rather her father did. We eagerly wrote down the address while Casimiro's immaculate ten-year-old daughter, Maria de Rosario, was sent out for freshly washed cockle shells for the children. There were many handshakes when we left and Casimiro's wife asked Jessica for a kiss, declaring that she was *guapa*. It was Maria de Rosario, however, who got the kiss. "I wish I could have a yellow dress like dat girl," said Jessica sadly as we left. She was destined to an unrelieved diet of blue jeans for many months to come.

Pura's father, the owner of the donkey, was called Rubio, and he had a farm 'somewhere near Santa Lucia'. Thomas and I once more sought out Clark Gable, who always kindly enquired after our search when I took Iago out to the late-night lamp post. He pointed out that there was only one word written on the scrap of paper we had given him, apart from 'Rubio' and 'Santa Lucia', and that was almost illegible. Nevertheless, somewhat unwillingly, he admitted us to the dove-grey interior of his limousine, which smelt faintly of incense. Soon we were swishing disdainfully along the tarmac road to Santa Lucia between toiling peasants. But not for long. After enquiring the way from one of these, our driver turned on to a dirt-road, and as soon as it began to climb, explained that he could go no further; he had to consider the car. We were abandoned with two kilometres still to walk, all uphill, and no prospect of getting back to Santiago except by hitch-hiking. The great walk was starting sooner than we had expected.

Certainly the track was a perfect one for donkeys. It was wide and red and lined with three-foot-high poker-like flowers of palest lilac, known as burning bush, and small blue gentian-like ones. Larks sang above the gorse and once we met a cart loaded with gorse. We were to learn that gorse, so despised in our prosperous island, forms an essential part of the Galician agricultural economy, for it is used as bedding for the animals and then as manure for the fields. A peasant once told us that there is no Castilian word for gorse, only the Galician one, *tojo*, for gorse grows only in Galicia.

The cart was drawn by a pair of biscuit-coloured *Rubio Gallego* oxen yoked to a central pole. It was of an extraordinarily primitive design, the wheels being made of solid wood without spokes. As they turned they emitted a continuous ear-splitting howl which the Galicians regard as music and also as a potent talisman against the devil. These carts are thought to be a replica of the Roman *plaustra* in almost every detail. The husband rode on top of the prickly load and the wife walked in front of the oxen to guide them.

We trudged on for another twenty minutes, and came upon a complex of wooden stockades surrounding a stone cottage. Braving barking curs tied to ramshackle kennels, we penetrated the inner yard where an old woman stood with her back to us in an open-sided shed. She was ripping corn off the cob with work-blackened thumbs and did not turn round as we approached.

Eventually the barking of the dogs produced Pura's mother from the house, carrying a two-year-old boy. She explained that her husband worked at Pontevedra, but she was willing to show us the donkey, whose name was Rosa.

Rosa stood on dirty gorse in a dark shed of hand-hewed planks. She was the largest donkey I had ever seen, covered all over in nigger brown wool. Her ears would have reached from your elbow to your finger tips. The woman assured me that she was *tranquila* and that a child could ride her. Traffic didn't bother her. She often carried sacks of corn down to the mill, and that meant passing under the railway bridge.

I asked nervously if I could try her, and an ancient pack-saddle was produced with one dangling stirrup. With the aid of a stool I mounted and sat nervously waiting for the saddle to heave under me and deposit me in the dust among the chickens. Nothing happened, however, and a shout of *"Arré"* set Rosa in dignified motion. '*Arré*' is the time-honoured command given by Spanish muleteers to their charges. It is an Arabic word, which is not surprising, since for generations the Moors were the carriers of Spain. They were known as *arrieros*, or gee-uppers.

Although I knew the word for 'go' I was uncertain of the one for 'stop'; the woman told me to say something that sounded like 'oh show!'". I tried it and Rosa obligingly came to a halt.

Encouraged by my success I started to manœuvre her among the haystacks, pulling her by her head-rope to go one way and flicking her neck with it to go the other. Finally I drew up with a flourish in front of my audience of four. (Rubio's mother had now dared to emerge from her shed.)

"How much do you want for her?" said Thomas.

"Three thousand *duros*," said Rubio's wife without hesitation. A *duro* is the old Spanish dollar, worth five pesetas. Fifteen thousand pesetas seemed excessive, particularly as the woman did not wish to part with the saddle, and did not know where we could buy one. We had expected to get a donkey for about 5,000 pesetas (£40). We said we would go away and think about it. As we left, Rosa's yearling foal called from some other dark shed.

The next day was a Sunday, and a wet one. We had been reading Richard Ford, the eccentric nineteenth-century travel writer, who preferred riding round Spain dressed as a muleteer to the 'butlers, bores and button-holders' of pre-Victorian England. His first guide to Spain, published in 1844, was thought to be so discursive and outspoken that he was persuaded to suppress it, but later he published much of the excised material in *Gatherings from Spain*, a book which became our camp-fire reading for the Spanish part of our journey. Ford warned us that Galicia was 'more rainy than Devonshire'. Edwin Mullins, author of a modern book on the pilgrimage, had however assured us that we would be entranced by the beauty of the wet granite paving-stones on our way to High Mass. Alas, the associations of wet granite were too reminiscent of wet holidays in Cornwall to allow of any aesthetic satisfaction.

Luckily the famous Portico della Gloria of the cathedral was under cover, for although the three richly carved arches were on the outside of the cathedral in the twelfth century, they are now covered by an eighteenth-century narthex. Miranda was delighted to see that the figure of Gluttony on the left hand arch was eating an *empanada*, a Galician version of a Cornish pasty much favoured by her. She also enjoyed putting her fingers into the five holes in the Tree of Jesse.

The Tree of Jesse divides the main doorway of the portico. It was the custom for newly arrived pilgrims to insert their fingers between the twisted stems of this stone tree, and generations of hands have left five smooth holes. It is strangely moving to insert one's own fingers into these holes and imagine the feelings of joy and relief of one who might have done the same thing nine hundred years ago. In those days a mere fraction of those who set out for Santiago reached their goal. There were pathless mountains to cross, brigands to encounter, and, worst of all, poisoned rivers to drink from. What dangers, I wondered, would we encounter on the famous pilgrims' route into France?

The interior of the cathedral was impressive. The severe Romanesque pillars and arches contrasted with the burst of baroque exuberance above the altar where St. James is buried. The statue of the saint has steps behind it, so that a continuous file of pilgrims can give him the ritual kiss on the shoulder. Above is a tumbling pile of figures, and, at the very top, St. James appears again, this time on a white horse, as the slayer of the Moors.

The cult of St. James at Compostela was closely associated with the great movement to expel the Moors from Spain in the ninth century. The Spanish Christians needed a figurehead under which to unite, and the discovery of St. James's grave was timely. From then on the saint made numerous miraculous appearances in battles, turning the tide of victory in favour of the Christians. At Clavijo in 834 he slew 70,000 Moors. Two of the 70,000 clawed the air beneath the hooves of the saint's wooden horse and seemed in danger of toppling off the pyramid. Their agony was disturbingly at variance with the gospel of peace that was being preached below them.

In the late afternoon the sun came out for the start of the celebrations that would reach their climax on Ascension Day. Eight student couples danced the *lechera*, a Galician milkmaids' dance, in the Plaza de las Platerias at the back of the cathedral. The girls wore full black and red skirts which revealed white pantaloons and stockings when they spun. They carried milk-cans on their heads and alternated nimble footwork with a lovely, slow, dragging step. The band consisted of a man with a tabor and three players of the Galician bagpipes, which produced a plaintive wail very similar to that of our familiar pibroch. Indeed, as we travelled through Galicia we were often to be reminded of the Scottish Highlands. Both are remote areas of mountain, heather and mist; both support a poverty-stricken but sturdily independent population; both have a Celtic past. "It is inhabited by a hardy, independent, and rarely subdued population," Richard Ford wrote, "since the mountainous country offers natural means of defence to brave highlanders."

Monday saw us once more on the donkey trail. We decided to try the barracks of the Civil Guard, little knowing that these armed policemen, in their absurd patent-leather hats, were to be our enemies in the future. The six Land Rovers with windows of stone-proof mesh lined up outside, should have been sufficient warning for us, but Thomas plunged bravely in. He soon emerged, surrounded by a group of gesticulating guards, holding in one hand a scrap of paper bearing the address of a man called Sexto. Sexto was the *jefe* of a village called San Marcos. He owned the bar there and he was famous for knowing all about donkeys.

We knew of San Marcos, for it was from here that the approaching pilgrims caught their first glimpse of the three spires of the cathedral of Santiago. On nearby Monte Gaudi they traditionally shouted with joy to be so close to the holy city.

A bus took us to Sexto's bar, which was the only modern building in a hamlet of old tiled roofs. It was large and empty and the youth behind the bar did not look like a village elder. We ordered a jug of *ulla* from him. Ulla is fruity white wine named after the river that connects Santiago with the former port of Padrón. After a few glasses we felt brave enough to enquire for Sexto.

It took five minutes for Sexto to emerge, in a suit that he appeared to have eaten and slept in many times. He was a plump, unshaven man and very slow of speech. We explained about our proposed journey and showed him a map. He appeared to go into a trance over it, which must have lasted several minutes. Galicians are traditionally slow and stupid. Richard Ford, who seldom spoke ill of the Spanish peasantry, described them as "rude and agricultural". Even so, it began to occur to us that Sexto's prime was past and that he was fast submerging in a barrel of *vino de Ulla*. The only time we got a reaction from him was when we passed on the compliment of the *Guardia Civil*. This produced a slow and charming smile which gave us an idea of what he had once been. Finally we put the question about donkeys. After a very long pause indeed Sexto told us that the only place to find donkeys was the *Feria de Ascensión*.

It came as no surprise to discover, at four o'clock that afternoon, that the Chief Public Relations Officer had reached the same conclusion.

CHAPTER 2

How it all began

What were we doing anyway, trying to walk from Santiago to Smyrna, a distance of around 6,000 kilometres even by the most direct route? Basically we were in search of adventure, a chance to come down off the feather bed of civilisation and feel the natural world around us once more. In our centrally-heated house in Sussex we had all too successfully insulated ourselves against our environment. Moons waxed and waned unheeded outside the double glazing. Even when we travelled we went by car, content to let the world pass by us on what was little better than a television screen. For a period, at least, we wanted to feel the wind in our faces and watch the night sky.

This was not the first time such a yearning had hit us. Fifteen years earlier we had driven a Land Rover from Nairobi to Capetown, camping every night of the 8,000 kilometres safari. Andrew had been six at that time, and Cordelia four. Since then we had begun to form vague plans for a journey on a larger scale, which might last many months if not years.

Unlike most people, we had no jobs to tie us down. We both earned livings of a sort as writers. But our children had to be educated, and for years preparation for O and A levels kept us rooted in the vicinity of schools. Then, when Cordelia was twelve, Miranda was born, followed four years later by Jessica, and we had another reason for putting off the journey. Yet we were anxious not to postpone it too long. A start must be made before the serious education of the new pair of children began and, incidentally, before we ourselves were too decrepit for adventure.

Thomas's fiftieth year seemed right. Cordelia was established at university, Miranda was seven and Jessica three. Andrew, now twenty-one, was ready to share the adventure with us. But we had yet to decide what form it should take. Thomas had always wanted to buy a boat and sail round the world. When feeling particularly trapped by a job at an American university, he had even taken out a subscription to *Yachting*, and used to scan the small ads for second-hand fishing smacks suitable for conversion. I, however, had no faith in the sea and was bored by photographs of families at Falmouth waving good-bye over the taffrail. It was the land I cared for and, best of all, the wild lonely places where people still lived as they have lived from time immemorial. I wanted the children to see these people before they were swallowed up by the progress machine. Thomas agreed, but pointed out that the only way to see the wilder parts of Europe would be on foot. Only by keeping away from the main roads and taking footpaths could we penetrate the true backwaters. There remained the problem of how to transport the children and the baggage. Then we had the inspiration about donkeys.

We were not without experience of donkeys. We had owned one called Edward before we bought our two ponies in Sussex. Edward had cost us £15 and had been a pleasant enough beast though, like all donkeys, he had had his peculiarities. He hated being shod and would spin round in circles as soon as the blacksmith picked up his feet. And when he entered the church at West Hoathly carrying the Virgin

Mary in a nativity play, I had to dress up as a shepherd and drive him in long reins, since he absolutely refused to be led by the small boy of seven who was impersonating Joseph.

We never used Edward as a baggage animal, but on a five-day walking tour in the Yosemite mountains of California in 1966 we had hired a coloured jenny to carry our sleeping-bags. She had done her work well, if slowly, and we had been particularly impressed by her American pack-saddle, consisting of a crossed wooden tree front and back, from which two canvas bags were suspended and then roped.

More recently, when spending a winter holiday on the Costa Brava, we had borrowed a donkey called Pascual de Portugal to take Miranda on expeditions into the hills. Pascual, it is true, had not proved satisfactory. He was a jackass, and as soon as he got wind of a distant jenny he would start to spin, letting forth the most deafening brays to all the points of the compass. A donkey's bray at close quarters must be one of the loudest noises in nature, and Miranda was terrified. We vowed we would avoid *burros padres* in future (only the violently anti-clerical speak of *padres burros*).

If Pascual had faults, he also had qualities. He was sure-footed and strong, and above all, he thrived on a diet on which horses would starve. He was the only donkey at the riding stable at Lloret de Mar, and while the wretched nags in the stalls alongside him were swaying skeletons, he was plump and perky. Not for nothing has the donkey been described as the poor man's friend. It was Cobbett's ambition that every English peasant should own one.

It only remained to decide where our journey should take us. While looking at a family tree, Thomas came across an eighteenth-century ancestor called Joseph Chitty of Smyrna and Dagenham. What enchanting images the name conjured up! He wrote to Eric Chitty, who is a genealogist as well as an actor, and asked for information. It seemed that Joseph had made a modest fortune from trading in goat's hair and carpets in the city that is now known as Izmir, before retiring to a country seat in the pleasant Thames-side village of Dagenham. We decided that we would go to Smyrna and see if we could find any remains of Joseph.

Santiago was chosen as the starting-point for our journey because we had wanted to visit it ever since Thomas, as an assistant public relations officer for Shell in the mid-fifties, had helped produce a sumptuous book on the symbolism of the scallop shell. The book had given us a romantic longing to follow the pilgrim route all the way to the Pyrenees and into France. We were vague about where we would go after that, but hoped to winter near Lake Trasimeno in Tuscany, where we could use an abandoned farmhouse in which we had previously spent school holidays.

It was a friend we had met in Italy, Livingstone Pomeroy, who had
suggested that we should follow Hannibal's route from France into
Italy. After all, he pointed out, the Carthaginian slaughtered 15,000
Romans beside Lake Trasimeno — their burial pits there, incidentally,
are the only *archaeological* evidence for his whole fifteen-year campaign in Italy. Pomeroy recommended Sir Gavin de Beer's biography of
Hannibal, a book which discards earlier theories about the Alpine
pass over which Hannibal led his thirty-seven elephants, and argues
that he used either the Col de la Traversette or the Col de Mary. Neither
pass is crossed by a motor road but our map showed a good mule-track
over the Col de Mary. We decided to take it.

During the second summer of our journey we hoped to cross Italy to
the east coast and take a ferry to Greece. Back in Sussex it was Colin
Thubron, the travel-writer, who suggested that in Greece we should
pick up the route of the First Crusade and follow it right across the
country through Salonica, Serre and Komatini, before turning south to
the Dardanelles.

Meanwhile we were stranded in Santiago with four days to wait
till the *Feria de Ascensión*. No doubt a party of adults could have
happily passed the time in sight-seeing and drinking the local wine,
but these amusements were hardly suitable for two children and a
dog. We took to making train trips into the country by day, as the
buses would not take Iago. In the evenings we embarked upon a com-
parative survey of the *tortilla*. These Spanish omelettes are cheap,
delicious and substantial, being thicker than French ones and padded
out with sautéed potatoes. No two restaurants served *tortillas* that
were exactly alike. Some were crisper, some were moister, some tasted
more strongly of olive oil, some of garlic. For four nights we pursued
the Spanish omelette through the low eating-houses of the town. But
I never became quite inured to the chore of pulling up tiny pairs of
knickers in the foul-smelling caves at the back of those places.

CHAPTER 3

Hannibal and Hamilcar

The Ascension Day fair at Santiago is said to be the second-largest
cattle fair in Europe. For generations Galicia has supplied a large proportion of Spain's meat, and now she exports to her old enemy, France,

as well. Buyers travel great distances, and think little of paying well over a thousand pounds for a good beast. So much business is done that the fair now begins the day before Ascension Day, and it was for this reason that Thomas and I set off after lunch on May 7th, leaving Andrew to take the children and the dog to the park.

The market was a vast asbestos-roofed building some distance from the town. A steady stream of vans was already unloading animals on to the terrace in front of it when we arrived. The scene was one of the utmost confusion. Great yellow-horned *Rubio Gallego* were coming down the ramps of vans in blundering rushes, canoning into the hindquarters of black and white Friesians who blocked their way. Ropes were looped over the horns of the cows and they were tugged and whacked towards the market in a semi-stampede. Pigs and kids were propelled forward wheelbarrow-wise, bleating and squealing. Plump mushroom-pink calves came in groups. One man would go in front, hauling on their ropes, another behind, twisting the tails of the recalcitrant. Where there were too many to be led, pairs would be tied together by the horns with a length of cord, since they could be relied upon not to try to stray in the same direction.

The whole of this panting, bleating, bellowing, squealing mass was funnelled through one entrance, where an official stuck coloured tickets on to their rumps. In the midst of it all an old woman led a black and white cow so sedately that it was obvious she had taken the beast to pasture every day of its life. It seemed sad that they should be parted, but presumably the cow was barren.

Inside the building the noise became deafening as the bellowing of men and animals reverberated among the metal girders of the roof. There must have been 300 head of cattle in pens already, but there seemed space for ten times that number in this cathedral of meat. We searched anxiously for the equine section and eventually found five yearling donkeys tied to a rail at the far side of the market. A couple of half-grown ponies stood beside them. They were described as *potrencas* by their owner and were probably the local breed of Galician pony, famous for its ugliness and hardiness. A sorrel mare of about fifteen hands stood beside the ponies. She was a cob-like animal, mature and well mannered.

Our appointment with Senor Armada was at four o'clock. Armada was the chief veterinary officer at the market, and we had been given an introduction to him by the Chief Public Relations Officer. Could this twentieth-century Armada, we wondered, spirit up two mature donkeys for us, and finally heal the rift between our nations caused by that of the sixteenth century?

Armada was signing forms in a concrete kiosk at the entrance to the market. He was an affable young man, dark-haired but pale-faced compared to the peasants. His spotless fawn mackintosh looked out of place among the black smocks and berets of the market drovers. It turned out that he was from Madrid, had studied in England and could even speak English after a fashion. He wore thick spectacles and appeared to know absolutely nothing about donkeys. With him we returned to the rail where the yearling donkeys were tied. He agreed that they were unready for work, but could not guarantee that there would be more the next day, as donkeys were becoming rare. They were also becoming expensive, for the price of donkeys in Spain was governed by the price of meat in France, and the price of meat was high.

When Armada had gone, Thomas and I remained gazing sadly at the two ponies, the five donkeys and the sorrel mare. The sorrel mare looked round and fixed us with gentle eyes.

"Shall we have her?" said Thomas. "We could try piling the children *and* the baggage on to her." Fortunately at this moment an elegant old gentleman led her proudly away. He had just paid 25,000 pesetas for her.

Before we left the market we inspected every van in the parking area, in case a donkey had been left inside. The job was a strenuous one, for many of the vans had no slots in the sides and you had to climb up to the top and look over. We only saw one donkey. It was alone in one of the largest vans, a poor shivering foal covered in muck. It must have been trampled on by the oxen with which it had travelled, for it had a big swelling on its belly.

I slept little that night. Because it was Ascension Eve, bands of students roamed the streets of Santiago all night, shouting and breaking bottles. When I slept, the song they sang — a Spanish version of 'John Brown's Body' — seemed to get mixed up with a dream about crossing the Alps on the sorrel cob, the children swaying precariously above the baggage and vast precipices yawning beneath them. Most of the time I lay awake and felt guilty about the sick donkey. I should have reported it to Armada so that he could have had it destroyed. I had only refrained from doing so from a cowardly fear of antagonising him.

When we arrived at our usual café at seven o'clock the next morning it was packed with students who had obviously been there all night. It was impossible to fight our way to the counter, so we had to take the bus to the market without so much as a cup of coffee inside us — not the best frame of mind for making decisions that would affect our lives for the next year and a half.

The great sliding doors of the market building were still closed when we arrived, but outside the scene was even more animated than it had been the day before. Stalls and outdoor restaurants had been set up along the terrace above the market and old women were lighting fires under cauldrons of stewed squid, and setting up trestle tables covered in grey oilcloth. Today, at least, there was no shortage of horses. Open lorries were arriving regularly off the main road with six or seven anxious equine heads peering over the side of each.

As we reached the market Thomas pointed out a donkey that had only just been unloaded. He was a large hairy animal, but neither as tall nor as dark as Rosa. His coat was the colour of the underside of a young mushroom and his white belly-fur was caked with muck from the stable where he must have spent his days. His owner was a young peasant with a pink turnip-shaped face. He was asking 15,000 pesetas. The donkey, he said, was a four-year-old, and, although broken, had done little work and was therefore valuable.

Conditions could hardly have been worse for judging a donkey. I tried to remember what one was supposed to do on such occasions. I ascertained that he was a gelding and then I looked at his hooves, which were round and solid although unshod. I felt his knees, which were the largest and hairiest I had seen on a donkey. There was no sign of puffiness or swelling round them. I stroked his velvety white muzzle and he didn't bite me. I walked round behind him and he didn't kick me. It remained only to discover whether he was trained for riding. I suggested to the owner that he give me a demonstration, but he shook his head and pointed to his best market-day trousers. There was nothing for it but to get on myself and be led about among the jostling cattle. Twice I came perilously close to the heels of a pair of yellow cows with rolling eyes, and was aware that I was causing some amusement among the drovers, but I wasn't thrown off. I nodded to Thomas who hurried off in search of Armada while I stayed astride the donkey, hoping thus to ward off rival buyers.

Armada, still in his spotless mackintosh, sailed in bravely and brought all his guns to bear on the turnip-faced peasant. Fifteen thousand, he insisted, was sheer robbery. But the owner repeated that this was a good donkey with a lifetime of work in it, and started leading the beast towards the market. When he paused Armada renewed the attack. This happened several times, and every time the peasant and his donkey set off for the market we all followed, including the peasant's one-eyed father (who urged him to stick to his price) and his wife (who carried an eighteen-month-old baby which, she insisted, frequently rode the animal). Armada's gestures became more animated as we approached the doors of the market. It was a point of honour to get something off the price, but by now Thomas and I were desperate to have the donkey and ready to pay the full sum. Armada said that they were asking so much because they knew they were dealing with foreigners. At last we convinced him that we were willing

to pay, and the deal was clinched with a grip of the right shoulder
and a handshake. Hannibal was ours.

But there were still the formalities to be gone through. First the
veterinary certificate had to made out. Armada led us to an office,
where a bored elderly assistant, who had never set eyes on the animal,
filled in an interminable form. Armada brought rubber stamps from
neighbouring offices and decorated the form liberally with them. We
were later to learn what an important part in Spanish life the rubber
stamp plays. Then the certificate of ownership had to be filled in. And
still we had another donkey to buy and, until we had done so, no hope
of breakfast.

The pens were now almost all full, and more spirited young work
horses, often decorated with ribbons, were being led in, slipping and
clattering on the unfamiliar concrete floor. One animal, a fine *palomino*
with a silver-mounted saddle, was being trotted up and down by a
ten-year-old *caballero* to the peril of old ladies with baskets who
wandered everywhere. The bourgeoisie of Santiago strolled about on
the metal catwalks above. The noise of the day before had increased
by many decibels and it was hard to think clearly.

There were several groups of small donkeys with pricked ears, but
again they looked young. I was sorry to see the foal with a hernia
there too. At least it had stopped shivering, but it was hard to imagine
that anyone would buy it. Then I spied a fat little animal standing
quietly between two pony foals. His coat, like Hannibal's, was mushroom brown, but shorter and sleeker, and he had a charming head with
a white muzzle and large kindly eyes. I sauntered past him, trying to
appear uninterested, as I had been told I should. Having ascertained
that the donkey was shod in front and therefore, presumably, accustomed to work, we set off in search of the owner.

With some difficulty we hunted him out, drinking brandy in the
crowded café. He was an oily young man with black hair and a red
shirt, obviously a gypsy. Lolita, our landlady, had warned us against
buying from *gitanos*, but there seemed no alternative. He was asking
11,000. The donkey, he claimed, was eight years old, but the rings
of white hair round each fetlock suggested that the hobbles had bitten
into his flesh for a good many more years than that. When I asked
if the animal was trained for riding, the young man, careless of his
immaculate checked Oxford bags, jumped on to the poor brute's rump
and galloped it the length of one of the concrete aisles, scattering
drovers and calves as he went. After a rapid exchange of shots, Armada
brought down the price by 500 pesetas and a second deal was made.

We named our latest donkey Hamilcar, because we suspected he
was old enough to be Hannibal's father. We tied him up outside the
café, beside his large son, and stood back to admire them both. We

were donkey owners! And the owners, it seemed, of a remarkably calm pair of donkeys. While we watched, a cart-horse yearling, which was tied up next door, threw itself to the ground and all but strangled in its halter before its owner released it. Our *burricos* barely pricked their vast ears in its direction. While Thomas went back to the pension to fetch the children and the luggage I was left on guard. Within five minutes a wily old peasant, having lifted Hannibal's tail to ascertain his sex, offered me 17,000 for him. Another, younger man, perhaps a butcher, was ·meanwhile poking Hamilcar's plump hind quarters. "They are sold," I said proudly. "I have bought them." They shook my hands in the courteous manner of the Spanish, and wandered away. An hour later the older man returned to point out the *calamares* restaurant, in case I was hungry.

CHAPTER 4

Loading up

It was three hours before Thomas returned to the market with the children. Lolita was compensated for our sudden departure by the gift of the two St. Jameses in their boats and a faltering alarm clock. We wondered what she thought of Iago's travelling kennel, which we abandoned on the landing. No doubt she made good use of the ancient Marks & Spencer cardigan which had served him as a bed.

Our next task was to buy tack for the donkeys and get them shod for the hard work that lay ahead. Riding-saddles and pack-saddles, bridles, halters and saddle-bags, all brightly decorated, hung in clusters from the wooden framework of several stalls. The crowd of customers made it impossible to bring the donkeys close, so we tied them up below, and our saddler seemed quite willing to hop up and down the six-foot wall, trying different items for size. Meanwhile the children fed stalks of green barley to the donkeys, Iago tried to get down a drain, and Hannibal aimed sly kicks at the paintwork of a car that he considered had been parked too close for comfort.

We bought leather head-collars for each donkey, hoping they would also act as bridles, as the nosebands consisted of stout chains which would pull tight. We also bought two bells of different sizes which would make a harmonious sound when we were walking, and would help us locate the donkeys if they strayed at night. Hannibal, being large, was to be the baggage animal. For him we selected a pack-saddle bound in leather and embroidered in green for 1,000 pesetas. A leather and webbing surcingle which passed over the saddle and under his belly cost extra, and so did a breeching strap which circled his hindquarters and prevented the saddle from sliding forward. Andrew bought two six-metre lengths of stout cord and a stick from an old lady who traded by the market doors, and we then persuaded the saddler to show us how to load up.

We had stuffed all our possessions into four sausage-shaped khaki kit-bags, bought from an army surplus store. These were made of stout canvas, closing with a clip at the top. They were second-hand and still bore the names of the gunners and fusiliers in the British Army who had carried them. Our saddler tied a cord round each end of two of these bags, joined them with two lengths about two-foot long, and slung them over the saddle so that they balanced each other. The other two bags he joined together in a similar way but with shorter connecting lengths and laid along on top. We were doing up the last knots when Armada arrived with a plump, heavily scarred blacksmith who was described as *herrero muy bueno*, and a rather superfluous journalist.

We hoped we had seen our last journalist when the *Monte Umbe* sailed from Liverpool two weeks ago. The efficient young woman who managed public relations for the Aznar Line seemed to have informed every known national newspaper of our departure. Bribed with free brandy, we had lent ourselves to a variety of pseudo-nautical poses on deck for the benefit of photographers from the *Mail*, the *Express* and the *Liverpool Echo*. Growing steadily tipsier in the lounge on B deck we had related our plans for the journey to newspaper and radio journalists who varied from the young and eager to the old and bored. But at least these interviews had been conducted in English. We left the privilege of giving an interview to Spanish Radio to Andrew, an excellent linguist, and slunk off to the blacksmith's shop.

It was here that Hamilcar revealed the first of his many vices. He hated being shod behind. Perhaps that was why he only had shoes in front. Spanish blacksmiths, unlike English ones, do not grip the hoof they are shoeing between their knees. An assistant is required to hold it up for them. A scrawny little man, who appeared to be a passer-by, was called in to perform the unenviable task of holding up Hamilcar's off hind. He did not hold it up for long. As soon as the first nail went in, the donkey gave a tremendous kick and sent the poor man sprawling into the road, almost under the wheels of a passing cattle truck. He picked himself up, bleeding slightly from a cut in his head, and went in search of a stick. The children, who were sitting in the ditch out of harm's way, then burst into tears, not because the man had been hurt but because he hit Hamilcar. It has to be admitted, however, that Hamilcar behaved better after that. The six shoes cost 500 pesetas, about half the English price.

At last we were ready to set off. A busy main road seemed hardly the place for the children to try out a new mount. They were accustomed to riding their own Exmoor pony at home, but they had never ridden tandem. We feared, however, that they would be in greater danger on foot, as we were fully occupied with the management of the donkeys and the dog. We had brought a felt riding-saddle with us from England. It was insubstantial but had the advantage of being flat, since I was afraid that a leather one with a raised pommel and cantle would not leave enough space for two riders. I had also been careful to bring out elastic-sided safety stirrups from England. In Italy, the previous summer, we had done a twenty-hour trial trek with a tiny pony called Picchio and it had nearly ended in disaster. Jessica had fallen off going down a rocky slope in the Apennines; one foot had become entangled in the stirrups and she had been dragged for several yards under Picchio's belly. I was determined that nothing like that should happen again.

Over the felt saddle we laid the bright handwoven *alforjas* we had bought at the market. These basic peasant saddle-bags consist of a strip of cloth about eighteen inches wide with each end doubled up to form a large pocket. They have been a tradition in Spain since the time of the Moors, and indeed their name is derived from the Moorish *al horeh*. In the old days the owner's name would be worked on the edge by his mistress. Ours boasted no such refinement, but were nevertheless invaluable for carrying food and spare clothing, since, once Hannibal's kit-bags were in position, it was impossible to take anything out of them until we camped at the end of the day.

The donkeys minced along sedately, taking not the least notice of the continuous market traffic. Thomas and I led one each while Andrew brought up the rear with Iago who walked at heel, as befitted a graduate of the West Hoathly Dog Obedience Class. Miranda sat proudly on Hamilcar while Jessica clung to her waist. Nobody cried. It was a proud moment. The dream had materialised. All our worldly needs for a year and a half, bar food, were being carried along on eight furry legs. Four years and four months after the idea had first occurred to us we were finally on our way.

CHAPTER 5

First camp

That first day with Hannibal and Hamilcar was long in the way that days are long that are filled with new experiences. I still remember vividly every hour of it. This heightened awareness is, surely, one of the best arguments for travel. Days at home pass pleasantly enough, but one is very like another, and they leave little mark behind. By travelling you make each day extraordinary, and cheat time into giving you more than your share of memories. You also, of course, risk having your days cut short, as we were to discover on more than one occasion.

The great cathedral bell at Santiago had long since boomed the angelus when we parted with the blacksmith. We were all hungry, but it was an hour before we saw an area of grass and pines between the suburban smallholdings where we could picnic. It was an exciting moment, securing the donkeys with the stout tethering ropes we had brought from England and waiting to see if they would eat. They did eat. But both spurned the fresh green grass round the trees and pushed their way into a thicket of gorse where they nipped off the green tufts from the end of each branch, daintily lifting their lips to avoid the prickles.

The sun was hot and we spread out the *alforjas* as a rug and set to work on a meal of bright orange *chorizo* (a kind of gristly sausage flavoured with paprika and garlic) helped down with coarse bread and purple *Ribero* wine. Iago, free at last, smelt out rabbits, till, exhausted by the heat, he crept under a gorse bush. There he turned round several times, made himself a nest in the long grass, and fell asleep. In the next few weeks we were amazed at how quickly he adapted himself to a life not far different from that of his remote ancestors. The first summer of his adult life, and, alas, possibly the last, was to be a supremely happy one.

After lunch Thomas and Andrew heaved Hannibal's kit-bags back on to his saddle while I held his vast furry head. He had a most endearing way of dropping his nose to your knees when you stood in front of him and letting you stroke his preposterous ears. Those kit-bags, which probably weighed twenty kilos each, always seemed twice as heavy after a good meal.

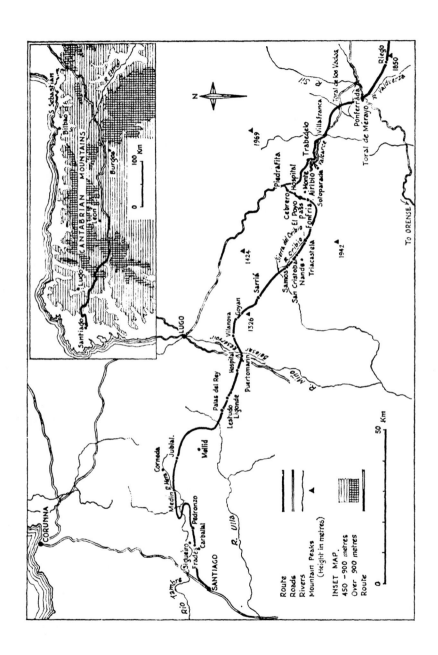

Donkeys for sale at the *Feria de Ascensión* at Santiago—Hamilcar second from the left. Below, a Spanish blacksmith at Santigao at work on him.

Above left, Miranda and Hannibal, right, Jessica and Hamilcar. Unsaddled at last, below, Hannibal rolls, Hamilcar waits his turn.

As soon as we could we turned off the main road on to a track in the general direction of a village called Carballal. Our plan was to keep parallel to the pilgrim *Camino de Santiago*, rather than on it, for long stretches of this, linking the famous cathedral towns of Astorga, Leon, Burgos and Pamplona, are now under asphalt. We were soon in open country, although a monstrous black bull on a hilltop advertised Osborne brandy. We also had to pass several city rubbish dumps and on one of these there was a decomposing sheep. I hurried Hamilcar past, hoping that Jessica hadn't noticed, but I heard her telling herself, "There was a red thing that was all bones with a funny face. And lots of shoes. Why do people throw away their shoes?"

The sun was sinking in a golden ball behind the Osborne bull when we found a patch of waste land enclosed by gorse at the edge of the track. There was feed for the donkeys and we could see no factories, although there was a sound like rocks being ground in a giant mincing-machine not far away. The track seemed almost unused, and in fact only one person passed while we were there. He was a plump-faced young peasant on a small motor bike, and we asked if it was all right for us to camp. It became our habit to camp in remote places, and only to ask permission if there was someone of whom to ask it. The peasant's reply was typical. *"Porque no?"* Why not? He added that he had seen us at the fair.

I took the donkeys back to a stream in the valley to water them, hoping that it had not been polluted by factory effluents. A friend's horse had dropped dead in the Pyrenees after drinking from a poisoned stream. We had already filled our own two-litre plastic bottles from a pipe in a wall, hoping that it was fed by a spring, but doctoring it heavily with sterilising tablets.

There was a scene of cheerful activity when I returned to the camp. Thomas had put up the tent, a Blacks' 'Good Companion', with a sewn-in groundsheet and aluminium pole. He had also built a fireplace of stones and was boiling a Sainsbury's packet soup in one of a pair of lightweight saucepans that packed inside each other. The lids of these doubled as frying-pans. Andrew was cutting broom to go under the sleeping-bags, as we carried no mattresses. Miranda was happily slicing up 'pemmican' (corned beef) in imitation of her current heroine, Captain Nancy of *Swallows and Amazons*. Jessica, as the ship's boy Roger, had been assigned the humbler task of collecting firewood. I tethered the donkeys to wild apple trees and Hamilcar immediately set to work pruning the gorse, as a gypsy donkey should. But Hannibal was restless and obviously missed his stable. He had an odd habit of treading the ground with his front feet, and every now and again he began a stifled bray, as if he had not quite mastered the art of it. Hamilcar was a more practised performer and, lifting his head and

B

opening his mouth wide, could let out a series of tremendous bellows ending in a rather disappointing whimper.

We spread the empty kit-bags round the fire as seats at supper-time and, balancing our tin plates on our knees, drank our soup. It was an awkward business, especially for the children, for the plates were shallow and the soup tended to slop. We vowed that next time we would buy wide-rimmed bowls which would be suitable for every-thing. Half-way through supper the sun disappeared behind the hori-zon, leaving us to grope our way to bed in the dark. We soon came to regard darkness as an enemy, always coming upon us before we were ready for it. Romantic evenings singing songs round the camp fire proved out of the question. Supper had to be eaten and washed up and the children put to bed while there was light to see what we were doing.

Clearing up for the night was the job I most hated. Stiff from the day's walking, and besotted with the evening's food and drink, I dreaded the incessant bending demanded for picking up our scattered possessions, and pushing them under the eaves of the tent. Frequently I would trip over the guy-ropes of the tent or crush the frail aluminium tent-pegs under my boots. A friend once remarked that civilisation was a matter of artificial levels, and how I agreed with him! Out of doors everything has to be done on the ground, and I for one have long lost the art of squatting in comfort. Crawling to the back of the low tent with the knapsacks of clothes that we kept behind our heads, I would groan aloud.

We had made it a rule that each adult should carry his own knap-sack of spare clothes. Needless to say these were soon whittled down to a minimum. Apart from a change of underwear I carried a spare shirt and trousers, 'Cosijamas' which doubled as warm underwear, a cotton bikini and socks and sandals. It was always a relief to slip my sticky feet into these sandals after a long day's walk in boots and woollen socks. We all found plimsolls useless as we could neither walk in them nor cool off in them.

There was just room for the five of us in the tent, provided our feet protruded under the fly sheet, which extended to form a canopy. We each rolled up our padded nylon anoraks for pillows and I for one took a couple of Soneryls that first night. I slept until four and then the agonies began. Andrew had collected broom, but it was not enough. I felt as if I were on a marble slab in the morgue. If I lay on my back I developed an excruciating ache at the base of my spine. If I lay on my side there was an instant pain in my hip. If I curled up, my knees were liable to dislodge the central pole or bump Jessica. She whim-pered occasionally but a few seconds of torch light seemed to comfort her. Thomas also could not sleep but whispered that we must stick

it until six o'clock. Then he crawled out, lit a welcome fire of crackling twigs in the darkness and brought a cup of coffee to the mouth of
the tent. I was so stiff that it was several seconds before I could sit
up and drink. Never had coffee tasted so good, although it was served
in a plastic mug and made by boiling coffee grounds in a saucepan
and adding condensed milk from a tube.

Striking camp in the morning was also a laborious task. The tent
had to be taken down and folded, the five sleeping-bags had to be
tightly rolled and the smoke-blackened cooking stuff replaced in its
bag. After the four kit-bags had been packed and securely roped, there
were still the donkeys to water and harness. Hamilcar's felt saddle was
not difficult to put on, except that he kicked when you put his tail
through the loop of the crupper and, like most donkeys, could kick in
all directions. Putting on Hannibal's pack-saddle was another matter.
He was skilful at blowing himself up, and it required a man to tighten
his surcingle so that the saddle would not slip sideways as soon as the
load was on. There was also the breeching strap to adjust. Finally we
set off at nine o'clock and congratulated each other on an early start.

CHAPTER 6

A lame donkey

The first full day of our walk was a windy one and took us through
rolling cultivated country. Family processions were harrowing on both
sides of the road. The wife would go in front, leading a pair of oxen,
while the husband was dragged along behind, standing on a wattle
hurdle. He in turn led a horse with a metal harrow at its tail. As each
little procession went over the horizon it disappeared in a cloud of
pink dust.

Our own procession proceeded in a less orderly fashion. We were
beginning to discover that Hannibal too had faults. As he was the
larger donkey, we had expected him to go in front but he turned
out to be one of those generals who prefer to lead their army from
behind. Yet neither did he care to be led. He was young, and no doubt
barely broken, and if you took a firm grip of his head-collar he would
either lean his considerable weight on you in a friendly way, forcing
you into the middle of the road, or make a blundering rush into the
barley at the roadside, dragging you with him. On these occasions his

top-heavy burden usually slipped round under his belly, taking his saddle with it. He then grazed for ten minutes while the whole thing was taken off and put on again. Not for nothing did Miranda nickname him Hannibal Ditchrunner. In the end Thomas found it better to leave his head loose and drive him from behind like a cow, keeping a close watch on any tendency of the burden to shift sideways. Much of the time he held it on laboriously by hand. We began to think that the old Spanish muleteers' habit of balancing their packs with stones was not so iniquitous.

Yet it was Hamilcar, not Hannibal, who brought the first day's march to a premature close. We had just reached the main road to a small town called Sigueiro, when he went lame. Not slightly lame, but dead lame. He literally could not put his off hind to the ground.

It was a moment of extreme dejection. We lifted the children off and stood staring at the cars crossing in front of us. Hadn't we been warned not to buy from gypsies? Hamilcar probably had some long-standing tendon trouble that only showed itself after a day's work. No wonder he was so fat. The only person who would buy him was a butcher, and a French butcher at that. But how did one get a lame donkey to France? Thomas brought me back sharply from the other side of the Pyrenees. "We must find somewhere better to stop than here," he said.

Hamilcar was eventually persuaded to hop across the main road to the heath on the far side. Deep among the gorse bushes we found a grass clearing. There was nothing for it but to see what a twenty-four-hour rest would do. It was a pleasant enough place. There was even a sawn-off tree stump for me to put my blue washing-up bowl on, and a bush of broom to decorate the corner where the tent was. Thomas, however, was worried about the delay. We had to be safely over the Alps before the snow came, and the first fall had been known to come as early as September. The fear of those frozen peaks was in the back of our minds the whole of that summer.

There was no shortage of amateur vets at Frades. The farmer who gave us water for the donkeys bravely removed a couple of nails from Hamilcar's lame foot and smelt them for blood. The quick had not been punctured, he said. The lameness must have some other cause. Perhaps the *burrico* was old. Hamilcar had no desire to have his teeth examined, an operation I had foolishly omitted at the fair. He rolled the whites of his eyes, but the grizzled peasant had a firm grip of his nostrils and chin and soon pulled his lips apart to reveal long yellow fangs. "At least fourteen years," he declared. Back in camp Antonio was equally ready to give an opinion on all matters equine, or rather asinine.

Antonio was a dark, wild-looking boy in ragged trousers. He came swaggering up to our camp, puffing furiously on a cigarette, an old jacket of his father's draped over his shoulder like a cape in the manner of the muleteers of old. As he could not have been more than fourteen and was short for his age, the effect was slightly absurd. Horses were his passion and he put the hobbles on the donkeys like a professional — a task which I had found impossible — giving them orders in a husky voice that they instantly obeyed. He confided that his ambition was to be a bullfighter, but that would mean going south to train, and his father did not approve. He had nine older brothers and sisters and all of them had studied at the University of Santiago. He alone was the stupid one. He worked as a hired farmhand. Before he left us he went home for an old green plastic bucket full of maize for the donkeys and showed the children how to push the grain off the cob with their thumbs and tie the bucket over the donkeys' heads so that not a morsel should be wasted.

That evening Thomas ventured beyond the routine packet soup. He created a risotto with a sauce made of smoked clams, tinned tomatoes, wine and garlic, which, as hunger is the best sauce, seemed as good to us as anything Madame Prunier ever served in her lately lamented fish restaurant in St. James's. Madame Prunier, incidentally, was perhaps unaware that St. James's Palace is named after a famous pilgrim monastery and leper hospital that occupied the site.

If hunger is the best sauce, then so is fatigue a featherbed. That night, although Andrew had abandoned the thankless task of cutting bedding, we seemed to float above the hard ground in delightful slumber. One of the nicest discoveries we made during the walk was the pleasure to be derived from savouring simple things. After a hard day's walk we had as much enjoyment from a glass of rough country wine as, at home, we might have derived from a bottle of Chateau Lafite. We looked forward as eagerly to our half hour of reading aloud by candlelight as we might have done to an evening at Covent Garden.

Our slumbers were terminated by a salvo of barks from Iago, who slept on the *alforjas* at the tent mouth. An ancient, ancient man was driving five biscuit-coloured cows straight through the middle of our camp. His face was bony as a skull and he wore plastic fertiliser bags as gaiters. Half an hour later a young cowherd with four Friesians took the same route, mounted on an old mare with a foal at foot. The foal came up to Hannibal, sniffed his nose, and galloped back to his dam with head and bottle-brush tail in the air. The mare had neither saddle nor bridle, and was guided by the gentlest tap on the neck with a stick.

After a breakfast of bread and fried *chorizo*, Thomas, Andrew and Jessica set off in search of a blacksmith who would remove Hamilcar's shoe in case it was this that was causing the lameness. The friendly farmer had told us that there was one who worked between nine and ten on Friday mornings in Sigueiro. Antonio, however, insisted that Tuesday was his day and that he called at a quite different village. As it was Friday we decided to go to take the farmer's advice.

Thomas and Andrew arrived at Sigueiro to discover that the farmer had been right but that our watch was wrong. The smith had returned to his remote home. Then began the game of hunt-the-blacksmith that was to become so familiar during the next six months. Andrew, as so often, nobly volunteered to go in search of him, leaving the donkeys tethered in the yard at the back of a barber's shop. He was away for an hour and a half, being sent off in a different direction by each person he asked. Meanwhile Thomas and Jessica shopped, and Jessica was given chewing-gum, for the first time in her life, by a shopkeeper. She must have swallowed it for it never reappeared. She talked about it wistfully for several days afterwards.

As soon as the young but gigantic blacksmith picked up Hamilcar's lame foot the donkey began to kick wildly in his usual fashion. The blacksmith then took a firm grip of the end of his nose, extended it nine inches and clamped the extended portion between the handles of a pair of pincers to form an improvised twitch. Hamilcar still kicked. Numerous ropes were then produced, the lame foot was tied to the ham and the whole connected over his back to his nose band. His sound rear hoof was tautly tied to the fore foot on the same side. Even then he struggled violently, kicking Thomas on the hand, but the black- smith managed to remove and replace the shoe and paint the heel with a scarlet tincture.

He would take no payment, for he declared he had done nothing. The shoe, he said, had not caused the lameness. It must be the result of a bruised heel. Perhaps the *burrico* had kicked a wall. Hamilcar had certainly kicked a good many things since we had bought him, but I could not recollect a wall. Then I remembered how his former owner had galloped him down the market aisle to convince us he was ride- able. Could he have lamed him in the act of selling him to us?

CHAPTER 7

The fateful Mera

Hamilcar was barely limping by the time we set off once more, but we decided he should carry no one for a day. We set Jessica on top of Hannibal's load, between the kit-bags, looking like a miniature maharanee in a howdah. She was delighted. Poor Miranda, who had to walk, was less pleased. We pushed our way through knee-high gorse with tall mauve burning bush coming up through the sea of yellow. We were making for a town called Mellid. The River Mera, flowing back towards Santiago, lay between us and it. There were glimpses of the fertile valley ahead of us, and of blue mountains beyond. Hamilcar was going well and, needless to say, before long Miranda was perched on the baggage and Jessica was on Hamilcar.

Thomas had decided that convalescent donkey or no, we must do five stages of fifty minutes that day and every day. The week at Santiago and a misapprehension about the scale of our maps had left us a fortnight behind schedule, and those snow-covered Alps loomed. There was to be a break of ten minutes between each stage, with a snack after the second and lunch after the fourth. Thomas carried the food in a large orange knapsack and shared it out between us at the scheduled stops. Everyone waited eagerly for the mid-morning snack. It consisted of slabs of coarse Spanish chocolate and oranges. The donkeys ate the orange peel with relish. We all made the best we could of the rest. The children played and Andrew did yoga exercises in a place apart. We would often see his army boots waving above the gorse as he stood on his head, restoring the life force to his heart. I lay back an an armchair improvised from kit-bags. But the ache had barely begun to drain from my back and legs when it was time to heave my knapsack on to my shoulders and plod on.

Walking with donkeys, we discovered, was a slow and exhausting business. Unlike ponies, they do not enjoy their work. They would walk rather than trot and rather stop than do either. Unless you constantly urge them forward they will turn on to the verge and start eating, which is their main interest in life. Hamilcar went best if he had the undivided attention of two of us. Thomas would walk behind, poking him periodically with a stick and shouting *"Arré"*. I would

walk in front giving him a lead, which he seemed to like. This arrangement worked well, because I too was developing donkey characteristics.
If allowed to bring up the rear I lagged further and further until the
little party had disappeared round the next bend. Then I was only too
liable to sit in a ditch and light a cigarette.

At this stage in our journey we were not following footpaths, but
striking boldly across country with the aid of a compass and maps.
The compass was a fine piece of Edwardian brasswork that Thomas
had inherited from an ancestor only slightly less remote than the
famous Joseph. The maps were 1/200,000 military ones which meant,
as Andrew constantly explained to me, that one centimetre represented
two kilometres. They were the best available, only recently released
from the secret list, but, as we were to discover, incredibly inaccurate.
Villages were missed out or put in the wrong places, and there was no
relationship between the size of print used and the population of a
town or village. The small river we reached at midday seemed to be
one of the things that had been missed out.

There was a low pack-horse bridge made of blocks of granite, but
Hannibal refused to entrust himself to this. He would put one hesi-
tant hoof on it and then back violently away in spite of active encouragement from Andrew behind. Then a young woman who was cutting
grass on the far bank started to wave her sickle at us, indicating
that we should lead Hannibal through the water. With some hesitation Thomas took his walking boots off and rolled up his trouser
legs. The water barely reached his knees and Hannibal followed
meekly.

There was a great deal of water in Galicia. "Come to well-watered
Galicia!", I muttered to myself as I splashed through the ruts, feeling
the damp patch on the heel of my left sock growing. Streams constantly crossed our path under little stone bridges or ran beside it in
raised stone channels. Sometimes they zigzagged merrily down the
track itself.

That evening we reached a village called Pedronzo which was a
Venice in miniature. Its cobbled alleys ran with water. Where mud
rendered them impassable, wads of gorse had been laid so that we
walked on a springy carpet. Vine pergolas stretched between the stone
houses and a mill wheel turned in a blossoming orchard, the water
cascading from its paddles.

Pedronzo was typical of many *aldeas* we passed through that week,
each with its central bandstand made of rough boards and poles. The
children could never resist scrambling on to these and dancing for the
benefit of three chickens and a pig. As we walked along the rough
tracks we always knew when we were nearing a village because there
was invariably a patch of smooth green turf with geometrical rows of

oaks on the outskirts. We never discovered what purpose this served, but we liked to imagine that the village fiesta was held there.

No village was more beautiful than Jubial, tucked between green hills where cuckoos called to each other incessantly. There was a decayed manor house there with a stone escutcheon on the outer wall. The great courtyard now held nothing but carts and the fine loggia was hung with washing. The wooden doors had gone from the gigantic hinges at the entrance, but doves were still alighting on the round stone tower on the hillside opposite, where some forgotten *seigneur* had raised squabs for the pot.

The beauty of the villagers, alas, did not match that of their villages. Often when we arrived at one it appeared to be inhabited solely by frantically barking dogs. These were either very small and looked like Pomeranians, or very large and looked like Alsatians. The large ones were cowards without exception and would flee from the delighted Iago, their tails between their legs. Only gradually would the human inhabitants show themselves. And when they did they were frequently grotesque, the men hugely inflated with goitres and the women kippered and toothless.

When I tethered the donkeys to graze in the copse where we were camping at Pedronzo, I was relieved to see that Hamilcar was quite sound once more. But now Hannibal had problems. The breeching had chafed his hams and there was also a raw red patch under the surcingle that held on his saddle. The skin of a donkey's underside, just behind the elbow, is soft and velvety and very easily damaged. I resolved to place the saddle further back in future, by shortening the breeching. At the same time I would raise it, since it was obviously interfering with the action of his hind legs. I tried to ignore a bald patch which was appearing on his withers.

We little knew, when we set out to cross the River Mera on May 13th, that it would cast as evil a spell as did the Guadalquivir over Penelope Chetwode on her ride through Andalusia. Our way took us first through woods of eucalyptus with naked white trunks. Their bark hung from them in festoons, and sheaths of it paved our way. Tall blue columbines grew between the trees. Suddenly, immediately below us, we saw the Mera itself, running through grassy meadows of an English lushness which were starred with equally homely pale mauve ladies' smocks. There was no path across but Thomas, trained to navigate in the Royal Navy, took a bearing with the ancestral compass and led Hamilcar boldly forward. About half-way across Hamilcar sank.

He did not just sink up to the hocks. He went right up to the top of his legs. From behind nothing of him seemed visible but his burden and his ears. I thanked God that the children were not on him — he was taking his turn as baggage donkey, to relieve Hannibal's sores.

The lush green grass had covered a bog of treacherous black mud. Thomas and Andrew splashed around, unroping kit-bags. After a tremendous struggle Hamilcar heaved himself out and immediately sank again. Now he appeared to resign himself to his fate — if anything with relief.

At this point we might have been forgiven for panicking. We might even have been tempted to hit with a stick those portions of the animal that were visible, to exhort him to exert himself. As it happened I had had a similar experience with our cob Cossack in a bog in Cornwall only a few months earlier. He also had gone in up to his belly. I knew that we must give Hamilcar time to rest. Sure enough, after three further heaves he emerged, his legs stockinged in black mud. He appeared quite unconcerned and started cropping the lush grass at the edge of the meadow. At this stage we realised that we had no idea where we were.

My memories of the next four hours are not happy ones. I sat under a dry-stone wall with the children while Thomas and Andrew scouted in different directions, looking for a way across the accursed Mera. We were on the move again, sadly retracing our steps uphill to seek a better crossing, when the rain started. It came down steadily and intensely. I pleaded to be allowed to put up the tent but Thomas was adamant. We had not done our daily fifteen kilometres. Rain was creeping down the back of my neck because I had taken my rainproof hood down to see where I was going. Miranda, whose feet had been soaked in the bog, began to cry, and Jessica said she would like to go home in an aeroplane, please. A cuckoo called heartlessly from a copse, echoing my own opinion of myself. At last, wet and weary, we came downhill again and found not only the Mera but also a good bridge across it. Glancing to our left we noticed that we were at the far side of that very same lush grassy meadow, exactly 100 metres from the point where Hamilcar had sunk.

We trailed on for another hour before Thomas at last permitted us to camp. As soon as we started to unload, the sun came out and within ten minutes our mood, as so often happened, changed from gloom to elation. I hung up our soaking anoraks to dry on the baggage ropes, the children went gaily in search of firewood, and Andrew lit a fire and arranged his steaming socks on an elaborate structure of twigs. On principle he owns only one pair.

It was at this camp that Andrew decided, understandably, to sleep in a different tent from the rest of us. He suspended a plastic space blanket between two trees some distance from the camp and, with difficulty, wriggled into the tunnel thus formed. This 'survival' shelter, as he called it, seemed to have an irresistible attraction for Iago. I once saw him dive in at one end and emerge from the other five minutes later, closely followed by my sleepy and dishevelled son. What had passed during the interval I never discovered.

As we busied ourselves with preparations for the night, we noticed that we had an audience. Two children, Mercedes and her younger brother Juan, were minding three cows and a black donkey among the gorse bushes. Both were extraordinarily fair, but Mercedes, a pale girl of about ten, wore a woollen cap and coughed continuously. She soon won Jessica's heart with the gift of a new peseta; Miranda, anxious not to be ignored, showed her how she could ride Hamilcar bareback. With a length of cord for reins, she trotted him up and down the lane, loudly lamented by Hannibal. After much giggling and hesitation Mercedes agreed to mount while curly-haired Juan minded the cows, turning any animal that strayed with a skilfully aimed pebble.

The remote control of beasts by stone-throwing is an ancient Spanish art. In the last century the stage-coaches of the peninsula were pulled by teams of six mules. The leaders were well beyond the reach of the coachman's lash and were kept at a full gallop by an able-bodied young man called a *zagal*, who ran beside the team aiming stones at the rump of any beast that was not pulling his weight. He carried fresh ammunition in a brightly coloured sash wound many times round his waist in the manner of a bullfighter.

Thomas, who had gone off in search of food, returned discouraged, after a five-kilometre walk to the nearest shop, which he described as a one-eyed bar at a crossroads. The people there were not only morose but also stupid. All they would sell him was sardines and when he asked where Mellid was they pointed the wrong way. I, meanwhile, had to give a bad report on the donkeys. Hamilcar, after carrying the baggage all day for Hannibal, was also developing a girth gall. We decided we must cut down drastically on weight.

Sadly we spread our few possessions on the ground, wondering how we could manage with fewer. No single item apart from the maps (with which we had been able to pave the entire ground floor of our house in Sussex) was heavy, but their cumulative weight was formidable. When Mercedes and Juan's parents arrived to hoe cabbages they were surprised to receive a gift of a yellow storm lantern, four padlocks, a bridle and a dandy brush. The lantern had proved useless. Not only did the paraffin bottle leak but also we were now living, like the birds, by the daylight. As soon as night fell we retired to our tent. Thomas would then read aloud to us for half an hour in our sleeping bags and for this a candle was adequate. As he completed each page he threw it away to save weight.

Mercedes' father was a typical Galician, plump and fair. In north-west Spain, we had discovered, swarthy dark-haired people whom you would regard as typically Spanish were usually gypsies. His wife was a poor scrawny creature but she had Mercedes' charming smile. She was probably not more than thirty and one could imagine that her daughter would look like her not so many years hence. We explained that we had lost our way, and the man drew a rough map for us in the sand with his hoe. The River Mera was here, he explained, and Mellid there. "Surely not!" Thomas protested. "The river is *there* and Mellid *here*." Gradually it dawned on us that we had been walking in the wrong direction. Thomas's ancient military compass was hopelessly inaccurate. Every one of the thirty painful kilometres we had covered in the last two days had been backwards, and we had ended by crossing the Mera in the *wrong* direction.

CHAPTER 8

Rain

After thanking us for our pile of unwanted possessions, the father of Mercedes called a couple of his cows out of the bushes and yoked them to a wooden plough. The plough was as primitive as anything the Romans can have used. It was similar to the one Ford had seen in 1830, insisting that it was none other than that invented by Triptolemus. It consisted of a wooden pole tipped with metal and was obviously extremely awkward to handle. Our good-natured peasant was soon transformed into a swearing fiend. Things went well enough on the straight, where one ox walked in the furrow and the other on the fallow, but at the headlands the plough had to be heaved out of the ground and there was no furrow for the ox to follow. The poor wife stumbled patiently ahead over the sods and Juan ran alongside throwing stones.

The next morning Thomas, with ceremony, threw the perfidious compass into a tributary of the Mera, where it could never again deceive unfortunate travellers, and vowed that there would be no more scrambling across country. In future we would stick to tracks and, as our maps could not be relied upon to indicate these clearly, we would ask the way to the next village of everyone we met.

Soon after crossing the Mera for the last time we found both a baker and a guide. Bread was elusive in Galician villages, and bakers' shops, when they existed, were hard to recognise. From the road, this one appeared to be no more than a shed stacked with sacks of flour.

At the end of a narrow passage between the sacks, however, there was a cluttered sitting-room where an old woman knitted behind a counter. When I asked for bread she hobbled into the room beyond, where long-handled wooden paddles for extracting bread from the oven were visible, and returned with a flat round loaf 60 or 70 cms. across with a knob on the top. It weighed two kilos and was still hot. The children devoured the knob standing outside the shop.

As we left, an old man rode up on a mare with a foal at foot, and tied her to a ring outside the baker's shop. He came out with a plastic sack full of loaves the size of ours, and slung it across the saddle behind him. It turned out that he supplied bread to the village of Medin which was on our route. It was five kilometres away and he would show us the mule-track.

Luckily the old man's progress was slow. His pony seemed almost as old as himself and her dun-coloured foal was inquisitive and often strayed. He stopped and talked about us with every group of peasants he met, and these in turn asked us boldly who we were and where we were going. Like all Spaniards, they seemed to find our motives completely incomprehensible. They could only accept the idea of walking by choice if it was for a bet. The children slowed our progress further. They had learned to quarrel on donkey-back. The chief bone of contention was who should ride in front. The waking words of each child were "My turn in front!" When feelings could no longer be relieved by quarrelling they resorted to fighting. Considerable damage could be inflicted by the rider in front jerking her head back, but the one behind had the advantage when it came to kicking. I knew that a great deal of this fighting was caused by the flat felt saddle which gave neither them nor Hamilcar much comfort. I swore that I would buy a better one at Burgos.

It was at this stage that we started to invent games that could be played on donkey-back. Mental arithmetic was popular with Miranda, and before long Andrew was setting her shopping lists of formidable length to tot up in her head. Jessica preferred the flower game, the winner being the child who spied twenty different species first. In Galicia this was no problem. The variety of heathers alone was amazing, ranging from giant white ones through all shades of mauve and purple to a dwarf variety of the deepest blue. Andrew insisted that the flowers be given their proper names. "You can't just say 'Dat yellow one'," he would tell Jessica, who was trying to score a point for a wild vetch. Stories, of course, were popular, as long as the energy and invention of the teller would last. But nothing helped the miles pass faster than singing. Luckily we had our own repertory of songs collected in Sussex by our neighbour Mervyn Plunkett, and several even coarser ones that Thomas had learnt in the Navy. It was important to know all the verses by heart, the more verses the better.

At a crossroads a young man driving a Renault van addressed us chirpily in English. He had worked at St. Catherine's School, Godalming, and was now living at a village two days' march ahead. We were constantly amazed at the number of Galicians who had worked or were working in England. Letters with British stamps were being regularly delivered at the remotest villages. The taxi driver who had driven us from the docks at Corunna had been a mechanic for several years at Mr. Day's farm at Forest Row, two miles from us in Sussex. We wondered whether Mr. Day knew that his Spanish tractor-hand spent his days off ferrying smuggled cigarettes from Southampton in a hired car.

We achieved our five fifty-minute stages that day and were satisfied to have clocked up eleven kilometres when we camped on a high and blasted heath under a louring sky. We were still walking over heathland the next day when the rain came. This was not just a prolonged shower like the one that had drenched us the day Hamilcar went into the bog. It was a continuous downpour that went on hour after hour after hour. Having now experienced the discomforts of extreme heat and extreme cold I can firmly announce that neither is anywhere near as bad as extreme wet when on the march. It is true that we were prepared for rain. We had lightweight nylon anoraks that were, anyway to begin with, waterproof, and trousers of a similar material, which, according to Andrew's Oxford Dictionary, are correctly described as antigropelos. But we had not learnt the art of putting up a tent in a rainstorm without getting the tent floor, and most of the things that went inside, soaked.

This, alas, was what happened when we were finally forced to a halt still some kilometres short of Mellid. The site was pleasant enough: a moorland slope overlooked a tree-filled valley where cuckoos called. But we had little heart to appreciate it as we sat huddled in our wet, crackling armour, while the rain pattered on the canvas roof close above our heads. Once a very old man, who was cutting gorse with a sickle, looked in at the mouth of the tent. He accepted a cigarette, squatting on his haunches and surveying us with interest. His clothes were in rags but his frayed shirt was spotless. He announced proudly that he was eighty-three, and he appeared to be unaware of the rain. Perhaps, in Galicia, that is the only way to be. Inspired by his example, Andrew spent the last hours of daylight sitting in front of a little heap of smoking birch bark, trying to blow it into a flame. In his dripping Australian bush hat and brown oilskins running with water, he was almost as strange a figure as the old man. All he had achieved by nightfall was fingers as brown as a hardened smoker's. We resigned ourselves to a bread-and-cheese supper and a night in damp sleeping-bags. It rained all night and in the morning the donkeys were a sorry sight, their curly wool coats sodden. Hamilcar was actually shivering. He obviously needed food and shelter. The Spanish do not feed oats to their beasts. The traditional fodder is *paja y cebada*, chopped straw mixed with barley. Andrew and I set off with the donkeys in search of *cebada*. We were now to learn something of the poverty of Galicia, a land where Wellington complained that campaigning was impossible for there was nothing for man or beast to eat.

The first farmhouse we called at was a wretched place, though no more wretched than its neighbours. Most of them had so many broken windows and so few curtains that one could only tell whether they were inhabited from the state of the vegetable garden. No attempt was made to beautify them with a vine or even a patch of marigolds. Occasionally, however, they sported a great square chimney with a little steeple on each corner, or a row of cork beehives on a balcony.

At this particular house an unshaven man leaned over the lower half of his front door. Behind him, in the dusty cobbled passage, a crone with one tooth peered. I asked if I could buy barley. There was none. What had we paid for the donkeys, he asked, and, suitably horrified, declared that the *burricos* would not be worth *one* thousand by the time we got them to France unless we fed them maize. No, he had no maize either. For that one must go to the mill at Corneda two kilometres up the road.

We called at each farm we passed on the way to Corneda, trudging across muddy farmyards and being refused corn by the sullen and suspicious inhabitants. These Galicians were as dour as proverbial Scots. In our dirty rain-sodden condition we looked, no doubt, like dangerous mendicants, and the dogs barked accordingly, circling us and sniffing our legs though never actually biting.

In defence of the Galicians I must add that, four days later, we had a very different reception at a farm further from the road. The farmer and his family, who shared their smoke-blackened ground floor with their cows, brought chairs into the yard for us and insisted on plying not only us but Miranda with iced beer. Even the donkeys were given cut grass. Miranda became exceedingly tipsy and giggly and some time later confessed to feeling 'rather unwell'. But I am looking ahead. On this occasion even the mill was closed to us. When we reached it, the miller was out and his wife, a bedraggled drudge in trousers, said she could not serve us in his absence. She advised up to go to Mellid, where you could buy *de todo*. There was a bus at five o'clock.

Although there was no food for beasts at Corneda there was a typically primitive *tienda*. A *tienda* is one up on a *taverna*, which sells drinks exclusively and can often only be distinguished from a cowshed by the plastic crates of empty bottles outside. This *tienda* was dark and dusty and in the gloom two men stood drinking *aguardiente*, a kind of *anis*, at the counter. The owner was an old woman in black. I went through the familiar motion of scanning the bare wooden shelves behind her for anything other than tinned sardines and washing powder. In the end I selected biscuits, matches, wine, and four tins of *calamares*, or squid cooked in it own ink. Then began the adding up. The woman wrote down the price of each item in large uncertain figures on a scrap of paper and then stared blankly at them. After some minutes she slowly wrote three further figures on the paper and passed it to one of the drinkers. He passed it to his friend, and after some discussion they decided that she had made a mistake and passed it back to her. This time she stared even longer at the sum before finally changing one figure and getting it right. These interminable calculations became familiar in Galicia. At one shop the woman, after a fruitless struggle, led Thomas to her husband's sickroom. A wasted invalid, lying on his back in a crumpled bed, he tried to do the adding up for her, till his biro gave out and Thomas did it himself.

The sun was out by the time we returned to the camp and Hamilcar had stopped shivering. The sleeping-bags had been spread out to dry and Miranda, Jessica and Iago had gone to dam the stream. We lunched and slept in the sun and then Thomas and I set off gaily to catch the bus to Mellid. After the peasant's dreadful predictions about the donkeys I was determined they should have barley before nightfall.

It was a strange sensation to move along on cushioned seats above wheels again. The green countryside went past so effortlessly. The sensation, I had to admit to myself, was delightful, though funnily enough I never felt envious of the people in cars who passed us when we were walking, even when things were at their worst.

As we arrived in Mellid the sky once more opened. The town was probably not beautiful at the best of times, although it was built on Celtic foundations and boasted two pilgrim churches. In the rain it was a depressing place. Groups of men stood around under umbrellas and there were loaded ponies tied up in the unpaved side-streets. We were soon, however, to discover that there was something very extraordinary about Mellid, and that was the shops. They had not changed for a century. I had only once before in my life walked through a door and immediately been transported back a hundred years in time. The place had been a small town in Nevada called Tonopar, and the establishment a saloon. Cowboys played poker under murals of Edwardian nudes and a plump *décolleté* pianist entertained them behind a hedge of potted palms. The draper's shop at Mellid was no less remarkable. Shelves of printed cottons rose to the ceiling, the higher ones being reached by a wooden gallery. A row of old ladies sat sewing behind a mahogany counter. They looked pale compared to the peasants to whom we were accustomed, but they were extremely friendly. They said they had heard about us on television.

The grocer's next door was equally amazing. Hams hung from the high, beamed roof and flour was stored in an oak chest with a wooden scoop for serving. There was a puddle of rain on the stone flagged floor, but the service ranked with that of Fortnum's. The proprietor himself, a bald middle-aged man in a white apron, attended to our needs. When we asked for chocolate he laid a sample of every brand in his stock on the counter before us, explaining that what we were asking for was in fact drinking chocolate, *chocolate de taza*. We did not mention that we were in the habit of omitting the *taza*. He particularly recommended a brand called *La Perfection*. He also had large juicy raisins, a delicacy we had sought in vain even in the larger villages. Each item was wrapped separately and, as we left, the proprietor held the door open for us and bowed us out.

Laden with a three days' supply of food, we wandered through the rain in search of a seed merchant who would sell us barley for the donkeys. A plump slut, with stockings rolled to her knees, saw us hesitating outside her shop and lured us in. She was cheerful and unscrupulous and reminded me strongly of one of our less satisfactory chars in England. She sold us a delicious home-made cheese, round, flat and creamy, and to compensate for having grossly overcharged us, locked up her shop and led us all the way to the corn warehouse in spite of the rain.

CHAPTER 9

Hail

A purple patch on the map meant that the dreaded Sierra del Oribio, a section of the Cordillera Cantabrica, was looming ahead. Our need for a post office was becoming acute. Thomas had films to send to the *Observer* and Andrew was suffering from the weight of two unwanted but much-loved books. One was about dental hygiene and was called *The Tooth Trip*, and the other was Adelle Davis's *Let's Eat Right to Keep Fit*.

These two books had haunted us since before we left England. At Charles and Blue Hodgson's house in Chelsea, where we had spent

the night before embarking, Andrew had sat up all night attempting
to transfer their contents to his private compendium. This compendium is a thick file containing all the knowledge he considers useful,
from the thoughts of Chuang Tzu to methods of telling the time by
the sun and collecting water in the desert. As his writing is minuscule
(all but his youngest relations have to read his letters through a
magnifying glass) a very great deal of information is stuffed into
it.

By the time we reached Liverpool Andrew was ready to post the
books, but there was no post office at the docks. Somehow he forgot
to despatch them at Santiago and it was when we were on the road
that the real trouble began. Village postmasters firmly refused to
accept even the smallest foreign parcel and our route was designed to
avoid towns. At Mellid the post office had been shut. The books posed a
problem not only of weight but of volume. Andrew has a theory that
the human frame is designed to carry a pack very high on the shoulders.
To make this possible it must be small and the shoulder straps short.
Accordingly he had only brought with him an army pack the size of a
school satchel, with straps so short that he had to lie on his back to
put it on. There was no room for the books in it and he had to carry
them in a red plastic bag, offensive both to his colour scheme and
whichever donkey he was leading.

We reached Palas del Rey after three days of walking over the gorse-
covered uplands above Mellid, but again the post office was shut. It
was a Sunday. As we wound our way up the long main street we looked
at our reflections in the windows of the closed shops. Certainly we were
a strange sight: the children humped like monkeys on their ass,
Thomas with his smoke-blackened khaki anorak hanging almost to his
knees and me with my scarecrow hat and the blue plastic washing-up
bowl hanging from my back.

Palas del Rey, like Mellid, was on the pilgrim route and boasted a
Romanesque church but no palace, apart from a *palais de dance*, doing
good business, judging from the empty bottles outside. Drizzle was
falling once more and we hadn't the heart to get much beyond the
campo de futbol to camp. Rain fell all night but it stopped in time
for us to roll up the sodden tent in the morning and leave in thick
cloud. The first kilometre was along the main road and, for the first
time, I was glad of the vulgar 'day-glo' orange of Thomas's knapsack,
which I had secretly regarded as fit only for a German hitch-hiker. It
might be visible to the juggernauts that loomed continuously behind us
with their lights on.

When we turned on to the cart track to the remote villages of Lestudo
and Ligonde, we left the twentieth century behind and plunged instantly into the fifteenth. It was market day at Palas and we met a

succession of people on their way to market. First came an old woman with a pig, then a man with two sheep walking primly in front of him like poodles, and finally a whole family in an ox-cart spread with shawls. A muzzled calf walked behind the cart. Everyone was wearing best clothes in spite of the mud and the mist.

We camped at Hospital on a high sunlit heath from which we had our first view of the snow on the Sierra del Oribio. Thomas and Andrew spread out the maps.

"Thirty-five kilometres along a ridge at 1,000 metres," said Thomas exultantly.

"And not a sign of a village," said Andrew with equal delight. I could only think how much I wanted a bath. I had not had one since we left Santiago twelve days ago. After sleeping in my clothes for so many nights I felt sticky and uncomfortable and was sure I was not nice to be near. Soon there would be no way of distinguishing me, physically and perhaps even morally, from a gypsy or a bomb-site derelict. There was a stream near the camp, and I laboriously scooped water into a bowl and transferred it to a saucepan on the fire. When it was hot I tipped it back into the bowl, filling my eyes with smoke and burning my fingers in the process. Then I retired modestly behind a gorse bush with my sponge bag, only to discover that I had left the towel under the eaves of the tent. When I returned, Hannibal, who had refused water at the stream, had drunk every drop of my hot water. He was a donkey who liked home comforts. I compromised crossly by washing my hair in cold water.

That night a young moon no thicker than a paring of a thumb nail hung above the snows of the Oribio, beckoning us forward. In the morning the mountains sent out a less friendly message. Their peaks were wrapped in a great black cloud from which Jove was hurling shafts of lightning. We had a brief quarrel about anoraks and anti-gropelos.

"They're so hot," said Thomas.

"The Lugo newspaper says fine weather," said Andrew. We had now crossed from the province of Corunna into the province of Lugo, a large town we were avoiding.

"But look at the lightning," I protested as it crackled on the horizon. We had been going about ten minutes along the main road to the bridge at Puertomarin when Thomas yelled, "Waterproofs!" It was too late. We were still tugging the children's leggings over their wellingtons when the storm burst with a deafening crash over our heads, turning day into night and drenching us in an instant. I pride myself on being brave about thunderstorms, although a craven ninny about wasps and dentists. This time, I freely admit, I panicked, and in front of the children. It was because of the sickle I carried on my back under the blue plastic washing-up bowl. I became convinced it would attract the lightning, which seemed to be snaking in and out of our legs like a demented firecracker.

"Take it off!" I yelled, howling like a banshee. "I only came on this bloody expedition because sailing round the world would have been w-o-o-o-rse!"

Then the hail started. Cone-shaped stones two centimetres across were being hurled in our faces with the force of gunshot. The donkeys firmly turned their rumps towards it and we did the same. I held Jessica in front of me. The gutter in which we were standing was soon piled high with chunks of ice large enough for a whisky on the rocks. There was no sign of Miranda. I discovered afterwards she had weathered the storm in a ditch, clutching Iago and singing 'The Jolly Ploughboy'. Neither of the children showed any sign of fear.

The storm vanished as quickly as it had come. From now on it was downhill all the way to the bridge at Puertomarin. We covered the distance without mishap, except that once Hamilcar shied and dumped both the children, howling, on the ground. Andrew's red plastic bag, which he had left beside the road for a moment, had finally had the effect I had long forecast and we vowed we would post it at Puertomarin, come what might. The sun was now out; the black road steamed and the red soil ran in rivers of Heinz tomato soup down the gutters. We sat on a felled pine tree and peeled off our antigropelos. The trousers underneath them were sodden with sweat. We agreed that the man who invents waterproofs that are not also airtight will be a true benefactor to humanity. There was a lorry ahead of us collecting milk. The production of each farm was pathetically small. A churn or a couple of open plastic buckets was often all that stood beside the road. The standard of hygiene would have made an official of the Milk Marketing Board weep.

The Belesar reservoir was in a deep cleft between the hills and was not visible until we were almost upon it. This vast artificial lake was formed by damming the Miño, a river that cuts Galicia in two vertically and debouches into the Atlantic at the Portuguese border. To the lover of the past it is a sad place, for the waters have risen to engulf the old town of Puertomarin, one of the most picturesque on the pilgrim route. Among the honeycomb of mud-covered ruins on the shore are the remains of the pilgrim hospital built by Pedro Peregrino in 1126. The traces of his bridge are also visible. The old church has been reconstructed, stone by stone, in the new town of Puertomarin on the hill above. To us it looked uninviting, and when we discovered that the post office was, of course, shut we decided to pass below it.

The climb out of the valley of the Miño next morning was but a foretaste of the climbs that lay ahead, but the peak of nearly 900 metres was higher than any in England. We rose slowly above the cloud, so that by the time we made our first stop we were able to look down on a sea of white. As we watched, the old pilgrim church at Puertomarin appeared above the swirling whiteness. Our reward, after a hot and exhausting struggle to the top, was a close-up of *las obras*, the television tower under construction near Vilanova. It was sad to see so lovely a place desecrated by something that could only lead to further pollution, for surely the chief effect of television on the peasants would be to persuade them to buy more things that come in bottles and plastic containers. At present the Spanish countryside, unlike the Italian, is amazingly free of these. Plastic fertiliser bags alone offended our eye, and these, it must be admitted, we found useful. Our kit-bags fitted neatly inside them and could thus be partially waterproofed.

By the time we had accomplished the steep descent into the village of Goyan we were so exhausted that we could hardly leave our chairs in the little shop for long enough to order provisions for the next three days (our usual habit when in a well-supplied shop). It was satisfactory to see the shopkeeper stretch his eyes when he heard we had come 100 kilometres on foot from Santiago, and had climbed the nearby mountain. He could not resist pointing out, however, that if we had taken the *carretera*, we need not have climbed at all. We drank two Fantas each and watched a group of workers from *las obras* having their lunch. Hunks of bread, raw ham and *chorizo* were followed by a rich red stew which they ate with their fingers, popping complete sausages into their mouths. The whole was washed down with many glasses of wine with *gaseosa* (fizzy lemonade), and followed up with cigars and brandy round a card table. How different from the lunch of our British workmen!

Although we, also, were tempted to eat, we knew that, filled with food, we would never get our aching bodies in motion again. We were well clear of the village before we found a camp site. It was a small gorse-edged field with a stone wall round it. Thomas put up the tent and handed out lunch. With my mouth still full of bread and cheese I fell asleep with my old blue denim hat over my face. It seemed only a few seconds later that I was awakened by a surly growl. A hideous toothless head, with a beret stuck on its side like a fungus, was staring down at me from the top of the wall. It informed me that we were camping on its cow pasture. In vain I pleaded for the exhausted children (meaning the exhausted mother). Every stick of our chattels, which by now were spread over many square metres like the aftermath of a car accident, had to be man-hauled to a patch of common ground on the other side of the road.

The day, however, ended happily. The common ground was paved with turf as smooth as a vicarage lawn and there were pines from which to string the washing. Two charming girls called Aurelia and Pilar led me and the donkeys to a fern-fringed spring. I was constantly to be amazed at how rosy-cheeked and well dressed were the Galician children, however shabby their parents. Their education also was evidently well taken care of. The only ugly building in any village was the school, a grey barracks. Galician schoolboys on their way to it in the mornings looked extraordinarily Victorian with their great farm boots and their umbrellas.

Pilar, the older of the two girls, accompanied me back to camp. There a charming sight met our eyes. Andrew, with Jessica in his lap, was giving her her daily reading lesson, stopping occasionally to wonder at the excruciating *chirrico* made by the solid wheels of an ox-cart passing down the lane. This was the time of day when he always taught the children. Jessica was learning to read and write from scratch. Her text book was Volume 1a in the Ladybird Reading Scheme series. Miranda had brought a mathematics textbook from West Hoathly Primary School with her. Answering questions from this and writing the diary of her journey largely constituted her education that summer.

While Andrew taught the children I usually wrote my diary. I was the chronicler of the trip, and it was essential to describe the places we passed through before the memory of them either vanished or became a jumble in my mind. Often in the future we were to ask each other questions like "Where was the camp where the one-eyed shepherd warned us of wolves?" Only the diary could tell. I used to write it some distance from the camp, so that I could not hear the children quarrelling. The pack-saddle served me for a back rest, and Iago and Felipe II (a cheap vanilla-flavoured brandy) kept me company. The delicious smell of dinner being cooked by Thomas would eventually woo me back to the camp fire.

On this particular evening we had *migas*, a kind of home-made bread that we resorted to when none could be had in the shops. Although classic *migas* requires breadcrumbs, it can also be made by frying a mixture of flour, oil and water, and is regarded as a great delicacy in the poorer parts of Spain. The sun was sinking in a red ball behind a hill green with barley as Thomas distributed the last fragrant panful. Iago sat up among the sleeping-bags and yawned anxiously. He had lain like the dead all afternoon, but he always knew when it was time for his supper.

He was proving a first-rate walker in spite of his short legs, and never faltered throughout the long, hot mornings. As the sun rose his shadow dwindled from the size of a porcupine to the size of a rat. If we walked twenty kilometres, he covered a hundred, for most of his walking was done in circles. Yet he knew how to conserve his energy.

When we stopped for a rest he would flop down as if dead. He never passed a stream without drinking from it. What he most enjoyed was a muddy puddle through which he would wade, belly deep, to cool his large paws, lapping as he went. At night he curled up like a football in the mouth of the tent and didn't uncurl until the sun was well up. Then he would go inside for a game with the children, who greeted him with cries of joy except on the days when he had rolled in pig manure. One morning I found two somnolent heads emerging from one sleeping bag. One was Miranda's and the other Iago's.

Sarriá, which we reached next morning, is famous for its church, its castle and the Convent of the Merced. For us it was the place where we finally found a post office and where Jessica started to itch. The post office was up a flight of dark wooden stairs in the old part of the town. To our amazement the ancient clerk behind the grille, guarded by an armed *Guardia Civil*, refused to accept our parcel of films because it was *too small*. While we were repacking this I noticed that Jessica had begun to scratch violently underneath her oilskins. I rolled up her tiny antigropelos to reveal a leg patterned with raised white patches like the continents on a relief map. They had pink edges and reminded me horribly of some eruptions Thomas had had when suffering from food poisoning in the south of Italy in 1953. I was about to rush her to the local hospital, if there was one, when I noticed that, with the hand that wasn't scratching, she was cheerfully sucking a lollipop (a gift from the saddler's wife). Perhaps after all this was a problem we could solve ourselves.

We hurried back to the suburban garden where Andrew was reading *The Meaning of the Quran* with the donkeys and stripped Jessica to her underpants. She was an alarming sight, blotched from head to foot. Needless to say the medicine box was at the bottom of the most tightly packed of the kit-bags. But there, amid tins of codeine phosphate tablets (for stomach upsets) and broad-spectrum antibiotics (for everything) was Miranda's phial of allergy tablets. We administered half of one, so small that it was barely visible. By the time we reached Samos, with its massive monastery and library, Jessica's skin was back to its usual tawny gold.

CHAPTER 10

Frost

As Jessica's condition improved, mine began to deteriorate. The sight of the great blocks of La Perfection drinking chocolate that Thomas had offered us before we left Sarriá now nauseated me. To my surprise the children also refused them. I began to wonder whether the choco-late de taza might not be the cause of Jessica's troubles and my own. Richard Ford had warned us that, even in its liquid form, Spanish chocolate was so thick that you could stand a spoon in it. It had been so concocted to circumvent the Church's laws of fasting. It was advis-able, he said, to follow it with a glass of water 'for the sake of the liver'.

Walking was becoming a painful effort now, and my throat was so dry that I thought I would suffocate. I cursed myself for not buying boiled sweets to suck in Sarriá, but Thomas assured me a pebble would do just as well. Finding no comfort without, I took refuge in fantasy. I had two favourite walking daydreams into which I retired when things were bad. One I called 'vin d'honneur'. In this, I was being received as a heroic walker in the place of some French town. Trestle tables had been decorated with tricolour bunting and the mayor was proposing my health in champagne. I rose to make a speech in reply, looking ravishing in a silk dress that displayed my sun-tanned legs. It was, however, into the other, called 'the hospital', that I retired now. It centred round a bed of spotless purity. The sheets of this bed had been freshly ironed and a corner turned down for my reception. Be-tween these cool sheets I, also newly washed and wearing a white cotton nightie from the hospital linen cupboard, gratefully slid. A gentle voice murmured, "I'll bring you something light on a tray after you've had a little sleep, dear."

By midday even the hospital dream was of no further avail, and, protesting that I could not take another step, I flopped by the bridle-path, refusing to move. I slept all afternoon and in the evening crawled into the tent with an interminable novel by Trollope, an author who can always persuade me I'm somewhere nicer. In the morning I still felt vile. I lay in my sleeping-bag moaning that it was no good, I wasn't a walker, I must have a pony. Meanwhile Thomas stripped the fly-sheet from the top of the tent. But when I continued to lie like a stone crusader on a tomb with Iago at my feet he realised it was useless to goad me further and announced a day off.

That stolen day was one of unalloyed happiness for all of us. We vowed that in future we would have a day of rest every ten days come what might. I had chosen to collapse in a beautiful place, a glade between the villages of San Cristobal and Nande. The grass was velvety under the trees and below us was the green valley of the Rio Oribio, a tributary of the Sarriá, laced with stone watercourses and fragrant with cow parsley. Everyone except me was quietly occupied. Thomas repaired Hamilcar's saddle with an awl made for him by Mr. Townsend, the saddler at East Grinstead. Andrew darned his only shirt, a khaki one given him by an untouchable in Delhi, and the children rehearsed for a performance of *Red Riding Hood*, with Iago cast as the wolf. A dusky peasant woman led her cows past at three-hourly intervals, her eyes a startling blue under the load of fodder she carried on her head.

As I lay in a sun-warmed trance I heard Andrew talking to Thomas. "We're not going to get her to the Pyrenees unless we lighten her load," he was saying. "And she's absolutely hopeless when it's hot." For a moment I was confused. Surely he knew the donkeys were geldings. Then I realised he was talking about *me*. "We must take off her knapsack and get her walking the minute it's light. That way we should be in camp before she starts to wilt." My son, not so long since cooing in his cradle, was bringing his cool, Oxford-trained mind to bear on my shortcomings. It was an odd sensation.

We spent the evening preparing for a lightning start the next day. All our knapsacks were ready packed and Miranda made a list of morning duties for each of us. Mine read: "Roll up sleeping-bags. Saddle Hannibal." Hamilcar entered into the spirit of the thing and woke us with a series of deafening brays at 4.30 a.m. because Hannibal had been tethered where he couldn't see him. It was dark and close to freezing and to save time we had cold coffee, promising ourselves a hot cup at the first café we passed on the road. The last thing to be packed, or rather unpacked, was Jessica. The tent was taken down around her and still she slept, curled like a little brown squirrel in her sleeping-bag.

We were now following the Rio Oribio up into the Sierra del Oribio. Above our heads the rocky crags of their highest peak, Monte Airibio, turned pink, while below, the grey stone roofs of San Cristobal looked like a herd of tortoises. At Triacastela, miraculously, a café had opened to supply coffee to an early busload of people going to Lugo. We stayed long enough to collect two leather wine *botas* that Thomas had ordered the day before. A *bota* must be seasoned for twenty-four hours with *aguardiente* before being filled with wine. The traditional way to dispose of this liquor is down the gullet of the purchaser. Perhaps it was for this reason that we climbed so gaily towards the first and lower of the two passes that would take us over the Oribio range to Piedrafita. I now carried only a stout leather handbag slung on my back. Poor Hannibal was saddled with my knapsack and the strange accumulation of objects that had dangled from it. They included the washing-up bowl, the sickle, a hoofpick and a scout whistle for recalling the children if they got lost.

The view from the first and lower pass, where we stopped to eat *turon*, our substitute for *Perfection*, was breathtaking. Ridge upon ridge of mountains stretched in all directions. The roofs and steeples of Triacastela clustered far below like a toy village. Larks sang, and so did the children, pretending that a row of pylons marching below the road was invading Martians. I attempted to recall my school Browning and quote from 'The Grammarian's Funeral', and to forget that we must spend the night up on the ridge. There was no hope of getting over the high pass of El Poyo (1,337 metres) before the next day.

We reached Fonfria at twelve o'clock, having completed seventeen kilometres in three stages before lunch. I was not even tired, in spite of the climb. Andrew's plan had worked. But we need not have worried about the injurious effects of the noon-day heat on my constitution, for the sun had vanished. Fonfria was rightly named 'cold spring' — a huddle of grey houses cowered round a fountain under a grey sky. The only relieving features were the brightly coloured blankets spread on every wall and hung from every window.

We camped, as so often, on a heath, where three locals combined minding their cows with observing us in an amiable manner. They advised us to move our tent, telling us that the north wind would be bitter in the night, and mentioning that a wolf visited the village in winter. I asked them when they ate their supper and they said ten o'clock, so there was nothing for it but to eat our own scrambled eggs and scorched bread in front of them.

That night I made the children sleep with their hoods up and gave each a stone from the fire for a hot-water bottle. Thomas read aloud from Christopher Hibbert's *Corunna*. The account of Sir John Moore's fearful retreat from the French over these very mountains in January 1809 made us feel warmer. His men had walked starving through the snow with only rags round their feet. The verges had been strewn with dead and dying. Well clothed and well fed, we slept snugly, although there was ice on our coffee in the morning.

The climb to the pass at 6 a.m. was bitter, for the sun had not yet risen over the mountains on our left, although it was setting fire to the peaks on our right. Poor Jessica was wearing a sock on one frozen hand because the mitts knitted by her beloved Sussex great-aunt had fallen into a gorse bush on which they had been put to dry. Miranda was not much better off. She was wearing sandals, because a wellington had been left outside a bar somewhere. Try though we would we seemed to be leaving a trail of our possessions along the roads of northwest Spain. The donkeys' tethering ropes were among the latest casualties, but we had discovered that the baggage cords did equally well.

At the top of the pass of El Poyo, the sun burst gloriously upon us, turning the ecstatically circling Iago the colour of flame. All round us peaks rose from a boiling cauldron of mist. Somewhere among them was Cebrero, the showpiece of the mountain route, where the monks of Aurillac had built a hospice for pilgrims in the tenth century, so great had been the loss of life in the crossing of the Sierra del Oribio. Cebrero is off the main road and its streets are of mud and cobble, patched in places with gorse. The Holy Grail is said to be preserved in its solid Romanesque church, where a miracle occurred five hundred years ago. A peasant from a neighbouring village, who had struggled to Mass through a thunderstom, saw the Host turn to tender meat, and the wine in the chalice to boiling blood. The children were disappointed that there were no longer monks in the monastery refectory, but there *was* ice cream gâteau. We were the only people eating there, apart from a plump middle-aged lady with a Pekinese. She wore a bright handwoven poncho and a knitted cap and was sitting in front of a half-empty bottle of wine. She reminded us strongly of one of our more eccentric neighbours in Sussex.

Round the church at Cebrero cluster the famous *pallosas*, stone huts with thatched conical roofs, no chimneys, and portholes for windows. The Spanish government is said to pay the peasants to stay in them for the sake of the tourist trade. It is to be hoped that their lives are not so hard as those of their ancestors during the Napoleonic invasion. A German officer described the interior of one of these hovels at the time:

The fireplace was in the middle and the smoke went wither it listed, up to the roof or out of the door. The fuel consisted of moist heath; they did not burn any light throughout the long winter nights; but illumined their huts with their heath fires, the smoke of which made the eyes smart horribly. The family in this particular hut consisted of a tall, old, black and yellow witch with three ugly children, of whom two were suffering from a hectic fever. Everything was extremely dirty; their hair was matted together, and they seemed never to have washed since the day of their birth. Round the woman's neck hung a rosary in three strands, ornamented with sacred medals, and she wore two huge earrings. She did nothing except sit over the fire and shake with cold and misery. The whole place presented a picture of the most appalling wretchedness.

Today one *pallosa* has been preserved as a museum. Among the well polished looms and samples of folk-weaving it is hard to imagine such a scene. We had breakfasted in a far more genuine peasant interior that morning at Hospital. (There are a number of places with this name on the pilgrim route.) A woman had beckoned to us from one of the glassed-in balconies that are typical of the region, and we had gone upstairs to a kitchen smelling strongly of pig. There she served us little cups of sweet black coffee at the most practical table in the world. It consisted of a wood-burning range with a tile-topped stone table built round it. Thomas wanted instantly to cable an insertion to our book about survival, *On Next to Nothing*, currently at the printer. Our hostess told us the village was under snow nine months of the year, so little wonder they dined off the top of the stove.

After we had eaten our bread and cheese she led us to the smoke-blackened cave next to the kitchen where there was a copper for pig swill. She told us they boiled up nettles, young bracken and flour and tipped the lot through the hole in the floor, from which, sure enough, hopeful grunts were issuing. Branched wooden racks were suspended from the ceiling to await *chorizos*, the final product. In the midst of it all Jessica, a well-trained child, yelled, "Big jobs!" and I had to rush her down to the wood-yard at the back of the house, not daring to face whatever served them for a privy. I was becoming an expert on wood-yards at seven o'clock in the morning.

At Piedrafita romance and Galicia ended abruptly. We were in a very ordinary little town on the main lorry-bedevilled road from Corunna. The sides of the valley of the Rio Valcarce were so steep that there was literally not a square metre flat enough to pitch a tent. It was coming up this ravine that Sir John Moore lost so many of his men after their excesses in the wine cellars of Ponferrada, and into it that he hurled treasure chests containing 150,000 *douros*. We ended up camping in a quarry by the side of the main road, with juggernauts thundering past our heads all night.

CHAPTER 11

Men with guns

The valley of the Valcarce is a smiling place in its lower reaches, giving the returning pilgrim a respite between the mountains of the Oribio that lie behind him and the mountains of Leon, that lie ahead. Everywhere there are weirs, sluices and irrigation canals. When we were there the sides of the valley were purple with wild lavender, and at Trabedelo they sold litre jars of dark lavender honey for ridiculously little. We sat by a stream and ate hunks of bread saturated with it, while laden donkeys tittuped up the hill behind us to Sotoparada, a village apparently entirely supplied by donkeys. We regretted having to bypass it.

It was in the valley of the Valcarce that we passed the only pedestrian pilgrim we saw the whole journey. He was a wrinkled brown man with an amused face, wearing a black felt hat turned up in front in the approved pilgrim manner and carrying a pack and a staff. He reminded us of the Pied Piper of Hamelin, and sure enough, soon after we had passed him, our road disappeared into a black hole in the mountain. We had arrived at a tunnel for motor traffic only.

"I'm not going through *that!*" I said.

"Of course you are," said Thomas. "It'll save three kilometres."

"We'll flash a torch at anything that comes," said Andrew encouragingly. "I can see a light at the end." I remembered the joke about the light at the end of the tunnel being the lights of the oncoming train. Luckily at this dramatic moment an ancient man pushing a two-wheeler trolley croaked "*Es prohibido*" and pointed at a notice. We went the long way round.

Villafranca del Bierzo was the first beautiful town we had seen since Santiago. It was so called because pilgrims, who were too ill to continue across the Oribio range, could obtain a free pardon here. They must have been glad to lounge on the bridges over the Valcarce and in the plazas of balconied houses. There were also two fine churches in which they could discharge their religious duties. It was here that Sir John Moore abandoned the supplies that could have saved his men from starvation in the Oribio mountains.

Beyond Villafranca the landscape changed once more. We were in the

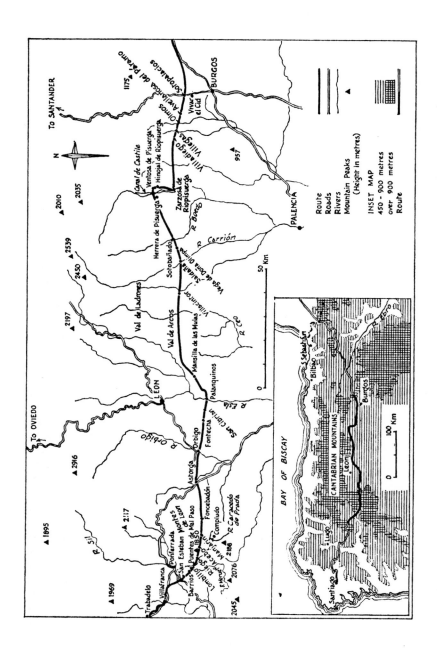

wide saucer-shaped valley known as the Bierzo, once the bed of an ancient lake, and now studded with vines. When we stopped under a tree hung with ripe cherries, we could see no less than ten assorted animals ploughing between them. Donkeys, mules, oxen and horses were all at work. Cries of "*Vaca vei!*" and "*Arré burro!*" resounded from near and far, and Hannibal, who is of a sociable disposition, became very excited. The ox-carts here had spokes in their wheels. Rude Galicia was behind us. The atmosphere was southern. A straw-hatted woman passed us, sitting sideways on a donkey, drumming on his flanks with red felt slippers.

We camped on a grassy hillside bright with flowers. Jessica picked wild roses, honeysuckle, orchids and gladiolus and distributed them. Andrew accepted a poppy and poked it neatly through an eyelet in his hat. Birds were equally abundant. Round our tent a complete orchestra was performing, the flute-like chatter from the bushes being regularly punctuated by a deep bell-like note from a tree. Into all this walked the Civil Guard.

Up the hill towards us they came. The man in front was fat and pink under his shiny black hair. He was unarmed apart from a pistol in a holster. The lieutenant, who walked twenty paces behind him and slightly to the side, rested an automatic carbine on his hip. It was pointed at us. I had not looked down the barrel of a loaded gun before. I felt an irreverent desire to make faces and giggle at such a crude form of intimidation. But for the fat pink officer this was no laughing matter. One of his colleagues had been shot dead that week in San Sebastian by Basque terrorists. Perhaps we were in league with them. He wanted to see papers, and we gave him the letter of the cultural attaché at the embassy. He looked at it blankly. "Stamps!" he said. "It is not stamped." I realised we were about to be liquidated by a slave of the rubber stamp. "The donkey papers," I whispered to Thomas. "I don't think he can read." Thomas drew Hannibal's veterinary certificate from his wallet, so liberally decorated by the official vet at the fair. The effect was satisfactory. Our unwanted visitors stumbled back down the hill to their car. Afterwards I wondered why we hadn't simply shown them our passports. Perhaps we had been more flustered than we admitted.

This was not the only time we were to be troubled by the Civil Guard, a sort of auxiliary police force or private army established in 1823 to enforce the absolute rule of Ferdinand VII and never, alas, disbanded. I think it was because we travelled on foot that we aroused their suspicions. Richard Ford had warned us that "no Spaniard ever walks for pleasure and none ever perform a journey on foot except trampers and beggars . . . Pedestrians therefore are either ill received, or become objects of universal suspicion."

Our road now lay towards Toral. There are two places called Toral
near Villafranca. They must on no account be confused. The first is a
grey place on the main road, the home of the Cosmic Cement Works.
The second is secret and enchanting, straddling the Rio Valduerza with
a Roman bridge. It was here that we celebrated the feast of Corpus
Christi with Cesar Garcia Lopez. Lopez was a stout, cheerful citizen
with an air of authority. Perhaps this was why we asked him about the
stork's nest. It was on the church tower in the dusty little plaza (Toral
was innocent of tarmac) and the great platform of twigs all but
obscured two stone pinnacles. I had never seen a stork's nest before.
I wanted to know about the strange dance the male was performing
round his three fledglings. He seemed to hover, flapping in slow motion
an inch from the surface of the nest. I did not understand Cesar's reply,
but after some questions about our journey he offered us a *vasito*, and
we accepted.

Both the cafés in the town were crowded with men in their best
suits. They sat round tables, drinking brandy, playing cards, and hook-
ing smoked mussels out of tins with toothpicks. But Lopez led us past
these, down a street where each house beckoned us to linger and
admire. Not one was without a fine wooden *corredor* or balcony running
round it and an outside stone staircase leading up to the front door.
The cows which were stabled below were being let out to drink in the
Valduerzo.

At last Cesar brought us through a small orchard of black poplars
to what looked like a broken-down stone shed. It was his *bodega*, and
contained two vast barrels on their sides. There was a table with a jug
and a few glasses ready, and he expained that all the best drinking was
done '*Alle boca della cuba*' (at the mouth of the barrel). There was a
square hole in the top of the *cuba*, closed only by a leather flap, and to
Thomas's amazement, Lopez simply dipped a glass into this. The wine
had not turned vinegary in spite of the exposure to the air. It was a
typical *clarete* of Leon, lighter in colour and flavour than the purple
vinegar of Galicia. There we had sometimes been reminded of the inn-
keeper who, on being accused of serving wine that was sourer than
his vinegar had replied, "Impossible señor! They both come out of the
same barrel!"

After three glasses of the wine of Cesar Garcia Lopez we agreed it
was the best in Leon, if not the whole of Spain, but there was no
escape. Two disreputable looking henchmen of the great *capitalista* had
arrived and they insisted we should follow them down a dark passage
to *their* barrel and, by candlelight, go through the ceremony of samp-
ling *its* contents. After two more glasses, we made our excuses and
prepared to leave. The great man was sorry we couldn't stay to *cantar
y bailar*. It was hard to imagine him dancing.

Camp at Jubial, Galicia.

Andrew and Miranda saddle up on the Val de Arcos.

We camped in a plantation of black poplars down by the Valduerza. Here an evil old peasant, surely the brother of the one at Goyan, soon arrived to ask us whether we had the señor's permission to camp. When we enquired the whereabouts of the señor he thumped his own chest and said, "*Soy el señor.*" He refused grazing to the donkeys near the camp and at the same time warned us against a *lobo* (wolf) whose pawmarks had been seen round the village in winter. We consoled ourselves with mashed potatoes and sardines fried in breadcrumbs, well smoked.

The potatoes came from the *bodega* of Cesar Garcia Lopez and had white tentacles a foot long, a sign of excellence, he had assured us. Certainly they were strangely sweet. It was when mashing them that we discovered the need for a fork for the first time on the journey. Luckily Andrew had his runcible spoon, that is to say a spoon with a forked tip, and this served. While travelling we had discovered, like Louis XIV, that forks as tools for eating were 'a useless luxury'. In dispensing with them we were merely following the custom of the country, for in many Spanish homes the *tenedor* is unknown. Andrew's sheath knife was adequate for cutting up our food and we each had our own spoon with which to shovel it into our mouths.

The footpath through the uninhabited gorge of the Rio Valduerza was one of the most beautiful stretches of the whole walk. The hillside was a mass of blossoming bushes of gum cistus. The flowers were like giant white rock roses with spots of purple velvet in the centre. Whenever there was a patch of level ground near the river, poplars had been planted. During the whole of the eight-kilometre stretch we passed only a fisherman and an old couple leading a donkey.

At San Esteban the gorge opened out. We shouted outside the closed bar until the señora appeared on her balcony and agreed to make Nescafé for us, since her coffee machine was not yet warmed up. Her bar was in a state of confusion, the tables covered with empty glasses and the floor with cigarette ends. Still in her pyjamas and dressing-gown, she explained that her customers had celebrated Corpus far into the night and eaten every morsel of cheese in the place. We breakfasted on a great flat loaf which we had just seen shovelled out of the oven in the bakery next door. Iago frisked with the señora's dog, Basilio, a longer and hairier version of himself, and apparently just as sex-starved.

There were several fine houses in San Esteban, with elaborately carved stone coats of arms. The lady at the bar said that nobody remembered the names of the seigneurial families to whom these *escudos* had belonged. "*Siamo todos eguales ahora*" (we are all equal today), she added. She told us that there were many more seigneurial houses at Barrios, the next village. She was right. Barrios was amazing.

c

A whole square was flanked with splendid palaces, partly in ruins, each proudly bearing the *escudo* of a long-forgotten family. It was like an undiscovered version of Santillana del Mar, the village in the hills above Santander, where they have converted one of the palaces into a luxury hotel. Perhaps one day they will do the same at Barrios, and the herds of cows will nose their way between parked cars with foreign number-plates.

At Lombillo we stopped to ask the way. The mountains of Leon lay ahead. The normal approach would have been through Molinaseca, but Thomas was anxious to take the short cut over the Puentes de Mal Paso, two ancient bridges at the bottom of a gorge. Two men filling buckets at the village fountain said the footpath leading to the bridges was open. Then a woman joined the group and declared that it was totally impassable on the far side. More people joined in, the discussion became animated and we, the cause of it, were forgotten. After watering the donkeys we set off once more. As we left the village we overtook a woman with a wheelbarrow. "For the love of God," she whispered to me, "don't attempt the Puentes."

CHAPTER 12

The bridges of evil repute

The Puentes de Mal Paso were not easy to find. By mid-afternoon we were on a plateau, covered with lavender and larks, high above Ponferrada in its industrial haze. Andrew set off on a two-hour reconnaissance and returned exhausted but triumphant to announce that he had indeed found two ancient bridges, almost overgrown, at the bottom of a deep gorge, but that we could not reach them that day.

We carried on along the lonely ridge, and finally camped on the edge of the gorge. Somewhere out of sight below us, were the Puentes de Mal Paso. It was a grim place. We could hear the thundering of the water and see, opposite, a distant road where an occasional fisherman climbed out of a car the size of a matchbox. The sides of the gorge were covered with broom bushes which Miranda said looked like flocks of yellow sheep.

As the sun set behind black mountains, an icy wind sprang up and moaned below us in the gorge. The children and I retired to the tent to fantasise about the home-made chocolate cake their Sussex great-aunt might be serving for tea in her Tudor cottage, cake known in the family as a 'Mrs. Norgate', after its skilful maker. We thought of the velvet curtains drawn and the bright fire in the grate. "Wouldn't it be wonderful," said Miranda, "if a cake could fall out the sky at this very moment?" Andrew meanwhile was crouching over the wind-demented camp fire, attending to the ritual murder of yeast. Adel Davis had informed him that it was a valuable source of most of the B vitamins, provided it was dead, but alive it would lurk in the intestines and, far from providing them, gobble them up. For hours it bubbled like toffee in the frying-pan, giving off a rich brewery smell.

I slept little that night. I was haunted by the loneliness of the place and by the impossibility of getting help if a child should be injured during the crossing. It also seemed to me a perfect habitat for wolves. Thomas and I were both up with the first tweet of the pre-dawn chorus, trying to persuade ourselves that the moon behind the mountains was dawn. It was a relief to see that the donkeys had not been nibbled at.

As soon as it was light we set off down the gorge by the footpath Andrew had discovered. Broom, gum cistus and lavender wet with dew had drenched our trouser legs in five minutes. In places the undergrowth was so high that Hamilcar appeared to be swimming. Sometimes it closed over him completely, engulfing the children on his back. The smell of lavender was so strong that Jessica looked back suspiciously over her shoulder and enquired who was eating sweets.

It was about half-way down that we came within an ace of losing donkey and children. The path, which clung perilously to the almost vertical slope, was barely wider than a human foot at the best of times, but at this point it was completely blocked by a large broom bush. While attempting to get round this, Hamilcar allowed his hind legs to slip over the edge. For several ghastly moments he scrabbled frantically in the loose earth while the children were suspended over the abyss. Then, somehow, he managed to get back on to the path. I don't think either Miranda or Jessica knew what had happened, and I, for some reason, didn't have hysterics, perhaps because it was all over too quickly.

At last the two bridges came into sight. They were certainly impressive. The first, over the Meruelo, was almost as overgrown as the path, and as I crossed it I was too occupied in keeping Hannibal straight to do more than glance at the cascade far below. The second, over the Caracedo de Prada, was a massive stone arch carrying a wide cobbled track. No one could tell us anything of the history of these abandoned bridges, but they were certainly used by the mule trains who supplied Spain's transport well into the last century. It was easy to imagine the bright and glittering line of animals emerging from the brushwood and filing across the bridges, the clatter of the leader's bell breaking the stillness. In north-west Spain the muleteers would have been the famous Maragatos, a picturesque tribe thought to be descended from highland Berbers. They wore wide zouave trousers and enormous hats.

It was not of the Maragatos, however, that I thought as I rested on the only flat patch of ground in the bottom of the gorge. My chief concern was to get out of it. The wall of vegetation above looked even steeper and denser than the one which we had just descended, and Andrew had not pioneered a way up it. Now, strengthened with dead yeast, he set about repairing the omission. After an hour Thomas went in search of him, and I was alone with the parapetless bridge, the roaring torrent, and the children.

For a time they amused themselves playing horses, their latest game. Jessica, trussed up in Iago's chain, was always the horse, while Miranda gave her complicated directions with two sticks. When this game palled, I imitated an opera singer doing her vocal exercises. Perhaps, like the Maragatos, who kept up a perpetual oriental chant as they travelled, I felt the need to fill the sinister place with human noise. We were down to our last heel of bread and our last canteen of water.

After another hour Thomas returned, saying the path had given out half-way up. An hour later Iago appeared, as wet as if he had been swimming, and finally Andrew himself. He said there *was* a path, if you looked for it. It was not easy but it was passable. Even he looked exhausted as he heaved the baggage on to Hannibal.

A path there may have been, for an active young man and an equally active dog. But for two loaded donkeys it scarcely deserved the name. The first hundred metres were rocky and, in places, no more than heaps of stones, but it was further on that the real trouble started. Here the path was almost completely overgrown with giant broom bushes which grew well above our heads. Worse still, many of them had been blackened by a forest fire, which made them brittle and scratchy. As Hannibal forced his way through, his burden was constantly dislodged and it was almost impossible to get alongside him to straighten it. Several times it swung right under his belly while we swore helplessly.

Then Jessica began to scream. Being constantly smacked in the face by blackened twigs was more than she could bear. She begged to be allowed to walk but we knew we would never get to the top if she attempted that. The sun was hot now and our soaked trouser legs were beginning to steam. Finally even Miranda's nerve began to crack and Andrew had to remind her that she was Captain Nancy of the *Amazon*. He invented a game in which she had to yell "Holy baggers" whenever she saw a branch about to dislodge his hat. She did this with great gusto while Jessica continued to scream hysterically.

At last we were on a plateau at the top, studded with flowering gum cistus. We rested and ate the last of the bread and drank the last of the water. The back of Thomas's shirt was soaked with sweat, Andrew's face was black from the burnt broom, Jessica's purple and tear-streaked. I daresay I was no picture. Ahead of us we could see civilisation in the form of an old man and his wife pasturing three cows. Above them on the ridge was a row of red sandstone cottages. We had reached the pilgrim village of Riego. It was two thirty and we had left our camp at six forty-five.

CHAPTER 13

The traffic warden of Astorga

At Riego a goat-herd joined us for tea. His herd of 260 beasts had chosen the patch of close-cropped turf where we were encamped as the place for their final feed of the day. They were of every colour, continually moving like the streams of a delta over the landscape, their communal legs twinkling. The evening air was filled with the sound of their bleating and their bells. As we sat and talked with their keeper, a handsome and well-informed man, the setting sun lit up clusters of slate roofs perched absurdly high on the mountains ahead. These were the ghost villages of the Montes de Leon.

We set off towards the pass across these mountains with morning mist steaming round the snow-capped peaks and often obscuring both them and us. As we climbed, with bursting lungs and knocking hearts, even Thomas began to falter under his orange load of food. I was more fortunate, for I had discovered that Hannibal did not object to my strap-hanging from his tail. We did at least have the consolation of knowing we were on the pilgrim route, for at our first village, Acebo, a notice in mock antique writing told us so, in French.

In Acebo it was hard to imagine tourists. The streets ran with muck and half the houses were in ruins. In one, the front had been torn off and a brass bed waited for an occupant in an upstairs room. The only living person we saw in the main street was a shepherd standing on a balcony with a skin slung over it. "It's a wolf!" cried Miranda. "It's got claws." The shepherd assured us that it was merely one of his dogs. The sheepdogs in these mountains were formidable brutes, bigger than their sheep. They were black-and-white and jowly, with evil yellow eyes and cropped ears that a wolf could not get a hold on and they wore collars with spikes two inches long. Iago was unabashed by them. He stole half the femur of a cow from under the nose of one, and carried it for a couple of kilometres, stopping to have a gnaw when he could get far enough ahead.

There was not a sign of a *tienda* or even a *taverna* at Acebo. A loafer assured us that refreshments could be had at a farm opposite the church and even thumped on the door to prove it. The Spanish habit of late rising was already defeating our plan to breakfast in cafés, but on this occasion we were lucky. A friendly farmer's wife took us upstairs to her small kitchen and lit the range with a bundle of broom while we sat round a table on backless wooden stools. As we ate our bread and cheese, her husband and her half-witted sister-in-law came in and declared Jessica *muy guapa* in spite of her peeling cheeks and food-smeared mouth. They were getting ready to milk the cows in the room below.

We did not blame the people of Manjarin, the next village, for abandoning it in favour of jobs in Madrid. Bleak moorland lay all around and nothing seemed to grow but cushions of dwarf broom on shale. The church was without doors or windows, and political slogans had been painted on the walls of the sanctuary. A donkey inhabited the front room of one of the houses and a herd of sheep had taken over several others. Foncebadón, still lauded in the guide books as *muy tipico*, had only one human inhabitant. She was an old woman, probably a Maragata, who had obstinately refused to leave her home. We saw her pale face peering out from black shawls as we passed on the main road.

It was a relief to come down, after a night on those rainswept mountains, to the sun-warmed plain where Astorga lies. Astorga is one of the five famous cathedral towns on the pilgrim route and we planned to take a day off to visit it. We were within sight of its twin towers by the unprecedented hour of eleven o'clock, and I decided to carry on into the town alone, eager for an afternoon of sightseeing, though my first port of call was not the cathedral, but the hairdresser, where for forty pesetas (30p) I enjoyed the luxury of a hairwash. For the first time in three weeks I was able to study my face in a mirror more than two inches across. It was dirty but shamelessly healthy. To my disgust it betrayed nothing of the sufferings of the last two hundred kilometres.

The interior of the cathedral gave the same sense of uplift as Salisbury, with its vastly elongated arches and fan vaulting. But the bishop's palace next door, designed by the celebrated Gaudi in 1909, could only be described as Walt Disney Gothic, with its toy turrets and stained-glass portholes. It did, however, house a fascinating pilgrim museum. Here a whole room was filled with small wooden statues from such village churches as Acebo's, often not even labelled. Most memorable was that of Santa Eulalia from Riego, looking distinctly flat-chested and carrying her breasts, like twin blancmanges, on a plate. There were also pictures and statues showing how the properly turned-out pilgrim should look. He travelled remarkably light, his whole luggage consisting of a water gourd suspended from his staff and a wallet from his belt. How different from us! An engraving that particularly interested me showed pilgrims passing through Astorga in an endless serpentine procession while the citizens waved from doors and windows. In the Middle Ages the town must have been given over almost entirely to sheltering them.

No such welcome awaited our little procession early next morning. We had foolishly decided to take the donkeys straight through the town, as the pilgrim route to Leon lay that way. The two figures in Maragato costume on the town hall clock were striking eight as we tied our donkeys to the benches in the square. A delicious smell of coffee was coming from the principal café and we went in eager for *mantecadas*, the little butter-flavoured cakes that are as typical of Astorga as the Maragato muleteers once were. We were not to enjoy our *mantecadas* for long. An imposing figure in an air-force-blue uniform, with a belt as white as his moustache, appeared in the café doorway. He was the traffic warden of Astorga and he indicated that there was no parking space for donkeys in the square. The cultural attaché's letter, explaining that we were pilgrims, cut no ice with him. The only pilgrims he understood came in charabancs. There was nothing for it but to stuff the children's pockets with cakes and slink off to a playground on the ramparts.

The ramparts of Astorga are of great interest. They are Roman and twenty feet high, and kept Napoleon's army at bay for two months in 1810. Tied to the railings along the top of them the donkeys, we thought, would have a fine view of the mountains they had just traversed and would bother no one. The children, meanwhile, could pretend to be buses in the acacia-shaded playground, which had been laid out as a miniature traffic intersection with zebra crossings, halt signs and traffic lights.

We shopped in shifts, Andrew going first. He said he would be away half an hour, but he has little time sense and was anyway in search of difficult items like dehydrated oranges and canvas with which to make pockets on his inadequate knapsack. He returned two hours later. By that time much had happened. Our old friend the traffic warden had turned up again. The parking of donkeys on the town walls was strictly forbidden. Fortunately he had a friend who was the proprietor of the nearby Funeraria Moderna. After a brief consultation with the traffic warden, he said the yard at the back of his funeral parlour was at the disposal of our donkeys.

Nobody, however, had consulted Hannibal. To reach the undertaker's yard he had to pass through a workshop where stood three coffins wrapped in brown paper. He refused absolutely to enter this place, planting his hoofs on the pavement and leaning his hairy rump against Thomas's shoulder. I tried bribery with a whole orange, not just the peel, and Thomas tried force with somebody's carpet beater, but all he raised was dust. Soon a small crowd began to gather, there was a good deal of laughter and even the traffic warden's white moustache was seen to twitch at the sight of Thomas's frantic efforts. Then a little man, as brown as a walnut, appeared from nowhere, went up to Hannibal like an old friend, put his greasy jacket over the donkey's great furry head, led him round in a circle three times and straight in past the dreaded coffins.

He was a man who knew about donkeys. He could tell from the way Hamilcar's tail had been clipped that he was a gypsy donkey, and from the length of his teeth that he was not a day under sixteen. Hannibal, on the other hand, was probably of Zamora stock. Only at Zamora did you find beasts of such stature and with so much bone. With donkeys, he said as he left us, you must be gentle and persuasive. Force got you nowhere.

When the time came to leave Astorga, Hannibal proved as unwilling to leave the Funeraria Moderna as he had been to enter it. Hamilcar went gaily past the coffins and stood outside ee-awing encouragingly. Hannibal would not budge. A fur-covered rock could not have stood more firmly. Calmly and confidently Thomas draped his khaki jacket over his head, but the trick wouldn't work a second time. Once more a crowd began to gather. This time a fat pink man stepped forward. Having given Hannibal's backside a thorough basting with his malacca cane, he let out a yell of "Arré burro", with a formidably rolled 'R'. The effect was instantaneous. Hannibal popped on to the pavement like a cork from a champagne bottle.

CHAPTER 14

Villages under the ground

On the red plain of Leon we felt real heat for the first time, and
Jessica was glad of the enormous flower-printed hat she had selected
for herself in Astorga. It was hot even before breakfast, and we almost
envied the Etonians who would be cowering under marquees with their
strawberries and cream, on the coldest Fourth of June on record. We
planned to breakfast at the famous pilgrim bridge at Orbigo, the
longest and one of the oldest on the pilgrim route.

Outside Orbigo I spied a modern café and motel with parked cars.

"Coffee!" I gasped, with all the urgency of a desert traveller within
sight of an oasis.

"We're not here for coffee, we're here to see the bridge," said
Thomas, giving Hamilcar's backside a firm poke.

"I don't give a damn about bridges, I want *coffee!*" I yelled. This
sordid wrangle went on for some time after we'd left the motel behind. I told Thomas he was mad if he thought he would find a café
anywhere near his damned bridge. Eventually we reached the bridge
and there was a café and it was open.

And what a bridge was the Puente de Orbigo! It wandered across
the shallow valley and spanned two streams on its countless low
arches. Its foundations are said to be Roman, although the present
structure is thirteenth-century, and it owes its miraculous survival to
the fact that the main road now bypasses it. We told the children about
the tournament held there in 1434, when the valiant Suero de Quiñones
knocked 727 knights from their horses because they dared dispute the
beauty of his lady.

To me the café seemed hardly less remarkable than the bridge, with
its picture windows, its hygienic plastic-topped tables and its long
well-supplied bar. No less than five different wall-paper patterns had
been used in the ultra-modern décor. Two women were shovelling up
the deep litter of sawdust and cigarette ends which covers the floor
of even the most civilised Spanish cafés, and Miranda danced between
their brooms, measuring the table-tops and the leatherette benches for
her mathematics project. Her textbook required her to list the dimen-

sions of the furniture in her classroom, and this was difficult when her classroom was usually an open field.

It was at the café at Orbigo that Andrew first persuaded me to try his dead yeast, a certain cure, he said, for my early morning lassitude and irritability. The children were already addicted to it, but were only allowed it provided both took it. Otherwise, Andrew said, the contests on donkey back became unequal. To my surprise my spoonful was crisp and tasted deliciously of Marmite. And its effect was instaneous. When we set off once more, I was no longer the weary drudge who whined for coffee, not monuments. I now strode across the plain, giving the children useful instruction on mirages (about which I am totally ignorant) and arrived fresh in camp after twenty-three kilometres. And this in spite of heat so intense that, for the first time, I unzipped the legs of my runcible jeans, converting them into shorts. These invaluable jeans had been made for me by Jenny Sturrock, a talented dress designer who lives at Ardingly, two miles from West Hoathly.

The plain, although hot, was not in fact a desert but intensively cultivated, and it was almost impossible to find a patch of waste ground which was not next door to a well. These wells were formidable affairs, several metres across and quite open. They formed part of an elaborate irrigation system. Eventually, near the village of Fontecha, we thought we had found the very place, three little glades of rich clover surrounded by trees. We should have known better. As the day declined a frog chorus informed us that there was the grandfather of all wells just behind our row of poplars, and a shepherd returning with two hundred sheep said we were crushing his best grazing. He relented, however, and said we could stay one night.

Miranda and I decided to ride the donkeys to the shop in Fontecha, she going ahead on Hamilcar and I following on the less manageable Hannibal. The village was built entirely of mud, whole streets of Iago-coloured houses glowing in the evening sun. Even the church was of mud, with a primitive ladder of tree trunks going up inside the tower. We stopped and watched a group of men and women repairing the wall round the cemetery. A framework of wood was filled with wet mud and removed when it was dry. These red walls would stand until the thatch along their tops decayed. Then they dissolved like sugar cubes in the rain.

On our way home Iago, who had always lived at peace with our nine hens in Sussex, disgraced himself. Miranda and I were riding peacefully through the terracotta streets when I looked back and saw, to my horror, a small red animal in pursuit of a very flustered hen. By the time I reached him he was plucking out her tail feathers at the feet of her ancient mistress. It was hard to say whether the hen or its owner was squawking more loudly. Luckily an old man threw his walking-stick at the miscreant, and he released his hold on the chicken and cowered screaming by the barn door while I belaboured him. By this time the denuded hen had vanished and there was nothing for me to do but apologise profusely to the old lady and offer to pay.

Iago was a much chastened dog when we returned to camp. I had never beaten him before, and he would not look me in the eye. He spent the evening curled up under a distant bush. For the rest of us, it was a perfect evening. As we sipped our *caldo Gallego* we watched a steady procession of tractor-mule combinations entering the village between us and the setting sun. All night long not one, but two nightingales sang relentlessly. To be honest I only heard them at dawn under the crescent of a waning moon, but Thomas reported that they got into his dreams, since they were being played as Musak over the loud-speaker system at the Ritz where he was having tea.

The next morning we followed a cart-track across uplands velvety with green barley. Cornflowers and poppies were brilliant under the early sun, and there were larks for Iago to chase, but he was too sad to chase them. Instead he trotted glumly at my heels, obeying every command instantly. I missed the sight of his pricked ears and tail moving along a distant horizon in the hopeless pursuit of small birds, and secretly feared I might have broken his spirit, or at least a rib.

It was up on this lonely plateau that we saw our first underground village, totally abandoned. The former inhabitants had literally bur-rowed into a hillside. Flights of steps ran down to the locked and numbered front doors, which were approached by rounded tunnels of mud bricks. One door was open and I ventured nervously inside. It was dark and cold down there, and a corridor ran a long way back with doors opening off it. I did not have the courage to pursue it.

We passed several underground villages that day. Most were deserted but at San Cibrian we photographed the only inhabited one which we saw. It was a positive palace, with a brick front, gaily painted railings and a garden of flowering rose bushes. Its shiny tin chimneys (or ventilators) went a long way back on the hillside. The lady who lived in it was anxious that we should include her three cows in the picture.

CHAPTER 15

Jessica's birthday

Jessica was going to be four years old on June 6th and we were anxious to reach the banks of the Rio Esla so that swimming and a trip to Leon could be included in the festivities. The lower reaches of the Esla had been the setting for a gallant cavalry action by Sir John Moore's rearguard during which a Major Jesse saw the arms and legs of several French *chasseurs* 'sliced off clean and neat like Berlin sausages'.

The line of poplars that marked the river took an eternity to approach and the day was the hottest we had had. The cow-herds in the water meadows stood under umbrellas for shade. At last we reached a bridge which carried us across the Esla's broad green waters, and on the far side found a dilapidated bar among clumps of willow. There were no customers and the owner did not lift his head from his paperback. We decided it was the place to celebrate Jessica's four years of existence. The mosquitoes were delighted and pestered us all night for invitations.

The birthday began with a special treat, eggs and bacon, eaten at dawn so that Thomas and I could catch the train to Leon from Palanquinos. We had exactly four hours in which to see the sights of the city, buy the ingredients of a birthday and catch the one o'clock train back. Amazingly, we succeeded.

Leon was by far the most sophisticated town we had seen since arriving in Spain. Smartly dressed women and highly starched little girls paraded the main street that ran up to the cathedral. They seemed to belong to another world, and it was impossible to believe we had once been as clean. There were even some tourists, chiefly elderly Americans, the first we had seen this trip. They were mostly in the shops, complaining about things.

The interior of the cathedral was dark, illuminated only by 2,000 (or was it 10,000?) square metres of stained glass, one of the finest collections in the world. The effect was electrifying. It was like being inside a kaleidoscope. We realised what the English cathedrals had lost when Cromwell's soldiers hurled stones through their rose windows, banishing the holy gloom.

With the minutes passing, and Jessica waiting hopefully by the Esla, we hurried on to the pantheon of the kings of Leon. The young man who had been forced on us as a guide was quite mystified by our refusal to see the famous treasury, a tour of which was included in the 100 pesetas we had paid. But the pantheon alone was worth it.

The Spanish are good at death, being perpetually preoccupied with it. My most vivid memory of El Escorial, which I had visited on our honeymoon, had been the octagonal golden vault where Charles V and his descendants lie, entombed in uniform black marble. The pantheon at Leon was an altogether more archaic affair, for the old saying is that Leon had twenty kings before Castile had one. Their plain stone tombs lay about in the gloom, under low rounded vaults covered with extraordinary Romanesque frescoes, mostly in yellow, prussian blue and terracotta. One arch was lined with twelve lunettes representing the months of the year. In May the peasant sowed his corn, in October he slaughtered his pig, and in December he sat in front of the fire and ate them both.

By a miracle we caught our train and walked the two kilometres from Palanquinos, with Jessica's birthday on our backs. After a siesta and a swim in the Esla, the celebrations began. The book-loving proprietor of the little café had given us permission to use one of his outdoor trestle tables, and we hung balloons from the awning above it and filled a tin with poppies. The children had both changed into crumpled cotton frocks and fairly white ankle socks, and raced towards us at a signal from Thomas. They found a feast awaiting them; a box of fancy biscuits, *turon*, potato crisps, and a slightly squashed cake called a *Torta Napolitana*, which looked as if it might indeed have travelled from Naples. The café had provided two large bottles of fizzy orangeade and lollipops on the house. There were carrots for the donkeys and a bone for Iago. Jessica was at first too occupied with unwrapping her presents to eat. She had a doll, a book made by Andrew, and a cot blanket to replace the one we had been using under Hannibal's saddle. When she surfaced she seized Andrew's sheath knife and carved up her *Torta Napolitana* with the rapidity of a practised chef.

Little did we guess that the day's excitement was not over. After we had put the children to bed with the mosquitoes, Thomas and I set off once more for Palanquinos to get drinking-water, there being none at the café. We had filled our two-litre plastic bottles and were peacefully eating ice cream in a café when two members of the *Guardia Civil* entered. They were half-way through their glasses of wine when they approached our table and asked us to accompany them to the *cuartel*. The village was evidently the site of a barracks full of them.

We were led down the dark street and into a harshly lit office, where sat a great grey slug behind a desk. He was addressed as *Commandante*.

The *commandante* was quite unimpressed by the cultural attaché's letter, which he seemed barely to read, but he did copy useless details from Thomas's driving licence in a slow, childish hand. We explained that our passports were in camp with our three children, and for a moment we hoped he might take us back there in his car. No such happy fate was to be ours. The *commandante*'s plan was to send some of his own men to our camp site (which he didn't believe in), wake Andrew (whose existence he doubted), and get him to produce the passports (which he thought we didn't possess). At this point I put on my hen-deprived-of-her-chicks act. It was dark, I howled, Andrew had no idea where we kept the passports, the children would be terrified. Why should innocent writers, not to say pilgrims, be molested? The *commandante* told me I was an experienced traveller and must be accustomed to these little inconveniences. I was near boiling point now, and swore inwardly at my primitive Spanish that would not allow me to tell him that indeed I had travelled through much of Europe, Africa and the United States, but had never had to endure the insult of being hauled into a police station on sight. Quite incapable of rendering all this into killing Castilian, all I could do was remark that Thomas was a *romancisto muy famoso* with fifteen novels to his credit, and go off into a childish sulk.

Things were beginning to look ugly. We had been in the bare little room for two hours now, with little to look at but the portrait of the *Caudillo* on the wall, and a machine gun on a stand in the corner. Six of them stood round us, and there was a nasty moment when the slug heaved himself from his chair and left the room. When he returned he shut the door behind him and laid something heavy and metallic on the filing cabinet. I thought the torture was about to begin, but he merely ordered me to empty my knapsack, which I did. It took some time to convince him that a small plastic jar contained glycerine suppositories, and was not a supply of nitro-glycerine.

And then, quite suddenly, the *commandante* said we could go.

"*En auto?*" said Thomas hopefully. A guard replied by lifting his orange knapsack and indicating he should put it on and *andar*. So home through the frog-loud night we dragged our leaden legs, our water bottles weighing more at every step. There had been a nasty burst of laughter as we felt the *cuartel*, but I only fully appreciated the incivility of the Civil Guard when, after one of the longest forty minutes of my life, we finally reached the camp site. At that precise moment a car stopped beside us and out climbed two men with a torch. They were none other than our old friends the Civil Guard. Evidently they had tried to find the camp on their own and failed. It was some consolation to take them down the steepest part of the bank in inky darkness, so that they would get their socks well filled with burrs, and maybe even twist an ankle, before inspecting our passports.

CHAPTER 16

Shoeless in the wilderness

The cost of maintaining a donkey, compared to that of a car, is infinitesimal, but there are four spare parts that must be replaced every six weeks, and these are the shoes. Hannibal's back pair were beginning to look perilously thin. Three wildernesses lay between us and Burgos. He would certainly need new shoes before we reached it.

The wildernesses of Leon were not barren wildernesses, for they were frequently cultivated. But they were vast in extent, monotonous and totally uninhabited. Spanish farmers prefer to stay together in villages, and the invention of the tractor has made it possible for them to live great distances from their fields.

Our first wilderness, fifteen kilometres of uninhabited country, began at Mansilla de las Mulas where they were busy obscuring the old town walls, known to generations of pilgrims, with hideous villas. It was called the Val de Arcos, but the name of a similar stretch just to the north, Val de Ladrones, seemed more appropriate, for pilgrims were frequently robbed while crossing both. I have not seen a cultivated plain so desolate in Europe. Open prairie planted with barley, a cereal that the Spanish seem to grow recklessly, stretched to the horizon. Andrew said it reminded him of Illinois, where we all once lived for two years. Later it became very hot. An occasional abandoned building appeared like a ship in the heat haze on the horizon, and still our tintinnabulating procession moved along the sandy road. The only living thing we saw was a small brown snake lying across our path. It was in the act of swallowing a green lizard at least twenty-five centimetres long. The legs and the tail of the lizard still protruded from the snake's extended jaws. Both children squatted, staring with horrified delight.

"Poor lizard!" said Jessica.

"Poor snake!" said Miranda. Certainly predator and prey seemed in an equally poor way.

We camped outside Villacintor by the village fountain, a lovely place where a spout of *aqua la más rica* (the richest water) fell into a stone basin. Nearby was a pond full of green frogs with their attendant stork, and beyond it the red mud walls and streets of the village. These soon became black with little groups of people staring at us. Miranda and Jessica were bathing in the fountain's basin, when we saw a procession of eight exquisitely dressed little girls approaching. Miranda dived for the tent and emerged in her only frock, just in time to receive them. Each child carried a rose between her teeth and presented it to her.

A deputation of boys arrived next, to be entertained by Andrew, and finally six gnarled peasants who displayed a most informed interest in our route, unlike their brothers in Galicia who had often barely known the name of the next village. One of them had brought a bottle of the light red *clarete* of the village for us to try. There was also a continuous stream of women bringing earthenware bottles with spouts to the spring.

The village cows, mostly mouse-coloured, all issued from the different streets at the same moment, drank from the frog pond, grazed for a couple of hours and then, as if acting on a signal, returned up their separate streets. Four old men, who had spent all the late afternoon on a bench against the village wall, watched them pass. Here, we felt, was a truly contented community.

There was a violent thunderstorm during the night and a rather damp Andrew crawled into our tent in the early hours. Of late he had abandoned his space-blanket shelter and slept in a kind of envelope made from a sheet of polythene held together with clothes pegs. It kept out all but the worst weather. As we left in the morning, the village was still asleep, but one old man was up to see us off. He wore carpet slippers inside clogs, and he had brought a little warm cake for each child. They still remember those cakes, after so many details of the journey have been forgotten.

There had been a blacksmith at Villacintor, but he told us that no one asked for donkey shoes nowadays and he had only mule shoes. We therefore approached our next wilderness with some trepidation. It was a fourteen-kilometre stretch of pine forest intersected by wide sheep-cropped valleys with streams, called *arroyos*, running through them. There was no track, but Thomas guided us across successfully with the aid of the map. As we passed the stone that marks the boundary between Leon and Castile, Jessica, clinging on behind Miranda and almost invisible under her multicoloured *sombrero*, counted up to ten for the first time. Andrew's patience in preparing her for this achievement surpassed belief.

Saldaña was a nice little town on the bank of the River Carrión, where the central square was surrounded by wooden arcades and overlooked by a castle. The *herrero* there had donkey shoes all right, but no nails small enough to fix them on with.

Now the sides of the poplar-shaded road were like a herbaceous border and Andrew had several fruitful sessions of the Flower Game with the children, who discovered ten species they had not seen before, including a bee orchid. Picturesquely placed along the valley were red mud villages with geraniums spilling from the house fronts and glimpses of more in courtyards beyond. The prettiest of all was Vega de Doña Olimpa. Doña Olimpa sat with a river running past her feet, wearing a church for a crown, and she was *en fiesta*. When we entered the main square we found a small crowd gathered round the door of the *taverna*, which was decorated with green branches stuck with marigold heads. Inside a group of men were drinking brandy and eating delicious morsels off toothpicks. There was some confusion about whom the fiesta was honouring.

"*Es la fiesta de la padrona*," suggested one old toper. "*Doña Olimpa.*"

"*Che cojones!*" replied another. (It was the first time I had encountered the exclamation outside Hemingway.)

"*Es la fiesta del padron, San Cristobal,*" declared the swarthy landlord with an air of tipsy authority. The feast of the patron saint of travellers seemed a suitable one for us to celebrate and we accordingly drank several glasses of the local brandy and promptly lost our way on leaving the village. We had been given authoritative directions, but, as so often, realised too late that the important thing for a Spaniard is not the correctness of the information he gives you but the manly and defiant way in which he gives it.

By four thirty we had climbed into a wide green valley. It was totally deserted and the *arroyo* that wandered down its centre was not much more than a bog. Here we decided to camp, hoping to collect water for the donkeys by digging holes in the bog and leaving them to fill.

We still look back on the night of the feast of St. Christopher as the best of all the nights in Spain. It was close on midsummer, and as the sun went down behind the green shoulder of the valley, a new moon took its place, standing like a flame on the skyline. Miranda and Jessica played wild games of dinosaurs with knickers over their heads till long after dark in this enchanted playground and Miranda for the first time, slept under the stars. As she lay looking up at them she said, "I want to be a tramp or a gypsy or a pilgrim all my life." Surprisingly, the water holes also filled.

Miranda was to be put to the test the next day, for we had to cross our third wilderness, and it was a dreary place. Oak scrub had been bulldozed and grey pine saplings planted in the grey exposed subsoil. The sunshine had given way to a matching greyness and a strong wind made a sound like a whiplash through the wires of the pylons above our heads. Once we got lost, and walked on and on, into a head wind, at last reaching a road that, according to our map, shouldn't have been there. The road ran dead straight to the horizon in both directions, and it seemed a question of tossing a coin to decide which way to go. To me that road, going on pointlessly for all eternity, seemed a fore-taste of Hell, or at least Purgatory.

After another four kilometres of hip-grinding, footsore slog, we reached Sotobañado, just as the thunderstorm burst. There was noth-ing for it but to shelter in the large porch of the Romanesque church and wait for it to be over. I could only pray that the *párroco* would not arrive and find the children bouncing a rubber ball against the faces of saints a thousand years old, or, worse still, Thomas with three days' growth on his chin, snoring like a clapped-out tramp on top of the baggage. Our camp by the Rio Boedo that night was as dismal as the previous one had been delightful. We pegged out the tent among broken glass and empty tins and when Hannibal indulged in a luxurious roll in the riverside sand, I saw, to my horror, that the back part of both hind shoes was completely worn away. The last of the three wilder-nesses had proved too much for them.

The search for a blacksmith was now urgent, and we felt certain of finding one in the next town, Herrera de Pisuerga. Surely a place with a name like that must have shoes and nails of every size. The farrier at Herrera did indeed have donkey nails, but he once more had no donkey shoes. Cursing ourselves for not having brought shoes from Saldaña, we camped on the banks of the Canal de Castile.

The lock by which we slept that night was built of giant blocks of red stone to last a thousand years. The water cascaded over the top of the upper gates into a great boiling basin overlooked by a bridge of superb masonry, surely the work of English engineers. Yet we later discovered that this section of the navigation, which runs parallel to the River Pisuerga, was the only one ever completed. According to J. Phillips, writing in 1795, the canal was designed to carry the produce of Castile to the Atlantic at Santander "receiving from the little rivers in its passage the tribute of their waters". In fact it petered out ten kilometres north of Herrera, halted, like so many Spanish projects of the period, by lack of funds. As Ford pointed out, "a Castilian would rather settle his debts with cold iron and warm abuse than with gold and thanks", and "the coldest spot in the hot capital" was the Stock Exchange.

Next morning, keeping Hannibal on the grassy verges for the sake of his shoes, we followed the tranquil Pisuerga southwards and finally ran a blacksmith to earth at Zarzosa de Riopisuerga. His forge was in an alley of whitewashed houses and he was hard at work beating out ox shoes. He set to work at once on Hannibal. When it came to Hamil-car's turn I was overcome by cowardice and slunk away to the bar, pleading an urgent need for Fanta on the part of the children. I knew that Andrew would have to hold up those savage back hooves and I could not face the prospect of seeing him flung sky high.

The bar at Zarzosa de Riopisuerga was in a dusty square, overlooked by a fine Romanesque church, locked, of course, as they all were. Backed up against the bar door was a two-wheeler cart of the type that Diggory Venn might have driven across Egdon Heath; its hood was of painted canvas lined with reeds, and an ancient pony dozed between the shafts. The interior of the bar was hardly less archaic. It was as dark as a cave and run by a villainous-looking couple, both showing signs of advanced alcoholism. A few regulars in carpet slippers were knocking back brandy at ten in the morning and I soon became involved in a lively discussion about which language was spoken by the largest number of people in the world. The party was just getting under way when, to my surprise, Thomas and Andrew appeared, apparently unscathed. They said that, by getting Andrew to take a firm grip of Hamilcar's ear and twist it, the smith had robbed him of all desire to kick, and nailed on his shoes in record time. To me it sounded about as probable as one of those Spanish fairy tales that Andrew was always telling the children, in which, at a magic word, donkeys vomited showers of gold coins.

CHAPTER 17

El Cid's castle

How many of the thousands of tourists who visit Burgos, I wonder, realise that it stands in the centre of a great limestone plateau, called the Páramo, meaning wilderness? I for one had been unaware of it when I wandered with Thomas along its shady embankment twenty-five years earlier. No one who approaches on foot, however, can ignore this skeletal setting of the Páramo, where the bones of the earth show white through sparse windswept vegetation, and where wolf and wild boar still roam. By way of consolation, the Páramo offers wild flowers in profusion, ewes' milk cheeses (for only sheep prosper here) and Romanesque churches of amazing beauty. As we approached Burgos these village churches improved continuously. The one at Villegas surpassed that at Avellanosa del Páramo, and that at Olmos outshone them both. All had elaborately carved portals consisting of rounded arches on low pillars.

The children were more interested in the prospect of Burgos post office. They wanted us to march straight to the centre of the city, donkeys and all, so that they could themselves collect their first mail for six weeks, but we bribed them with the promise of a camp at El Cid's castle. The castle was at Sotopalacios, ten kilometres from Burgos. It was a vast ruin, quite abandoned, with green barley lapping against its walls, as if the local farmers resented this obstacle to their ploughs. Storks from the nearby river flapped about nests on its battlements. We never found written proof that the famous knight of Burgos lived in this castle but since the next village was called Vivar El Cid we decided to agree that he had.

El Cid, who was a native of Burgos, is closely associated with the history of the pilgrimage. When he fought the Moors at Coimbra in the late eleventh century it was none other than St. James who stood at his side and turned the tide of battle in his favour. The story of his adventures is told in the twelfth-century epic poem, *Cantar de Mio Cid*, the Spanish equivalent of the *Chanson de Roland*. Unfortunately the true Cid bore little resemblance to the hero of the poem. His real name was Rodrigo Diaz. 'El Cid' derived from the Arabic title *Side*. He fought the Moors not because of high Christian ideals but because he was paid to, and was an unscrupulous mercenary leader who would sell his services to the highest bidder.

Andrew was the first member of our party to visit Burgos. He went on foot that afternoon, and we waited up to hear about his adventures. All he had seen, however, of the eleven-centuries-old city was the inside of the ironmongers' shops. He had been in search of a washing-up bowl that would exactly fit into his diminutive knapsack. And he had found one, what was more a brown one, his colour. He proudly demonstrated how, when inserted into the knapsack, it gave it rigidity and at the same time acted as a drawer from which his possessions could easily be extracted.

The following day Thomas and I took a train into Burgos, determined to do it justice. I enjoyed that day in Burgos more than any day in a city on the whole trip. Perhaps it was because the icy wind from the Páramo had dropped and the sun was shining, or because we were not rushed as we had been at Leon, or simply that Burgos is an exceptionally beautiful place. Certainly there is nothing like an unrelieved diet of country life to give one a taste for what Ford calls 'the fleshly comfort of cities'.

Our first port of call was naturally the post office, where a friendly man, imprisoned behind a grille, shook hands with us through it, told us our post was *mucho*, and handed us a bundle of books and letters to prove it. Among them, we were relieved to see, was a new Arthur Ransome — Miranda had now read *Great Northern* seven times. Bearing our precious wad we made for a pavement café, and, while we drank sherry, Thomas read aloud accounts of the scandalous goings-on of our friends in England. It all seemed as remote as the campaigns of the Cid, but not the less entertaining for that.

In the basement of our café there was a tap, and out of this tap came water, and the water was hot. After six weeks of camping this seemed to me almost miraculous. It was strange enough to have water without having to carry it, but stranger still for it to be heated without the assistance of a fire.

We had one important practical objective in Burgos, and that was to find a pack-saddle for Hamilcar on which the children could sit comfortably. The complete dearth of saddlers throughout northern Spain had been an unpleasant surprise and we were determined to find one here. A lethargic man at the tourist office gave us the names of three cordoneros, but two of these had been reduced to making alpagatas and fishing nets. Our hopes were raised when we read the magic word guarnicionario painted on a weathered sign above the entrance of the third. Again we were to be disappointed. The owner led us to an upstairs cupboard where he showed us a fine collection of stuffed mule collars and bridles made by his father which he never hoped to sell, but there was not a pack-saddle among them. He had no call for them now, he said.

At last we were free to head for the cathedral. From my last visit I remembered something overpoweringly ornate and Gothic, like the duomo at Milan. I was to be pleasantly surprised, for Burgos cathedral is cosily surrounded by mediaeval houses on various levels, and its three towers are as light and open as cobwebs. I was immediately reminded of the great thirteenth-century cathedrals of the Rhine — Cologne, Freiburg and Strasbourg — and was pleased to discover that the architect was none other than Juan de Colonia, the man who had built Cologne cathedral. The interior had neither the inspiring purity of Astorga cathedral nor the stained glass of Leon, but it had an impressively monumental quality. Each of the elaborate side chapels was the size of a normal church. We followed a young man who was displaying the place to three Frenchwomen of impeccable breeding. He made a thorough job of it and did not miss out the tomb of El Cid and his wife Ximena, but he struck me as an excessively servile creature. Not only did he kneel at the foot of the postcard stand when selecting cards for the old ladies, but he was carrying all three of their handbags.

A pleasure which we did not deny ourselves at Burgos was that of eating. We had come into the city like meat-starved savages, and any succulent display in a restaurant window excited us shamefully. All through the morning we had kept a watchful eye on restaurants with a view to lunch; at one we had seen four live lambs being carried in by their legs, and at another hogskins of wine being delivered by a burly cellarman. The use of hogskins in place of barrels is a time-honoured Spanish custom, and according to Ford the adoration of the *borracho* "disputes, in the peninsular, with the cigar, the dollar and even the worship of the Virgin". The entire skin of the animal is used so that the wine-skin preserves the shape of the pig, legs and all. The hairy coat lines the interior which is pitched, like a ship's bottom, to prevent leaking — hence the tarry taste of some Spanish wines. *Borrachos* were the big-bellied monsters which Don Quixote attacked, and a drunkard in Spain is called a *borracho*.

The restaurant we finally selected had tables on the pavement and was named, rather surprisingly, Parry's. By the time we reached it, we were the only customers and had the undivided attention of a plump and fatherly waiter. Our tourist leaflet had told us that fish soup and lamb from the Páramo were the classic dishes of Burgos, and these we ordered. What a fish soup it was! A divine, garlic-flavoured juice with fresh-water crayfish floating in it. And the miniature pink joints of lamb that followed were no less succulent. With them we ordered a bottle of Pacenta from Haro, for Haro would be our next city, and no Spanish table wines can vie with those of the Rioja.

The sun was descending like a fiery ball behind El Cid's castle as we returned to camp, and the Páramo wind was beginning to blow again. We found Andrew taking notes on Spanish colloquial usages as demonstrated in *Zippee-Zappee*, his favourite comic. Spread about him on the grass was his entire wardrobe, now dyed nigger brown in his new bowl. The children, he reported, had played schools all morning and hospital all afternoon. At the school Jessica had been the sole pupil, and, at the hospital, the sole patient and the survivor of several prolonged operations.

As Thomas cooked the lamb chops we had bought at Burgos, sheep started to come down from the Páramo. The first flock of 192 was led by a wild-looking boy of about twelve who swaggered (and staggered) under the weight of a man's coat over one shoulder, a man's leather bag over the other, and an outsize stick. He had a dog that looked like a black poodle without a tail and, when we praised it, declared it was no more than *regular*. Perhaps he was right. It stood with its eyes glued to his face and went to any place where he threw a stone, but the stone seemed to have more effect in moving the sheep off the crops than did the dog. The next flock was under the care of an old shepherd, his leathery face white with stubble. His dog was even less satisfactory. He said he would happily make a present of it to us, and that it quite often took the sheep by the throat and killed them.

We met our third Páramo shepherd the following morning. He looked like a plump tractor-driving farmer except for his handwoven hooded cloak. We were glad to find him, since, not for the first time, we were lost on the Páramo. The only indication of the path to the Ermita de Santa Marina near Monasterio was a double line of signs forbidding hunting. They marched across the interminable chalk plateau and were presumably the work of neighbouring proprietors, each equally determined that the other should not have his birds. Unfortunately, halfway across, both landowners had tired of the game.

The hermitage at Monasterio compared, in a more civilised way, to our paradise above Vega de Doña Olimpa. A Romanesque church sat, like a child's toy, on smooth green grass, protected on all sides by the cliffs of the Páramo. For the comfort of travellers there were stone tables and benches and, best of all, a constantly replenished tank of fresh water the size of a small bathing-pool. Into this the children immediately jumped like a pair of water-babies. For fear of the *párroco* I insisted they should wear their bathing briefs, but every time I looked round these had come off again. A black dot sitting on top of a cliff was a shepherd guarding his sheep. The sound of his pipe came down clearly to us. Much excited, Miranda got out her descant recorder and, sitting cross-legged on a stone table, began to play. Soon Andrew joined in with his alto. They were still at it long after the shepherd had taken his flock home. Under the waxing moon Jessica flitted round the tables like a shadowy sprite, hopping to their music.

CHAPTER 18

An accident

From the *meseta* of Castile, the returning pilgrim descends to the Rioja district, where the banks of the Ebro are striped with vines. For us, the wine country began at the village of San Millán, where winejars clustered round the doors of the houses. It was a relief to have descended to an altitude of 573 metres and no longer to feel the winds of the Páramo round our necks. To combat them I had been obliged to knit a polo neck for my sweater with wool bought at Burgos. An added luxury, also bought at Burgos, was a thermos flask which enabled us to have hot coffee with our picnic breakfasts, since we had finally given up our attempts to rouse Spanish café owners at this time of day.

San Millán, the patron saint of the village, was one of the many hermits who lived in caves in Castile in the sixth century. It was his successors, men like Santo Domingo de la Calzada, who were to do so much to make the route safe for pilgrims, building roads and bridges, often single-handed. Such work was, of course, not possible for San Millán, since the bones of St. James had not yet been discovered in his day. Instead he wrestled with the devil and cured the blind and afflicted.

The present-day people of San Millán were evidently fond of cats. Groups of white ones with tabby splotches regarded us sedately from behind geraniums on several window sills as we passed through the village. Round holes to admit them had been cut in the barn doors. In general we were impressed by the kindness to animals shown in northern Spain, where we never saw a mule ill-used or a dog underfed. On several occasions, indeed, it was the Spanish who chided *us* for thoughtlessness, one man pointing out a sore place on Hamilcar's nose where the halter had rubbed, and another reminding us that the wind had changed and the *burricos* should be moved to the leeward side of a bush.

If the people of San Millán loved cats, those of its larger neighbour, Treviana, preferred dogs. The population of *braccos*, a type of spotted pointer, almost equalled the human population. The first *bracco* I saw lay sprawled in the gutter, quite motionless. I was ahead of the others because I had mistaken the electronic church bell for the chimes of a travelling shop. I stopped and watched the flies crawling over the poor creature's muzzle, and cursed the people of Treviana for not disposing of their dead pets decently. I would have to drag the corpse into the undergrowth myself for I could not let the children see such a sight. I had just taken a firm grip of its enormous back paw when it jumped up, gave me a withering glance, and slunk away.

We had a special reason for wishing to visit the vinous town of Haro, though it was not strictly on the pilgrim route from Burgos to Pamplona. In 1957 we had become much addicted to a moderately priced Rioja, the product of Bodegas Bilbainas at Haro. So great had been our enthusiasm for this wine that we persuaded our London wine merchant to give us a letter of introduction to Señor Diez, the manager. On our way to a fortnight's holiday in the south we had stopped at Haro and made a memorable tour of the cellars, which seemed to extend under a large part of the town. We now planned to visit them once more.

Just outside Haro we put up our tent beside the ponderous Ebro, and immediately set about cleaning ourselves. As we knelt beside the blue washing-up bowl and scrubbed our hands and faces, I could not help wondering whether, after forty-five nights under canvas, we would even get past the gate of Bodegas Bilbainas this time. Thomas's only

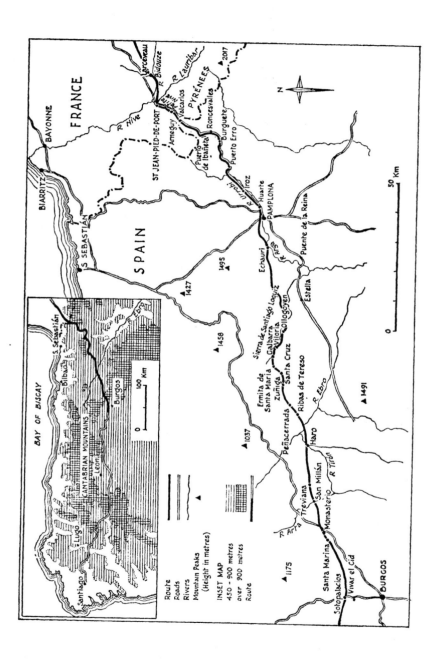

clean shirt had split from wrist to armpit and even our best jeans were dusty and baggy at the knee. Fortunately the first person we spoke to on arriving at the *bodega* was none other than Señor Diez himself, the young man who had shown us round the cellars eighteen years ago. He had now lost his hair and grown a corporation and did not pretend to remember us, but at once took us into a large office decorated with painted tiles. He told us that he had been promoted to director on the death of his father, and he offered us the usual tour.

Fortunately the annual fiesta was about to begin, so we were only subjected to one hour in the catacombs, though Thomas, who takes a professional interest in wine, would happily have spent longer. Down there, tunnel after tunnel lined with bottles vanished into the gloom around us and the whole place was pervaded by that slightly vinegary smell inseparable from cellars. We were at a distant point of the tour when all the lights went out, and for five minutes we were left in Stygian darkness many metres below the ground where the temperature is a constant ten degrees centigrade. It was a relief to return like Persephone to the dazzling light of day.

In the bottling-shed we missed the rows of women corkers we remembered from our last visit. This work was now done by machines. The cat population on the other hand had gone up. Señor Diez assured us that there were now twenty of them and that he knew them all by name. To prove it he addressed a heavily pregnant tabby as Nelson.

When we left the *bodega* he handed us a large parcel. We carried it back to our hide and, like bandits with unknown booty, eagerly tore off the wrappings. Inside were four superb bottles of a rich and fruity Rioja red wine called Pomal. We agreed it would be cruelty to Hannibal to make him carry them, so we demolished a litre and a half there and then. When you have spent an hour treading reverently round the cathedrals of wine, communion must follow even if it is only eleven o'clock in the morning.

After a lengthy siesta and a swim (rashly promised to Miranda) in the icy municipal pool, we walked into Haro itself, where the main square was decorated for the *Batalla de Botas*, when the populace squirt leather *botas* of wine over each other's best clothes. The battle was not due to start until the next day, but all night bursts of song were carried down the river to our camp. At dawn we heard the municipal band strike up, and the first fireworks go off. It required an effort to turn away from all this gaiety and set our faces towards the slow ascent to the Pyrenees.

The Sierra de Cantabria gave us our first taste of the mountains ahead. As we crossed over the shoulder that lies between the villages of Ribas de Tereso and Peñacerrada we left the wine country behind. The change of vegetation at the summit was dramatic. Behind us was a dry, rocky slope of juniper and rosemary. Ahead was a green, Atlantic landscape. Descending through a thick forest of beeches and oaks, we felt strangely nostalgic for England, and the children shouted with excitement as they recognised the birches and ashes of our forest of Gravetye at home. Even the humid quality of the heat was reminiscent of an English summer day, but the clouds of butterflies told us that we were in a land that had not yet been poisoned by insecticides. Now we understood why the business men of Bilbao have surrounded Haro with hideous villas. Only a heavy annual rainfall could produce such a forest, and no doubt they wanted to get away from it. Because of its dry and healthy climate the whole Rioja district is known as the lung of Spain.

Two days later, just beyond the town of Santa Cruz, we crossed into Navarre. Navarre was once one of the kingdoms of Spain and, although the majority of the people who live there are Basques, they call themselves Navarrais, because Navarre is not one of the three official Basque provinces. These are Guipúzcoa, Álava and Vizcaya. Nor do the Navarrais share the characteristics of the Basque (a private and intensely nationalistic race) but, by contrast, are gay, hospitable and generous as we were soon to discover. In one village we passed through we found the bar locked but a bottle of wine cooling in a horse trough outside. We sat eyeing the bottle enviously as we ate our mid-morning raisins at an outdoor table of a totally deserted café. When the landlord returned with the rest of the population in a procession from Mass, he insisted on making us a present of the bottle and providing Fanta for the children as well.

Our first camp in Navarre was above the saw-milling village of Zuñiga, at the foot of the Sierra de Santiago Loquiz. For the second time we found an enchanting hermitage waiting to receive us, with stone benches round its base and a green-shaded lawn beside it. Unfortunately there was somebody there already: a fat lady in a black bathing costume sun-bathing under the guardianship of an ancient duenna. Discreetly we wandered off among the mountain scrub in search of an alternative camping place, but in an instant the Señora had wrapped a black skirt round her ample thighs and, with a hasty "Adios", was gone, followed closely by her attendant crone.

It was shaming to discover how quickly, in the face of necessity, our public-school standards of morality crumbled. Our currency allowance was small and, like tramps, we walked with our eyes on the ground purloining anything usable we found in ditches. By the time we reached France both Thomas and Jessica were kitted out in smart cardigans, Miranda had a new shirt and shorts, and we all had new scarves and handkerchiefs. The camp at the Ermita de Santa Maria had everything a gypsy could desire. Besides nightingales and a waning moon (the moon that we had seen born at Doña Olimpa) there was a conveniently placed field of broad beans.

When I examined the donkeys in the morning I was sad to see that Hannibal was developing sores under his pack-saddle. There was a small raw patch on his withers and one just in front of each hip bone. Because of the necessity for haste, all we could do was put the baggage on Hamilcar for a day. With the children mounted on Hannibal we set off across the wooded mountains, passing two lonely villages nestling in pockets of green among the trees. At one of these a man travelling with a pig asked if we were musicians going to the fiesta at Galbarra. It was at the village beyond Galbarra that the accident occurred.

Hannibal was not a vicious donkey, but he was young and excitable. He was also quite tall. As we entered Viloria, a mule, tethered on the mountain pasture overhanging the road, made a rush towards us out of curiosity. Startled, Hannibal reared, throwing the children over his tail on to the newly gravelled road. Miranda picked herself up and ran up the bank, clutching her head. There she curled up in a ball, screaming. Jessica, also screaming, lay in the road, her new hat soaked in blood.

CHAPTER 19

The charcoal burners of Viloria

It was Andrew who picked Jessica up off the road and comforted her. This was not the last time that we were to rely on his coolness in an emergency. He called for water, and I do not even remember rummaging for the canteen in the saddlebags. I do remember the awful moment of not being able to unscrew the top with my shaking hands, making a superhuman effort, and succeeding. Andrew soaked his handkerchief in it again and again, mopping away the blood. To my relief, no gaping wound was revealed, just a puncture on the temple and a large lump.

The sun was now high, and we carried Jessica to the only scrap of shade we could find beside the road. Some men had gathered round, and a woman arrived with a first-aid kit and painted Jessica's forehead a lurid red. The poor child was a pathetic sight as she lay whimpering on the grass, for, besides her new troubles, she already had one eye closed from a mosquito bite the night before. I sat watching her pupils for signs of concussion, while Andrew told her Chaucer's story of Chanticleer and Pertalotte, and Miranda, who had been only slightly hurt, offered her her last sweet.

We had not planned to camp at Viloria, but there was no alternative. We found a grassy shelf above the stream and spent a hot and uncomfortable afternoon lying under a hedge, trying to keep in the constantly shrinking shade. We were plagued by flies, and both children complained of headaches and had to be given aspirins. It was only when evening came that we discovered that we had made our forced landing in a place of great interest.

Viloria was a village entirely inhabited by charcoal burners. Under a walnut tree outside the village we watched one at work. He was as black as a coal miner and stood guarding his great pile of earth day and night, occasionally throwing a shovelful of soil on it to damp the fire within. Smoke came out continually from holes round the base. Slowly and courteously he told us how, by controlled burning, wood could be reduced to *carbon* without being consumed. (Coal he described as *carbon mineral*.) The wood must be wrapped in straw before it was buried and must burn for fifteen days and nights. If the fire was allowed to go out during that period, the charcoal was ruined.

That evening, through the velvet darkness, bursts of music and singing came to us from the fiesta at Galbarra, two kilometres away. After Thomas had read the children to sleep with *Kidnapped*, we decided to set off for the bar at Viloria. As we climbed the village street we paused to look at the stone escutcheons on the corners of houses. These are typical of the Spanish Basque country where any family, simply by virtue of being Basque, is considered noble.

We found the bar in a small square with a walnut tree. The entrance was through a stable-door without any sign above it, and once through this we had to pass several stalled cows before we reached a bare little room where men were drinking. The furniture was of the simplest. Apart from the counter, there was only a kitchen table and three wooden stools. The array of bottles behind the bar was sparse, and wine and Coca-Cola were kept cool in a stone sink through which spring water passed continuously. Yet, strangely enough, presiding over all this squalor was one of the prettiest girls we had seen in Spain, a slim señorita with most delicate feaeures and a perfectly filled pair of jeans.

We soon discovered that all five of her brawny customers were charcoal burners and very drunk, and that one was the owner of the mule that had caused Hannibal to shy. By way of compensation he offered us a squirt from his *porrón* of red wine. He said that he drank four litres of this 'black wheesky' daily and that it did him nothing but good. We had our doubts when he pulled up his plaid shirt to reveal a formidable scar on his solar plexus, the result of an ulcer operation. It looked as if the surgeon had gone about his task with a broken bottle.

Later, two stout men wearing flashy ties and rings came in. They were strangely out of place in that primitive setting. One looked like a leader of the Mafia, and the other his bodyguard. The *Mafioso* called for Scotch whisky and cigars and treated the company. It took the beautiful señorita several minutes to find the half-empty whisky bottle, which she brought from another room and which was probably kept under her mother's bed. It was obviously not called for often. After a couple of rounds the *carbonero* with the scar started to strum on the guitar. As we left, he and his friends were settling in for an all-night session.

At dawn the sound of music from the Galbarra fiesta was continuing unabated. Bursts of shouting and singing, interspersed with tunes from a band, were as loud as they had been at midnight. It remained a source of constant wonder to us, this fierce passion for enjoyment of the Spanish. Not even the pleasure-loving Italians have such staying power.

The old man burning charcoal under the walnut tree had told us of the mule-track we must take over the Sierra de Santiago Loquiz to Estella. He had told us at length, repeating his directions twice, and ending with a courtly speech which went something like, "If you do as I say, and follow the directions that I give you, you will surely, with God's blessing, reach the end of your journey in safety." We did as he said, and for several kilometres climbed a well-marked track between arbutus, myrtle and juniper. It was when we began the descent that the path deteriorated into a staircase of rock and finally disappeared in a grove of holm-oak. This was frequently our experience when following mountain footpaths in Europe. They radiate from villages and for the first few kilometres are well maintained, but the stretches which linked one village to another are today frequently missing, leaving the traveller to fight his way through the undergrowth until, if he is lucky, he hits upon one of the tentacles radiating from the next village. On this occasion we were not lucky and, when we finally saw the roofs of Ollogoyen below us, there seemed no way to reach it except down the face of a deeply eroded chalky ravine.

Estella is one of the richest towns in Navarre, and Navarre, according to a taxi driver we met, is the richest province in Spain, with a car to every three in the population. At Estella we learned what it feels like to be destitute in the midst of plenty. When we camped seven kilometres outside the town we discovered that Jessica and Hamilcar had rubbed each other raw coming over the mountains. The donkey had a nasty place on his backbone and the child had a red spot the size of an old penny on each buttock, with two corresponding holes in the seat of her jeans. There was nothing for it but to walk into the town to buy sticking plaster for Jessica and powdered penicillin for Hamilcar.

I volunteered to go with Thomas, little guessing what seven kilometres on the blistering tarmac would do to my bare feet in sandals. The afternoon heat had reached its zenith and, to make matters worse, the road was lined with summer villas, each with its own swimming-pool. Dante could not have devised a torture more exquisite than that of constantly hearing the splash of someone else's body hitting the cool water, while one's own ran with sweat under sticky clothes. At the first bar in Estella we emptied a litre bottle of iced mineral water in a matter of seconds.

We had last been in Estella when Miranda was aged one and we remembered it as a shabby little town where there was a fiesta going on. Seven years later it was still shabby and a fiesta was again in preparation. Decorated floats full of trumpeters were being paraded round the streets, and in the main square children in their best clothes were jigging to the music of a string orchestra issuing from a first-floor window, where a wedding reception was in progress. It was our misfortune to arrive in Estella on a Sunday. As usual we had a shopping list as long as both our arms, and the only shops open were fancy-cake shops and, mercifully, the chemist. There was nothing we could do but sip cognac at a pavement café and stare at the closed shutters of butchers', bakers' and grocers' shops. We could not find so much as a loaf of bread or an egg, and we knew that, back in camp, we were down to emergency rations: half a bag of rice and a tin of tunny.

If there is a medal for cooks who can make something out of nothing, Thomas deserved it that night. By adding sultanas bought at a confectioner, a pickled onion from the bar and a handful of thyme from the roadside to our tunny and rice, he achieved a triumphant risotto for all of us, including Iago. We ate it again, cold, for breakfast.

CHAPTER 20

Bull fever

Pamplona is the capital of Spanish Navarre. It is an ancient city, founded by the sons of Pompey in 68 B.C. to guard one of the main gateways into Spain from France. Its original name was Pompeiopolis, which the Moors corrupted to Bambilonah when they occupied it. The present walls are ringed on the north side with the remains of many previous ones, which bear witness to a history of continual sieges and sackings.

Approaches to big cities are seldom pleasant, and Pamplona sent out poisonous tentacles a long way into the country. We breakfasted by a river ten kilometres from the town, realising too late that its banks had been used as a dump. Among mountains of broken window glass, one of the choicer items was a crate of rotting sheeps' heads. Iago had no objection to them and was unapproachable for many hours afterwards.

We next had to pass the city slaughter house. The doomed cattle, bellowing from parked lorries, were to haunt Miranda's dreams for many nights to come. The cement works, which went on for a kilometre, blowing a fine white dust in our faces, were followed by a brief respite at a workman's bar, owned by the *pelota* champion of Navarre for 1964. His presentation beret, complete with tassel, hung in a yellowing plastic bag above the bar, and his array of silver cups badly needed polishing. He himself looked in pretty good shape, and spent a lot of time throwing sticks for a noisy Alsatian. He had a complete *pelota* court in his back garden and from time to time small boys came in and asked for the loan of the hard ball, covered in dogskin, used for the game. They bounced it against the back wall of the court with their bare palms. Professional players use a large basketwork glove called a *chistera*.

It was a mistake to take the donkeys through one of the busiest streets of Pamplona, but on our map the road appeared to skirt the town to the north, and it was the only way to reach Huarte, the next village on our route to the Pyrenees. At a busy intersection, a traffic policeman frantically waved white-gloved hands at us and shouted that the road was not suitable for animals. He was quite right, but we persuaded him to hold up all four streams of cars and heavy lorries while we crossed. The next hour was not one I would care to live through again. The sun beat down, the traffic roared, and delivery vans and cars, often double parked, forced us and the donkeys right out into the main stream of the traffic. We realised how wise we had been to give large towns a wide berth in the past, and vowed that we would do so again in the future. At last we reached a quiet wood by the River Arga (a tributary of the Ebro), and put up the tent.

We were not the only people eating lunch by the river at Huarte that day. A Spanish family, in a motorised caravan, was there before us. They had the greater part of a small pig laid on a grill and looked, from their shapes, as if they devoted a large portion of their lives to

Cebrero, high point of the pilgrim route, on the Galician border.

Susan writes the diary.

Passing through the village of Banuncias.

eating similar meals. They had brought all their children and pets. Even the goldfinch was being given an airing in his cage on the roof of the caravan. We sat at a discreet distance eating bread and *pamplonica*, a particularly delicious brand of *chorizo*, which closely resembles *salami*, made, of course, in Pamplona. But even the taste of the best preserved meat cannot compete with the smell of freshly charred flesh. We all of us, including Iago, sat with our noses eagerly to the wind, barely mastering the temptation to beg bones for him. After many courses, and many bottles, the father of the family attempted a few notes on a guitar, but soon fell asleep in a deckchair.

Thomas had promised me a treat in Pamplona. I was to have a bath there, the first for two months — not only a bath, but a night in a bed with real sheets and a pillow. I took the bus to town feeling like a gold prospector hitting the bright lights for the first time after months in the outback. I was determined to squeeze every ounce of pleasure from these twenty-four hours of civilisation. I had not reckoned with the feast of San Fermin. The great bull festival lasts a week, with Spain's most famous matadors drawing crowds to the bull-ring every day. But the most exciting events of the festival are the morning *encierras*, when the bulls that are to fight in the afternoon are driven through the streets to the Plaza de Toros. The agile Basque youths, wearing red berets and sashes, run ahead of them, usually (but not always) missing mortal injury by centimetres. Only the Spanish, with their obsessive death wish, could give over a city centre to such a wildly dangerous sport.

San Fermin was not in fact due to begin until July 5th, in four days' time, but the city was already packed with tourists. Six hotels in succession told me they were full, and in the end I sought the assistance of the tourist office. Twenty Americans, all no doubt determined to live out their own version of Hemingway's *Fiesta*, were doing the same thing, and the three girls behind the counter looked ready to drop; indeed, one did while I was there. At first I thought she was searching for a leaflet for the paunchy mid-Western post-graduate ahead of me in the queue. Only when she failed to reappear did the post-graduate and I peer over the counter to see what had become of her. The poor creature had passed out cold on the floor.

One of the remaining two girls eventually told me that the Little Slaves of Christ the King were the only people who could put me up in Pamplona. They ran a hostel on the outskirts of the city, and thither I set out to walk. Walking had now become a habit. It was no longer any effort to set the automatic pacing machine in motion and to enjoy the sights and sounds of the city as it carried me along.

The hostel was on the fourth floor of a modern apartment block. A smiling nun opened the door and took my 200 pesetas before leading

D

me to a cell which contained little beyond a white painted iron bed-
stead and a crucifix. The rules, however, which were printed on the
back of the door, did not appear too strict. I could do more or less
as I liked provided I vacated other people's rooms by eleven thirty,
came in by 1 a.m. and did not share my bed with anyone. And the
bathrooms were lovely. There was a whole row of them, all empty, all
with hot water coming out of the taps. I chose the one with the largest
bath, filled it to the overflow hole, and slowly lowered myself into its
warm embrace until nothing of me emerged but my nose.

No wonder that the Romans devoted so much time and energy to
erecting elaborate baths. No wonder mediaeval monks considered personal filth a form of mortification and therefore holy. It took Charles
Kingsley and the cold-water brigade to turn bathing into a penance for
Englishmen. As I reflected, the steam rose, and a thick brown layer of
scum formed round the side of the bath. Nobody knocked on the door,
and I stayed in an hour.

It was getting dark when I set out once more to explore the town.
Had I been the gold prospector, no doubt I would have had the intention of painting it red, but mine was a humbler ambition. I wanted to
find a saddler who would sell me a pack-saddle to protect my children
from my donkey and my donkey from my children. The girl at the
tourist office had given me the addresses of three, amidst much laughter, but one had turned over to upholstery and another to tarpaulin
making. I was pinning my hopes on the third, who operated in the old
part of the town.

My way lay through the fairground, and an enormous fair in honour
of San Fermin was in full swing. There were at least three sets of
everything from bumper cars and roundabouts to machines with flail-
ing arms that hurled cabs through the sky. All were brightly lit and
each belted out its own music at a deafening pitch. The ghost train
was surmounted by a mechanical monster who periodically raised
a life-sized girl to his fangs. She was bleeding profusely from wounds
in her naked thighs and breast. After eating a frankfurter at one of
the three gigantic demountable bars at the fairground I continued my
journey.

The saddler's shop was in a narrow cobbled street near the church
of San Nicolo. Peering through its grille I could see that it was a veritable Aladdin's cave whose contents excited me far more than gold or
pearls. New leather mule collars hung from the ceiling like hams, and
pagodas of military saddles perched on the counter. At the back of the
shop were gigantic bells attached to wooden collars to prevent cows
straying in the mountains. Vowing to return first thing in the morning,
I walked back to the convent. It was after midnight by the time I
reached it, but the nun on the door was still smiling.

Sleeping in a bed was to be the culmination of all those waking dreams about freshly laundered sheets and cool plumped-up pillows that had kept me going on the walk. Yet, strangely enough, when the dream came true, it was nearer to a nightmare. The pillow seemed too high and the bed too soft. Being used to the rigidity of the ground, I felt as if I was in a badly sagging hammock. In the morning I had the kind of headache that normally results from sleeping with the windows shut, but on this occasion the window was wide open. Perhaps I was growing unsuited to normal civilised life.

When Thomas came to rescue me from my convent the nun on duty informed us it was St. Thomas's Day. We set off gaily for the saddler's shop, only to be disappointed yet again. The leathery old Navarrais who owned it told us that he had not made a pack-saddle for years. He did however have some felt pads an inch thick and nearly a metre square. They were expensive, but we bought two which, we hoped, would ease the donkeys' backs by day and our own by night.

Then we gave ourselves up to the pleasures of the bull-mad city. Teams of workmen were putting up massive barriers in the central square where we drank our aperitifs. Posts as thick as railway sleepers were being lowered into permanent metal-lined holes in the street and secured with wedges. In three days' time they would withstand the impact of half-ton bulls in pursuit of juicy lads. In the shop windows there were posters describing the exploits of famous man-killing bulls, and even the priests inside the fifteenth-century cathedral were not unaffected. One was conducting a male-voice choir of fifty and another was rehearsing a concelebrated Mass for San Fermin's Day. The three young priests under his direction bobbed and bowed in dumb-show round the altar while he gestured like a *maître de ballet*.

After lunch in a restaurant full of greedy French people, we walked to our bus stop by the bull-ring. Outside the Plaza de Toros, which is a modern one, we saluted Hemingway's gigantic bust carved in pink granite and wearing a polo-necked sweater. It seemed to us that old 'papa' stared balefully at the double line of young Americans jostling each other at the ticket office. Certainly the sight of them all but cured me of my own passion for bull fighting. Before I knew that San Fermin had been taken over by the American universities I had planned to nip back over the Pyrenees by bus for a day at the festival. It was as well that I didn't for if I had arrived on July 9th I would have witnessed a serious accident at the morning *encierro*. Somebody tripped, there was a pile-up, and six bulls ploughed through a heap of people, wounding twenty and killing a local hotel clerk.

CHAPTER 21

Roncesvalles

The Pyrenees now lay ahead. The great range is in fact a continuation of the Cordillera Cantabrica, which we had been skirting to the south for the greater part of our journey. Now we had no alternative but to cross it. The Pyrenees proper extend from the Atlantic to the Mediterranean, for a distance of 400 kilometres, being both broadest and highest in the central portion. We proposed to take the pass at Roncesvalles, near the western end of the range, forty-seven kilometres from Pamplona.

There are no dramatic peaks in this western section, which is thickly forested to the summit. Neither are there any footpaths up to the pass, so we were obliged to take the road, but we had the consolation of knowing that this was the route the pilgrims took. For the whole of the first day we followed the river Arga towards its source. By the time we sat down for breakfast at Iroz its waters had already cleared and were running over pebbles. Although it was only eight o'clock we were surprised to see a Spanish businessman drive right down to the edge of the river, remove all his clothes except for his trousers, which he rolled up to his knees, and proceed to wash his car slowly and methodically. Car washing was, we knew, a favourite riverside occupation of Spaniards, but it was one usually indulged in by family parties on picnics. When our businessman had thoroughly polished his car and shaken out all the mats, he dressed once more and drove off. Within ten minutes he was back. He had left his watch on a boulder. The poor man must have expected to find both it, and the strange gypsy party with donkeys, gone by the time he returned.

The whole of that morning walk was fragrant with the smell of mown hay, for haymaking comes late in the Pyrenees. At night we camped in a little triangular meadow that nosed its way up into a fold in the mountains, Along one side of it ran a lane where an ox-cart loaded with hay creaked past from time to time with many warning cries from its driver, for the way was steep and rocky. On the other side of the meadow was the Arga, now dwindled to a mere stream, descending through a series of rock basins, each about the size of a kitchen sink.

These sinks made perfect baths for the children, although very cold ones, and they spent an hour splashing about in them.

The donkeys found entertainment nearby. Beside the ashes of a large brushwood fire they fought for rolling precedence: that is to say, Hannibal showed his massive hindquarters to Hamilcar, who stood impatiently on the sidelines awaiting his turn. But Hamilcar's roll, when it came, was superior to Hannibal's. He went over and over, squirming with delight, and lashing at the ground with his tail. Then he got up, shook himself and did it all over again. Hannibal had merely flailed about on his side blowing at the dust and grunting with contentment. He had always been a clumsy roller, and there had been a memorable occasion in Galicia when he had selected a dry ditch for a roll and stuck fast with all four feet in the air.

By the following midday we had reached the River Urrobi near Burguete and had found an island on which to camp. Camping on an island, we soon discovered, had its inconveniences. Within the first ten minutes both children had fallen into the water fully dressed. But at least the river protected us from a herd of horses who inhabited the park-like plateau pasture through which it flowed. The donkeys, who did not share the island with us, appeared only mildly interested in these wild and beautiful creatures, which galloped round them in circles, tossing their manes and emitting rubbery farts.

We reached Roncesvalles early in the morning of our third day in the Pyrenees. The climb was not steep on the Spanish side and the forest through which the road passed could have been an English one, with the sun's rays illuminating the mist between the beech trees. The famous abbey at Roncesvalles looked like a barracks, being roofed with corrugated iron, and indeed it seemed to be inhabited as much by soldiers as monks. Yet its history is long and honourable. It was founded for the succour of pilgrims by Sancho the Strong around 1230, and the tomb of that seven-foot slayer of the Moors is still preserved in the church. The Augustinian monks to whom it belonged had owned a chain of pilgrim monasteries, which offered the same facilities to pilgrims setting out from Bordeaux as the Cluniacs did to those coming from Le Puy, in the Massif Central. At no monastery could the hospitality compare with that at Roncesvalles, where pilgrims who had struggled to the top of the uninhabited pass found not only good food but also real beds instead of the routine straw, and even baths. Right up until the eighteenth century a monk always stood at the gate of the monastery offering bread to passers-by.

When we reached Roncesvalles there was no bread on offer, and the owner of the little bar beneath the monastery walls was at Mass. We sat down to make the most of what food we had beside a notice that expressed the wish that it should never be said of us "This place was beautiful until you came." We were, as always, careful to pick up our litter, but we left behind us something far more important, as we were to discover five hours later.

The famous pass at Roncesvalles is a kilometre or two above the monastery, up the steep defile of the river Urrobi. It was in this tree-filled valley that the heroic Roland died, making the name of Roncevaux famous for four centuries before the monastery was built. Roland was one of the knights who accompanied Charlemagne on his Spanish expedition against the Moors in 778. His name was immortalised in the famous *Chanson de Roland*, one of the earliest of the *chansons de geste*, committed to paper in the twelfth century but possibly composed much earlier. The *chansons de geste* were sung by the *jongleurs* who accompanied pilgrims on their journeys, and their themes were often taken from the chronicles of the monasteries on the pilgrim route.

Many of the adventures of Roland were, alas, fictitious. Even the famous events leading to his death were falsified in the *Chanson de Roland*. It is true that Roland commanded the rearguard of Charlemagne's army as it left Spain. It is true that he was ambushed and would not sound his horn for help until all his men were dead and he himself was mortally wounded. His murderers, however, were not Saracens but Basques, avenging themselves for the sack of Pamplona by Charlemagne, who had thought thus to reimburse himself for the expenses of the expedition.

Rather surprisingly, the summit of the pass, which is called Puerto de Ibañeta (1,157 metres) does not form the boundary between Spain and France. The frontier is at Valcarlos. As we stood by the isolated chapel at Ibañeta we could see, opposite us, the green wall of the mountain that we must descend. It looked steep and it was, and the donkeys' back hooves slipped continually. Fortunately in many places there were wide newly mown verges. As the hours went by the heat became intense and so did the traffic coming from France.

It is a remarkable fact that although the slope on the French side is far more precipitous than that on the Spanish, it is from the French side, up the defile of the Petite Nive, that most of the tourists come. Nor is this phenomenon recent. The romance of Roncevaux has had a magnetic power over the French for two centuries, and Richard Ford described parties of ladies, who would not have dreamed of penetrating further into the Spanish Pyrenees (where dwell "the smuggler, the rifle sportsman, and all who defy the law"), coming up by carriage to the *Breche de Roland* to view *les bels horreurs*. No carriage loads of ascending ladies greeted us, but we met cars with number plates from almost every country in Europe and some from beyond. Six New Zealanders in a Land Rover, apparently naked but for their beards, gave us a cheery wave. At a wayside spring where we stopped to eat the last of our food three German hikers, flushed and sweating, plodded up the mountain towards us. They carried very new, and no doubt very heavy, knapsacks, hung about with saucepans and spare jackets, and looked dead-beat as they flopped on the ground to drink.

By one o'clock we were hungry again, but there was no prospect of food for another two hours. At this moment Miranda suddenly let out a wail of agony. She had left her survival belt, her most treasured possession, strapped round one of the trees at Roncesvalles. I would have gladly replaced the belt and every item in the leather 'housewife' suspended from it, rather than retrace our footsteps, but Andrew was made of sterner stuff. With a heroism worthy of the Chevalier Roland he offered to climb back to the abbey in the heat of noon. He would meet us in the first restaurant we reached at Valcarlos.

It was now my task to urge Hamilcar on. I simply had not the energy to combine this with telling the children a fairy story, as Andrew always did in the last stage of the day. It seemed as if the descent would never end when, suddenly, at a bend in the road, we saw the roofs of Valcarlos close below us. So many red and yellow Spanish flags were flying between them that we feared it might be the frontier and that Andrew, without a passport, would be unable to pass. However, the only challenge we received was from an enraged dog. It was a large boxer imprisoned in a garden above our heads. So passionate was its desire to sink its teeth into us that it plunged fifteen feet on to the road, landing on its head but not, alas, knocking itself out. The alarm of its two owners, who were running about trying to catch it, made us suspect that the animal really was dangerous. It first made a rush at me, and I gave it a hearty whack with my pilgrim staff. Next it went for the children who were walking because of the steepness of the street. At this point Thomas ran forward and landed two cracking blows on the snarling brute's skull. He felt, he later said, as if he was avenging himself on all the dogs that had rushed barking at us from every farmyard in Spain.

Valcarlos was a cheerful place, full of slightly tipsy French tourists who had come over the frontier in charabancs to eat large cheap lunches. We were soon following their example. Halfway through our third lamb chop Andrew arrived, waving the survival belt in triumph. He had hitched a lift halfway up to Roncesvalles, but had been obliged to walk all the way down. He said that the abbey was now almost unrecognisable, swarming with cars and tourists.

We spent our last night in Spain in a barn, for there were not two square metres of flat ground in the valley of the Petite Nive. The barn belonged to a fat and hospitable farmer who was piling hay into cocks in an almost vertical field. It seemed like a palace to us. The loft could be entered from the high ground at the back and there was a pile of straw to sleep on. Outside, a mountain spring perpetually replenished a stone trough. The farmer told us that, in winter, the stalls below were inhabited by his two hundred sheep, at present grazing in the mountains. The hillside opposite us, beyond the Petite Nive, was French territory.

In the morning we walked our last kilometre in Spain, to the frontier post at Arneguy, with fear in our hearts. Would we be allowed to take the donkeys and the dog into France? We were soon among the maze of halt signs that led to the Spanish customs. A group of soldiers inspected our passports and took a friendly interest in the donkeys. But they expressed doubts as to whether the French would allow our animals in. "*Hasta mañana,*" they called as they waved us on to the bridge.

Two

FRANCE

I have learned that the swiftest traveller is he that goes afoot.

Henry Thoreau, *Walden*

CHAPTER 22

The Basque country

The *gendarme* on the far side of the Petite Nive was as French as the Arc de Triomphe. There was not a speck of dust on his navy-blue cape and tunic and his complexion had just that tinge of yellow that denotes the discriminating gastronome. He surveyed us and our donkeys as balefully as if we had been last night's *boeuf en daube* warmed up. Meanwhile the three Spanish soldiers leaned over the railings on the far side of the Nive, grinning expectantly. There was a long pause while the *gendarme* retired to his office with our passports, the donkeys' papers, Iago's rabies certificate and our letter from the cultural attaché at the French Embassy in London.

When the *gendarme* emerged he said that we must wait an hour until he could telephone headquarters at Bayonne. French time was, improbably, an hour *behind* Spanish; the only explanation we could think of was that the Spanish government set their clocks so far ahead in an effort to get the people out of bed before midday. But a café was open and, having unloaded the donkeys and tied them up in a *pelota* court, we went in for breakfast, wondering whether this was the only breakfast we would be allowed to eat in France. As soon as we entered the café we knew that we were no longer in Spain. Gone was the litter of sawdust, cigarette ends, peanut shells and prawn heads inseparable from a Spanish bar. Here were fitted carpets and fumed oak panelling. The butter on the *pain grillé* was creamy as only French butter can be, the coffee came in thick white china cups and the bill was staggering. We could have eaten for a day in Spain on what that breakfast cost us in France. At eight twenty precisely a handsome uniformed officer with a red stripe down his trousers approached our table and informed us that we might proceed into France. The cultural attaché's letter had done its work.

Arneguy was an emphatically French little town. On the outskirts we passed an ornate, square grey house of the type you see in every French provincial town. At an open window an old lady with a chignon on the top of her head and a crocheted shawl round her shoulders was drinking her *café au lait* from a flowered bowl. She seemed to sum up, in her person, a certain orderliness that is typical of the French, and that the Spanish lack. Equally French was the first of the many châteaux we were to see. It stood, framed in trees, at a discreet distance from a village, a square eighteenth-century building with a steeply pitched roof and decorated mansard windows. It was strange to us to see an isolated country house after so many weeks in Spain, where they barely exist.

Our entry into the busy holiday town of St. Jean Pied-de-Port, at the foot of the pass, was little short of triumphal. The sight of our donkeys elicited a babble of baby talk from almost every Frenchwoman we passed. " 'Gardez les petits ânes!" they crooned, as they dragged their children to windows and doors, and even from the sacred dining-table. An old lady standing in her garden murmured "Comme c'est joli!", the clerk at the post office from whom we collected our letters said "Bravo!"; and a woman taking twelve long loaves of bread home on her bicycle rack concluded a running interrogation by declaring that she was ravie by our histoire. After the incomprehension of the Spanish all this was strange to us.

In the old part of the town we could hardly force a passage between the holiday crowds. The narrow cobbled streets were filled with family parties, and there were herds of little boys dressed in identical mini-shorts and peaked caps under the guardianship of bored student overseers. As we crossed the bridge over the Nive itself and passed under the gateway of the old citadel, we realised what it was that had brought the tourists to St. Jean, and what they had succeeded in destroying. Thomas wanted to take photographs, but he was too weighed down with a bag of irresistible croissants to handle his camera. Instead it was us who were photographed. The fat fathers with cameras who knelt in front of us on the cobbles thought we were some kind of strange travelling people who had come out of Spain, which indeed we were.

This was the street down which pilgrims bore palm branches made into crosses. They would plant these in the ground when they reached the summit of their route across the Pyrenees at the pass of Ibañeta. It was the place where pilgrims from all three routes across France met for the first time. One route came from Paris, one from Vézelay, but the most easterly, which we would follow, originated deep in the Massif Central at the cathedral city of Le Puy.

In France Andrew took over the duties of navigator. Our French maps were to a scale of 1/50,000, four times as large as our Spanish. They were also far more accurate. By following them carefully we found we could keep to pleasant country lanes or reliable footpaths. The heat of summer was approaching and Andrew planned each day's walk to end beside a river. Our first river was the shady Bidouze, and we were in it almost before we had unloaded the donkeys. Even Thomas,

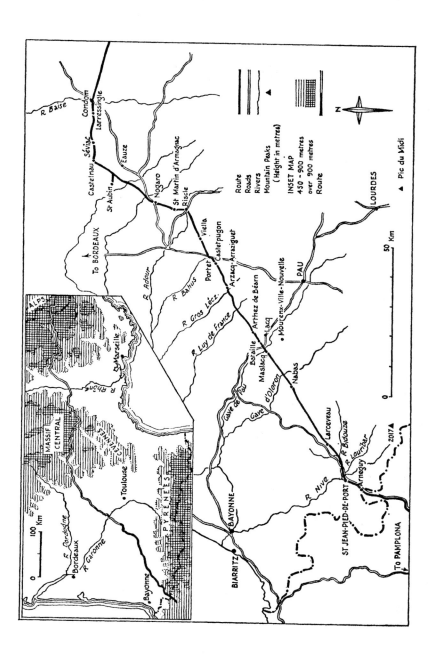

who has not cared for water since they made him take cold baths at Winchester, lowered himself cautiously off a fallen tree and struck out for the far bank.

One of the charms of that first camp by the Bidouze was a pair of water rats. They lived in a muddy backwater and frisked unafraid on a half-submerged log. They looked surprisingly round and fluffy out of the water, and their tails were shorter than those of land rats. Miranda, who was brought up on *The Wind in the Willows*, watched them enchanted. When she tired of rat-watching she played at carriage horses with Jessica. For some days now they had been a matched pair of palominos who invariably beat Mr. Jones's brilliant but erratic chestnuts at shows. When playing the game Miranda held Jessica's hand and trotted her round in circles, lifting her knees high and talking in a bleating manner like Larry the Lamb. This was supposed to resemble the neigh of a horse. I began to wonder whether, after five hours a day in the saddle, my children were not turning into horses.

The landscape round Larceveau, through which we walked the following day, reminded me of Westmorland. Wild, bracken-covered fells rose on either side of the lanes which ran between dry stone walls, and the donkeys, to their delight, found gorse for the first time since leaving Galicia. They fell upon it eagerly, and, after a night of prickly feasting, were practically unmanageable. Hamilcar threw me when I attempted to ride him into camp in the morning, and Hannibal went all day at his most maddening pace, a series of baggage-dislodging rushes, with Thomas dragging on the rope behind him and yelling "Stoppit, you bloody brute!" Iago also had feasted well during the night. We had failed to put a lid on the tinned tripe we had had for supper.

In the valleys between the fells were the farms. We followed a wooden cart, drawn by a pair of beige oxen with sheepskin headdresses, to one of these. Typical of many we saw in the Basque country, it was a large, chalet-like building, painted white, with four red-shuttered windows on the first floor and three on the second. A wide, centrally-placed door led into an imposing front hall, as we discovered when we were invited inside to buy *fromage de brébis*. Cheese made from ewes' milk is the speciality of the French Pyrenees and we had disturbed several groups of the famous Marech sheep when we took footpaths over the fells. They are fine milkers but their coarse fleece, although well adapted for keeping out the Atlantic rains, is only fit for stuffing mattresses. The furniture of the farmhouse hall interested us even more than the cheese. Fine antiques stood about the great beamed room, including a refectory table, a grandfather clock and a genuine Basque *zuzulu*. A *zuzulu* is a wooden bench with high back that can be folded to form a table.

Above the door of the house was a tablet bearing the date it was built and the name of the man and woman who had built it. We saw many of these inscriptions above farmhouse doors, for the Basques cling tenaciously to family traditions. The father of the family, the *etcheko jaun*, has complete authority and chooses his heir from among his sons and daughters. The rest must seek their fortunes elsewhere, and many have emigrated to South America.

Perhaps as a result of emigration, we found the Basque country sparsely inhabited. Few of the villages had shops, and we had to rely on erratic vending vans for food. On one occasion we were lucky and hijacked a van that was collecting eggs from the farms. The driver let us have six for a franc (an unheard of bargain in a land where food for the five of us was costing £50 a week). But we went three days without coinciding with a baker, and had been once more reduced to cold kedgeree by the time we reached the communal forest of Nabas.

Vast tracts of land in the Basque country are still owned and administered according to ancient laws by village councils, and the Forêt de Nabas was one of them. It had a wide verge and a notice saying *Interdit aux Nomades*. Beside this we settled down to our breadless breakfast. I was just pouring coffee from the thermos when a farmer approached, pushing a bicycle behind four beige cows and a large Friesian. He had a typical Basque face, mostly consisting of a nose and a smile, surmounted by one of those berets that members of his race only remove for church and bed. All proceeded in an orderly manner until the leading cow caught sight of the donkeys tethered to the 'No Nomads' notice. It was obvious she had never seen a donkey in her life. With hardly a moment's hesitation she swung her great head round and retreated at a gallop up the road, accompanied by her four sisters, their vast udders swinging, their flanks wobbling like jellies. The Basque waved his bicycle in the air in an attempt to turn them, but nothing would arrest the stampede. Only when the donkeys were well hidden in the forest would the cows finally pass us. Fortunately their owner regarded the whole incident as an enormous joke. After shutting the cows in a field he came back, still laughing, and said *"Vous faites le scout, alors?"* We had been taken for pedlars and travelling musicians, but never boy scouts.

When the Basque had departed Miranda told us she had composed a poem in honour of the occasion. It went as follows:

> Our friend the cow
> Carries a map
> The sea is white
> And the land is black.

Everyone applauded except Jessica who, after five frowning minutes of silence chanted

> Our friend the dog
> Is a hog
> Because he eats all our food.

CHAPTER 23

14 July

The Pyrenees continued to cast their spell over us after we had entered Gascony, for as we travelled eastwards through Béarn, we crossed a series of rivers which had originated in the mountains and were on their way to join the Atlantic at Bayonne. These were no ordinary rivers, but racing torrents known as *gaves*, a word said to be Basque in origin.

We camped beside the Gave d'Oloron, which cut a canyon through rich fields of maize and tobacco. The descent to the river through dense scrub and periwinkle was steep, but at the bottom was a shady beach lapped by green foam-capped waves. The children opened a pebble shop on a rock there, and Iago dug river-whitened bones from the sand.

The Gave de Pau was sluggish and polluted by comparison, no doubt because we crossed it downstream from Pau. Beyond, the countryside of Béarn began to resemble our own Wealden hills, ridge lying behind ridge with thickly wooded bottoms between. The farmhouses were beautiful here, many of them eighteenth-century with roofs of weathered red tiles overhanging decorated cornices. Their barns, built of round boulders from the *gave*, were fragrant with new hay, and their gardens filled with roses, hollyhocks and gladiolus. At the village of Bataille we found ourselves at the top of a ridge with breathtaking views on either side. It seemed well named partly because we had climbed up to it with such effort and partly because it divided the heavily industrialised vale of Lacq to the south from an unspoilt valley to the north.

At Lacq, alas, they have struck oil and gas, and from our ridge we looked down on a line of rigs, standing like great pecking birds on the valley floor. The flaring chimneys of a refinery were just visible through the smog, and even from that distance they emitted a steady roar.

Andrew called them the dark satanic mills, sucking up an evil brew from the bowels of the earth to lay waste the land, and produced some startling statistics from Ivan Illitch on modern transport. Apparently if you divide the number of passenger miles travelled by mechanical means by the number of man hours put into the manufacture, manning and maintenance of transport machinery and its fuels, you come out at a figure of four miles an hour — exactly Hamilcar's pace when on top form.

Our dislike of the oil field was not shared by the people of Béarn. A farmer at Bataille proudly told us how the Societé Nationale des Petroles d'Aquitaine had struck oil at Lacq in 1949. Lacq's thirty wells now produce more natural gas than almost any other field in the world, and this is conducted all over France in 6,000 kilometres of pipeline. More is used for the manufacture of chemicals and plastics. He strongly recommended a visit to Lacq's oil museum. Although we might affect to despise the chemical industries of Lacq, I was painfully aware that our journey would have been much harder without them. The lightweight plastic and aluminium equipment we used was all directly or indirectly the product of such industry.

As we approached Arthez de Béarn along the ridge we moved into villa land. Some of the houses were converted farmhouses, beautified with wrought iron and renamed *La Rustica*; others were bungalows with names like *La Maison des Nids* and *Vent de Roses*. They were in fractionally less awful taste than their Spanish equivalents, although up-ended concrete dice a foot square, painted red and white, were a common decoration on gate posts.

Arthez itself is a little French town like hundreds of others that merits no mention in Michelin, but not without charm for all that. A decorously ornate *hôtel de ville* and *gendarmerie* face each other across the main square, and at 7.30 a.m. the *boulangerie*, the *charcuterie* and the *épicerie* were all open. Blessing the French for their early-rising habits, we sat on a park bench on the parapet and ate a superb breakfast of fresh bread, pâté, cream cheese and honey. Beyond the smoking chimneys of Lacq we could see what looked like a mediaeval walled town with towers, but Andrew assured us it was the futuristic city of Mourenx-Ville-Nouvelle, built to house the oil men.

It was mid-July now and the heat of summer was upon us. Walking, even early in the morning, had been hotter and more exhausting than we had ever known it. I was wearing shorts even for these first stages, and my legs for the first time in my life were turning a satisfactory shade of brown. The donkeys had lost their shaggy wool coats and were sleek as mice. Only Iago's wiry coat remained unchanged, but he had added four centimetres to the length of his legs since leaving Santiago. For three more days we struggled up and down the ridges of Béarn, collapsing thankfully on the banks of small rivers to camp each night. Those riverside camps were delightful. The Luy de France, the Bahus and the Gros-Lécz all gave us a cool welcome at midday, and were still warm enough to wash in at six o'clock the following morning.

It was the Luy de France, in its alder-shaded water meadows, that we enjoyed most. The children were in and out of it all one afternoon, playing at pirates with a plank for a ship. They had just started collecting minnows in our washing-up bowl when the farmer arrived. He was dark and handsome, but his jaw was set a little too firmly for comfort. I launched into an eloquent appeal, aware that I was defending my home, and he seemed satisfied, but remarked that it was as well we had not come a fortnight earlier. There had been an *ouragon* in the night and the Luy had risen two metres in as many hours. People who had lived at Arzacq-Arraziguet for seventy years could not remember such a thing. Our camping meadow had been waist-deep in flood water.

There was a fête at Arzacq that night and Andrew went, after spending the whole afternoon darning his trousers. The town band, he told us next day, had processed through the town, led by drum majorettes who, although pretty, lacked the length of thigh of those who paraded at ball games in Illinois. Children carrying flaming torches followed the *pompiers*, and afterwards there was massed dancing, but by six o'clock the next morning the arcaded square was deserted. The French evidently lacked the staying power of the Spanish.

As we left Arzacq, clutching hot loaves from the bakehouse, we had our first view of the High Pyrenees, four days after leaving Roncesvalles. A marvellous series of jagged grey pyramids capped with snow hung against the blue sky on our right. These were the great central peaks ranging from the Pic du Midi de Bigorre (2,865 metres) to the Pic d'Anie (2,504 metres). Beyond them, barely visible in the heat haze, were some of the peaks on the Spanish side of the frontier.

Our third day of struggling over the Béarn switchbacks was the *Quatorze Juillet*, and it was the hottest so far. Our way lay through a series of hilltop villages. No sooner had we reached Castetpugon than the road plunged, only to rise once more to reach Portet, and again to reach Viella. After Viella the road flattened, but the sun grew still hotter. We were determined to reach the small town of Riscle, on the Adour, for the celebrations of the Fourteenth, but it seemed an eternity in coming. I walked ahead, as usual, indulging in a new daydream. I was attired in a faultlessly cut riding-habit, mounted on a horse that required only the lightest touch of the heel to guide it.

Thomas had now taken charge of Hamilcar and the children, for Andrew had run out of Spanish fairy tales, and anyway preferred the solitude of walking behind with Hannibal. By forming the rearguard of the cavalcade he could stop when he wanted and gossip with the insatiably curious natives. Thomas entered upon his duties with the zest of a newly arrived schoolmaster. He played 'Animal, Vegetable or Mineral' on the first stage, during which Andrew had always imposed a rule of silence, and told a story during the second stage instead of reserving it for the third. The story was the first in the popular Betty Anne-Marie series. Betty Anne-Marie was four, and had often to be rescued by her seven older brothers, Abraham, Benjamin, Crispin, Duncan, Ephraim, Frank and George. The boys were kind-hearted but somewhat rough-spoken, with the exception of Abraham, whose ornate sentences came straight out of a Victorian children's book. Ephraim was the bookish one and Frank was greedy. Although Thomas is a novelist, and had been a father for twenty-one years, he had never before invented stories for his children.

By mid-morning we had the burning road to ourselves. The solitary middle-aged men bicycling in track-suits, whom we had passed in the early morning, had all retired to the shade of their homes. Only an occasional car went by. It was one of these that stopped when we were sitting on the parapet of a bridge eating yoghurt (Andrew was under the bridge, wallowing like a hippopotamus in a small pool of water). Out of the car stepped a cheerful elderly gentleman. When we told him we had walked 1,000 kilometres, he said, "*C'est bien, ça!*" and shook us all by the hand before driving on.

An hour later we met the same old gentleman, standing by his parked car. This time he introduced himself as the mayor of Viella and handed us a piece of paper authorising us to have five drinks at his expense at the Café de France at Riscle. We had not planned to stop at Riscle, intending to go straight through the town and camp on the banks of the Adour, but the mayor of Viella's invitation changed everything. As Miranda later remarked, the two halves of the Fourteenth of July didn't seem to belong to each other. When we entered the main square of Riscle our weary walk suddenly became a triumphal progress. M. Boeilh, the proprietor of the Café de France, came out to greet us, and ushered us into his smart establishment, where we were given the place of honour at a table near the front. We had only dared venture into a French café once since crossing the frontier. At Maslacq they had charged us £1 for five tiny glasses of fizzy lemonade each containing fifteen centilitres, and we had vowed in future to buy our lemonade in large bottles at village shops and drink it in the street. Sweating and dusty, it was lemonade that I now longed to order, but honour dictated beer. The children had a whole Coke each, the first since Pamplona. We sat sipping our iced fizzy drinks in a state of stupefied bliss. There was even a bowl of water for Iago.

Monsieur Boeilh appeared to own half Riscle. He said that, for twelve francs, we could dine that night at his restaurant, Chez Mimi, and that the car park of his cinema was at our disposal as a camping ground. The cinema was admirably suited to our purpose, for it only opened on Saturdays, and an abandoned walled garden went with it. Here we put the donkeys, to wander through grass as high as their ears. We had hoped that Hannibal, free at last of his rope, would entertain us with a dance he had once performed unofficially all over somebody's potato field, but instead they both stood eyeing us sadly through the gate, ee-awing whenever we went by.

During the afternoon a journalist, also the property of M. Boeilh, interviewed us, and a nice young woman with a small boy invited us to tea. Her name was Madame Dauphine and she had a large shady garden just over the wall from the cinema. We soon found ourselves sitting round a table under a cedar tree eating homemade strawberry jam on biscuits and drinking *café au lait* out of bowls. The conversation turned on Southend-on-Sea where Madame Dauphine had been an au pair girl. It was the first time we had been invited into a bourgeois home since leaving Santiago, and it made us realise how much we had come to feel outsiders on this journey.

In the next stage of that amazing dream we were all being driven down to the Adour by Monsieur Dauphine (who was a television repairer) to swim. The place where we had planned to camp turned out to be one of the largest camp-sites in France. Our donkeys would have been woefully out of place among the 200 blue and orange tents, each with its attendant car. But the three swimming pools, one for each age group, were just what we wanted. After so many days of sunshine the water was tepid, and Jessica jumped continually into the enormous paddling pool and had ecstatic splashing matches with the Dauphines' small boy. Miranda, in the children's swimming pool, learned to float on her back. Luckily for our fellow-swimmers, a hot shower was obligatory before entering the pool.

We had decided to dine at Chez Mimi because it was July 14th. The little restaurant was already crowded when we arrived. Thirty peasants, supervised by a beaming nun, were hard at work with knives and forks along two trestle tables. All were elderly except for a savage-looking girl with a Neanderthal brow and a bosom that heaved with boredom under her flowered blouse. She ate voraciously and spoke not at all, which wasn't surprising considering that she was surrounded by pig-faced men three times her age. Soon we were being served with a five-course meal that we have eaten again in memory many times. It progressed with Gallic dignity through Julienne soup and terrine with cole slaw to the main dish, a succulent slice of grilled lamb. This was followed by French beans cooked as only the French can cook them, with butter and garlic. A lettuce salad then made way for a triumphant finale in the form of a chocolate éclair stuffed with real cream. The local Cabernet *en carafe* was included in the miraculous twelve-franc menu. Half-way through this feast we noticed that Jessica was gaily tipsy; she had downed the last half-inch of a glass of Ricard.

At midnight, as we wriggled into our sleeping-bags in the cinema car park, we heard the sound of music and fireworks coming up from the camp-site on the Adour. The *Quatorze Juillet* was being celebrated in the proper manner.

CHAPTER 24

A land flowing with Armagnac

The Department of Gers is famous for the production of Armagnac. We were determined to buy a bottle of the famous *eau de vie*, considered by many superior to cognac, and if possible to buy it at one of the cellars where a free tasting precedes purchase. Armagnac cellars are not easy to miss, for a vast warehouse is required, as the brandy grows more desirable (and more expensive) with every year that it matures. We came across our first at a road junction just outside Riscle, but as it was still before breakfast we decided to wait for the next.

Our donkeys were once more due for shoeing and when we saw an animal that closely resembled Hannibal wandering loose in a farmyard we enquired the name of his blacksmith. The white-bearded owner, having first assured us that his *mulet* was not an *âne*, told us that there was a blacksmith at Riscle. Cursing ourselves for not having made enquiries before leaving Riscle, we voyaged on, in search of a telephone. We were now in a remote network of country lanes between Riscle and Nogaro and telephones were rare, but he had told us we would find a *point publique* at the big white house a kilometre down the road.

When we reached the white house it was big indeed, standing amid lawns and groves of bamboo. There was no telephone sign outside and it was with some trepidation that I mounted the curved flight of steps leading to the front door. My embarrassment was increased by the fact that it was still barely eight o'clock in the morning, but it was imperative to telephone Riscle before travelling further away from it.

The door was opened by Monsieur Gandy of St. Martin d'Armagnac himself, a diminutive white-haired man attired in beige silk pyjamas piped in brown. He assured us that he did indeed permit local people to use his telephone. He was sympathetic about our need for a *maréchal ferrant* and led us into an elegant but not recently decorated dining-room with a porcelain stove in the fireplace and eighteenth-century plates on the walls. It turned out that the farrier at Riscle had been in retirement for four years, but our host refused to admit defeat. While Madame Gandy, wearing a flowered housecoat, plied the children with biscuits, he telephoned five horse-owning friends, but in vain. All of them, it seemed, were in the habit of putting their mounts into boxes and transporting them a hundred kilometres to a blacksmith in the Landes. When we left we promised to visit Madame Courte, the owner of another château in the Gers.

At Nogaro, a town slightly larger than Riscle, we were accosted by a professional animal-lover of a type that I had thought existed only in England. She was a middle-aged lady with a shopping-bag and a walking-stick, and she bore down on the donkeys with a determined air.

"*Les pauvres ânes,*" she cried, tearing off the end of a loaf of bread she had just bought and giving it them.

"Shall we tell her?" whispered Miranda anxiously, for she knew that fresh bread gets stuck in donkeys' teeth.

"*Le pauvre petit chien,*" she said, handing out more to Iago who treacherously wolfed it down.

"But you must admit, madame, the donkeys are fat," said Andrew.

"Ah, but their poor legs!" said the lady, who was herself both fat and lame. By now her loaf was half gone. She gave another mouthful to Hannibal who was still in difficulties with his first.

"Animals are so much nicer than people. They never let you down," she said, giving us a withering look as she waddled off in the direction of the butcher's shop.

For two days we walked through fields where vines grew as thickly as barley had in Spain. We began to understand why the farmers of Gers were obliged to distil some their wine into brandy. At a small shop that stood at a crossroads among vineyards, we bought a copy of *Sud-Ouest*, the local newspaper, and saw ourselves marching stalwartly under the headline *Nouveau voyage avec un âne dans les Cevennes*. We had not known that Monsieur Taris, the young journalist who had interviewed us at Riscle, had been a lover of Robert Louis Stevenson. The woman at the shop was delighted and agreed to sell us her entire spare stock of three copies of the newspaper.

No sooner had we appeared in print than a good fairy materialised, a large one. We were sitting in the ditch, not far from the shop, folding up our cuttings, when she climbed out of her car and flung her arms out to us. "How wornderfool to see you," she cried, teetering on the edge of the ditch. "I saw your peecture in the papurr." Which of the elderly French ladies of my acquaintance was I failing to recognise, I thought frantically.

"You must come to my house. You shall have tea, coffee, champagne, anything you like." The woman from the shop had joined us now. "You should see the house of Madame Courte," she said. "It is typical of the Gers region." I remembered that Monsieur Gandy in his silk pyjamas had also pressed us to visit Madame Courte. Throwing caution to the winds, we agreed to make the two-kilometre detour to her house. It was a decision we were not to regret.

The Château de St. Aubin was of brick and timber, one storey high, and built round a quadrangle. At each corner there was a square tower roofed with red tiles. In the courtyard Jean, the gardener, was watering roses which grew between miniature box hedges. The spoiling began as soon as we entered the vast kitchen of the château, which was hung with copper pans and had French windows opening on to a smooth lawn. Two bottles of sparkling *Vin Fou* were produced for us, and the children had great bowls of strawberries and raspberries. Their eyes grew round with delight at the sight of them. Madame Courte took an immediate liking to Miranda, whom, to that child's secret disgust, she insisted on calling Ophélie. Through the layers of grime she professed to see a typically English face, so *comme il faut*, so like the little girls of good family she had known in Eastbourne in 1913. Miranda responded admirably by making a daisy chain for her.

Madame Courte, who was, unbelievably, seventy-five, was the widow of an admiral. She lived alone, cared for by Jean and Isabelle, a nice couple from the neighbouring Department of Landes. While Isabelle cooked and Jean attended to the donkeys, Madame showed us the house, which, like so many châteaux, appeared to consist of a series of salons, each more formal than the last. The suites of eighteenth-century furniture and the Italian paintings (workshop of Raphael) contrasted admirably with the rustic character of the whitewashed rooms with their beamed ceilings and brick floors. "I don't care for all this stuff myself," said Madame, indicating a pair of fifteenth-century Flemish tapestries. "It belongs to my daughter. I prefer something simpler."

We lunched democratically in the kitchen with Jean and Isabelle, at a long refectory table, and no distinction was made between the menus of mistress and servant, except that we drank a 1973 Madiran (the famous red wine of the district) and they drank white wine made on the estate. For the second time in three days we ate a meal that will go down in family history. The crowning delight was Isabelle's *confit de canard*. To make this dish you first raise a black barbary duck on an exclusive diet of crushed maize, kill it at six months and render it down in a copper preserving pan. It must then be kept for a year in an airtight jar under a layer of its own fat. Madame said she had tasted better, but we disagreed. The six-course meal ended with a very old Armagnac made on the premises and served, apparently correctly, in our coffee cups.

There was to be another gastronomic treat before that eventful day ended. The day before I had suggested to Thomas that we should buy a broiler and stew it for supper. Iago must have heard me, for as we approached Castelnau late that afternoon, he suddenly appeared with a dead chicken in his mouth. Before I knew what was happening Thomas had removed the still warm bird from Iago's jaws, stuffed it in the saddlebags and administered a beating to the culprit. When we reached camp we discovered that it was no more than a *poulet*, but, boiled up with an onion, some wine and a couple of soup cubes it produced a superb gravy which we mopped up with bread. Thanks to our afternoon of self-indulgence with Madame Courte it was long after dark before we gathered round the fire to destroy the evidence of Iago's crime. Our faces lit by the camp fire, we looked a true robber band.

The Armagnac cellar at Castelnau was one of the largest we had seen but, alas, we arrived after it had closed. Nor was the *degustation gratuit* on offer at six o'clock the following morning. I was beginning to fear that we might pass through the Armagnac region without being able to buy a bottle of the liquid that I had tasted at the Château de St. Aubin, for we were now heading towards the remote village of Séviac.

The attraction at Séviac was a newly excavated Gallo-Roman villa dating from the first century A.D. Madame Courte had given us an introduction to the archaeologist in charge, Madame Launet-Aragon, and, as the place was roughly on our route, we decided to make use of it. We arrived at the excavation during the lunch hour, which, in France, lasts from twelve to three o'clock. It was in high open country with views all round, and there was a ruined farmhouse nearby, behind which we camped. We were half-way through our siesta when Madame Launet-Aragon arrived in immaculate white trousers, accompanied by a female assistant who was not introduced. She had been expecting us, she said, having met the indefatigable Madame Courte at a lecture the night before. We crawled out of our sleeping-bags to shake hands. She was a dark woman approaching sixty, rather plump, with a lot of gold teeth and a handshake like a man's. She told us to finish our rest and then come and visit *les fouilles*.

By the time we reached the excavation there was quite a crowd there, with Madame Launet-Aragon at the centre of it, not easily recognisable now in shorts and a man's straw trilby. The villa must have belonged to a person of some importance, for the ruins extended over several acres. Galleries, courtyards and rooms had been floored with mosaics in elaborate geometric patterns, many of which were still intact and came up in brilliant blues, yellows and terracottas when rubbed with oil and resin. To Miranda's delight much of the central heating system also remained. Jessica preferred a pair of Merovingian skeletons discovered hand in hand among the ruins and nicknamed *les amoureux de Séviac.* "The poor people," she said. "Have they always been dead?" The skull of the woman had a hole in it, for which Madame admitted responsibility. *"Malheuresement ma pioche a passé par son crâne."*

The story of how the site was rediscovered was remarkable. Excavations had been initiated in 1868 by a local doctor but had ceased on his death. By the time Madame Launet-Aragon was born the exact location of the villa had been forgotten. As a child she had been brought by her father to the fields under which it lay and he had told her that it was somewhere in the area. The idea of the palace under the corn had fascinated her, but it was not until 1959, when she was approaching middle age, that she found the time to start excavating. She spent a Sunday digging with her teen-age children and found nothing. The next day her son struck a mosaic pavement with the first stroke of his pick.

The excavations have continued spasmodically ever since, whenever money was available. In 1971 the Department of Gers provided funds for buying the land under which the villa lay, and so far 5,000 lorry loads of earth had been removed. During the summer vacation students provide the labour force, and pay for the privilege. They work only in the mornings, however, and on the afternoon when we were there three portly gentlemen in bathing trunks were labouring in one of the trenches. Madame Launet-Aragon encouraged us to make admiring noises at them. She was a woman who knew how to get people to work for her. I had always imagined that digging up the past was done with a toothpick and a camel-hair brush, but these three Gascons were going at it with mattocks. Their finds were laid on polystyrene trays and consisted chiefly of oyster shells, confirmation of the Roman passion for this delicacy, since the complete Department of Landes lies between Séviac and the sea.

That night we slept under a full moon, knowing that there might be mosaics half a metre below our tent. Perhaps pale Romans trod the galleries, but they did not enter Jessica's dreams. She sat up screaming at 2 a.m. convinced she had fallen down the abandoned well near our tent. "I did keep hold of the rope," she sobbed. In the morning Madame Launet-Aragon was on the site at six o'clock to see us off. She had brought with her a large-scale map on which a learned abbé had traced the exact route taken by the pilgrims between Condom and Lectoure. Madame was accompanied by a different assistant this time. He was dressed in a skin-tight suit of blue denim and also was not introduced. He dodged about obediently in the background taking photos of our departure.

We were now in the heart of Gascony, not far from the birthplace of d'Artagnan, of *The Three Musketeers*. It was in this area that the religious wars of the sixteenth century had been most fiercely fought and many fortified villages, known as *bastides*, still bore witness to those troubled times. The most beautiful of all the *bastides* was Larressingle, five kilometres from Condom, built by the Bishop of Condom as a bolt-hole. It was entirely surrounded by walls and consisted of a fortified Romanesque church, a castle and a row of flower-covered cottages selling hot *crêpes*. Most improbably it was at the little *tabac* beside the entrance arch that we finally ran to earth a bottle of Armagnac. It was of the medium grade and was called, suitably enough, Larressingle.

Condom, with its fortified cathedral, its narrow mediaeval streets and its river, merits a page in any guide book. We hurried through it, eager as usual to find pasture for our donkeys. Not far beyond the city we picked up the abbé's pilgrim way. It started off along a suburban lane, past neat villas, and finally brought us to a pleasantly scruffy farm with a superb view of the cathedral. The old man who lodged at the farm was the retired owner of a shoe shop at Toulouse, and had toured England with the French rugger team in 1926. He invited us into a room which he shared with several hundred pairs of stiletto heeled shoes, dating from the 1950s, and offered us Armagnac made by his landlord, the farmer. It was a clear fiery liquid which burnt a way direct to the stomach. When we left to camp in the field at the back he insisted that we accept a bottle in honour of the *entente cordiale*. Our third bottle of Armagnac that day was of an altogether superior variety, elegantly packaged and expensively matured for twenty years in Condom itself. It was given to Andrew by a French Canadian couple whom he met when he was being shown the cathedral cloisters. We needed the consolation of Armagnac before the day was out; Miranda came to supper carrying one of Hamilcar's cast shoes.

CHAPTER 25

An appointment at Moissac

Hamilcar could not have chosen a more inconvenient moment to lose a shoe. It was now Saturday, July 19th and we had an appointment with seven friends and relations, including our eldest daughter Cordelia, at Moissac on Wednesday, July 23rd. The blacksmith at Fleurance could not see us before 6 a.m. on Tuesday, and this left us two days in which to reach Moissac — fifty-five kilometres away. We normally covered twenty kilometres in a day.

Our spirits were low as we limped along the hot grass verges of the main road, trying to think up questions on Roman history for Miranda, whose head was still full of the Roman villa at Séviac. Not only had we been obliged to abandon the pilgrim route to Lectoure, drawn out for us by Madame Launet-Aragon's abbé, but also we were in danger of missing the long-awaited birthday concelebration we planned for July 23rd (the anniversaries of my sister and of Cordelia and Miranda all occurring around that day). We reached Fleurance in the heat of noon on a Sunday and made straight for the blacksmith's shop, which was naturally closed. His home was on the other side of the town, near the River Gers, and thither we made our way, pausing first to cool ourselves at the fountain in the market place. There was an empty stone trough under the spout, and we were just pumping water into it for the donkeys when the apparition materialised. She was a splendid gypsy woman, brown as an Indian, and dressed in a crumpled purple and yellow silk skirt that reached to the ground. Her arms clanked with gold bracelets and she wore a deeply fringed shawl. Striking a splendid pose, her hand on one hip, she enquired where we were going. Her company was going to Spain, but would visit Lourdes first.

On the way to our encampment we passed hers, which was an altogether superior affair. Five large caravans were drawn up beside five American-style limousines in a car park. Inside them we caught glimpses of china ornaments, brass lamps and purple velvet curtains edged with bobbles. Our friend from the fountain beckoned us over to speak to her

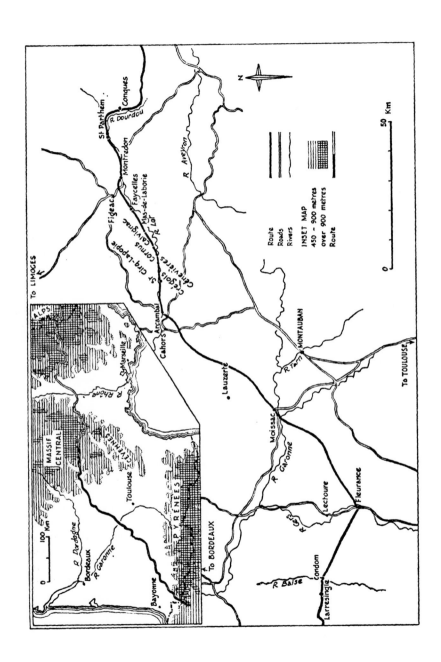

husband, a fat man in a lounge suit. His womenfolk, all in fancy dress, gathered round us while he questioned us closely about prices in Spain, particularly the price of petrol, of which we were, of course, ignorant. He seemed obsessed with money, and proudly declared that his weekly food bill for a family of five was double ours. We in turn questioned him about his travels and were surprised to hear that he had spent four years in Scandinavia, a country most hospitable to his tribe. In England they had barely survived a fortnight. We forbore to ask the one question that occupied all our minds, which was where they got their money.

The blacksmith lived in a little street of colour-washed terrace houses, mostly inhabited by artisans. A strong smell of varnish came from the picture-framer's next door, but number fourteen was firmly locked. The picture-framer told us that Monsieur Larroque would not return from his place in the country until the evening, so Andrew composed a lengthy appeal in his minuscule handwriting and dropped it through the letter box. We camped that night in a poplar grove beside the municipal pool in which we speedily submerged ourselves. We were just turning in, at nine thirty, when Iago set up a frantic barking. A band of people was approaching through the darkness. It was the blacksmith and his family. He would 'do' us at ten o'clock the following morning. By midday on Monday the donkey bells were jingling once more. We were on our way.

Two mornings later we crossed the wide confluence of the Tarn and the Garonne, a few kilometres west of Moissac. We all laid bets on which of the four separate parties expected on the post-office steps at six o'clock that evening would actually turn up. In theory there should be Cordelia with her sixteen-year-old cousin Sebastian; Tamara, a rather senior civil servant, with her schoolboy son Tim; and John Enos, the Oxford economics don. Most improbable of all, my sister Lyndall and her husband Lorenzo, an Italian count, had suddenly announced their intention of joining us from Cortona on their way to London. We hardly knew whether we would be more alarmed if we found none of them there, or all of them.

The post office was in a shady street by the Garonne canal. We reached it at midday and found a letter there from John Enos announcing the first defection. It was a sad letter. There had been a muddle about times and places and he had followed us on foot for two weeks from St. Jean Pied-de-Port, but had finally been obliged to return home without finding us. At Riscle he had been only twenty-three hours behind us, and had talked to people who had seen us. At Nogaro he had seen donkey droppings on the road and been shown our photograph in *Sud-Ouest*. He had been given eight versions of the donkeys' names, including 'Mathematics' and 'Philosophy'.

As we were leaving the post office we saw an elegant young woman with dark glasses and a floppy hat crossing the road and realised it was Cordelia. After joyful embraces all round she led us to Sebastian, who was sleeping peacefully beside the canal, propped up by their two knapsacks. They had taken only two days to hitch-hike from Dieppe and had camped the night before on a hillside above the town. It was to this hillside that our enlarged party now repaired. We asked permission to camp at the first farm we came to, although it was barely clear of the suburbs. Our luck was incredible, for the farmer's wife was a pretty elfin-faced woman of great generosity. Not only did she ply us with the famous peaches of Moissac, cool and fragrant from her 'fridge, but also she gave us permission to sleep in her husband's barn. She offered us a lift into the town after lunch, so that we could keep our remaining appointments on the post-office steps at six o'clock.

Our afternoon in Moissac was not unlike our morning in Leon on the day of Jessica's birthday six weeks earlier, except that we were now catering for *three* birthdays instead of one. We confined our sight-seeing to a swift circuit of the famous Romanesque cloisters, which so closely missed demolition in the last century to make room for the railway station. Our own treatment of them was hardly less irreverent, for each of the intricately carved capitals deserved ten minutes' scrutiny. They are said to resemble closely those at St. Domingo, near Burgos, also built by Cluniac monks for the pilgrims.

When we returned to the post office at six o'clock we found a very small figure sitting there beside a very large knapsack. It was Tim, aged thirteen, who informed us that he and his mother had taken four days to hitch from Calais. "Mum's under the drier as usual," he added, with disgust. We told him to look out for Lyndall and Lorenzo, and repaired, with our mountain of shopping, to the chestnut-shaded tables of the Hotel de la Poste. We were halfway through our first Ricard when Tamara herself appeared, grinning broadly under an orange helmet of hair. She carried a knapsack three times the size of Tim's, and coloured a brilliant red. Twenty minutes later Lyndall and Lorenzo arrived in their motorised caravan. They had driven non-stop from La Spezia that day and had barely survived a failure of the steering in the centre of Toulouse.

The field in front of our barn was a perfect place for a hyper-picnic. There was a view on three sides and, later, an orange moon overhead. Lyndall had brought a tablecloth, and on it we spread champagne, melons, pâté, cold chicken, salad and, best of all, an elaborately decorated birthday cake. It was iced with coffee cream and came from one of those terribly expensive French *pâtisseries* we did not normally dare to put a foot inside. Lyndall, whose actual birthday it was, cut it skilfully into eleven sections. Miranda, who was officially admitting to being eight that day, although her real birthday had fallen on the fifteenth, bit blissfully into it. "At last a real Mrs. Norgate cake," she sighed. Jessica, who had survived eating her melon, skin and all, was already asleep in Lorenzo's lap.

CHAPTER 26

Camp followers

Readers will by now have observed that I am a reluctant and not very efficient walker. They will therefore perhaps forgive my satisfaction in discovering there were others who were even more reluctant and even less efficient. For Tamara, I am sure, would now freely admit that walking is not her greatest gift. She was, however, unaware of this when we strode forth boldly on our first morning together. Our band of five had expanded to nine and, as we straggled along the road to Cahors, we resembled an eccentric cub outing. Lyndall and Lorenzo had continued their journey to England, mercifully carrying a large quantity of Tamara's excess baggage, including about a kilo of cosmetics. She had clung firmly to the remaining half-kilo, insisting that without it no lorry driver would give her a lift back to Calais. Our resemblance to a cub outing became more marked when we made our first camp. Instead of one orange tent, there were four, and a certain amount of tent-hopping went on, for Miranda was entranced with Tim, and spent the evening swapping the words of interminable folk-songs with him.

Now that we had extra hands, Andrew decided to visit friends in the Auvergne, meeting us in three weeks' time at the mountain resort of Aubrac. He spent his final evening making preparations for his departure. While Cordelia sewed a nosebag into which he could stuff dandelions while he walked, he taught Sebastian the Spanish words of command that the donkeys understood. Fortunately Sebastian likes animals and was planning to become a vet. At midnight Andrew left to walk 200 kilometres in six days. He was in high spirits, for the moon was bright and he was eager to have the road to himself, unencumbered with children and donkeys.

Our progress the next day was even slower than usual, for we were now climbing up on to the wild limestone *causses* of Quercy which lie between Moissac and Cahors, and Sebastian and Cordelia were unaccustomed to directing the cumbersome Hannibal. Even so, Tamara and Tim gradually lagged further and further behind. We breakfasted on a ridge overlooking the mediaeval fortified town of Lauzerte, which stands on a hill rising from a fertile valley. When Tamara, pink and perspiring, caught up with us, she admitted that not only had she always suffered from 'rolling ankles', owing to being overweight as a child, but that she had recently had several bones removed from her toes. Tim trailed pathetically in her wake, dragging boots that looked too big for him, but he brightened at the sight of food, and was soon giving a spirited rendering of 'The House of the Rising Sun'. Tamara had stripped to a bikini so that from behind all you could see of her was a pair of broad pink legs below a red knapsack, a blue sleeping-bag and a yellow bubble pad. Unfortunately it was not often that we saw her from behind. On the fourth day she wisely decided to spare her filleted toes. She and Tim would hitch to Arcambal, a village outside Cahors, where we would meet them.

We followed the *Sentier de Grande Randonnée*. These *sentiers*, or footpaths, are a fairly recent invention. Groups of earnest French ramblers have pioneered them, marking rocks and trees with elaborate red and white hieroglyphs, and the youth of the nation is encouraged to follow them. The preface of our guide to G.R.65 consisted of an ecstatic description of the joys of walking that only a Frenchman could have written. It began with quotations from Rousseau and Lamartine and concluded with the reflection that life itself is, after all, but a prolonged walk on a G.R. whose destination is heaven. Admittedly the section of the G.R. that crosses Quercy does in fact follow the pilgrim route for 160 kilometres. It was a rare treat to find cross-country sections of the *Chemin de Saint-Jacques*, which has, alas, so largely disappeared below tarmac.

The footpath to Cahors led us over wild upland country covered with oak scrub. It was the hottest day so far and when we reached Arcambal we found Tamara and Tim sitting enviably in the shade. They had been there since 7.30 a.m. and had found no shop. They had however managed to pass an hour exploring the pilgrim church.

That night, deep in the forest above Arcambal, Tamara dispensed wine and led the singing round the camp fire. From folk-songs we progressed to unprintable student rounds, of which she knew a surprising number, and finally to dirty stories of which she knew more. It was a rare pleasure to make merry in this way. For once we had no compunction about staying up late, for the next day was a day off.

Our day in Cahors was chiefly devoted to shopping for the donkeys. Hannibal's sores were almost cured, but Hamilcar still had a raw place on his backbone, and I hoped that a foam-rubber bath-mat might help him. Since Prisunic, the only place for *flocon mousse*, did not

Crossing the Puente de Orbigo, longest pilgrim bridge in Spain.

Celebrating Jessica's fourth birthday beside the River Esla.

Above left, brookside laundry. Right, Hannibal takes an interest in the route. Below, civilised camping at the hermitage of Santa Marina.

open until three o'clock on a Monday, we were free to enjoy a morning of sightseeing in the lovely mediaeval quarter near the cathedral, with its narrow streets of brick Renaissance palaces. Thomas and I lunched triumphantly at a small restaurant, run by another retired rugger player. He was called 'The Rock' and gave us a signed photograph before filling our plastic bottles with the red wine of Cahors, 'the preferred drink of popes and the Russian Orthodox Church'. At Prisunic we bought Hamilcar's bath-mat and a bottle of rum (France's cheapest spirit). From the train, as we crossed the Lot on our way home, we saw, or hoped we saw, the famous mediaeval bridge of Valentré.

That evening we were entertained by a nice English professor called Ruth, who lived at Arcambal with a French professor called Marie Claire. Both taught at Toulouse University. They were bringing up a pair of Indian orphans found in dustbins by Mother Teresa, and owned a grey parrot which could reproduce exactly the voice of Ruth's mother, who had died four years earlier. "What a strange family!" said Miranda, who is fascinated by human relationships. "Let's talk about them."

At six the next morning Tamara set off to hitch back to Calais, painted like a film star, with a Union Jack pinned across her fine bosom. Tim was due at a bird-watching course in Yorkshire in five days' time and was anyway beginning to tire of the exclusively feminine company of our two girls. He and Miranda now exchanged kicks more often than folk-songs, although he still remained touchingly attentive to Jessica. We were sorry to part with Tamara. No longer would our camp-site be enlivened by such gay cries as "Golly, I haven't washed my bottom for six days!"

CHAPTER 27

The race to Conques

The River Lot, which we had first seen at Cahors, was to be an intermittent companion for many kilometres and a frequent source of refreshment as the summer heat approached its zenith. The pilgrim route at first ran parallel to it to the south, keeping to the high *causses*, but descended into its valley at St. Cirq-Lapopie.

St. Cirq-Lapopie is described in the travel brochures as the premier village of France. Its turreted stone cottages tumble self-consciously down the side of an escarpment, offering *crêpes* and caricatures for

E

sale. Luxury charabancs were lined up outside them as we descended to the wide Lot. Sebastian at once plunged in. An hour later he returned to the camp, his muscular brown body glistening and his yellow hair wet. He had just swum the river both ways. He slept like the dead for the next four hours, failing in all his donkey duties, and could only be aroused with difficulty for supper.

The next day we followed the south bank of the Lot below limestone bluffs, passing Crégols, Cornus, Cénevières and Calvignac, villages that we preferred to St. Cirq, for they had the same architecture without the fuss. After we had crossed the Lot we began to climb and the sun climbed with us. Once again it seemed hotter than ever before. Even the indefatigable Iago trailed along with his tongue hanging out, and the children, on their shared donkey, grew fretful. At the top was a village called Mas-de-Laborie and, to our amazement, a shop.

We must have presented a strange spectacle as we lined up at the counter, frantic for cold lemonade. Thomas tells me my face was blotchy and swollen from the heat and he himself could hardly see for the salt sweat in his eyes. The shopkeeper took a lively interest in our adventure and allowed us water from his almost exhausted cistern. He even spared a bucket to pour over the children's heads, which they accepted with squeals of joy. We camped in a grove of sparse oak and juniper just beyond the village, where every tree had its familiar spirit in the form of a rattling cicada. That night, under a waning moon, other spirits haunted the grove. Iago kept dashing out of the tent, barking frantically. Cordelia was convinced that she heard the sound of sheep-bells in the middle of the night and saw a man, a woman and a boy drive a herd past. It took us a long time to convince her that she had been dreaming.

On the outskirts of Faycelles the next day, we found the answer to a question Miranda had frequently asked: "What noise does a mule make?" The mule who answered the question for us was a magnificent shining bay that could have passed for an Irish hunter but for its monstrous ears. It galloped up and down its paddock, popping its great head over the wall, and, as it saw us disappear, let out an extraordinary sound which perfectly combined the vocal effects produced by each of its parents: a donkey's 'ee-aw' but with the tremulousness of a whinny added to the 'ee'.

Faycelles was built dramatically on a hillside and had obviously been 'discovered'. The old houses had been converted into holiday villas and even the water tower on the hill above (where we camped) had been given a red tiled roof in keeping with the local architecture. The siesta under that water tower was the hottest of the whole summer. It was the first day of August and even lying in the shade we sweated continuously, the flies stinging our bare ankles below our pyjama trousers. In the end Cordelia, Sebastian and I gave up the attempt to sleep and took the children to the village wash-house. Here a cool spring gushed from the rock face and they spent an hour cavorting in its stone troughs.

Faycelles was only five kilometres from Figeac, a town I had always wanted to visit, but I could not summon up the energy to go there. Sebastian was made of sterner stuff, and announced his intention of hitching a lift. Back in camp Thomas, who can usually resist the temptation to wash, was crouching over a fragrant frying-pan. The last week of blazing sunshine had ripened the peppers and tomatoes on the farms, and with the addition of a dozen eggs he was making a *piperade*. When it was ready we divided it religiously into six sections, setting Sebastian's on one side. Helped by Cahors wine it went down only too fast. Thomas, Cordelia and I sat with well-wiped tin plates on our knees and gazed longingly at Sebastian's ration.

"He can't get in and out, and see the town in less than three hours," Thomas said.

"And it won't be good cold," I said. Only Cordelia, who is a nice character, remained silent. We had just finished the last mouthful when Sebastian arrived home. We had not allowed for his elfin charm which had commanded instant lifts both ways from ladies whose cars were already crammed with children, nor for his ability to see the sights of a mediaeval town in half an hour.

Long sections of the walk the next day followed footpaths between walls that seemed to trap the heat and form it into something solid that you had to push your way through. It was a feat of enormous endurance to keep the muscles in our thighs working, and the sweat ran in rivulets down our chests. But we had the consolation of knowing that we were on the true Chemin de Saint-Jacques, and it was not hard to imagine meeting a party of pilgrims round the next bend.

Montredon was also on the top of a hill, and the angelus was ringing across the dusty square as we arrived. Here we bought our first newspaper for many days and discovered that we were not the only people who were feeling hot. The whole of France was wilting under a heat wave; sheep were dying in the Pyrenees and people were being poisoned by the water from stagnant wells all over the south. On the Spanish border the "Aoûtians", that is to say the people who take their holidays in August, were sitting in a 160-kilometre traffic jam, slowly roasting alive in their cars.

A nice old farmer let us camp in a field above the road, and from our tent we were able to see the Aoûtians for ourselves, for a continuous stream of them drove past. Many had towels soaked in water hung across the windows to protect the row of hot children in the back from the sun. What amazed us about these vacationing Frenchmen was the amount of ironmongery they carried. Not only were their cars large and new, but also many of them trailed even larger and newer caravans and, not content with these encumbrances, bore a row of shining inverted bicycles on the roof rack. One car with four cross children inside and a trailer behind stopped to collect water at the spring below us. The parents oozed bad temper as they fiddled around with the load and snapped "*Couche toi!*" to an enormous panting dog which attempted to escape every time they opened the back door. On the whole we did not envy them, even though that was the day Hamilcar escaped and stole four oranges and a loaf of bread from under the fly-sheet of the tent.

We were sitting round the camp-fire watching the lights coming on in the view when Thomas dropped his bombshell. We had to be at Conques, thirty kilometres away, by twelve o'clock the next day, if we wished to collect our mail from the post office. Otherwise we would be obliged to wait two days until it reopened on Monday morning, and would miss our appointment with Andrew at Aubrac. Conques was for me a place of fable. My father, a great lover of France, had many times urged me to visit the great abbey church of Charlemagne there, the last shrine of importance encountered by pilgrims returning to Le Puy. In its treasury is preserved the archaic gold figure of Ste. Foy studded with precious stones. Ste. Foy was a young girl martyred in Agen in the late Roman period. The *Majesté de Ste. Foy* escaped the Revolutionary armies through the cunning of the abbot, who buried her.

The next morning we set off in darkness, overtaken by the occasional *Août ian* with his headlights blazing. Hannibal's soldiers, on a forced march through Gaul, could hardly have bettered our pace. We all hoped for letters, and the cries of encouragement everybody gave the donkeys filled the wooded valley of the Lot. At St. Parthem they were hanging up flags for a fête and people cheered us from the bedroom windows as we rattled past.

Thomas allowed us a timed breakfast break of twenty minutes by the river and then hustled us on to the road again as the sun began to gather strength. He had just urged Hamilcar back into a jog when a man with a camera jumped out of a car and frantically signalled us to stop. "We are the press!" he cried.

"Can't be helped!" we gasped. "Must get our letters from Conques."

A younger man with a notepad now appeared and, undismayed, attempted to keep pace with me while he asked routine questions. He might have succeeded if he had not been wearing a pair of Indian sandals that were attached to his foot only by a loop over the big toe. These fell off continually.

"How do you spell Chitty?" he called after me desperately as he re-adjusted his footwear for the third time. The photographer's task was even harder, for he was obliged to hurry ahead of us backwards to get a shot.

"That's the way to deal with the press," grunted Thomas, as the exhausted and dishevelled men finally climbed back into their car, telling us to look out for the story in the *Depêche du Midi*, Decazeville edition.

By now we had crossed the Lot and were labouring up the steep gorge of the Dourdou. Thomas had not revealed to us that our thirty-kilometre dash would include climbing up the side of the Massif Central. It was no accident that Conques almost alone of the great French ecclesiastical foundations, preserved its treasure from the greed of Revolutionary officials. It would have been a determined tax-gatherer indeed who could have unearthed the church plate from the scattered farmsteads of that mountain fastness. As the slope grew steeper the heat increased and, shout at our donkeys though we would, the minute-hand of my watch seemed to fly round. At last we saw the grey cliff of the abbey church, shrouded in trees, almost directly above us. Another precipitous two kilometres brought us to the post office ten minutes before closing time.

We were a strange sight as we gathered round a café table to deal out the letters and books from home and drink lemonade. Our hair stuck to our foreheads in wet fronds, our faces were red and shining, and Thomas's shirt was so drenched in sweat that it could have been lifted out of the Lot. Tourists loaded with cameras passed us in a continuous stream on their way from the car park to the basilica. When strength returned we followed them up the cobbled street, only to discover both the church and the treasury on the point of closing for lunch. The magnificent façade rose above us, high as a cathedral, dwarfing the semi-circle of mediaeval cottages that squatted at its feet. There was nothing we could do but admire the 'Last Judgment' carved on the Romanesque tympanum, buy a postcard of the famous golden statue of Ste. Foy and vow to come back to see the original in the late afternoon.

We never went back. We camped two kilometres below the village, by the cool and gentle Dourdou, and by the time we had swum and eaten and slept, the great bell of the abbey church was chiming closing time. Even if the treasury had remained open all night I doubt if I could have climbed the hill again. The muscles of my calves and thighs were sore and stiff from the morning's exertions.

Twelve hours later we were once more on the road to Aubrac. As I walked ahead of the donkeycade, with Iago jogging at my heels, I tried to compose a suitable message for the postcard of Ste. Foy I had promised my father. Dared I admit I had walked the pilgrim way from Santiago to Conques and not seen the famous statue? Only a fellow-walker would understand that such things could happen.

CHAPTER 28

Andrew lost

There were three days left before our date with Andrew at Aubrac, and seventy kilometres still to cover. It was at Estaing, the day before the rendezvous, that Cordelia began to feel ill. She lay all afternoon beside the Lot. In her sea-green bikini with her chestnut-coloured hair round her shoulders, she looked like a drowned Ondine. The next morning, pale as death, she insisted on walking the nine kilometres to Espalion. When we stopped to breakfast in a field below the ruined castle of Calmont d'Olt she could only eat yoghurt, and Sebastian, who by now was also feeling queer, abstained with her. As soon as we started to walk again she was sick into a roadside drain. Faint and dizzy she sat on a milestone to recover.

"We can't make her walk in this condition," I pleaded.

"We've got to get to Aubrac," growled Thomas. The walk had brought out a grim determination in him that, in the past, appeared only when he was defending his right to work at his current book. I suddenly realised that, before we were through, any or all of us might be sacrificed to it. Cordelia raised herself wearily from the milestone. "I'm all right," she said. But her hands shook as she tried to lift her knapsack, and we put it on top of Hannibal's burden instead.

Espalion was a nice little town. There were prim nineteenth-century villas on the outskirts, of the type that the old lady in the Baba books would have favoured, and a busy central square full of cafés with bright awnings. For us, however, Espalion has few pleasant memories. The addition of Cordelia's knapsack to Hannibal's burden proved the last straw. It promptly swung round, saddle and all, and hung under his belly, where it had hung so many times before. Cordelia sat on the curb while we reloaded him and only shook her head when I asked her how she felt.

We were trying to find the pilgrim route to St. Côme, also on the Lot. We had just struggled to the top of the town when a fat farmer with a red flag, riding a motorised bicycle and driving four cows, told us it was at the bottom. Twice we got lost again. Again Hannibal's burden came off again. We passed a mini-ranch with a log cabin and

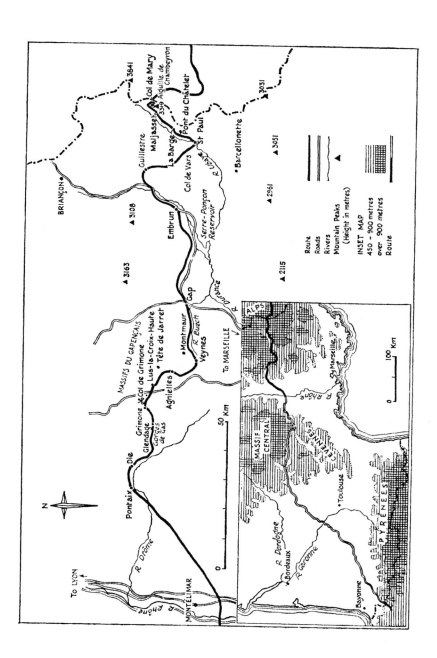

a tethering rail on the outskirts. It belonged to the fat farmer. He redirected us across further water meadows and we got lost again.

St. Côme d'Olt ('Olt' was the older, Celtic form of the name Lot) was a walled citadel of mediaeval houses with overhanging first floors and layers of balconies. Just beyond it we must leave the pilgrim route and turn east if we were to accompany Hannibal over the Alps. The sandals we had bought Jessica in Santiago seemed to consider their work was done. They finally disintegrated that afternoon by the Lot, giving us an excuse to explore the little town. Though there were three general stores in the cobbled *place*, they stocked chiefly stale groceries and beach goods for the camp-site. There was not a leather sandal between them, but Jessica seemed delighted with a yellow plastic pair which looked as if they'd been cut from banana skins. Thus equipped, we set out the next morning to meet Andrew at Aubrac.

Our way lay across the Lot, by the old bridge at St. Côme, and up a steep and rocky footpath barred with brambles. A white mist in the valley formed a background for the towers of St. Côme as they turned pink in the dawn light. By the time we had climbed a further 300 metres, a wider landscape opened behind us and the donkeys were sweating. Several signs directed us to ski resorts. We were approaching the high Cévennes. The going was not easy for our two invalids who had only partially recovered. By ten o'clock it was obvious that they would not reach Aubrac churchyard by midday. We would have to find somewhere to camp and send Thomas ahead to meet Andrew. At Le Pouget Jeune we found the unspoilt peasant we had come so far to see, a dear old granny in a wide straw hat who lived with her slightly retarded son in a stone-roofed farmhouse by a spring, subsisting on six cows and some barnyard fowls. She allowed us to camp in a shady field where the drought had retarded the second crop of hay. "It rains only under the hat," said her son with an idiot grin. It was his only joke and he made it every time he passed our camp which he did frequently, carrying an assortment of improbable objects.

When Thomas set out for Aubrac he took our only watch with him, leaving us to a long afternoon in the widow's hayfield. It was one of those rare periods of peace and timelessness. Far from the shining tourist cars, we sprawled on rugs in the shade. Cordelia played snap with Jessica while Sebastian read aloud a chapter of *Zen and the Art of Motor Cycle Maintenance* to Miranda. I should have been putting new seats in the children's trousers. Instead I lay gazing inanely into the leaves of a tree and listening to the sawing of a thousand grasshoppers out in the sun. Like them, I could take no thought for the future, for there would be no food to prepare for supper until Thomas returned with it on his back. Over a smoky cup of tea, prepared by Miranda on a secret camp fire in the bushes, we speculated idly upon whether Andrew would be at Aubrac and whether Adrian and Rachel would be with him.

Rachel had been a fellow-worker with Andrew in Voluntary Service Overseas in New Guinea. Adrian was a social science graduate from Yorkshire whom she had acquired since her return. They were due to meet Andrew by appointment somewhere in the Massif Central and then walk with us for two weeks. The likelihood of their keeping their rendezvous with Andrew had always seemed slight, but we had little doubt that the reliable Andrew would be on time.

As the tree shadows began to engulf the field, Cordelia and I went to the farm for milk. The widow and her son sat at a refectory table eating bread and milk in a great beamed kitchen. The television set was on, and above it the widow's husband stared from a silver frame. She insisted that our donkeys should be allowed to roam free in the calf paddock overnight. "It's nothing," she protested. "For one night! I'm sure you would do the same for me." The idiot son showed us the way to the calf paddock, leading us from behind. Both Cordelia and I were uncomfortably aware of his eye on our bare legs. "Very Zola," she remarked under her breath.

As darkness fell Thomas returned to the camp alone. He had walked twenty kilometres and had carried a three-day supply of food for half of them. Andrew had not been in the churchyard at Aubrac at midday, nor had he been there at three o'clock when Thomas woke up from his siesta among the tombs. There was no shop in the village, but the proprietor of one of the three hotels had a message and a phone number. When Thomas called it he found Andrew sitting at a café table at St. Flour, a village many kilometres to the north. Rachel and Adrian were with him, but he had underestimated their walking capacity. They would meet us in three days at Chirac.

CHAPTER 29

Excessive travels with a donkey in the Cévennes

Between Le Pouget Jeune and Chirac we walked across a vast plateau that lay close under the sky. It was grazed by herds of biscuit-coloured cattle with wide black-tipped horns. This was ranching country with barbed-wire fences marking boundaries every few miles, and occasional abandoned farmhouses. The children trotted gaily along the turf on Hamilcar. About half-way across we saw two red dots approaching. A couple of students were walking across the plateau in the opposite direction. It was the only time we ever met ramblers on a G.R.

After about three hours we were lost. In a fold between the hills was a farm, as large as a village, called Plagnes. A stony track led down to a yard, flanked with massive stone barns. The place seemed to be manned by students who gave us water but said it was not *tellement possible* to camp and directed us up to the Col de Bonnecombe (1,246 metres). After leaving them we got lost again, disobeyed orders, and camped on top of a hill in a field full of very inquisitive cows. Every now and again Miranda, Iago and I had to drive them half a mile down into the bottom of the valley.

Round the tent the turf was studded with flowers. Wild pinks, harebells, cow parsley, thyme, clover and wild pansies formed a living tapestry for us to sit on while we ate our supper. The idyllic meal, however, was brought to a premature close by one of the most dramatic thunderstorms of the whole summer. All afternoon great clouds had been piling up on the horizon and thunder had growled in the distance. We were just scooping up our last fried sardines when the sky went dark and a violent wind burst upon us. We crowded into the tent and stared out anxiously as the gale flattened the flowers at the tent mouth. Then the thunder and lightning began in earnest and a thick grey cloud drove down the valley in front of us, completely hiding the hillside opposite.

Thomas lighted a candle and prepared to read aloud our evening chapter of *Zen*. He had barely started the first sentence when the lightning appeared to hit the ground just in front of the tent and there was an instantaneous crash of thunder directly overhead. The children squealed with laughter at the idea that the storm was jealous of Thomas 'stealing its thunder'. Our jokes became more frantic as the danger increased and the rain came down. Soon the noise of the water on the canvas above our heads was louder than the noise of the thunder. Rain fell steadily all night.

In the morning we set off across country for the Col de Bonnecombe. We followed a path that was no more than a muddy cowtrack, till it petered out in a boggy plateau. On a distant hill we could see two stone barns with what might be a car parked between them. We started to climb once more. One barn seemed inhabited but was locked. A large number of chickens was cackling in the other. We followed the marks of tyres across the summit of a turfy down and came upon a sight we shall probably never see again. A vast herd of cows and calves stood in a temporary enclosure of wattle hurdles, and

among them moved five unshaven men carrying wooden pails hooped
with metal. They went from cow to cow, squatting a few minutes beside
each on a one-legged stool which they carried strapped to the back of
their belts and sticking out behind like a tail. It was a scene of summer milking that seemed to belong to Thomas Hardy's Wessex.

The milkmen directed us to a well-marked *sentier* over the heathery
heights of the Col de Bonnecombe and down into a domesticated landscape of round green hills chequered with cultivation. It was while we
were descending the pretty valley of the Pepinière that Sebastian fell
out of love with the enamelled *Défence de Cracher* notice that he had
carried on his back from St. Côme. He decided he must reach Chirac,
where we were due to meet Andrew, before midday, in order to post
it home, and set off, driving Hannibal ahead of him at a formidable
pace. We followed as best we could, but it was not easy. When
we reached Chirac we discovered that both children's bottoms were
afflicted with prickly heat, that Hamilcar had a raw place on his backbone, and that Hannibal had a loose shoe in front — only two weeks
after being shod at Fleurance.

The camp at Chirac, like most town camps, was not a happy one.
We set up the tent in long grass by the river at the back of a row of
houses and waited for Andrew and his party. During the late afternoon it began to rain heavily. I was worried about Hannibal's shoes
and I was even more worried about the incompatibility of the children's
seats and Hamilcar's back. Both parties obviously needed a rest from
each other, but already we were behind schedule for our Alpine crossing and a few days off were out of the question.

An hour later Iago barked at strange noises among the trees.
Thomas, Andrew, Rachel and Adrian had arrived, drenched to the skin.
Rachel and Adrian crouched in the mouth of the tent to be introduced.
He was a bleached little man in wire-rimmed spectacles, his hair and
beard clinging in wet strands round his shoulders. She was powerful
and high-coloured, draped in a sodden ground-length peasant smock.
Both wore matching straw hats and outsize scarlet packs. I seldom
felt less like a hostess as I crouched morosely in the back of the tent
to make room for them. By now the rain was driving down and cooking
supper was out of the question. Instead we listened to the tale of
Andrew's adventures while we drank rum out of plastic mugs and ate
bread and pâté.

It was a tale of disaster. He had, as we suspected, walked fifty
kilometres by moonlight after he had left us near Moissac, and the
same on the two succeeding nights. On the fourth night a blister on his
left heel became so bad that he hung his boots round his neck and
walked in plastic sandals. After forty kilometres in these the soles of
his feet began to burn intolerably and he collapsed into a camp site

and telephoned the people at the château he was planning to visit, only to discover they were away. The tenants at the home farm came and rescued him in their little Renault and after a brief stay with them, he embarked on his return, aiming to pick up Adrian and Rachel on the way.

Then his real troubles had begun. Again he had discovered that, undramatically and, as it seemed, almost accidentally, our ability to walk had become formidable. Escorting Adrian and Rachel south, he had felt like a man in normal health helping two invalids along the Bournemouth promenade. To make Aubrac on time had soon become out of the question and even to bring them to Chirac had been a problem. ·

With the arrival of Andrew and his friends our party again expanded to nine and Thomas's task as cook and quarter-master became exacting. Every time we sat down for a picnic he had to cut thirty-six rounds of bread and spread them with pâté and camembert. More serious, our two saucepans, carefully judged to feed five, were too small comfortably to feed nine. It was the sort of problem which had not occurred to us when we had gaily invited several dozen English friends to come and walk for a stretch with us.

Our second camp with Adrian and Rachel was as beautiful as the first had been beastly. It was amid sparse pines beyond Marvejols above the village of Goudard, with a view down to fantastic flat-topped mountains which reminded us of the Grand Canyon. Adrian and Rachel practised 'Tai' among the bushes, a strange bent-kneed walk which was supposed to enable them to draw up strength from the earth. It looked exhausting to me.

They overslept the next morning, and were still rolling up their sleeping-pads when we ungallantly left. During all the time they were with us they never seemed to make up the two kilometres they lost that morning, in spite of constant practice of the earth-strength walk. Our way lay downhill that morning and Miranda walked all eight kilometres of the first stage in order to rest Hamilcar's back. In the cool of the day she found this no effort provided she was entertained, and I managed to spin out the plot of *Oliver Twist* over fifty minutes. The murder of Nancy was particularly appreciated.

We were now deep in the mountain province of Lozère, and, as we came round a bend, Mende, the capital of the Department, was suddenly spread below us on the floor of a wide valley, its mediaeval houses clustered round the cathedral. At Mende, however, it was not the *Cathédrale* signs that we followed but those marked *Centre Equestre*, Sirvens. Hannibal now retained only a fragment of each of his front shoes and we felt sure that a riding-school would know where to find a blacksmith.

The riding-school was beside our old friend the Lot, now greatly diminished. It was a typically French establishment. The only installation visible from the front was a bar elaborately disguised as a Western saloon, for, with the French as well as the Italians, riding and drinking are inseparably linked. Thirty horses were locked away somewhere at the back but no one was around, for the luncheon hour still had an hour and a half to run.

We had pitched our tent, bathed and fed when the proprietor arrived. He was a blond and booted young man who received us courteously in an elaborately furnished office. Enormously enlarged grainy photographs of Camargue horses splashed through lagoons round the walls and the smell of horse dung came only faintly. Our luck was in. The *maréchal ferrant* was arriving that very afternoon. He lived a hundred kilometres away and came only once a month. *Voilà!* That was his car, outside!

The *maréchal ferrant* was in fact two blacksmiths, both gigantic and dressed in leather. They were sympathetic and friendly but, alas, they carried only horse shoes with them. There was no call for donkey shoes in France nowadays. The twin Vulcans stood at their anvil scratching their well-thatched heads. There *was* Monsieur Mazurat. He was old and a bit cranky. But he did have donkey shoes. If you rubbed him up the right way he might be persuaded to attach the one to the other. He lived at le Pont-de-Montvert.

Admirers of R. L. Stevenson's *Travels with a Donkey* would no doubt welcome the opportunity to visit le Pont-de-Montvert, buried deep in a secret valley in the heart of the Cévennes. We did not. It lay two days' march due south, and our way was east. Furthermore, Mont Lozère, the highest mountain in the Cévennes, lay between us and it. We were not a cheerful party as we sat round the camp fire that night. My thoughts were on Hamilcar's sore back, and Adrian's were on his upset stomach.

"It's no good," he said to Rachel, as he spooned down a liberal helping of Mende veal cooked in wine and served with rice and almonds. "It'll only come straight out the other end." It did, audibly.

"Mind those nasty prickly things behind the wall," Rachel called anxiously into the darkness.

My night was punctuated by the sounds of Adrian's discomfort. Peering out of the tent at one moment I dimly saw Rachel creeping about the hillside locating a safe spot for him to squat. I turned painfully on the hard ground, worrying about Hamilcar and the children. At two o'clock I had an inspiration. Since going to le Pont-de-Montvert involved a detour, it would not be cheating to take the children there by bus and so give them and Hamilcar a two-day rest. In the morning, to my amazement, Thomas agreed to the plan.

CHAPTER 30

The terrible gorge
at Thines

Le Pont-de-Montvert was a charming place, built in a gorge of the Tarn. The streets were steep and cobbled and often turned into flights of steps, but along the river front was a row of cafés crowded with holiday-makers. The children, Cordelia and I arrived well ahead of the others, in spite of spending a night at a hotel in Mende, and then hitch-hiking (the bus having proved illusory). We sat at the café by the old stone bridge and wondered if we were near the château of the notorious Abbé du Chayla whose death at the hands of the Camisards in 1702 Stevenson so graphically describes. The insurgent Protestants, singing hymns and carrying torches, broke into his house and stormed the stairs. The Abbé escaped by jumping from an upper window, broke a leg, crawled into hiding, was discovered, dragged to the market place and there received a separate stab from every member of the mob of fifty.

It is Stevenson rather than the Abbé du Chayla who is now remembered at le Pont-de-Montvert. When we told the café proprietor that we were travelling with donkeys he said, "We have two or three like you through here every year. They all follow the Route Stevenson but none of them find as much to say about it as he did." This did not surprise us. It had always struck me as remarkable that Stevenson in fact only spent two weeks in the company of Modestine.

At midday, as arranged, we met the donkey party in the churchyard of the Catholic church (not to be confused with the Protestant temple). Relations with Adrian had evidently deteriorated during the ascent of Mont Lozère. He sat silent and apart while Cordelia and I handed round the food we had bought in Mende.

"I couldn't eat *that*," he said, and stared down his spectacled nose in disgust at a variety of cheeses from Prisunic. Eventually he went to a shop with Andrew and Rachel and was bought a quantity of fruit yoghurts and bananas.

"He tells me that at home he only goes once a week," Sebastian said. "I expect it's the shock of a daily motion that's bowling him over. We had an awful job getting him up Mont Lozère."

"But he ran all the way down," said Thomas. "Anyone who can do a five-hour jog over rough country because he prefers a public convenience to the bushes . . ."

The conversation was brought to a close by the reappearance of Adrian who set about demolishing a hand of bananas behind a tombstone.

Old Monsieur Mazurat, the blacksmith, whom we had come so far to see, was as temperamental as a prima donna. He lived up a series of steep alleys in a cottage that opened on to a cobbled yard. Our appointment with him was for two o'clock but he was still at table when we arrived. When eventually he did emerge, a small toad-shaped man, he picked up the donkeys' eight feet and declared that he could do Hannibal but he had no shoes small enough for Hamilcar. It was here that Cordelia's command of colloquial French came to our rescue. After a passionate appeal that lasted a full five minutes, Monsieur Mazurat relented and said he would have shoes ready for both donkeys if we cared to return at six thirty the following morning.

That night we camped on a grassy terrace above the town, encircled by mountains and overhung by a half moon. Only when we walked to the edge of the terrace could we see the two hundred illuminated tents below, corralled in what we dubbed Camp City. It was on this terrace that Adrian, zipped tightly into his tiny yellow tent to keep out the tempting smell of chicken risotto, announced, through his ambassador Rachel, that he must rest for a couple of days and would join us somewhere along the route.

There were more problems with Monsieur Mazurat the next morning. The shoes he had made for Hamilcar were too small, for he had not taken the precaution of measuring the donkey's hoof. Once more he was on the verge of giving the whole thing up, but by now he was surrounded by a ring of interested passers-by, mostly farmers with scythes on their way to harvest oats, and his honour was involved. While we waited he forged a second set. Hamilcar celebrated the occasion by behaving worse than ever before. He kicked, he backed, he jumped forwards and sideways in spite of having a man attached to each ear. The remaining bystanders, by now a sizeable crowd, lent moral support. Three hours later we were free to set off across the Parc National des Cévennes.

The road led upwards, following the gorge of the Tarn, and for several kilometres we were able to look back to the ledge where we had camped, now occupied by a solitary yellow tent, now zipped against the morning chill. Eventually we reached a high grassy plateau where cows grazed among real gentians of an unbelievably glowing blue. We passed Hôpital and several other largely abandoned villages consisting of fine stone houses with massive stone lintels over the doors that made us think of Stonehenge. Sometimes one or two had been converted into holiday homes and there were tents round them.

After a few hours, cars and cultivation entirely ceased and the great plateau rolled on under the sky, broken only by occasional beech copses. It was in such a landscape, we felt, that the fearful Bête de Gevaudan had had his lair. The Bête was a gigantic wolf who, in spite of the prayers of the Bishop of Mende and the soldiers of Louis XV, ravaged the region for three years. By the time he was finally killed by a peasant in 1767 he had devoured fifty young women and children.

Camping was strictly prohibited in the Parc National but we had no alternative. We were punished for our disobedience by a restless night, for Andrew had acquired the siesta habit on his solitary walk and this left him with energy to expend far into the night. He crashed about the undergrowth by the light of a candle stuck in half a plastic Evian bottle, performing a variety of noisy chores and at one o'clock there was a blood-curdling yell. Iago had eaten half the yeast he was about to cook. Miranda uncurled from her sleeping-bag to burst into tears, not because the yeast was gone but because Adelle Davis says that raw yeast stays in the intestines and gobbles up all the other vitamins. "Iago'll die," she sobbed. "He won't have any vitamins."

The next morning, however, Iago's intestines were forgotten and Miranda was running across the sparkling plain barefoot, splashing through streams with soaked trouser legs. We followed the G.R. footpath which led us more or less vertically down the side of a mountain, once again teaching us that, when planning to take a footpath, it is vital to observe how many contour lines it crosses. Our reward was a rich harvest of the myrtle berries which we had seen filling succulent tarts in the windows of the *pâtisseries* at Mende. Below us, range upon range of rocky-topped mountains glowed pink in the light of the rising sun.

The day did not fulfil its morning promise and our memories of Villefort, in the valley, are clouded by heavy rain and an extortionate shopkeeper who asked £7 for a pair of children's sandals. Our spirits improved as we swung down the mighty gorge below the town, led by Miranda singing hymns. There was something biblical about the precipice opposite, with an ancient mule-track and broken wooden bridges clinging to its face. Thomas at the rear chimed in with a splendid bass for the chorus of *Onward Christian Soldiers*. We were in a hurry once more, for, rather unwillingly, we were due to meet Adrian and Rachel at Lafigère the next day. Evidently they were equally unwilling, for they weren't there.

We were now in the Department of Ardèche, a land of gorges. Once and only once did we make the mistake of attempting to cross one of these gorges without using a bridge. It was at a point where the village of Thines lay ahead of us, perched on a flat-topped hill. The road eastwards ran along the top of the ridge behind Thines, and Thomas became convinced that we could reach it more quickly by taking a short cut, avoiding the village.

At first there was a footpath and even an occasional cottage. At each cottage they gave us different opinions about the possibility of reaching the ridge with donkeys, but all agreed that the one person who would know was *le gare*, who did the trek three times a week carrying a sack. Eventually we had the good luck to come upon *le gare* in person. He rose hurriedly from a squatting position behind a large boulder where he had been relieving himself. He was a paunchy peasant who had not lately shaved and sure enough he carried a half-full sack. Adjusting this on his shoulder, he informed us categorically that it would be impossible to reach the ridge, for a deep gorge lay between us and it. He took Thomas with him and showed him the river and the cliff-face on the far side, which we would have to scale. For once even Thomas agreed that, with donkeys, it was impossible.

But there was another Chitty in the party, even more impatient of delay, or perhaps merely younger. Sebastian loved short cuts. On a zigzag mountain road he would frequently run down near-vertical banks and then wait to be discovered at the roadside a kilometre ahead of the rest of the party. Now he scouted ahead, determined to find a way across the river. An hour later he returned cautiously triumphant. He had discovered a path which, though steep, might be possible if we unloaded Hannibal and carried his burden across the river for him.

At this point a second hero took the stage. Fully loaded, Hannibal climbed down the rocks (steeper than most stairs) to the river, stepped nimbly across the giant stepping-stones, and heaved his way up the equally steep rock face on the other side. No horse could have done it. We stood watching his passage with bated breath, expecting the fatal fall at any moment and only daring to cheer when he and Sebastian had safely reached the path along the ledge on the far side.

The climb up to the ridge was very steep and I had constantly to gasp to Sebastian and Andrew, who were leading the donkeys up the zigzag path ahead, to slow down. At times I felt the weight of my knapsack (I was carrying the contents of Hamilcar's saddlebags to relieve his back) would pull me backwards into the abyss. Jessica scrambled up ahead of me, amazingly resilient for a four-year-old.

About half-way we came upon an area of smooth grass with an old stone barn where sheep had recently been folded. There was a stream and a view of range upon range of mountains behind which the sun promised to set splendidly. The temptation to camp was irresistible.

Once before, in Spain, we had found an earthly paradise in the mountains. In each of our paradises one element had been missing. At Doña Olimpa we had had to dig in the mud for water. Now, above Thines, it was food that we lacked. Sablières was eight kilometres away on the road and the road was still half the hillside above us. Again Sebastian offered to go ahead and Cordelia went with him.

Their journey to Sablières proved even more dangerous than our crossing of the gorge, for they were given a lift by a drunken speed maniac who carried a half-empty bottle of Ricard in his glove locker and accelerated on bends. He offered them each a hefty pull out of the bottle which helped to anaesthetise them. "On sait conduire," he yelled as he flew towards limitless space with both hands off the wheel.

That was a beautiful evening. The moon had expanded to the shape of a lemon and lit the mountain so brightly that the children could go on playing long after sunset. In the last week they had ceased to be horses and had become Oliver Twist and his friend Dick at the orphanage (the one who died of T.B.). Touching deathbed scenes now took the place of cantering in matched pairs. We were all asleep when a tremendous wind came up and would have taken the fly-sheet with it if Thomas, cursing heartily, had not crawled outside to replace the pegs. It was like being in a schooner adrift in a typhoon with the canvas flapping over our heads.

In the morning we paid the price for our mountain escapade, for there were still almost forty kilometres to go to Joannas where we had an appointment with the Katys. A year earlier Sebastian had done an exchange visit with Jean Paul Katy, a boy whose parents owned a camp-site at Joannas. Forty kilometres over mountainous country in a day seemed an impossible undertaking, but we set off in good spirits. After the children had scrambled on foot up the rest of the gorge, an ascent so steep that they and I were often forced to go on all fours, we took the ridge road which seemed to float across heather-covered mountain tops. Thines, which had towered above us the day before, was now a pimple at our feet.

We were just settling down to breakfast when a great black beast came trotting down the road towards us. It was an outsize goat carrying an outsize bell round its neck. Its coat was as long and silky as that of a regimental mascot, and its horns were formidable. Soon the goat-herd appeared and introduced the beast as 'Le Buq'. His appearance was hardly less strange than that of his charge, for his clothes were rusty with age and he had the dark oriental face we had seen on several of the local peasants. I was apprehensive, for the peasants of the Ardèche are said to be hostile to tourists. On several cliff faces we had seen such slogans as "Paysans pauvres, touristes riches" and, worse still, "Tourists, we'll get you." This peasant, however, proved friendly. He told us he had heard our donkey bells and had come to see if his animals were straying on to the road.

Several hours later we descended into a valley where vines were growing and reached the village of Ribes. We were quite exhausted. For the last half-hour I had only been able to prevent Jessica from falling asleep on the donkey by feeding her with blackberries. The sun burned down and there were still nineteen kilometres to go. Crouching under a wall at the village cross-roads, we argued. I was for giving up. Everybody else wanted to go on and reach the comforts of Joannas that night — even the children. I agreed to do another stage and then see how we felt. But I could only keep going like a machine. My hips began to grind in their sockets, then my knees and finally my ankles. I could no longer talk or even give a civil answer and I could only keep putting one foot down in front of the other and dream of proneness. At last Sebastian, striding ahead, let out a cry of joy. We had reached the point on the River Baume where he used to bathe with the Katys. I will draw a veil over the last few hours which included a short cut over the top of another mountain and down the far side. By then even the untirable Hannibal was hanging his head on a level with his knees.

The camp-site at Joannas was everything that Sebastian had said it would be. There was a little river that he had helped the Katys to dam for a swimming-pool; there was the peach orchard among whose foliage the tents nestled discreetly; best of all, there was the shower block disguised as a thatched cottage. As we descended the mountain we recognised on the perimeter the tiny yellow triangle of a tent we had last seen at le Pont-de-Montvert. From it emerged Adrian, his wire-rimmed spectacles triumphantly a-glitter.

"We've been here four days," he said and proceeded to describe course by course the gigantic meal he and Rachel had received from a French couple who had given them a lift all the way from le Pont-de-Montvert to Joannas.

CHAPTER 31

High wind on the Rhône

Monsieur Katy was a thin, dark, serious man who had given up his job in Paris as an engineer draughtsman to earn a precarious living as an amateur architect and contractor among these mountains. His cheerful round-faced wife and his three sons showed us to a piece of waste ground outside the camp-site where the donkeys could graze undisturbed. We felt we had arrived in Paradise.

The following day was my birthday and each of us spent it according to his fancy. I passed a large part of it in contact with hot water in the shower block; the children chose the cold water of the river; and the five young persons of the party went shopping in Largentière. Andrew was in search of the ingredients for a new knapsack. By normal standards his present knapsack was small enough, but he was obsessed with the desire to cram his gear into an even smaller space. As Sebastian remarked when they returned, it would be so much easier if one could just swallow one's possessions and carry them in a paunch. And that, virtually, was what we did that evening. They had all bought me consumables for my birthday. There was local goat's cheese from Thomas, Montélimar nougat from Cordelia, cigars from Andrew, and Calvados from Sebastian. The Katys arrived in time for the birthday dinner, bringing two bottles of the local wine, and Adrian got tight and rolled squealing on his back without his spectacles while the children tickled him. At the end of the meal (at which he had two helpings both of the veal in marsala and the peaches in wine) he told us that he and Rachel would be leaving in the morning, a week early, as they had just remembered a wedding at Cambridge. Relieved as we were that they had recognised that our sort of pilgrimage was not theirs, we also felt sad that we had probably contributed to their failure, as well as making ruthless use of their troubles to cement family unity. When they went they left us some good tales but an unexpected gap.

By a strange coincidence our only two introductions in France were both in the Ardèche. At Alba, a charming stone-built village of archways and alleys near Montélimar, the Bruces, neighbours in Sussex, had a cottage. Our only fear was that, as we were two weeks late, they might already have returned to England. It took us two days of forced marches, in appalling heat, to reach Alba. On the night of the first we camped by the River Ardèche, where we were occasionally disturbed by chattering flotillas of canoes mostly travelling broadside on. The second day we went badly astray. As the sun climbed to its zenith we were forcing our way along a steep hillside through ever denser scrub where there should have been a cart-track according to our map, but clearly wasn't. So we retreated through orchards heavily loaded with Golden Delicious, and used roads for the rest of the day, walking for hours on dreary tarmac. When we reached Alba at half-past two Hendry Bruce was just carrying the last load of suitcases to the car. As Betty handed over the key she told us they should have left an hour ago, but had been held up by a farewell drink with their friends and neighbours, 'the potters'.

Within ten minutes they were gone, and the house was ours. It was a charming place, built over an archway, up a flight of steps. We had not spent a night under a roof for four months and we entered the spacious whitewashed kitchen, with its pine furniture, like a band of awe-struck savages, wondering at the convenience of it all. Perhaps what amazed us most was the ease with which a cup of tea could be made in a house where there was a stove, a tap and a table, all within easy reach of each other and all at waist level. As we sat around the table, drinking Earl Grey tea out of china mugs, Iago snored contentedly. He had already found the dog basket in the fireplace and was curled up in it as if he had never known any but domestic comforts.

Dinner was a convivial occasion. We indulged in all the things we could not have in camp: spaghetti bolognaise (because it needs a big saucepan), tomato salad (because it requires oil and vinegar which cannot easily be carried) and, best of all, conversation. This was something we had missed out of doors — the chance to sit back and expand mentally after we had eaten. The new custom interested Jessica, whose head only just came above the end of the table. "Is this the talking bit where nobody eats?" she enquired.

As I lay in a soft bed the next morning, warmed by the rising sun, I felt I never wanted to leave the comforts of a home again. Yet, strangely enough, twenty-four hours later I was glad to go. The free day went well at first. We spent the morning sorting and washing our possessions in preparation for the assault on the Alps. Again and again we filled the bath with hot water, which speedily turned black. On the burning terrace even the donkey blankets dried in half an hour. We lunched well with the two jolly trousered ladies who ran the pottery next door and had allowed us to put the donkeys in their field overnight. It was only in the evening that, suffering, no doubt, from too much rich food and too little exercise, I started to find fault with the state of the house. The spacious rush-matted sitting-room that Andrew, Cordelia and Sebastian were sharing, now looked like a hippy pad, with filthy objects covering every square centimetre of floor space. My annoyance was increased by the refusal of any of that idle tea-drinking lot to go out and water the donkeys. By the time I realised I would have to do it myself, a thunderstorm had burst and the cobbled alleys of Alba were running rivers. Dinner, as a result, was not a cheerful meal and the night brought little peace, for Andrew decided to devote it to assembling the jigsaw of his new knapsack in the kitchen and Sebastian sat up with him making cups of tea. The result of this was periodic trips to the lavatory which opened out of our bedroom. When, at 3 a.m., a muffled figure opened the bathroom door yet again, flooding my pillow with light, I let fly. Unfortunately it was not Andrew but Cordelia, who was in the throes of a bilious attack. She dissolved into tears. Overcome with guilt, I gave up the attempt to sleep and spent the rest of the night in the kitchen reading a senseless novel about cultured people in North London. Such things never happened in camp. We were glad to be on the road again at dawn, in spite of a steady downpour.

Andrew was a strange sight in his new knapsack, still largely held together with safety pins. It looked like a life jacket, with two oblong breasts in front and a square hump behind. It obliged him to adopt the upright stance of a woman carrying a water-pot on her head and made bending awkward since his breasts then clonked against his knees. On the other hand it was certainly compact, so compact that quite a number of his possessions had to be carried by Hannibal.

Ahead of us now lay the Rhône, and beyond that our next historical trail, the route which Hannibal had taken with his thirty-seven elephants in 218 B.C. Hannibal, as every schoolboy knows, was the Carthaginian general who set out to defeat the Romans by taking them in the rear. The easy way to attack Rome from North Africa might seem to be through Sicily, but Hannibal chose to make a vast detour through Spain and France and invade from the Alps which were considered impassable in winter. But just where he crossed them is uncertain. Sir Gavin de Beer, whose biography of Hannibal was our guide, writes, "The identification of the actual watershed pass over the Alps which Hannibal crossed has been a sport for 2,000 years."

Sir Gavin proceeds to develop his arguments for his own choice. Mainly they depend on the work of Polybius, the historian who wrote closest to the time, though even his account was not composed till seventy years later. It does, however, provide such key data as the distances Hannibal marched on each day of his passage from the Rhône to the Alps, and descriptions of the terrains over which the First and Second Battles of the Alps were fought. From this and other evidence Sir Gavin concludes that Hannibal crossed the Rhône some way south of Viviers, where we now crossed it. He did not have the advantage of the great suspension bridge which we used. Looking down at the river, we were not surprised that his elephants took a dim view of being asked to ford this broad and powerful flow of water. Eventually he built rafts for them, disguised these as projections of land, walked the elephants on to them, and before they had time to discover the trick, detached them from the bank and floated them across.

On the far side we turned north and made for the Drôme, the river up which Sir Gavin believes Hannibal made his way to the site of the First Battle of the Alps at the Col de Grimone. The Col was still far ahead of us as we fought our way forward through the mistral, often bent double to keep going against this northerly gale which tears down the Rhône valley. Sometimes exceptional gusts brought us to a complete halt.

The wind reached its peak when we were doing a stretch on the busy D6. Suddenly a car overtook us with a loose tarpaulin over its roof-rack which was making a roaring flutter, and I heard screams behind me. Hamilcar, with both children swaying precariously on his back, was careering loose towards me! In spite of my remonstrances, Thomas had taken to driving him ahead of him and now he had been left far behind. "I won't have my children treated like this," I yelled into the wind. "I won't speak to you till you cease to be hysterical," he yelled back. Fortunately on this occasion all ended well.

The wind dropped when we turned eastwards into the beautiful valley of the Drôme. Now at last we had truly joined forces with Hannibal. To our left rose a three-tiered landscape. At the bottom was the wide, boulder-strewn river-bed, then came steeply pitched green vineyards, then organ-pipe mountains white against the blue sky. And wherever there was a patch of flat land the lavender grow. The children sewed the flowers into bags for me that night in camp and once we passed an open shed where they were extracting the essence of the flowers by packing them into a steaming underground pit.

Of more interest to Thomas, however, was the sparkling white wine of the region, called Clairette de Die. Philippe Jullien, a friendly wine-merchant of Pontaix on the Drôme, gave us two bottles of the demi-sec. At Die itself, home of the famous wine and also on the Drôme, we briefly joined the *Route Annibal*, as this section of the N93 is called. To celebrate the proximity of the Alps I bought Iago a new collar and lead. Next day we all let out a spontaneous cheer at the sight of a signpost which read "Col de Grimone. Ouvert. 26 kms."

CHAPTER 32

A night on the bare mountain

It is hard to say exactly where the Alps begin. They form part of a mountainous region 300 kilometres wide, and we were to cross two major ranges before finally attempting the Col de Mary over the main watershed pass.

Like Hannibal, at least in Sir Gavin's version of his route, we approached our first pass, the Col de Grimone, up the valley of the Bès, a tributary of the Drôme. Our party was now reduced to its original size, for we had regretfully parted with Cordelia and Sebastian before Die and seen them reduced to a red and yellow dot on the road behind. About mid-morning we arrived at the place where the valley narrowed into the formidable Gorges des Gas. It was here that Hannibal's baggage train was ambushed by the Allobroges from above. He lost many men and animals as a result of panic which caused them to fall into the river-bed below. It seemed indeed a perfect place for an ambush and we were chiefly amazed that, without the advantage of today's road, an army's baggage train could have made its way up this gorge even unmolested.

The sheerest part of the road has now been improved by four short tunnels, one of which is entered by a bridge which flies the river before entering a hole in the rock face. According to an inscription, these tunnels were the work of the people of Glendage, a small village which lay in a wide saucer of cultivation higher up. From Glendage the Col de Grimone was visible, a green flat-topped mountain towering above us.

We were labouring upwards under a hot sun when a car stopped beside us. A young man and a small girl got out and told us they had heard about us on Radio Monte Carlo. Once more, mention in the media worked its magic. We were invited to lunch at the young man's holiday house in the village of Grimone, three kilometres below the pass.

It was only as we toiled those last eight kilometres towards the Col that we began to question Sir Gavin's siting of the First Battle of

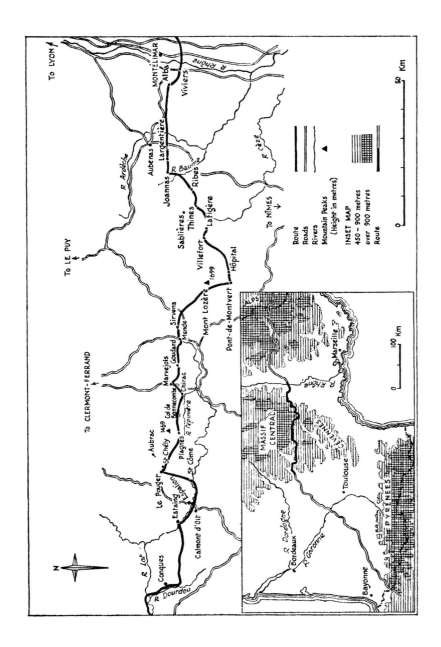

the Alps, and his choice of this pass. As Polybius described the battle, Hannibal discovered the Allobroges' ambush at the gorge, waited till night when he knew they would return to their villages, then passed his light troops through to occupy the pass itself. When his baggage train was ambushed on the following day these troops were then in a position to return and catch the Allobroges in the rear. It seemed to us that they would have had a long way to go to carry out this manœuvre.

Grimone village consisted of eight or nine large stone houses with a permanent population of two ancient *célibataires* who were not on speaking terms. The Rousne brothers, with their wives and children, had rented one of these houses for the summer. They both worked in Paris, one as a telephone engineer, the other as a motor mechanic, and seemed hardly to have heard of Hannibal, let alone his battle at the Col de Grimone, but this did not affect the warmth of their welcome. Four tables were put end to end in the garden, an awning was made by throwing cotton blankets over a couple of clothes lines and we sat down twenty-three to a vast family lunch. As we left, somewhat confused by the *vin du pays*, the fat electrician from Lyon, who rented the house next door, waved from his balcony. "Going to Turkey?" he called. "It's just up the road."

We did not tackle the Col until the next morning. It was possible to reach it by a steep and stony track suitable for jeeps and Land Rovers. The top was smooth and sheep-cropped, with a solitary house by the roadside and a still more solitary blue tent. We were at 1,318 metres. A tarmac road descended steeply from the pass, clinging to the almost vertical side of the mountain. Ahead, a series of mountain peaks appeared to be cut out of grey paper, with the rays of the sun fanning out behind them. Far below, the roofs of farmhouses were in shadow. We were about half-way down when the clouds came up and hid the silhouetted peaks in steam.

Lus-la-Croix-Haute was a nice little town full of French children on mass holidays. In the main square we consulted our maps. Ahead lay the Massifs du Gapençais, a mountainous region of natural forest. Across the middle of it was marked a tempting footpath leading to a village on the far side called Montmaur. We fell for the temptation and set off, following a stream called the Rioufroid by a wide track paved with red pine needles.

Up and up we went, the forest feeling more and more remote. We had been walking for a couple of hours, through ancient firs under a sky which became blacker and blacker, when the rain began. At this exact moment we came upon a log cabin whose door swung invitingly open. Half the floor was covered with straw for sleeping. The female section of the party quickly set about home-making. Jessica swept the floor-boards with a pine branch while Miranda laid out the sleeping-bags in a row on the straw. Soon we had our anoraks hung on hooks, our food ranged on shelves and a candle burning in the middle of a table improvised from loose planks. For much of the night a heavy thundery rain continued to fall and we were grateful indeed for our tin roof and straw bed.

The following morning, now even higher in the mountains, we were following a track along the contour of a pine-covered slope when we met the day's first obstacle, a trap obviously laid by the Allobroges to halt the progress of Hannibal's army. For half a kilometre the path was entirely blocked by the trunks of felled trees. Miranda went ahead leading Hamilcar, while Thomas and Andrew each shouldered one of Hannibal's four kit-bags. Still partly loaded, the stout-hearted donkey did some amazing leaps over fallen trees from a standstill. I came behind with Jessica and together we shouted *"Olé"* every time he cleared an obstacle.

For a stretch of open but precipitous pasture we joined a G.R., driving a dozen Hereford cattle ahead of us along a narrow ledge and averting our eyes from the drop to our right. As Andrew remarked, the French do not consider a footpath worth walking unless it is almost perpendicular. Otherwise, *"Pourquoi pas le Solex?"* (motorised bicycle). We breakfasted over a splendid view of sun-struck peaks with cloud forming a white ocean round their bases. Then we joined a Forestry Department track newly hacked out with bulldozers. It was after we had followed this for a couple of kilometres that things started to go wrong. A great two-humped peak, the Tête de Jarret (1,815 metres), was beginning to loom to our left, but it was too far to the left. According to our map we should by now have been circling its lower slopes. Gradually it occurred to us that the track we were following was no longer the G.R., but had been designed solely for the extraction of timber from the forest.

This horrid supposition was soon confirmed. Rain was already falling when the track came to a dead-end in a deeply furrowed turning circle. No path of any sort led out of it except for the one by which we had come. Thunder now began to growl, the temperature dropped rapidly, and the Tête de Jarret disappeared into cloud.

The next hour was not a happy one. We sheltered between two beech trees while Andrew cast about for a track. To pass the time Miranda lit a fire of twigs. Little did we guess how important that fire would be. As the downpour became torrential, first the trees and then our anoraks ceased to keep out the water. Frantically we gathered twigs that would keep alive our only source of warmth, but soon it seemed that the rain must overpower the fire. "Keep it going, or we're dead," said Andrew between clenched teeth. He was erecting a waterproof cotton blanket over the fire, suspending it between the beeches and pegging it down with guy ropes made of saddler's thread. Miraculously this improvised umbrella worked. Under its shelter the sodden children held their frozen feet to the fire. They had been wearing sandals when the downpour began.

For what seemed like hours we pulled wet branches out of wet leaf-mould, breaking them and piling them to dry beside the fire, being careful not to stumble over Andrew's frail guy ropes from which we felt our lives were suspended. As I stooped for branches, water trickled down my back and my toes squelched in pools of tepid water inside my boots. It was only when the rain finally slackened that we could consider putting up the tent. Fortunately Thomas had meanwhile had the foresight to spread out our aluminium space blankets in the turning circle, where each had now collected a basinful of rather muddy water — there was no question of going on that day, even if we had known which way to go, and we had exhausted our drinking-water at breakfast. When I lifted the third space blanket from the piled baggage I discovered Iago sheltering under it. He rolled his brown eyes up at me and thumped his tail apologetically. Unlike the rest of us, he was quite dry.

As soon as I had got the children into the tent I stripped them of their wet garments. Fortunately their spare clothes had remained dry, but not their sleeping-bags. Jessica's was soaked round the top and Miranda's had several dark sodden patches. Nevertheless they crept gratefully into them as the rain started again. While the three of us sheltered, Thomas and Andrew made soup and fought to keep the fire going. We were down to our emergency rations of flour and rice, and neither could be eaten raw. Over the same fire Thomas cooked enough kedgeree (from rice, hard-boiled egg and bacon) to last us and Iago two days. The wine had run out but there was no shortage of rum and rainwater.

For the next three hours the children played an elaborate game of mothers and babies. Jessica stuffed the doll from Leon up her jumper. Staff-nurse Miranda then enacted the whole ritual of birth and first hours on earth, asking me occasionally for advice on baby care. The rain lasted a very long time and before it finished the new child, dressed in paper nappies, was embarking on her first day in class six.

At about five o'clock on that eventful day a watery sun appeared and Andrew volunteered to reconnoitre a route to Montmaur for the next day. Carelessly we allowed him to go supplied only with his 'thoughts pad' and a polythene sheet. Almost as soon as he had gone the rain began once more and four hours later darkness came too, but no Andrew.

As we ate our supper we tried to convince ourselves that he had accepted hospitality at some peasant's cottage, well knowing there were no peasants' cottages for many kilometres in any direction. It must have been about ten at night when we heard what could have been the call of a distant owl. We yelled at the top of our voices. It came again. It was human and very high up. A series of shouted but incomprehensible phrases followed. It was Andrew all right, but was he calling for help — or what?

Thomas disappeared, yelling "Are you all right?" into the darkness. The children and I huddled alone in the dark tent straining our ears for every sound. Had Andrew fallen over a precipice? How would we ever find him? And if we found him what could we do for him? It was two days' journey back and we did not know the way on. At last the wet little figure of Iago ran shivering into the tent, a sure sign that Thomas would be back in a few minutes, and soon we saw the gleam of a torch.

"He's at the top of the Tête de Jarret and missed the way down. He's spending the night up there," he said.

What a horrible thought! Soaked to the skin, without food, light or a sleeping-bag. I went to sleep feeling guiltily warm, but woke in the early hours and found my ears straining for any sound from the mountain. Suddenly there was a hideous strangulated shriek from that direction. Of course it was only an owl.

From first grey of dawn I expected Andrew's footsteps outside the tent. But as it grew lighter the rain started again. There was no point in getting up and no hope of lighting a fire. We lay miserably in our bags pretending to be asleep till the children asked what was happening. It was full daylight and the rain had ceased when Iago rushed out of the tent barking frantically. Five minutes later Andrew peered in, looking just as usual, although his nose was a trifle red. He seemed perfectly cheerful, but glad of cold kedgeree.

He had discovered the path we had missed, but it was steep and blocked by barbed-wire. So much for the firm blue line on our map. He had then returned to the spur where he calculated from the map that we should be camped. Not finding us, he had climbed the Tête de Jarret and shouted in each direction in turn. By then it was too dark to descend safely and he had made a bed of pine branches and wrapped himself in his sheet of polythene. He had not been cold but had become sodden with the condensation from his own body inside his plastic tube. Later he admitted that, if he had not stopped during the afternoon to record a thought in his now soaked notebook, he would have reached the tent before nightfall.

CHAPTER 33

Accident in the Alps

We extracted ourselves painfully from the Massifs du Gapençais by returning to a point where we had seen men loading timber the day before. The track was now quagmire, but the sun had returned and a plume of white cloud hung in the blue sky above the Tête de Jarret as if, after a rough night, the old mountains were peacefully smoking a cigar. In ten kilometres we reached the abandoned village of Agnielles, and not long after that the main road. After a further ten kilometres on the tarmac we came to the busy little railway town of Veynes in a valley full of fruit trees. That night we camped in the bed of the Buech and there was another thunderstorm.

I cannot exactly explain my state of mind when we started walking next day. I should have been full of gratitude for the delivery of my son from the hump of the dreaded camel. Instead I felt depressed. We had not been really dry for days and when it was wet we could wash neither ourselves nor our clothes. Furthermore, I was losing the fight to keep the children's trousers intact. Huge holes were appearing in all four knees simultaneously and there never seemed time for mending after writing the diary. Once more, as in Spain, I had the nightmarish feeling that we were moving progressively downhill to some point of nameless degradation.

I remember exactly where these gloomy thoughts passed through my head. We were on the main road from Veynes to Gap. When the Paris–Briançon express rushed past, full of clean comfortable people, I burst into shameful tears of self-pity, wishing I was with them.

We reached Gap, the last sizeable town on the French side of the border, the following day and made straight for the trim lawns and shrubberies of the city park where we tethered the donkeys. It was our custom to skirt large towns but we were short of time and there were things I needed before I could face the crossing of the Col de Mary. I needed new boots (after 1,500 kilometres my French Patrick walking boots had cracked across the sole); a waterproof anorak (mine leaked like a sieve); and advice. Our adventure in the Massifs du Gapençais had frightened me. If that rain had been an Alpine blizzard we would have been in real trouble. I wanted to be quite sure of the route over the col and have some idea of the terrain we were likely to encounter.

The pleasant but preoccupied ladies at the Syndicat d'Initiative had never heard of the Col de Mary. They advised us to visit the local *alpiniste*, Dr. Arnoux, at his surgery. After a shave and a shampoo in the toilet of a café, this was what Thomas and I did. The doctor, a stout middle-aged man in a white coat, looked flustered as he opened the door of his modern apartment. He was obviously in the middle of examining a patient and did not invite us into the elegantly furnished waiting-room we could see beyond him, preferring to leave us in the hall. After half an hour he hurried back, glanced at our map, declared that he had no knowledge of the Col de Mary and that it would be best to make enquiries locally. Fortunately our search for boots and waterproofs was more successful and by mid-afternoon we were on our way.

After two more days we reached the valley of the Durance up which Hannibal led his army. The point where he crossed it is now many metres below the surface of the Serre-Ponçon hydro-electric reservoir. At Embrun, a pretty old town at the head of the reservoir, we sat on the rim of the fountain and read newspaper accounts of catastrophic thunderstorms in the high passes ahead. At Embrun, too, we met a farmer who told us that by this time last year he had been obliged to bring his sheep down from the pass because of early snow. At Guil-lestre we saw, for the first time, the peaks that are eternally snow-covered. Only the Col de Vars (2,109 metres) now lay between us and the Col de Mary.

The final kilometres of the road below the Col de Vars had been hideously developed as a ski resort by Expan-Vars and Develo-Vars. Even the bare top of the pass was embellished with a miniature zoo from which a plump lady tourist ran out to take a photo of us. I think she imagined we were one of the exhibits. But as we descended into Hannibal's valley of the Ubaye, all development ceased, and we had the smooth green mountainside to ourselves. The only sign of human habitation was St. Paul d'Ubaye's cluster of grey slate roofs far below us. Half-way down we made what we imagined would be our last but one camp on French soil. Facing us was the snow-capped peak of the Aiguille de Chambeyron, the further slopes of which descended into Italy.

The sun was rising behind the Aiguille as we set off the next morning, and frost sparkled on the turf. We passed the peasant who had grudgingly given us permission to camp the night before. He enquired grimly whether we had cleared up our mess and put out the fire. It was not far from here that the Dominici murders had taken place. As we swung down the road strange shrill cries came from the mountainside above. We traced them to pairs of what appeared to be fawn coloured penguins, until Iago made a dash at them. They turned out to be marmots the size of badgers and vanished into their burrows.

At St. Paul d'Ubaye we stocked up with food for what might be a four-day crossing of the Col de Mary. The shopkeeper there was the surliest I had encountered. He took a poor view of our chances of getting over. There had been a fall of snow up there the day before. We would have to enquire whether it had melted from the *refuge* of the Club Alpin Français at Maljasset. We breakfasted beyond the village and quarrelled about the police. I said we should consult them before crossing the Col (secretly I wanted to be sure that a search party would know where to look for us). Thomas, who has an innate dislike of authority, said they would be sure to raise objections about importing donkeys into Italy. In the end Andrew and I walked back to the police station where we were assured by a very young policeman that the path to the Col was marked all the way with blue and white arrows.

From St. Paul, like Hannibal, we followed the gorge of the Ubaye up a narrow road in need of repair, stopping to photograph the unbelievable Pont du Châtelet, which joins the two sides of the gorge like a spider's web at a height of 100 metres. Walking ahead, I now listened to some jovial exchanges between the children and Thomas about a fine peeled stick, probably a shepherd's, that he had just picked up at the roadside. Suddenly I heard the children's screams. I will allow Miranda to continue the story of which she was about to become the central figure: "When Hamilcar saw the stick he galloped away down the slope. Off we came, saddle and all. Bump! Jessica landed on top of me. Suddenly my arm went numb. Andrew came and picked me up. I was crying very much. A white car drove by. It stopped. A shepherd got out and tried to lift my arm up. No, I wouldn't let him. He told Andrew to lift it up by the thumb. I let him lift it half way. Then I couldn't stand it any longer. Andrew got out his first-aid book. 1. Do not panic. 2. Do not drink spirits. 3. Undo top buttons. 4. Keep him warm. 5. Don't let him look at the sky."

The gorge at this point was not sheer, but just a steep grassy slope. At the moment when the children's screams forced me to turn I saw Hamilcar trotting briskly down this slope. A second later, with Jessica still clinging to Miranda's waist, they both shot together over his left shoulder. Both were crying as we ran to them. I picked up Jessica who was rubbing the back of her head, but Miranda's left arm was hurting so much that she could not bear to have it touched or even have the sleeve rolled up for us to see what was wrong. At that moment a battered white Renault passed us slowly, going up the mountain. I rushed

Miranda and Jessica watering Hamilcar at the River Arga.

Madame Courte receives Hamilcar in the courtyard of the Château of St Aubin in the Armagnac district of France.

Miranda and Jessica study the Roman mosaics at Séviac.

up the bank and waved to it to stop. A dark unshaven man of about forty got out, followed by a gangling blond student. "We've had an accident. I think the child's arm is broken. She may need to go to hospital." I must have spoken in appalling French, for the student evidently thought I didn't know the language and kept laughing. The dark man, after briefly examining Miranda, said he was a shepherd and had *troupeaux* on the mountain which he couldn't leave, but his friend would come down in about ten minutes. We must wait by the roadside.

Very gently we carried Miranda up the bank and made a bed for her out of blankets on the verge. Andrew ran down to the river, where the two donkeys were now grazing, and dug our first-aid book out of the bottom of a kit-bag. It said that a broken arm should be padded and strapped to the patient's side. We used Miranda's socks for padding and a selection of our scarves to tie her arm to her side. The upper arm was aching badly and she cried whenever it was moved. Otherwise she lay very quiet. All the colour had drained from her face.

It seemed the car would never come. Not another passed; indeed the shepherd's old Renault had been the first we had seen since we had left St. Paul. The road we were on was a dead end, leading only to Maljasset. At last our shepherd himself returned from the mountains and Thomas and I lifted Miranda on to his back seat. His breath now smelt strongly of drink but his mood did not seem to have improved. As he took the bends at alarming speed, he pointed out that he had been intending to get a week's supply of food and now the whole day would be wasted. Whenever there was an accident it was always the locals who had to come to the rescue. The tourists never stopped to help. He was anxious about the snow coming. There had been a light fall two days earlier, but a shepherd that morning on the Col de Mary had said that it had melted.

Barcellonette was a crowded little town with narrow streets. The hospital was an old house standing in a garden, with the date 1756 over the door. The front hall was dark and empty. All I could see as I rushed in were three cooks at work in an even darker kitchen. They pointed up the stairs. I took them two at a time with the desperate feeling that there was nobody in the building and that nobody cared. At the end of a long passage I saw a grim-looking elderly woman sitting at a desk. She seemed annoyed by my appearance. "I don't know if there's anyone who can deal with her," she said. Finally she led me to a dingy operating theatre. "If it's only a broken arm she can walk into the hospital," she said. But Thomas insisted on carrying Miranda. Presently a bearded young doctor, who looked little more than a student, appeared. Miranda, lying on the operating table, smiled up at him and touched his wrist lightly. He smiled at her, the first

F

person who had smiled since we entered the place, and skilfully removed her sweater, revealing a badly swollen elbow.

The doctor and the lady started to wrestle with the X-ray machine, arguing with each other about the way it worked. How I longed for the cool efficiency of an English hospital and a clean white uniform somewhere! The doctor let out an audible '*Merde!*' as he prepared a morphine injection. He had broken the ampoule. Then they lowered a great plate so low over Miranda that it touched her forehead, and started to move the arm about, no doubt to place it correctly for the camera, but making her cry out with pain. For several seconds the room was plunged in darkness. Then the grim-faced lady retired into a cupboard to develop the photographs, after ten minutes miraculously reappearing with them. It was a dislocation of the elbow with the bones crossing, and a fracture as well. She would have to go to the big city hospital at Gap. They then relieved Thomas of almost all that was left of his ready cash and called an ambulance.

The ambulance was owned by a private company. An immaculate young woman arrived with a stretcher on wheels of shining chrome. That seventy-kilometre ride was a sad occasion. Thomas and I looked ridiculously out of place in our patched and dirty clothes amid all that white enamel and chrome. The elegant young woman, who now drove us, pointed out places of interest as we flew along the opposite bank of the Serre-Ponçon reservoir from the one we had so laboriously struggled up a few days before. Within an hour we were in the outskirts of the town.

"Back to bloody old Gap," said Thomas. I had never seen him look so dejected. He was sitting in the back with Miranda while she slept peacefully, a morphine-induced smile turning up the corners of her mouth.

Once we reached the shining clinic at Gap, presided over by the admirable Dr. Coronat, our medical troubles were over. Miranda's arm was set, secured with a vast metal pin which protruded through the flesh, and encased in several kilos of plaster. We both spent the night on the floor of her little room with its view of the mountains.

But in the morning Thomas had to return to Andrew and Jessica, who were camping at the scene of the accident and presumably short of supplies. It was a difficult parting. Miranda was frantic at leaving Thomas, whom she adores. I was worried about money, for Thomas could only give me travellers' cheques which *he* had signed. He could not wait till the banks opened on Tuesday to cash them.

The drama of that Tuesday, when I had to force my way into the bank manager's office uninvited, and burst into histrionic tears before he would accept Thomas's cheques, is no part of this story. Nor is the appalling moment when the cashier handed me only £40 worth of francs instead of £400 — she had misplaced the decimal point. It is only necessary to say that four days later, after affectionate adieux to the nursing staff, Miranda and I set off for a month's convalescence in England. We travelled overnight to Paris on the Paris–Briançon express.

CHAPTER 34

Hannibal's Pass

Thomas continues: By the time Miranda had had her arm set in the clean and efficient clinic at Gap it was late afternoon and I hurried out, leaving her asleep with Susan, to cash travellers' cheques. I had intentionally reduced my French cash to 140 francs before we should cross the frontier into Italy, and, as Susan has said, most of this had already gone on fees at Barcelonnette. Despite what they had said there, I hardly expected to find the banks open on a Saturday afternoon, but hoped a travel agency would help me. The first agency I tried said that I would just be in time for the banks if I hurried. They shut at five. I hurried — but I was not in time.

At the first, the iron grille was shut and though I could see several clerks moving about in the clients' area, smoking in a relaxed way now the week's work was over, and called loudly to them they wouldn't come. No doubt in my orange-patched trousers I looked like some unsavoury tramp. At the next, clerks were busy counting money and eventually by calling out my story in broken French I enticed one to the door. "A moment," he said, and returned to his caboosh. After five minutes a woman cashier approached. With enormous relief I saw her reach to the top bolt then bend to the floor bolt. What generous continental flexibility, I thought. In England you would never find such willingness to waive bureaucratic regulations in a case of human need. Now she was fitting a key into the door . . . Now she had turned her back and was walking away. She had not been opening the door, but finally locking and bolting it for the two-day weekend.

For the next hour I hurried desperately between the town's two travel agencies and five or six different hotels. None of them would change travellers' cheques, but eventually I found one which would take my last English five-pound note. This gave me just fifty-five francs on which Susan must live till Tuesday and I must get back to camp and reach Italy. More serious, before she and Miranda could leave Gap for England she would have to pay the clinic and ambulance bills, which we had been told would be about 2,000 francs, and buy rail or air tickets. But our travellers' cheques were all in my name. So I would either have to stay in Gap myself till Tuesday, leaving Andrew and Jessica for three days with little food and no idea what had happened to us, or find some other way for her to get cash.

Meanwhile Susan had been told that, although she could stay the night in Miranda's room, sleeping in the extendable armchair, I could *not*; the doctor/director of the clinic had specifically forbidden it. I had by then used some of the fifty-five francs on provisions — bread, cheese, yoghurt and wine — and as darkness fell we sat in that small clean but sterile little room, Miranda still sleeping peacefully, ate most of it — we had had nothing since breakfast — and drank several large tumblers of red wine. There was a hotel opposite, the nurse said, but I was long past trying it. As soon as the night staff came on duty, hoping they hadn't been told that I must leave, I laid my coat on the floor where there was just space for it, though I was half under the bed, and fell into a heavy sleep. Susan tried the extendable armchair, found that its leg section instantly collapsed, so used its cushions along the opposite wall.

I was too exhausted to notice the rock-hard vinyl tiles, but ironically, for only about the second time that year, we were pestered by mosquitoes. After my first heavy sleep I seemed to lie awake for hours, swatting at them or scratching the many bites they had already made on my hands and ankles. I distinguished two types: quiet, insidious ones I could barely hear, and those which approached with that fierce drone which to civilised man must be one of the most maddening of noises. In my dreams these became identified respectively with attacking fighters and heavy bombers. Adding to the ominous flavour of that long sad night, a thunderstorm rumbled for hours over the distant Alps, occasionally descending on Gap but producing no relieving rain. My good luck was that the various night nurses who came and went with tisane, thermometers and *supostes* (drugs in suppository form), didn't turn me out, and at about half-past seven next morning a particularly friendly one gave all three of us huge breakfast cups of French coffee and liberal slices of toast and jam.

Long before then Miranda had become ravenous. Was she now allowed to eat, we had asked at about six o'clock. It was twelve hours since her operation. Oh, good heavens no, the nurse had said. Nothing all day. But a quarter of an hour later she came back to admit that she had mistaken Miranda for an appendix case.

Some time around dawn one of our trip's most anxious crises occurred. Susan had decided in the night that she must also take Jessica home. I was sure that if she did we would never see any of them again and our whole expedition would disintegrate. I became fiercely obstinate and, to a background of Miranda telling us not to quarrel when she had a broken arm, Susan gracefully gave way.

The money problem remained, but as always seemed less insoluble by daylight. The clinic lent Susan 400 francs and agreed to wait for its fees till my insurance company paid. And I gave Susan £400 of signed travellers' cheques with a letter to the bank asking it to cash them. As she has described, this arrangement ultimately worked but in case it didn't the clinic's loan gave her cash for calls to a British consul.

Just the same I left them with anxiety at eleven that morning when I caught the daily bus to Barcelonnette — about thirty kilometres from our camp but the nearest point to which public transport would take me on a Sunday. Miranda and I both cried when I left her in her hospital bed, looking pathetically frail in her enormous plaster cast, and keeping my maroon scarf — the one we had used to bind her broken arm to her side — to smell to remind her of me. The day of the accident had probably been the most disappointing in my life and a background sadness remained for many days, only gradually lifting as it seemed we could save something of our trip, not finally disappearing till Susan's letter a month later at Fivizzano told me that she and Miranda would rejoin us soon.

At the same time I was guiltily pleased to be escaping from the practical problems I was leaving Susan with. My spirits rose as they often do when I am suddenly alone with only myself to protect. The day was sunny and warm and the two-hour bus ride through pretty villages and mountain valleys was pleasant enough in the T.V.-armchair way which had become so unfamiliar — a lot pleasanter than the same ride the day before in the ambulance.

Barcelonnette seemed deep in Sunday midday sleep, with scarcely a person in the streets and even fewer cars. Putting on my bright blue waterproof anorak to distract attention from my tramp's orange-patched trousers, I set out to walk the next thirty kilometres. It was a worrying prospect because I had left my Astronauts in camp and though I had walked in those boots for 2,000 kilometres without a blister, I had developed a sore heel in one hour the previous afternoon as I'd hurried round Gap in sandals.

So it was with great relief (and some sense of triumph, since Susan tells me I'll never hitch-hike successfully, dressing as shabbily as I do) that I saw the second car I thumbed come to a halt. I was even luckier: the friendly driver, who was turning off my route in one kilometre, gradually took me further and further as I told him our story and eventually right through St. Paul up the dead-end road of the Ubaye valley to the camp itself.

As we stopped I realised that that fantastic bridge, Pont du Châtelet, above its 100-metre vertical-sided gorge, was actually in sight from the point of the accident. Closer, down fifty metres of grassy valley side, I saw the little orange tent with Andrew and Jessica squatting at its mouth. They had just lunched on potatoes and sardines and Andrew was giving Jessica a reading lesson.

As Susan and I had guessed, the blue bowl was full of Andrew's clothes — he was taking the opportunity to launder his whole wardrobe. Iago had found the bones of a largish mammal and was grinding away at them in the grass. The donkeys were pegged out on a lower terrace. The previous evening, when Andrew was returning from watering them, Hannibal had bolted. Not remembering where he had left Jessica, he had held on heroically and been dragged twenty metres on his side, getting several now suppurating grazes on his hands. Soon afterwards Jessica had found the strangest caterpillar she had ever seen, ten or twelve centimetres long, as fat as a finger, black and red with brilliant yellow spots and a two-centimetre red horn with black tip. I've since identified it as the caterpillar of the poplar hawk moth. These had been the main incidents since I had left.

When the Frenchman finally drove away and the three of us stood by the roadside, feeling a more than usually small and vulnerable party, I noticed that the stick which had caused the whole incident still lay just where I had dropped it. Our optimism that morning as we had gone striding up towards our Alpine crossing contrasted dramatically with my present sadness and I could hardly believe that the accident only happened twenty-four hours ago.

We gave ourselves no time to mope. We would make the crossing next day while the weather held, before the return of another of those ten-day stationary cold fronts which are an Alpine weather feature. Last year there had been a blizzard on September 20th which had blocked every pass; it was already the 7th. The distances weren't great: eleven kilometres of road to Maljasset where we planned to get final advice at the French Alpine Club's refuge; six kilometres of track up to the Col de Mary; then eight more down to the first Italian village of Chiappera: on level road a long but quite possible day's walk. All depended on the steepness of the track and the difficulty of finding it.

We set off early — I can give few times during the next six weeks as Susan had kept our only watch and we intentionally remained without one. As we climbed up the small road which follows the Ubaye on its northern bank, the valley grew steadily narrower and more picturesque, with steep pastures and then high rock walls and clinging pines rising high on either side. Though we walked in shadow the tops of these were soon lit by the morning sun.

On the lower pastures we again saw marmots, those strange burrowing animals we had met on the descent from Vars, which shriek like a a seagull. They seemed as curious about us as we were about them and sat upright on rock tops to peer down at us. We never got close to them because they were perfect sport for Iago who spent all morning bounding up rocky slopes in vain attempts to catch one, invariably arriving about thirty seconds after they had dropped on to all fours and disappeared into their holes.

As we climbed we passed several parked cars, their male occupants all dressed in olive green anoraks scanning the rocky walls of the valley with binoculars. Customs officials checking for smugglers, I thought guiltily. But no, they were chamoix hunters. I don't love people who kill animals for sport, unless perhaps the animals are pests or the hunters also eat them. These men were thin-faced, dour French pocket Hemingways who only grunted when we spoke to them.

Far more sympathetic were the two or three inhabitants of La Barge, the last-but-one tiny village on the road, who turned from barrow and pitchfork to stare at us with typical French keen astonishment. Here I posted a final card to Miranda in a rusty yellow box which looked as if it had last been cleared in 1939. It reached her in England ten days later.

Tiny dwindling villages like La Barge far up remote valleys often make me try to picture the lives of their inhabitants before cars and bitumen roads connected them to the rest of the world. The simple food, hard work, lack of knowledge of anything beyond walking distance, and the intense curiosity about visitors are easy to imagine. Harder is the religious fervour which so often gave them churches grand out of all proportion to their populations. Two-thirds of the productive power of the mediaeval world went to the building of its cathedrals, I'm told. It had seemed credible in Spain when I contrasted those fantastic Gothic cathedrals at Leon and Burgos with the ant-hill underground communities in the country outside. The churches of these tiny French villages were no doubt examples of the same pattern on a village scale.

By the time we reached Maljasset, two kilometres further up the valley, the sun was high enough for us to breakfast in its warmth, sitting in a grassy paddock directly above the refuge. The warden was away but his jolly family, also at breakfast, told us that the pass was easy, with blue marks all the way and no snow. It was forbidden to take animals into Italy, they added. I remembered how, two months before, the Spanish frontier officials at Arneguy had alarmed us with a similar warning as they ushered us across the bridge towards France. Less reassuringly, I remembered a call I had made to the Italian commercial attaché in London five months before. "Dogs must be in-

oculated against rabies," he had read. "Donkeys! . . ." There had
been a pause while he had seemed to be hunting through his handbook, occasionally muttering, "Goats, rabbits . . ." "No requirements,"
he'd said at last. "Prohibited from Spain." Would ours still be tech-
nically from Spain, I had wondered, but decided against puzzling him
further.

So we began the ascent. Using a combination of the blue marks,
which were fairly frequent, and our French 1/50,000 map, 1930 edition,
we easily found the track which ran, not up the Vallon de Mary itself
as the ancient one had done, but up a gentler valley to the north, and
only reached the River Mary when we were above its precipitous-sided
gorge.

Looking down from here I began one of my commissions: to photograph this gorge, without showing modern features, for a series of
filmstrips on Great World Exploits — surprisingly difficult, since far
below us the little village of Maljasset kept intruding. This particular
filmstrip would describe Hannibal's famous crossing of the Alps with
his thirty-seven elephants, and it was in the Vallon de Mary that he
may have fought the Second Battle of the Alps.

Here the game of guessing Hannibal's route was reaching its climax.
The rules are that the actual Alpine watershed pass which he used must
have the six or seven specific features which Polybius or Livy, or both,
attribute to it. These include a narrow gorge for the battle, during
which Hannibal's troops were ambushed by the Gauls on the heights
above; a prominent rock at the head of the gorge to which he led his
advance guard and where he rallied his army; from there a relatively
easy ascent on the French side of the pass, followed by an extremely
difficult descent on the Italian side (on this section Hannibal lost many
men and animals because they trod through the fresh snow, were unable to get their footing on the encrusted snow left from the previous
winter, and as a result slipped over precipices into deep gorges below); a point on the descent into Italy where the way was blocked by
large rocks which had to be split with fire and vinegar; and a large
open space high on the Italian side where Hannibal assembled his army
and delivered them a speech of encouragement, showing them an extensive view of the plain of Piedmont below.

Sir Gavin de Beer concludes that the pass which most nearly provides these features is the Col de la Traversette. In his first book on the
subject, *Alps and Elephants, Hannibal's Pass* (1955), he gives no
alternative, but in *Hannibal*, written thirteen years later, he rather
mysteriously adds,

> If, instead, Hannibal's route was over the Col de Mary, he would
> have reached it by entering the valley of Ubaye south of Chorges

but after Barcelonnette he would not have gone on to the Col de l'Argentiere (which might have been his original intention), but would have been misled northwards, through St.-Paul-sur-Ubaye to Maljasset and Maurin. Opposite these villages, the Val de Mary debouches by a gorge, and that would have been the site of the Second Battle. The large bare rock would have to be found in one of the mounds of gypsum on the northern slope of the Val de Mary.

Sir Gavin's conclusions are well known and others have tested them against Col de la Traversette, some agreeing, some differing. The Col de Mary was another matter, and nowhere could I find further reference to it. Nor did I feel from the above that Sir Gavin himself had investigated it very thoroughly. Here, it seemed, was our chance to make our contribution to the 2,000-year-old sport. The Col de Mary had the added attraction that, at 2,654 metres, it was slightly lower than the Col de la Traversette (2,950 metres).

Looking back down the Vallon de Mary that bright sunny morning, it seemed the perfect site for the Second Battle of the Alps. I felt stirrings of the sort of satisfaction which surely fuels such controversies, and realised how tempting it must be to discover the features you need for the support of your own candidate. Looking up and to the left I saw two or three large rock masses set forward from the valley side. One of them could well have been the rallying point which Hannibal used for his advance guard while his main army was blocked in the gorge by the Gallic ambush.

And a relatively easy ascent followed — easy at least for soldiers and animals which had already crossed Spain from south to north and France from west to east, though occasionally too steep for a four-year-old on a donkey, and at several points we dismounted Jessica, leaving her to come puffing and clambering up behind. In Italy this was to become a common necessity and I always preferred her to follow, so avoiding the danger of being run down by one of Hannibal's sudden blundering rushes. But although many later climbs were more difficult, this one continued for a long time and the fine peaks which rose high above us to right and left, lit tawny orange by the sun, gave the crossing as a whole a grandeur matched by nothing which came before or after.

Presently our climb led us to even gentler upland country and we saw, ahead, an unmistakable dip in the mountain skyline, the col itself. It was the barrier which had lain ahead of us all summer and there was nothing now between us and it. True, we still had to make the descent 'of great difficulty' on the Italian side, but I nevertheless found it scarcely believable that we were going to arrive at this climax of our journey with such ease. Twenty minutes later we did indeed arrive there. The track ran straight over the summit with nothing but a simple wooden name-board to mark the point at which it began its descent into Italy.

All might have been different if we had had rain or snow (the following year the Alps had their first snow on September 5th), or if we had lost our way or suffered an accident in such a remote place. As it was, our ideas about arctic mittens, emergency rations — Susan had wanted to take a supply of barley for the donkeys in case the rocky col was bare — and of leaving messages for search parties to go out if we weren't sighted on the other side, seemed somewhat ridiculous. A chilly wind was blowing — the mountain tops were already in cloud — and we were glad of the shelter of a rock to eat a celebration Petit Munster (Miranda and I have a peasant taste for this smelliest of cheeses) and drink several glasses of red wine, but this was our sole discomfort.

When I look back on that crossing as a whole it seems a modest success. It is only when I picture the three of us crouching there with our cheese and wine that I remember my disappointment that we were not five to share the celebration of a moment we had all thought so much about. It was September 8th, four calendar months to the day since we had left Santiago.

So we began the descent and, glancing back, saw our only patch of the previous winter's snow, a huge brown deposit just below the col itself. But it was to one side of the track and I now began to face the fact that our candidate for Hannibal's pass was going to be a loser. The Italian descent was certainly steeper than the French ascent, but never very steep. The climate may, of course, have changed (though Sir Gavin's researches into climate, which are his most original contribution to the great debate, lead him to conclude that it was little colder in 217 B.C. than now), but even if there had been impacted winter snow here in Hannibal's time, on which the floundering Carthaginians could have lost their footing, there was no sign of any deep gorges into which they would have tumbled. The theory that an army could have suffered serious losses in this way on the descent from the Col de Mary is simply not credible. Nor is the descent at any point so narrow that rocks could have blocked it and needed to be destroyed by fire and vinegar. And though we did eventually find a place where Hannibal could have assembled his troops and made them an encouraging speech, it could not possibly be said to have an extensive view of the plain of Piedmont. During the whole descent we saw nothing below us except occasional far-off glimpses down the long narrow valley of the Maira of the tiny village of Chiappera. I can only guess that Sir Gavin included the Col de Mary on hearsay evidence which he never checked on the ground.

As for modern obstacles, by the time we had descended six kilometres we still hadn't seen a single Italian, let alone a frontier official, and the only evidence that we were in Italy had been an empty vermouth bottle with an Italian label.

About two kilometres above Chiappera, where a dramatic waterfall cascaded two hundred metres down a black rock-face, we made our first Italian camp. Though Andrew calculated that we had progressed twenty-three kilometres horizontally, climbed a thousand metres and descended six hundred, I don't remember feeling exhausted. On the other hand I vividly remember, as Jessica and I picked wild gooseberries after lunch, that the clouds which had grown darker all the descent became so louring that I expected a torrential storm. They produced a gloom which would have suited the most extravagantly neo-realistic film of *Macbeth*. We re-pegged the tent, all the time glancing up apprehensively, and it wasn't till about an hour later, by which time it had grown even darker, that I realised that what I had taken for the gathering of the most ferocious storm was in fact night falling.

Three

ITALY — THE NORTH

All paths are the same: they lead nowhere. They are paths going through the bush or into the bush. In my own life I could say I traversed long, long paths, but I am not anywhere. My benefactor's question has meaning now. Does this path have a heart? If it does, the path is good; if it doesn't it is of no use.

Carlos Castaneda, *The Teachings of Don Juan*

CHAPTER 35

Torrente di Gesso

Accidents are said to come in threes, but I didn't spend the days after Miranda had broken her arm expecting two more. Perhaps I should have done.

I was anxious to reach the post office at Borgo San Dalmazzo to get news from Gap, and we hurried forward down the deep green and very long valley of the Maira. Each time a steep descent seemed finally to bring us to its floor, we would find a further descent beyond. High above us, its mountainous sides were crossed, according to our maps, by mule-tracks; for the moment we rejected these and stayed on tarmac.

But as a result Hannibal's shoes, last renewed a month ago at le Pont-de-Montvert before we had even crossed the Rhône, were fast wearing out. We shut our minds to the problem till we reached Borgo; even if we had tried to solve it I doubt if we would have succeeded since we were to discover that Italian blacksmiths, at least in the north, have become as rare as French ones.

Below Chiappera we passed through a series of little villages each with its pretty square-towered church painted in blue and orange washes, some with huge external holy murals as well. At first these villages were in the process of depopulation but we presently passed an invisible dividing line and reached one which was expanding, with new holiday homes under construction and prospering shops. This was Acceglio, and here I bought our first Italian food: bread (most necessary since we had only half a stale loaf from Gap), and mortadella and gorgonzola to assure us that we had really arrived. Anxiously we compared Italian with French prices. They were lower, but by a smaller margin than I had hoped. To my surprise the shopkeeper spoke to us in French; today there can hardly be much border contact up the Val di Maira, and the nearest motor route to France would run all down the valley to Dronero then back up the parallel valley to the Col de Larche, a distance of perhaps 100 kilometres.

Sooner or later the chief event of our descent to Borgo San Dalmazzo was surely going to be an encounter with the Italian police and I wore my clean unpatched trousers ready for the officials who would

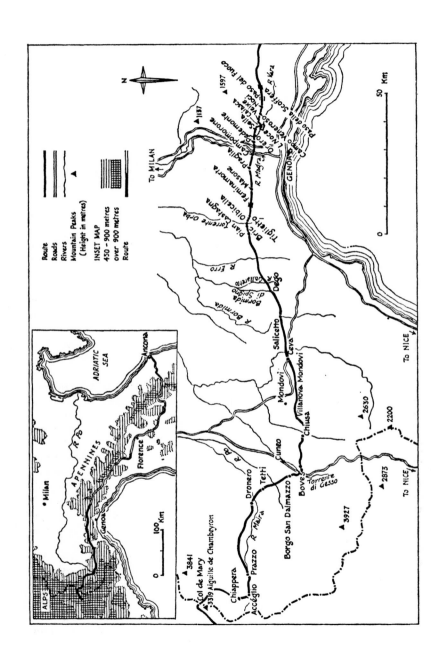

be waiting somewhere down this valley to make us unwelcome. I imagined internment for the donkeys or, at the very least, a long delay to satisfy bureaucratic proprieties. They would certainly be ordered a medical examination, since their only certificates of good health came from Santiago and were four months old.

Italian villages which have a police post are labelled at their entrance with the word *Carabinieri* and a phone number, but I must have missed the notice at Acceglio because it was not till we were on our way out that I suddenly saw the *Carabinieri* sign above the doorway of a sombre yellow house. Too late to muffle the donkeys' bells, we urged them past on the soft verge as quickly as they would go. The door stood ajar but no uniformed figure appeared.

Half an hour later, however, as we breakfasted in the stony bed of the Maira, two of them came striding down the road close behind us. We kept our backs turned and may have been hidden by the scrubby willow. Whatever the explanation they didn't investigate us.

But at Prazzo we were definitely seen. As we passed the official post a bemedalled officer appeared on the first-floor balcony to stare down at us. Perhaps indolence got the better of his curiosity because he too left us alone.

So it continued. At Dronero, our first real town, the *Carabinieri* post again made me nervous but we saw no one. By the time we reached Borgo San Dalmazzo I was hoping that any officials we did meet would no longer consider protecting the frontier to be their duty. A hundred years ago no doubt the valley of the Maira was as thoroughly policed against smugglers as any other crossing from France. I was grateful for those much-used and policed motor crossings which seem to have left remoter ways wide open.

On the second day of our three-day descent to Borgo, as we came into the tiny village of Tetti I heard live music. A fiesta? No, just a single roadside café in celebration, two youths strumming guitars among a crowd of a dozen locals. One of them remains conspicuous and memorable. Standing at their centre, hat tilted back, a miniature spirits bottle in one hand and a glass in the other, swaying from side to side and leering inanely at us as we passed, he was totally drunk. He was like the presence of Bacchus at a feast and the others seemed either ashamed of him or, more fancifully, to be unaware of his presence.

Those miniature drink bottles which litter Italian roadsides delighted Jessica. She has always been a child who can devise games from basic materials — a small heap of sand and grass, a few stones and sticks. A real miniature bottle was by her standards a proper manufactured toy, exactly designed for the suckling of her doll. The doll required wine, I was told, and by filling the bottle with water and then adding a single crystal of potassium permanganate I produced a most realistic purple liquid.

I now realise that it was as we were leaving Tetti that Iago may have sealed his fate. A wild flapping and squawking in a nearby farmyard told me that he had again got among the poultry. I yelled and roared, and after about ten seconds he came slinking after us, his tail between his legs, his mouth dripping feathers, though this time with no actual bird for our gypsy pot. We hurried on, expecting at any moment to hear angry shouts and not feeling safe for a couple of kilometres.

As a result, we kept him on the lead for the rest of that morning and for the whole of our final day's walk to Borgo. Soon after we had pitched camp there and collapsed in our usual afternoon exhaustion I realised that he had gone, lead and all.

I wasn't worried. It had happened before and we were at least 300 metres from the nearest road. No doubt he had felt under-exercised and the many local dogs he had scented as we passed through the town had proved too tempting. It was only when his supper-time came and he didn't return that I grew anxious. While daylight lasted we began to search, but there wasn't a sign or sound of him in all the surrounding scrubby bush and though we went far up and down the nearest roads there was no little brown corpse in the ditch. We put out his supper and went anxiously to bed.

In the morning his mash of bread and sardine lay untasted in its blue bowl. Again and more thoroughly we searched the surrounding bush. All the five days we were camped there we made further searches for him. We reported his loss to the local *Carabinieri* and called regularly at their office. We have never again seen or heard of him. The most hopeful guess is that some Italian child found and fancied him. "We should have realised that in Italy he was our third most valuable asset," Andrew said, tying up the donkeys more securely, "to prevent further depletion of our numbers."

His loss cast a new sadness over the expedition and I spent many anxious moments during the next weeks wondering how to break the news to Susan and Miranda.

We had reached Borgo at midday on September 11th. Though the foothills of the Alps still rose picturesquely to west and south, the town itself was on the plain, our least favourite sort of country for camping. But a kilometre beyond the town the river-bed of the Torrente di Gesso seemed a wilder area even than the map had suggested, a hundred and fifty metres across, part open, part thickly bushed with willow and acacia. Boldly passing the usual *Strada Privata* notice, we pitched our tent in a small, grassy open space past which the grey-white murky Gesso flowed in a modest eight-metre channel.

Here we examined our mail, collected as we passed through the town, including many letters from English friends, nine out of ten of which gave details of Antonia Fraser's affair with Harold Pinter, several including cuttings. The balance was corrected by Tolstoy's *Resurrection*, kindly sent by Tamara. It became our night-time reading-aloud book for the rest of that year's walk, drawing us relentlessly forward with its brilliant succession of characters, though confirming my view that even the greatest novelist can be a bore when he knows his message too clearly. A more unqualified success was James Reeves's selection of rhymes and poems for children, *The Merry Go Round*, which Jessica loved, her favourite changing as the days passed from 'The Farmer's Daughters' the eldest of whom drowns the youngest, to 'Soup, Beautiful Soup'.

Letters and new books set the tone of our camp at Borgo San Dalmazzo and if it hadn't been for the loss of Iago and for the event still to come, my chief memory would be of our sense of relaxation there. The big hurdle which had stood ahead all summer was now behind us and we could coast easily home. Autumn was coming but the weather was warm and sunny; in Italy it would surely remain so for the next six weeks. The problem of finding a smith no longer seemed urgent as it so often had in France and Spain when each day's delay meant a later crossing of the Alps. We set about solving it without hurry.

The only autumnal inconvenience I did begin to notice was the shortening of the days. For the last fortnight the moon had been waxing, thus extending our evenings, but now it was past full and rising later each night. In this phase it became an actual nuisance because, waking in the early morning without a watch, I found it impossible to distinguish between moonlight and dawn. As a result I took to sitting up in my sleeping bag and writing or reading by candlelight for an hour or so while I waited to see what happened. If nothing did I went to sleep again.

Later I learned to use the stars to tell the time. This can be done by treating the two pointers of the Plough as the hour hand of a twenty-four-hour clock which is turning in an anti-clockwise direction. For example, while we were at Borgo a clock-reading by these pointers of 7.0 represented 9 p.m. and a later clock reading of, say, 4.0 meant that six hours had passed and so represented 3 a.m.

But the system has drawbacks: it is only approximate, since without instruments it is hard to distinguish between readings like seven, seven thirty, and eight, and your calibration must be periodically changed, since the stars rise four minutes earlier each night.

During the day on the other hand, we found it restful to be without the exact time. We were usually in agreement about when the stages of our walk had gone on long enough and we needed a rest. I became

fully converted to the theory that the key technological advance, leading to all that is most neurotic about western civilisation, was the
mechanical clock. One has only to imagine an office day without clocks
or watches to realise that they are responsible for its most disagree-
able features.

The romantic idea that the watchless man learns to tell the time
by the sun is true only in a sense in which it is not usually meant.
The time he learns doesn't have numbers attached to it but events or
phases of his day which, as a result, fall into a more natural pattern.
We had noticed that our day became reorganised in the most striking way after that first timeless crossing of the Alps, and we continued to find that our lunch had often been late in the afternoon
since it was quickly followed by darkness.

One afternoon, still searching for Iago, I climbed to Borgo's
pretty church of Monserat. Its forecourt gave me a vast panoramic
view of the plains below. I could clearly see our river bed though
the tiny orange tent must have been hidden by bushes. When I arrived
a wedding was ending: two little bridesmaids in pale blue velvet stood
on the gravel while several dozen relations in their best suits milled
about the steps. The only discordant figures were those of the bride
and bridegroom, she little and middle-aged with a nose which almost
met her chin, looking in her gay hat the epitome of mutton dressed
as lamb, he hulking, toothy, fifteen years younger but already balding.
I was worried to imagine them making tender love.

The crowd allowed me only a glimpse of the brightly candle-lit
interior. Instead, I circled the outside and found nineteen nuns (I
counted them) sitting in a row on a low wall in the hunched position
nuns so often adopt, muttering their beads. This did not stop nineteen pairs of hooded eyes following my every movement as I picked
my way across their feet.

Another afternoon, crouching among riverside bushes for a quiet
crap, I heard an engine approach, a car stop, doors open and male
voices. Hastily pulling up my trousers and peering out, I saw the
strangest sight: four young men holding down some creature which
struggled on the sand while a fifth bent towards it with a long knife.
The creature — a pig I realised — made no sound and presently ceased
to struggle. I took a rear exit from the bushes back to camp, where
these same young men presently came roaming around collecting firewood.

My first idea that they were busy at some illegal trade I now abandoned, but my second, that they were engaged in some secret ritual, was
closer to the truth. What followed might be described merely as a Sunday-night roast-pig barbecue, but this all-male affair which went on
around a vast fire till perhaps 11 p.m., then abruptly ceased without any

climax or merriment, had more the flavour of a Masonic rite than of a family picnic. They left no scrap of meat or bone behind, just half a dozen plastic cups, several huge half-burned logs and a bundle of charred straw which I guessed they had used to singe the pig's bristles.

On our first afternoon at Borgo, Andrew visited Cuneo, the provincial capital, taking a bus along the ten-kilometre flat road which led there, a road continuously edged with ugly modern houses and small factories, reminding him of the outskirts of New Delhi. Italian taste in modern houses, we soon realised, was as bad as Spanish, if less flamboyant.

His purpose was to advertise for Iago in the local paper and to find a cobbler. Our boots were collapsing in turn. Susan's had split at Gap. My Astronauts, the most comfortable footwear I had ever possessed, giving me not a single blister the whole trip, had begun to wear at the heel, but as they were soled in Dr. Martin's patent plastic aircushions I didn't dare trust them to a local cobbler who might drive crude nails into them. Andrew's — £4 ex-army — were even more down at heel. But the cobbler at Borgo had pointed helplessly to the pile of waiting work on the floor beside him, and at Cuneo it was only at the third attempt that Andrew was more successful, and then only by beginning instantly to tell the tale of our trip before the cobbler could make a similar gesture.

By this time we must have been counting Iago's loss as our second accident because next morning when Andrew gently toppled the thermos, full of hot coffee, on to its side and its bulb shattered I optimistically scored it as our third. About lunchtime that day, our fourth day at Borgo, a steady rain began. There was nothing to do but crouch in the tent and wait for it to stop. Though the awning dripped, we were dry inside the tent itself, which I was now pitching more steeply by extending its centre pole, so preventing the fly-sheet from sagging on to the inner tent. It was the sort of afternoon which Miranda had often longed for, when we could do none of our normal camping duties but, safe and snug from some foul storm outside, would tell tales and sing folk-songs.

Hour after hour the rain went on, falling out of an even grey sky. When I saw rain coming in the afternoon I often cooked supper at once in case lighting a fire was impossible later, but that day it had begun too early and as dusk fell we realised that we must be content with bread and cold canned tunny. We had almost finished this and it was entirely dark when the rain entered a phase of even more drenching downpour, accompanied by flashes of lightning and rolls of thunder. In a momentary calm I put on my boots to make a sally for a pan of blackberries which I had stewed that morning — all our kitchen equipment still lay round the extinguished camp fire. Setting my feet out-side the tent mouth, I felt them sink into nine inches of black water.

It was flowing fast but in a sinister noiseless way. Our tent was pitched a few inches higher but now, feeling about below the awning, I found that this whole area was also awash.

At once I knew that we must move. I'd heard too many stories of river-bed drownings to risk staying a second longer. But the problem of doing it with Jessica, in the pitch dark, through thunder, lightning and violent rain was daunting. The terrain made the task still more appalling. Apart from being thickly set with scrubby willow and acacia, the whole area was cut up by ditches and gullies.

All I remembered was that the river-bed ended about 100 metres away in a steep bank, above which there was a flat grassy meadow. To this we floundered carrying Jessy in her sleeping-bag, my knap-sack, and as much else as we could manage, including two space blankets. Under these we made a waterproof nest for her and for every-thing else.

Throughout the whole evacuation she remained entirely calm, except when she thought she might be left alone; so now Andrew had to stay with her while I made a succession of journeys for the rest of our equipment. Finding my way back to the camp was slightly easier be-cause the candle still burned, but often after I had plunged about for five or ten minutes I would see its little orange glow in some entirely unexpected direction. Even by the time I first returned, the situation had changed and the tent was entirely surrounded by water. In the vivid flashes of lightning I saw that our whole cooking area was now a rushing torrent.

Returning loaded to Andrew and Jessica was far more difficult be-cause the shallowest of the gulleys was now knee-deep in water. On each journey, when I judged I was somewhere near our new dump, I needed Andrew to guide me there by shouting continuously to show where he was.

After the fifth journey the tent was empty but also floating. There was nothing to do except put out the candle, remove the fly-sheet and hopefully collapse it. At once it filled with water and even when I had collected the pegs its weight was so enormous that I thought I would never lift it. Eventually I realised that I must empty it from back to front like a gigantic canvas bucket. After ten minutes' heaving I at last had it bundled into a huge armful of sodden canvas, and staggered away with it.

As soon as we had re-erected it we swabbed it out with a damp shirt and put Jessica in the driest bag into a back corner, where she at once fell asleep. I made one more journey and stood splashing around our kitchen area, fishing up any hard pot or metal object I felt myself tread on, but everything light had been carried away.

Andrew made a final trip, taking off trousers and boots and rolling his long underpants to his crotch. The donkeys had been tethered further from the river, but he found Hannibal marooned on an island surrounded by thigh-deep water. Luckily he didn't panic but let himself be led calmly to safety. Sitting waiting for Andrew to return from this rescue I felt cold for the first time and realised that I was soaked to the skin. I had foolishly not made time to put on my waterproofs but had worn only Susan's 'showerproof' anorak.

By now it must have been around midnight and suddenly a brilliant moon appeared between heavy racing clouds. By its light we drank several large glasses of wine, took off our wet outer clothes, put on everything dry or nearly dry which we could find, and got into our sodden sleeping-bags. As we settled down to a very damp but surprisingly warm night, Andrew reminded me of the opening words of the chapter on "Being flooded out" in his back-packing book. "The very first thing to do as you prepare to evacuate your flooded site is to swear to yourself that NEVER NEVER will you let it happen again." We swore.

CHAPTER 36

Army-shod

We had passed through Borgo San Dalmazzo on our first arrival there when I heard behind us the welcome sound of horses' hooves on the road. Where there were horses there must be smiths, I still assumed, though in France they had often turned out to be many tedious kilometres apart. Glancing back, I was disappointed that these were not peasant beasts drawing an agricultural wagon but two strong mules pulling a smart khaki limber led by two *Alpini* in camouflaged uniforms with the traditional feather-decked *Alpini* hats. The army would have private shoeing arrangements.

But in the town next day Andrew was directed to the regimental farrier. This was the only person who could help us. The large barracks stood on the outskirts of Borgo and there he went late that afternoon, to be told that the farrier had left for the weekend.

Early on Monday he went again; by mid-morning the farrier himself, a dark-haired young man, had visited our camp in his smart new Fiat, taken the donkeys' measurements and promised to return in the evening. That had been the day of the flood and once the rain had started we ceased to expect him.

By twelve the next morning he was with us again, bringing eight new shoes, shoeing tools and a portable anvil. Clearly his military duties were not too closely regulated by the mechanical clock. During the next hour and a half he did a fine job, fitting heavy-duty shoes with seven nails each (four is normal for donkeys) on all eight feet. While he worked on Hamilcar Andrew held up his hooves and I held his ears in a vicious twist, so preventing him from giving the farrier more than the one kick on the head he had got when measuring him.

Was his job an easy one, we asked the farrier — he sweated heavily as he worked. At first he had thought so, he said, but the longer he did it the more difficult it seemed. Did his mules kick? No, no, they were all *molto bravi*. His regiment had forty-eight of them and they only needed shoeing every two and a half months. It was tarmac which caused wear; on grass or earth tracks there was little.

The day was cloudy but dry, with occasional weak sunshine, and we spent the rest of it draping our possessions over bushes. By evening we were three-quarters dried out, though certain items, for example *Resurrection*, remained obstinately sodden for many days. We also returned to the site of the flood. At first it seemed that many vital pieces of equipment were missing — Hannibal's girth, one of Jessica's sandals, the blue bowl full of washing, tooth-brushes, pots, pans, cutlery, and a plastic bag containing Andrew's money — but now the water had receded leaving the whole area coated in a fine grey silt, we gradually began to recover them.

The heavier articles were still in place but the lighter ones had been washed anything from twenty to fifty metres away and were often deeply embedded in rushes or driftwood. Amazingly, by the end of the morning the only missing item was one dessert spoon. Even the bowl of washing had turned up, poised uneasily on the edge of the river but still containing my old grey shirt and Jessica's socks and pants. Our good luck was due to a deep gulley with a narrow exit just below the site which had acted as a filter for the lighter items.

Our five-and-a-half-day break must have been making me restless. I was up early next morning and spent an hour packing before deciding that it was still the middle of the night. When a grey dawn eventually broke we were on our way before sunrise. Though reluctant to give up hope of finding Iago, I was anxious to reach our next postal address at Fivizzano for we still had no news from Gap.

But at our normal speed Fivizzano was only twelve days ahead and our less cumbersome party might move faster than that. Full of confidence, now that we were at last on our Italian 1/25,000 maps, we also planned to take the farrier's advice and use only paths and mule-tracks, thus making the donkeys' shoes last till our winter quarters near Lake Trasimeno.

These maps, bought from their official source in Florence, covered a direct route from the Alps to Trasimeno, only deviating to avoid Genoa and Florence, but the band they formed was only about ten kilometres wide. Just this narrow band needed fifty-eight sheets. I realise now that I had made two mistakes: I should have chosen maps of 1/100,000 scale to give a wider choice of route. True, these show fewer small paths, but in mountainous country such footpaths turned out, anyway, to be too rugged for our donkeys. The mule-tracks, which they do show, suited us best. I should also have looked at my maps' contours before I bought them.

As they succeeded each other to the east, the contour lines became thick and black, thinned again when the sheets began to mark them every twenty metres instead of every five, then once more became a dense black maze. The heights themselves were not alarming — around 1,200 metres at most — but at any height this density of contours meant continual steep ascents and descents.

We had to choose between a direct route over difficult country, or abandoning our new maps for a more northerly, longer but gentler route. We chose the direct route.

Even if we had had other maps they would all have been based on a 1936 survey, last revised in 1951, thus preceding the whole of Italy's post-war development, the development of a people who have a road-building tradition which goes back to the Romans, and an enthusiasm for damaging their countryside with the bulldozer which is like a child's with a new toy. Our salvation was that, just like violent little boys, they have often dropped the new toy after the first destructive game, and few of these tracks which they have bulldozed across hills and mountains have ever been surfaced, a welcome contrast with France where we would walk for many hours, passing only an occasional farmer's battered Renault 4, and never escape from tarmac.

We began at once to notice another contrast. In France, even more in England, the suburbanising of life has penetrated deeply. In Italy, even in the industrial north, a hundred metres from a main highway you can still be back in its peasant past. As soon as we had left Boves and taken to tracks, we began to see houses with great open verandas shared by humans, animals, and every sort of crop hung up to dry. In the fields peasants were turning their final hay by hand. Even odder, while whole families worked as their ancestors must have done for centuries, a small tractor would often stand, looking on but unused. Perhaps, like the bulldozer, it was a new toy which made them happy even when their peasant wisdom taught them that old methods were more economical.

On that first day, which soon became one of cloudless autumn sunshine, we met a more sympathetic Italian trait. At the pretty little town of Chiusa, where we were sitting on the parapet walls of the covered market place eating our yoghurt and raisins, a small boy came pushing through the circle of gaping older children holding out to Jessica on a piece of grease-proof paper half a steaming roast chicken. For a moment I thought it was something he should have taken home to his mother (he had seen Jessica and been overcome by love at first sight) but no, it was a present from the lady who kept the shop opposite. She waved and returned to her counter.

The least we could do was to buy our supplies there but when we did she asked us not a single question. We were to find this typical; the gift would be given and the giver would disappear, wanting no thanks. Before we left Chiusa, Jessica, her mouth still full of roast chicken, was also holding a packet of boiled sweets in one hand and a cylinder of cream-filled biscuits in the other.

As we progressed through Italy she quickly learned to exploit her success, and *we* learned why begging gypsies are often accompanied by children. She always asked to go with me into shops and was aggrieved when she didn't come out with at least a couple of *caramelli*. "I like lady shops," she told me. It was true that these gifts rarely came from male shopkeepers.

Our day's walk ended in hilly country near Villanova Mondovì where we found, ready and waiting for us between a grove of chestnuts and a plantation of pines, a rustic table with wooden benches. Despite the remoteness of the place, we had barely unloaded when an aged Italian came striding through the trees, telling us it was his pine plantation but that he would be honoured if we would camp here and use his table. He must have been six foot three inches tall and broad in proportion; he carried a strong stick in one hand and with the other held out a terrifying red and green fungus which he invited us to fry in butter.

I tried to imagine myself extending a similar welcome to, say, three curiously dressed Italians on a couple of motor scooters about to camp in our paddock in Sussex, and thought sadly how we have been spiritually crippled by being crushed together in our over-populated island. Before he left he shared half his lunchtime grapes with us, poured us several large glasses of wine from his bottle and asked me to photograph him among his pines. If he ever reads this I hope he will forgive our equally crippled English appetites: as we went to bed I dropped that alarming fungus into the red-hot ashes of our camp fire.

We continued to move steadily forward by earth tracks through pleasantly wooded country, only gradually realising that we were making half our usual daily progress. The mood of relaxation after the Alps was still with us and if we got lost, as we did once or twice each day, it didn't matter. Far more important, the feel and flavour of our journey was at last what I had originally hoped it would be. For whole days we would see no cars or only catch distant glimpses of them, busy glittering little digits humming along tarred roads in the valleys far below.

But we weren't alone, because Italians use their countryside in a way which the English and French have ceased to do. Every wood we passed through had its *funghi* gatherers, each carrying his plastic bag and his stick for poking among the fallen leaves. They must, I guessed, be gathering them for sale. No single family could eat these bulging bagfulls. We continued to abstain. In a café I noticed a big coloured chart of the different species. '120 Edible', the caption read. 'Only 4 Fatal'. That seemed quite enough.

The following evening we camped deep in another chestnut wood where by contrast we saw no one from our arrival till we left at dawn. In England an Italian friend had told me pessimistically that he doubted whether we would ever find places to camp in crowded Italy. Such ignorance of his own country seemed more and more amazing. Night after night we would be quite alone, and all day would pass equally remote and perfect camp-sites. At this one we found our first ripe chestnuts; as the autumn advanced they became an increasingly important part of our way of life.

Next day was one of the few when we did find it difficult to camp. Our plan had been to pass Ceva, but our slow wanderings soon made us realise that we should never get that far. Towards the end of the morning our path ended in a wide hill-top meadow where a typical peasant family was turning its hay crop with rakes and sticks. Here another splendid but younger Piedmontese in short-sleeved singlet exposing vast red neck and brawny shoulders, put us back on our track as well as giving us details of Napoleon's Italian campaign of 1796 against the Piedmontese. I had never met such a well-informed peasant. He also knew all about nearby sources of drinking-water. There weren't any.

At the next farm a witch-like woman with grey hair allowed us some for the donkeys but refused us any for ourselves. It wasn't fit for humans, she said, showing us the green scum it had formed in various stagnant buckets. We trailed on downhill, passing many good sites, all useless without water, eventually ending on the main road where we found a piece of waste ground beside a half-built house. Here a young man who was apparently building it single-handed made us welcome and showed us his tap. Towards dusk a smart grey Fiat 500 drew up and out climbed a large smiling, smartly dressed driver in pressed fawn trousers, suede shoes and fawn cardigan. It took me all the fifteen seconds of his grinning approach to recognise our brawny peasant hay-maker.

The following morning we revised our water arrangements, bought a three-litre can which would hold our essential needs for one night's camp, and determined, now it was autumn, that the donkeys must if necessary have their final drink in the afternoon.

Ceva, which we passed through early that day, is Italy of the plains at its most depressing. Hideous new blocks of flats are growing out of it on all sides. Those towards the motorway were decked with huge coloured advertisements for themselves, shown as clean white shapes among green trees and sky-blue swimming pools, bearing no resemblance to their sordid grey reality and arid brown surroundings. The wide valley with river, motorway and railway in which the town stands was the first of a succession of communication corridors we now began to cross. For two or three days we would be in remote hills; then suddenly below us another of these corridors would appear and we would wind painfully down into it. Each connected some coastal town — Savona, Imperia, Genoa — with Turin, Milan or another city of the Po valley to the north.

Our journey was leading us from west to east on a course roughly parallel to the stretch of the Italian coast which runs from the French frontier to Genoa. It was also taking us across the mountains which lie just inland from the coast. At Borgo San Dalmazzo we had been north of these mountains. The gentle hilly country of Piedmont which we had walked through had sloped down to the upper tributaries of the Po. By the time we reached a point due north of Genoa we had crossed them into Liguria and were on their much more rugged southern side, which slopes down to the Mediterranean. Though Piedmont annexed Liguria in 1815, gaining the port of Genoa and the power to be the rallying point for a united Italy, the two provinces remain vastly different in character, as we soon discovered.

At Dego we reached our second communications corridor. It lay somewhere below us, hidden in a thick lake of autumn mist. The date was September 21st, the autumn equinox, but I felt little anxiety as one day of glorious sunshine followed another. We were led into Dego by vast orange-painted arrows and huge letters N. I thought they must mark the course of a local motor-cycle scramble, known in Italy as a *motocross*, but later learned that they followed one of the routes taken by Napoleon's troops during the 1796 campaign.

When Napoleon was appointed to command the French army in Italy early that year he found it outnumbered and demoralised, hemmed in against the sea by the allied Austrian and Piedmontese forces. In a manœuvre which became a classic of its kind, he attacked the enemy's centre with his full strength, drove the Piedmontese north and, after defeating them at Ceva and again at Mondovi, forced them to sign a separate armistice only seventeen days after the start of his campaign. The footpath to Dego was used by the troops of Massena, the general who protected his right flank during these operations.

Unlike the French, who mark their footpaths sparsely, the Italians when they mark a footpath at all do it with fine exuberance. Again I seemed to detect the work of a child, this time let loose with brush and paint pot, in these great orange daubs on every rock and tree.

Dego itself was prettier and less expanded than Ceva, and the Bormida di Spigno by which we breakfasted was less brown and frothy than the last little river we had passed at Salicetto, where one bank had been formed by a rubbish tip including several dead animals and two gutted cars. We were now becoming familiar with Italian litter, which far exceeded French, let alone Spanish. It does not seem to occur to Italians when they picnic to remove or bury their plastic cups and plates. These, often still smeared with *pasta*, litter every pretty roadside stopping-place. Close beyond in the bushes, the unburied turds and brown-smeared newspaper begin.

As for the streams and ditches, they are invariably treated by factories and builders as open drains and lined with tips of refuse wherever they can be reached. A few days later, in an area where the streams had recently been in flood, we found the bushes and trees decked in trailing plastic up to four metres above their normal level. It was like some crazy water-nymphs' fiesta. Andrew informed me that Indians litter their countryside in the same way and that different nations had different litter habits as a result of the hygienic borders they set around themselves. Italians, like Indians, have the highest standards for their clothes and persons, but there it ends. Englishmen who accept this theory may feel less superior if they note the corollary: that we keep our persons no cleaner than our pavements and ditches.

Three days later at Masone, our third corridor, the motorway was still under construction but already vast and destructive. Whole sides of hills had been sliced away, acres of concrete had been laid, and heavy lorries and earth-moving equipment were churning about. When I meet particularly dismaying motorways I try to imagine them as the canals of the future: unused, their bridges collapsing, mushrooms splitting their concrete; perhaps they will then have a nostalgic charm.

We were glad to reach Masone because the descent had been the steepest yet, Jessica having to follow down a path that was more like a rock staircase. Her little figure came scrambling after us, although she needed all her concentration to stay upright. She was learning to call to us to wait when she got left behind, and not to sit on the ground and burst into tears. At the moment when Masone and its ruined valley finally came into view, Hannibal's breeching-strap burst, as a result of his load continually straining forward against it, and we spent an anxious twenty minutes cobbling it together.

Fortunately these traffic corridors were narrow and the country between them delightful; some of it was more remote and spectacular than any since the Massifs du Gapençais, that great mountainous area before Gap which we tried to cross but glanced off sideways.

Between Ceva and Dego we were still among chestnut woods, alternating with green hills. The emerald green of these against the pure blue but hazy autumn sky gave a strange sense of walking through an over-exposed colour photograph. It was a scene entirely without the harsh blacks and greys of the real world, and the little villages with their chiming clocks on faraway green hills seemed to consist exclusively of clean white houses with red tiled roofs. It was at our second camp after Ceva, in a grove of tall young oaks, later haunted by the cries of owls, that I heard Jessica behind a nearby tree giving her doll reading lessons in exactly Andrew's style and tone. "I don't know that word." "Yes you do, we had it yesterday." "I don't." "Of course you do . . ."

After the Dego corridor we continued for one more day in this hilly but kindly country till we crossed the Gallaretto near its junction with the Erro. Then all abuptly changed. The green banked streams became little torrents rushing over bare rock, the trees turned from chestnuts to pines and the undergrowth from bracken to heather and juniper.

Passing one more *Strada Privata* notice, we climbed steadily higher into this wild country by a narrow but puzzlingly tarred track. Suddenly we reached a formidable brick gateway with private shrine and huge iron bell to clank if we wanted attention. Undeterred, we passed through but were only half-way round a huge semi-circular driveway when a yelling woman appeared from a retainer's cottage at the far end. Hadn't we seen the notice, she cried. Couldn't we read?

But as soon as she heard we were English, her whole manner changed. "O, *scusi*," she said and in few moments she and her husband were leading us to water, giving Jessica bread and home-made cherry jam, insisting we take away the remains of the pot for the *povera bambina*. The house of the *padrone* we only saw later, a red roof far below us among the trees as we climbed, and who he was we never discovered. The word she used about him meant, according to our dictionary, 'crab'. His character? Or perhaps a millionaire crabmeat canner?

That night's camp was in high woodland near Pian Castagna, but it is the following night's that I remember better. It was the climax of the stage of our journey which ended near Genoa, and one of the most remote and serene of our whole trip.

The day had begun unpromisingly. Bric Berton, shown on our map as an uninhabited barren ridge, turned out to have become a village of holiday homes. Perhaps 150 square yellow boxes, separated by chain-link fences, their gate-posts topped by giant coloured dice or full-colour replicas of Snow White and the Seven Dwarfs, stood packed together on newly tarred tracks. Even in such dismaying surroundings Italians can be dauntingly kind. Though it was still only 6.30 a.m., two unshaven men stood for half an hour pondering our maps and trying to direct us across the next stretch of roadless country, while one of their wives fed Jessica with chocolate-coated peanuts. We left with two alternative routes, each of which had so often been recommended and unrecommended that we were in total confusion, and this was increased as the more helpful of the men passed and repassed us in his toy jeep, stopping locals who could give us more authentic advice. It was only by good luck that we breakfasted at Bric itself, a charming abandoned village consisting of three white cottages set among chestnut trees and green lawns.

A steep descent brought us to Olbicella at the foot of the next mountain ridge we must cross. Here at least there seemed no mistaking our way, for the bulldozer had been at work and what was marked as a mule track on our map had become a wide earth roadway. Up we went for a couple of kilometres till I saw Andrew unexpectedly halt ahead of me, posed on the skyline where the road seemed to make a sharp right turn. It turned indeed, but it also ceased to be a road and became the narrowest of tracks winding into the distance along the valley side, bordered the whole way by vertical rock above and by a 200-metre drop to the bed of the great green Torrente Orba below.

For two or three kilometres we followed this dramatic, alarming path, Andrew leading Hannibal ahead, Hamilcar following on his own, Jessica and myself behind, firmly gripping each other's hands. Then abruptly, where the road-building funds had given out at the other end, the freshly cut roadway began again. By now a new budget has probably provided money — the track was marked with red surveyor's paint — and another Italian feat of mountain road building has been completed. I am glad that I saw that earlier track because of the vivid idea it gave me of the pre-twentieth-century world, of the sheer physical effort this world needed to make just to keep in contact with its remoter parts, let alone create a civilisation. Though we were in Italy, not Spain, I remembered Richard Ford's description of the mule trains which serviced this mule-based world: "Mingled with droves of mules and horsemen, the zigzag lines come threading down the mountain defiles, now tracking through aromatic brushwood, now concealed amid rocks and olive trees, now emerging bright and glittering into the sunshine, giving life and movement to lonely nature, and breaking the usual stillness by the tinkle of the bell and the sad ditty of the muleteer."

Now we climbed steadily past the village of Tiglietto and reached a high, remote mountain track which, we were told, led to the pass of Feminamorta. I hoped it did, because there was no longer anyone to ask, just empty mountain-sides of scrub oak and heather. Late in the day we at last reached it and stood on a high saddle looking down into equally empty country ahead. We camped close below this saddle in a tiny grassy valley with a clear mountain stream running past our tent mouth.

It was my favourite sort of countryside, combined here with total solitude. As the sun set in a cloudless sky and brilliant stars began to appear, I abandoned the mildly diverting marriage problems of Trollope's Mary Thorn to listen to Jessica questioning Andrew, who was washing his clothes downstream.

"Mens don't wash so much as ladies?"

"Some do and some don't," he told her cautiously.

And a little later, thoughts of mortality prompted perhaps by our alarming walk that morning, "When these peoples die, do the new ones come with clothes?"

After our descent to Masone with its motorway devastation, I had hoped that we would climb again into wild country, but our camp at Praglia was by comparison suburban. The view below our tent on its windswept hillside contained two little holiday homes. The strong wind which made the tent flap wildly and continually brought up sea cloud to dissolve and re-form around us, was a further sign that we were nearing Genoa and the coast.

Next morning we began to descend into our final traffic corridor which connects Genoa with Milan. Rain was falling lightly. It grew heavier, and for three hours we walked through violent squally showers, which stung our faces and made the donkeys try to turn their backs, then through a steady drenching downpour. Often the newly tarred road was bordered by parking places, designed to give distant views of a blue and sunlit Mediterranean, but all we could see was thick grey cloud driven inland by the gale.

Only waterproof anoraks and trousers made walking possible in such conditions. Even so we grew hungrier and hungrier as the rain continued and we found no shelter for breakfast. At any moment Jessica might start to cry with cold and misery, though in fact the sounds which occasionally made me glance back at her little orange-coated figure on Hamilcar were snatches of Miranda's folk-song she was humming to herself. We were on the outskirts of Campomorone before the rain eased and we risked stopping in a steep abandoned orchard.

Passing high above the Serre-Ponçon reservoir, which now floods the valley of the Durance at the point where Hannibal crossed with his army.

Thomas feeds the latter-day Hannibal.

Miranda lies at the roadside after her accident in the Alps.

Survivors at the summit of the Alps, the Col de Mary, possible crossing point into Italy for Hannibal and his elephants.

Soon the sun shone, our clothes began to steam dry, and we experienced one of those violent changes of mood which were now familiar. One moment we would be wandering lost, cold and exhausted in some dank wood, deeply depressed at the long retracing of our path which seemed inevitable. A quarter of an hour later we would be striding briskly along a well-marked sunlit track, feeling warm and energetic and knowing exactly where we were going. I had learned to cultivate a state of empty-minded endurance during bad times. The euphoria of the good times I also tried to modify but there was no suppressing it that morning as we quickly became warm and dry and found ourselves sitting among such an abundance of crisp red apples that they weighed down the lower branches of the trees to the ground.

But we were down in the traffic corridor all right now. The valley road we had joined was one of the pre-*autostrada* routes to the north. Worse, after a kilometre of streets and shops we realised that Campomorone was no longer a separate little township but a suburb. Round a bend we met a large blue sign announcing GENOA itself.

A strange guide arrived to help us as we halted, wondering what to do next. We had noticed him earlier, staring at us as he passed first in one direction then the other, on a motor scooter. Short, broad and dark, he wore his hair in a curly pony tail gathered with an elastic band and strongly suggested a sixteenth-century Genoese seaman, so that I kept peering round his head for a gold earring.

Drawing us into a bar and buying us wine — although we had just breakfasted it was one o'clock — he gave us advice which, unlike so much we were given, still seemed sensible three days later. We must make for the pass of Scoffera, he said. There we would find the sort of tracks we needed. Meanwhile, turn left at the Aramco petrol station and climb past the cemetery.

We turned left and climbed, and a couple of hours later, after another swift descent and climb, were perched on the wooded summit of a hill inside the crumbling walls of an ancient fort, exactly at the centre of the Genoa–Milan corridor. Behind and below us lay Campomorone, a long suburban sprawl filling the valley for fifteen kilometres above Genoa, together with the old main road, river and railway. Ahead, we looked down on the rumbling double tracks of the Genoa–Milan *autostrada*.

Here we settled for a day's rest. It seemed astonishingly secluded for somewhere so close to Genoa — a good place also to look back on our progress since Borgo San Dalmazzo and judge the success of our policy of tracks not tarmac. On the one hand it was now September 27th, the day when I had hoped to reach Fivizzano, and we were still less than half-way there. On the other hand, we had walked through prettier country by pleasanter paths in a more relaxed state of mind than at any time before, and those fine military donkey shoes were so little worn that their bold-headed nails were still each leaving their individual prints in the dusty soil.

CHAPTER 37

By watershed to Emilia

Andrew went to Genoa. Our progress had been pleasant but effortful and we had long realised that the best way to cross this sort of country was not to labour up out of one valley and then collapse into the next, but find ridge-top tracks. To find these we needed more maps, giving us a wider choice of routes. Jessica and I would rest quietly in our hill-top fort. Two violent explosions before day had fully dawned disturbed our plan.

They were far closer than any Italian hunter's shots I had yet heard. Others followed, and presently I realised that what I had taken for a summer-time fire-watching post rising on stilts into the tree-tops about fifteen metres from our tent was in fact a hunters' hide. Because of the curve of the hill-top its wooden platform was about on the level of our heads.

The firing continued, and as the day grew lighter I could see gun barrels silhouetted against the sky and the shot spraying out from these. A second or two later it would come rattling down on the acacia leaves above us. God knows what they were firing at, as no birds seemed to come anywhere near. The whole scene was more like an episode from *Treasure Island* than the shooting of game as it is practised in England, and I suspected, as so often in Italy, that the real point was not the sport itself but the making of loud noise and the creating of a sense of well-armed male togetherness. Mixed with the shooting there were voices and laughter.

When it was fully light I showed myself, gesturing violently and yelling, "*Bambina*". A youth's head appeared over the pallisade. "*Si si,*" he called cheerily. But the sporadic fusilade continued. Only at about midday did it die down and I presently realised that the hide was empty.

Our route to Fivizzano must now turn south-east, as the coast does. Soon it would leave Liguria and take us into the ancient province of Emilia. Here our new ridge-top policy seemed particularly possible. A watershed separating the valleys of the Magra and the Vara runs for many kilometres in exactly the direction we needed, before dropping into the mountain basin in which Fivizzano stands. Along much of this watershed Andrew's new maps showed good mule-tracks. There remained the problem of escaping from Liguria and reaching these tracks which were several days' march away. The next three days while we were trying to do this were undoubtedly the most physically exhausting of my life. They also took us through the most beautiful and remote country I have seen in Europe.

Our progress on that first day if drawn in cross-section, would look like the folds of a concertina. At dawn we were descending into the valley of the *autostrada*, through fertile gardens of fruit and tomatoes down such steep and dew-soaked grassy paths that I was almost as often on my arse as my feet. At the bottom, just before the accurately named Pedemonte, our path was blocked by a rickety wooden bridge which no donkey would ever cross, and while a friendly fellow with trousers rolled to his knees and bare feet told us a way out, Hannibal's load fell off.

It was keeping his load in place even more than the walking which I found tiring, particularly on steep, narrow descents. Then it would slip forward over his neck and often at the key moment I would be unable to get alongside him to heave it back into place, because there was no space on the inside of the path, and to work from the outside meant that one of his sudden sideways blunders could push me over the edge. But unless I was there the instant a small tilt developed it would quickly become a fatal one, and he would come to a halt, a look of dumb innocence on his face, with his saddle, padding and four heavy kit-bags hanging under his belly.

On such descents I sometimes tried going ahead, glancing back to see what was happening as he lumbered down behind me, but this put the load completely out of my reach. So I would more often follow behind, stretching forward across his back to heave at the kit-bags and correct their tilt, but often losing my footing and being carried downhill like a fifth piece of baggage, overhanging vegetation sweeping past my head, my feet and ankles scrabbling at the sides of the rocky track. This sort of involuntary acrobatics gave me my only painful injury of the trip, when I bumped my ribs so hard on his knobbly spine that for a fortnight I thought they were cracked. The accident gives an idea of the sort of angles we were working at.

Ascents like the one we now began, by wide mule track from Pedemonte to Orero, were easier for me but harder for Hannibal. Their steepness made him stop every twenty or thirty metres to get his breath before heaving himself up some new forty-five-degree slope or over some tall rocky step in our path.

Did we form warm friendly relationships with our donkeys, I've often been asked. At such times my feelings came closest to something of the sort, especially for Hannibal. He laboured with a heavy brainless courage. When he stopped on these slopes, panting for breath, his chest and shoulders sodden with sweat, I knew that he really did need to pause for new energy and wasn't being lazy. There was something heroic about his character. If eunuchs can be classified, he was the plump willing variety, Hamilcar the mean spinsterly kind, continuously glancing out of the corner of his eye to catch you not watching him so that he could slow down or begin to graze.

But though I admired Hannibal's strength and dumb persistence, his stupidity was profound. Five months at heaving at his head whenever he walked on tarmac in preference to a soft grassy verge entirely failed to teach him this elementary lesson and each morning I would have to begin again. Equally maddening, he would invariably choose the moment when I was struggling with some rain-sodden knot to lurch forward, pulling it out of my hands, setting an iron-shod hoof on my toes. I began to sympathise with all those brutal peasants I had seen cursing and beating their asses instead of showing them kindness.

It was appealing that the donkeys often preferred to be near us rather than grazing sensibly on some distant and more nourishing fodder. Unfortunately, as soon as our backs were turned they would pick out a fresh loaf of bread from a knapsack, or nose open a bag of oranges and stand smugly munching them, the juice streaming from their clumsy mouths.

They were at their most likeable when they were unsaddled after a day's march and would find a piece of dry earth to roll on. There was a fine abandon about their rolling and I could understand just how they felt as they squirmed their uncluttered backs into the dust, the two together raising a great drifting cloud of it. But Hamilcar, if given the slightest chance, would roll *before* we had removed his saddlebags and I spent several half-hours picking out wet groceries and anoraks from crushed cartons of milk.

Even these admissions are a censored version of what was sometimes the truth, particularly at the end of the summer when Jessica and I were alone with the donkeys. At this time I often hated them with a passion that frightened me. I was crazy with exasperation that they seemed barely to feel the heavy whacks I gave them. My hate for them was nothing to do with the accidents they had caused. I was just driven into a frenzy by their persistent stupidity. Though Susan and Andrew had sometimes shared my exasperation, they were always more patient and forgiving.

During the second year much changed, and we realised that our irritation had been largely due to our incompetence. Once we had them properly harnessed and loaded, all of us, especially Miranda, developed real affection for them, particularly for the great furry brainless Hannibal. At the end I could honestly say that I had never known a more lovable, gentle and affectionate animal.

By breakfast-time that first day on from Genoa the path had grown thin; we had begun to cross deep gorges on the hillside and eventually been blocked by the day's second impassable bridge. There was no doubt that we were lost.

Food brought us new energy, as it often did. We were now eating enormously and our breakfasts had grown from the slice of bread and *chorizo* which we had thought enough in our first days in Galicia, to four or five vast hunks of bread topped in succession with cheese, *pâté* and *mortadella*, preceded by a great handful of peanuts and washed down with coffee. At each stop we would repeat this meal and lately we had added huge draughts of milk to cure the cracking at the corners of the mouth which Andrew diagnosed as vitamin B2 deficiency. Three of these substantial picnics followed by a cooked supper made a four-meal day. In addition I was giving Jessica and myself a good slice of bread and butter at dawn, and Andrew was feeding us spoonfuls of yeast which he continued to kill and dry laboriously over the camp fire. We needed every mouthful, though, surprisingly, we were eating less and less sugary food. It was protein we wanted, because the energy it gave us lasted a couple hours instead of half an hour.

That day's second climb, when we had rediscovered our path, led us up an ancient mule track paved with granite blocks and was steep enough. Emerging at Orero, we shopped, descended sharply beside a mountain railway line where a little two-carriage blue train whistled at us, and then began the ascent which really tested us. It was the steepest of the whole trip.

"Straight up there," the man at the bottom said, pointing to a tiny farmhouse on the skyline which stood at the pass of Sella. "You can't mistake it," and he followed us up the first hundred metres in carpet slippers, holding his little daughter by the hand. Up and up we went, hour after hour till I knew that we certainly had mistaken it. More worrying even than the sixty-degree narrow muddy paths, steep banks and rocky walls we were scaling was the thought that at any moment the track would finally disappear on the face of the mountain, as so many had before, and we should be forced to go back down all we had climbed. Though Jessica normally rode up ascents and only found descents alarming, much of this track was so steep and the drops beside the narrow path so sheer that she was forced to clamber up behind us on foot.

Drenched with sweat and shaking at the knees with exhaustion we still climbed, now through dense chestnut groves. All signs of the firm granite steps which we had found near the bottom had long disappeared. Now we seemed to be crossing the face of the mountain, and this was in fact what we found we had been doing when at last we collapsed on to a grassy ridge. The farmhouse we had aimed for was nowhere in sight and the pass we had reached was not Sella but another at least a kilometre to its north.

That night our tent was pitched on a narrow terrace above Lake Noce; it was so late when we arrived that the sun was setting and lunch became supper. Unlike most reservoirs, Noce is pretty, the water turned a deep green by the tree-covered sides of the valley, sides so steep that Hamilcar's braying echoed backwards and forwards for fifteen seconds after he had finished and must have been audible for twenty kilometres up the valley if there had been anyone to hear it.

How few people there were we discovered next morning when we set out to climb the northern side. We were in the country of my child-hood geography books, where milk from summer pastures came down into the valleys by enormous steel cables. "Look, it's flying," Jessica said the first time she saw a huge silver churn in mid-air high above the tree tops — but though a few of the lower of these devices still functioned, at higher altitudes they stood abandoned, their cables rusted and great timber anchor posts sagging. Even the sizeable village of Caiasca seemed uninhabited except for one woman working the milk cable.

She gave us confident advice. Straight on, a good mule-track led up to Campo Veneroso and then to Paso del Fuoco. Breakfast again found us lost, this time in a nearly vertical chestnut wood. While Andrew reconnoitred, Jessica and I crouched on one ledge, guarding the donkeys who swayed about terrifyingly on an even narrower one below. Returning to the milk woman at Caiasca, Andrew discovered that she had forgotten to mention a 140-degree left turn which we should have taken the moment we left the village.

Our climb up that valley side may have been slightly less steep than the day before's to Sella, but it was steep enough and even more spec-tacular. Below us we soon began to see the great green valley-side at the foot of which we had camped. Among its thick trees the abandoned terraces consisted more of vertical wall than of horizontal earth. Above them stood empty farms with fallen walls and gaping roofs. At Veixe we passed a whole one-sided street of abandoned houses, many of three or four storeys. Not even a shepherd now disturbed their sunlit peace — the last person to direct us, a gigantic peasant naked from the waist except for a thick collar of shaving foam, had been far back and below. Yes, there was a path, he had told us, but it was *strada brutta*. It certainly was. Again we climbed sweating over huge boulders which blocked the way, swayed perilously over precipitous edges, and staggered mile after mile, shaky at the knees with exhaustion, up steep overgrown paths. Again it was late before we sank exhausted on to the rocks of a little pass.

It was even later before Andrew had returned from the village of Noci, where he had only seen more gaping roofs, and we had carried the baggage, a kit-bag at a time, across a hilltop too rugged for loaded donkeys. But now at last we were on a ridge track of the sort we had longed for, and though it was often alarming, especially where it skirted a peak and landslides had carried away sections, it was also sensationally beautiful. For the most part it ran along a knife-edge of rock with sixty-degree slithery grass slopes beginning a few feet away to our right and to our left.

When we camped that night we seemed to be at the junction of two worlds. Behind us lay the vast empty valley up the side of which we had spent the day toiling. In the dark it tinkled with cowbells though we had seen no animals all day. Just beyond the tent we looked ahead into an equally dramatic valley, but one set about with many little red-roofed villages, each with its white-towered chiming church. Beyond them we could at last see the pass of Scoffera.

Those two days had included our most difficult ascents. The 400 metres of rock and scrub down to Scoffera next morning were our most testing descent. The motorist meets passes at the summit of long twisting climbs, but to us as ridge travellers they were now dips in our skyline route and often deep ones. Again Hannibal's baggage was constantly tumbling around his ears and I was afraid that at any moment the metal hoop on his *arreo*, to which everything was tied, would break loose. Jessica and I were again as often on our trouser seats as on our feet.

At Scoffera we shopped — more expensively than at any place yet. I had known that food would be a problem in the mountains, but I had forgotten that any shops we did find would be in small villages where prices are always high and where such things as the mysterious low-priced bread made from flour type O were rarely available but only bread from type OO costing twice as much. The prices in passes, where the food shops sell depressing souvenirs for exhausted motorists, are still more exorbitant. While we re-loaded, a hand threw Jessica a mixed bag of biscuits and sweets from an upper window which at once closed again. Even so, we left the pass of Scoffera with relief to climb back to our remote and beautiful ridge-tracks.

One more ordeal remained, though of a different kind. That night we camped just short of Barbagelata ('Frozen beard', a name which gives a vivid idea of its winter climate) on a pretty grassy slope with a view south down another wooded valley. A gusty wind was bring-

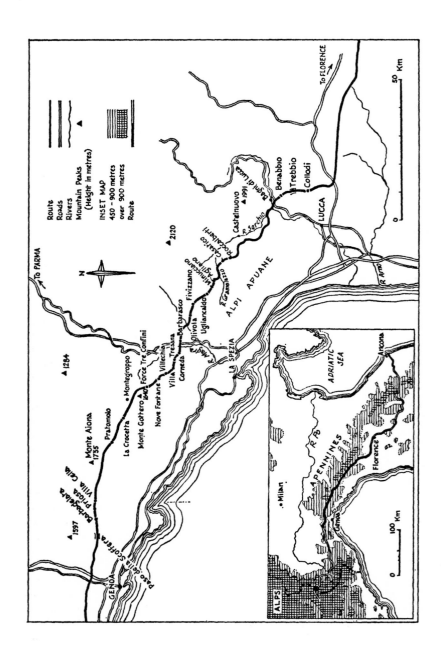

ing cloud up from the sea, in just the way it had on the night before our soaking descent to Campomorone, and after supper we had our first shower, but we still had not learned to recognise the pattern.

Soon heavy rain began, then still heavier. Lightning flashed, thunder rolled, and the wind rose, bellowing out the fly-sheet. In a dry interval Andrew pegged it down more firmly, but the next violent gust of rain-filled wind threatened to blow it completely loose and I hurried out, barefoot but in waterproofs, to push in pegs which had been torn loose and to lower the poles of the awning.

I was just getting snug and warm again and listening to the now torrential rain, the individual drops no longer distinguishable but merged into a single continuous whoosh of falling water, when a still more violent gust tore out the front pegs, tilted the tent sideways and snapped off the wooden bottom section of the central pole. There wasn't a moment to lose. Soon we would be out there unprotected in that gale-driven rain. While Andrew held up the pole, I again floundered round the tent, thrusting pegs into the sodden earth, completely removing the awning poles and pegging the fly-sheet down to the ground all round.

For about an hour the storm still raged. Then I fell asleep. When I woke there was an astonishing stillness. I crept to the edge of the tent and peered out from under the fly-sheet, like some strange mole putting its head out of its burrow. Far away, tiny and confined, the sky flashed picturesquely above a range of mountain tops but not a sound reached us and the sky above was bright with stars. Apart from a brief nightmare when she had imagined Hamilcar was eating her, Jessica had slept through the whole thing.

The serene camp at Feminamorta had been the climax of our stage to Genoa, but I think of the next eight days as the climax of that whole year's trip, the period when our walk became all I had hoped it would be, and I was only sorry that there were just the three of us to share it. As in Galicia, but on a more majestic scale, we seemed to become glutted with natural beauty.

In a way the fantastic mountain scenery was the least important part of that amazing time. The Grand Canyon, the Black Canyon of the Gunnison, the high sierras of Yosemite, had all been more remarkable sights and no doubt I shall see others just as fine. More important was that we were out in this landscape, a part of it, feeling its rock and earth under our feet as we walked and below our hips as we slept, breathing its cold morning air and hot midday winds, brushing through its bushes and eating its wayside fruits. We were not merely a part of this total experience but a marvellously healthy part. The physical act of living seemed no longer just a neutral background for more titillating sensations, but a positive pleasure in itself. At this time our sensibly devised diet seemed pointless, because our health triumphed over whatever we ate, our splendidly active metabolisms burning up the lot in one glorious crackling unwavering bonfire.

Earlier in the summer we had read *Zen and the Art of Motorcycle Maintenance*, in which Pirsig makes a similar claim for motorcycle travel. Smugly, but I think correctly, we felt that his twenty-eight horse-power engine would have disturbed the true contact with the earth which he claims, and that we were more genuinely in touch with the roads we travelled: both experiences showed car sightseeing to be what it is: capsule travel in a cinema seat with a TV window. For the first time I understood the dissatisfaction I had often felt after driving through beautiful scenery, the sense that something had prevented me from having the experience I should have had.

Each of those eight days had its special flavour, individual sights and events, and I pick from them at random. I remember one brilliant early morning as we came slowly across the dry grassy face of a mountain, seeing far below us a strange grey rock balanced on top of another. For some time I watched it, surprised by its shape and balance. Suddenly a little patch of smoke drifted away from it. It was a hunter crouched there, totally still in the quiet morning. I am no lover of Italian hunters, but the peace and solitude of those days is captured by that still, sunlit hunter crouching on his rock.

I remember the day we circled the foot of Monte Aiona, when the brilliant sun had brought up every family from the valley below to harvest the *funghi*. At fifty-metre intervals the beech woods were labelled *Divieto Racolta Funghi e Frutti Silvestri*. It made no difference. They pullulated with Italians of every age from little children to ancient grannies, poking among the dead leaves, carrying everything from the ubiquitous plastic bag to great wicker baskets. A single red and green monster was no prize here — these containers overflowed with every sort of terrifying growth from livid yellow saucers to grotesque pea-green warts.

That evening, near the mountain refuge of Pratomolo, we camped among dwarf beeches, and watched the sun go down in a brilliant glow of purple and scarlet like nothing I had seen since sub-zero winter evenings in Illinois: no pretty clouds with pink-lit undersides, just fierce still bands of colour darkening from fiery red to a purple so intense it was almost black. This was true mountain country — we were above 1,500 metres — and next morning when the sun rose in an exact repetition of those colours it was instantly too bright to look at.

I remember waking a few days later near Montegroppo where we had camped on a slope of newly planted pines, and finding we were in a dense cloud which every few seconds was lit by summer lightning, a scene so dank and threatening that I went back to sleep to wait for it to clear. It didn't, and we spent the whole morning wandering lost in cloud on the wooded side of Monte Gottero. Frequently we met rushing torrents in impassable ravines and were forced to climb higher up the mountain. Each time we seemed to find new and more beautiful upland clearings under tall beech trees, but it was one of those mornings when we could only endure and were in no mood for natural beauty.

After three hours of such wandering I realised — with alarm at the omen — that it was publication day for my new novel. But I could hardly be better insulated from the reviews which pessimistic novelists fear on these occasions.

We came at last to Force Tre Confini, the pass where the ancient kingdom of Emilia began and where the three modern provinces of La Spezia, Parma and Massa meet, marked by two stone gateposts each mysteriously labelled 1780–1825. A hundred metres below, we met one of the weirder samples of Italian desecration: a wide bull-dozed roadway which must have been fit for cars ten years ago when it was cut but had been allowed to revert to nature. Great landslides of rock made it barely passable for donkeys, let alone for a wheeled vehicle. At several places it had become the new bed for a mountain river which had cut sheer-sided gullies as it tumbled from level to level, shortcutting the hairpin bends. I wondered what political intrigue had produced this grotesque result.

Near Villa Cella I remember the ancient peasant who came slowly uphill through our pine-wood camp, driving three cows, two calves, a fluffy white sheep and a donkey. They became hopelessly entangled with our own donkeys and for fifteen minutes while we disentangled them he cursed steadily but impassionately in operatic style: "*Maledeto!*" Earlier that day at Priosa we had passed a team of six fine working mules, all harnessed like Hannibal but wearing shoes with heels, standing beside the great pile of logs they had brought down from the mountains. For the first time since we had left the Spanish province of Leon we were among people who still knew about working animals and whenever we stopped ancient peasants would approach our donkeys and without invitation examine their teeth.

Later that night a strange pattering noise, which I thought was rain, turned out to be the escaped Hannibal licking our supper plates clean and consuming our whole apple supply. It was a camp of accidents, for at dawn, while removing the fly-sheet, I accidentally shook the tent, forgetting that we now balanced the candle on a tin shelf tied to the centre pole. Thirty seconds later Andrew woke with a yell. "Hey, what's happening?" His sleeping-bag was alight. By the time we had beaten it out there was a gaping blackened gash. Jessica had sat up in bed watching the whole incident, apparently mesmerised by it. "I forgot to say," she told us.

I remember the blackberries at La Crocetta, more luscious and abundant than I have ever seen, the figs at Adelano, and the grapes, apples, pears and chestnuts everywhere. By now these last had become our staple food and we contrasted the Italian passion for *funghi* with their total neglect of chestnuts. Perhaps they are too closely associated with their peasant past. Day after day we began by collecting the chestnuts as they lay in glistening brown clusters all over the track, then gave up because we could carry no more. Night after night we filled ourselves with them, baked, fried in butter and garlic, curried, or made into a crude version of *crème de maron*. In the winter in Tuscany, where we collected seven sacks of them (here there *was* local competition), we made chestnut bread of three-fifths flour, two-fifths mashed chestnut and baked it under red-hot ashes; and also a dish we named Tuscan Delight, consisting of a tart case made from chestnuts mashed with butter and sugar and a filling of Japanese strawberries, the round red fruit of the arbutus.

Our wayside morality had at first been a problem. Apples and chestnuts presented no difficulty because they lay everywhere unwanted — there were days when I calculated we munched through fifteen apples each during our three marching stages; nor did such things as juniper berries, fennel seeds or mint for our daily mint tea. But actual crops like tomatoes, beans and sweetcorn we began by taking only occasionally and with guilt. Long before the summer was over we had become boldly gypsy, picking from fields wherever we could, refraining only from raiding domestic gardens — though I must add that this changed the following year, when Greek generosity made theft unthinkable.

More generally I remember mile after mile of leafy forest track where we could saunter along and let our thoughts stray. All those days we seem to have walked under a blue sky through glorious autumn sunshine which lit the beech woods every shade of brown, yellow and orange. Those hillsides may not have had the scarlet maples of the New England fall but in a less flamboyant way they were even more beautiful.

Best of all I remember the final day of our mountain passage. Again we had been walking all morning in perfect sunshine under a cloudless sky. Suddenly, as we came slanting down a mountain side towards Nove Fontane, we saw the Mediterranean. Far below to our right, faint and misty but unmistakable, lay the Gulf of Spezia. At almost the same moment we saw ahead of us, orange and formidably jagged, the four peaks of the Alpi Apuane. We were to meet them again in less comfortable circumstances, but that morning they stood up with the majestic peace of true mountains against the misty blue sky, the tallest

things we had seen since the Alps. They were already beyond Fivizzano in its mountain cup.

Next day we began our descent. At once we saw that while we had
been in the mountains the harvest had happened. At the tiny village of
Villechia the pavements were spread with golden maize grains drying
in the sun. At Villa the porches were hung with stripped cobs, strings
of garlic and onions, while sieves and tablecloths were spread with
drying beans, and wooden boards with strips of aubergine and *funghi*.
At Tresana great wooden hoops decorated with fresh acacia branches
crossed the street in harvest celebration, and at Corneda huge sledges
were bringing in the grapes. Made of basketwork, the size of a modest
double bed and mounted on sloping poles, they were dragged by white
oxen up the steep stone alleys, each holding six or eight overflowing
bidoni, those horn-shaped wooden tubs which are traditionally used
for gathering grapes. Everywhere we smelt the strong smell of new
wine; in every ditch, among less romantic refuse, lay purple heaps of
pressed skins and pips. Often I caught glimpses of some sturdy man
straining at the metal lever of his press, or standing on top of it
crushing it full with his wellington boots. At Barbarasco I saw a cooper
at work on a barrel which, even on its side, came up to his chin. This
year, we were told, the wine would be the best ever. Rain to swell the
grapes, and then sun to ripen them had come exactly when they were
needed. Later, but not much later, I tried some and guessed that the
verdict was right. Once in Tuscany I asked a farmer how many years
he matured his wine before he began to drink it. About eight days,
he said.

The night of October 8th we spent near Olivola, just eight kilometres short of Fivizzano. "Why does no one ever tell you what a
fantastic month October is in Italy?" I wrote to Susan. We spent the
next ten days discovering.

CHAPTER 38

Race for shelter

At Fivizzano we had good news. Susan and Miranda were safe in Cornwall and Miranda's arm was mending. We set out confidently again.
Our mountain tracks had been slow and exhausting. The way we had
begun to scatter possessions along the road behind us — a tethering

rope one day, Jessica's anorak, her waterproof trousers and one boot the next — showed that we were tired. But in every other way the tracks had been the greatest success. Of course we would continue to use them, first climbing out of Fivizzano's rocky saucer, then skirting the Alpi Apuane by a high mountain road which ran through their foothills. After that we aimed to descend the Serchio to Bagni di Lucca, then turn east and ascend the Arno, always keeping to the valley sides above the rivers themselves. This would lead us north of Florence to our next postal address at Pontasieve.

So we set out on October 10th to by-pass the Alpi Apuane, and camped that night in a chestnut wood well up their lower slopes. The tarmac, we were told, ended a few kilometres ahead at the pass of Ugliancaldo. Above the tree-tops the stars shone brilliantly — till shortly before dawn when the sky clouded and there was distant thunder and lightning.

I wasn't worried. We had had a morning shower the day before and an hour later the day had brightened into hot sunshine. Even the early part of the climb to the pass was pleasant, the newly cut hay smelling like an English summer, the grey sky producing the sort of climatic gloom in which I can indulge. The first stages of our daily walks were anyway best. Rested and energetic, the tedious packing completed, as the sun rose over the mountain tops I would feel an optimism I hadn't felt since childhood. Unknown adventures were ahead and, good or bad, I had the strength to meet them. Just to walk through such beautiful and remote country when the rest of the world was asleep was a delight.

This early euphoria corresponded to the excitement of writing the first chapters of a novel; indeed the complete day formed a parallel, with its tedious second stage when I would count the kilometre posts, just as I count my daily quota of words, enthusiasm only gradually returning when we reached the half-way point. A similar parallel could be made of our whole summer's walk: the steady building up of tiny daily achievements into something which amazed us by its size, the early excitement of Galicia, the heavy slogging in Castile and France, the climax of the Alps and now the relaxed cruising to the end. Even when the rain grew heavier on that leaden grey morning I still expected nothing but the calm completion of this final phase.

For two hours, as we climbed, the rain went on increasing. It ran off our noses, soaked the bottoms of our trousers and began to seep down the backs of our hoods. Even Jessica no longer sang. At last we were at Ugliancaldo, a drab grey street of stone houses half in cloud where chained dogs ran at us with more than the usual senseless barking and a few dour inhabitants stood staring at us from below great black umbrellas. Still it rained, but here at least we found a shabby lean-to garage of corrugated iron, occupied only by a derelict motor scooter, in which we could shelter. Might we breakfast there, we asked the friendliest local, who wore a bold AGIP on his shirt pocket. He did better for us, leading us down dark alleys to the local bar. Here we sat eating our peanuts and cheese, listening to the rain cascading down the scaffolding outside, unable to believe that it ever did anything else at Ugliancaldo.

Though we were sheltered we now began to feel even colder than before. The whole place was being rebuilt and icy gusts of rain-filled wind blew at our backs through glassless windows. Occasionally we had the dim grey light of a neon strip but after a few minutes the witch-like owner would appear from across the yard, a sack over her head, and switch off. In the grey gloom I never got a clear idea of her features, and now see her only as a pair of eyes under that hessian hood. She didn't even brighten when we bought large glasses of *grappa* to restore the circulation in our hands, which were blue with the cold.

Our first attempt to leave was a failure: just the fifty yards to the lean-to garage made us wetter than at any time before, the rain now falling in a thunderous torrent. Back to the appalling café we went and bought more *grappa*. It was midmorning before the rain seemed to be easing and, half-driven out by that hooded hag, we risked a real start.

At once, as we had been promised, the earth track began. Presently, below us, I saw Minucciano, a mountain village which typified all the mountain villages we had been seeing in Italy. Tiny and compact on a protruding knoll of hillside, with round church tower at the top, it was more like a communal human nest than the collection of individual houses we picture when we use the word village. Every building abutted the one below and the one above, and the slope they were built on was so steep that they gave the impression that if the lowest collapsed all the rest would tumble too. There can't have been a right angle in the whole place. Entered in a competition for *avant-garde* village design, it might today win the prize, but I don't believe any architect could invent the complexity and harmony which local builders had created over the centuries.

Soon afterwards the day's second ordeal began. A hillside track, well marked on our map, should have taken us quickly down to Agliano. After a few hundred metres it grew narrower and we detected the familiar signs of an ancient path which had been abandoned and became a dead-end.

We were wrong. Through dense broom, bramble and giant heather which often rose a metre above our heads, this one ran on, but only as a low narrow tunnel about the height of our thighs. Every bush and branch was drenched with the morning's rain and instantly we were too. There was no question of Jessica riding and, though in fact she was a better height than we were and came trotting merrily along this tunnel, she too became soaked. Occasionally we came to open stretches where brilliant yellow and black salamanders lay among the sodden leaves, but at once the path dived again and we were fighting our way through dense bush. When we emerged at the end into more steady rain we found this almost a relief.

It was dusk before we arrived at last above the river Gramolazzo, a tributary of the Serchio, on the slopes of a valley so steep that for kilometre after kilometre we couldn't find a flat place to camp. At last I saw a little road winding down the valley side below us. Even a dilapidated Italian Electricity Authority notice warning us that sirens would sound when the valley was about to flood didn't deter us.

Late that evening, in a brief clear interval, while Andrew and I sat at the fireside baking dry our soaked socks and sodden feet, we saw the headlights of two cars descending from the main road above us. We watched them with curiosity as they came closer, then stopped, holding us in their bright beams. Out leaped four *carabinieri*, our first Italian police and the largest posse we had raised since that alarming encounter with the *Guardia Civil* on the Esla.

As in Spain, they came in pairs, the front to question while his supporting trooper stood behind, machine carbine at the ready, occasionally clonking and slamming its moving parts. But although they started fiercely I didn't feel the alarm I had felt in Spain. The moment they discovered we were *stranieri* even their fierceness collapsed. The senior — short and plump with gold-framed glasses — was apologetic. These were troubled times, he explained. They asked for no donkey papers, were mildly curious about Jessica's collection of hunters' cartridge cases which lay scattered on the road, and only a little more suspicious of Andrew's passport which contains two photographs and was issued in Chicago and renewed in Sydney. Did it always rain so much at this time of year, we asked. It had been drier, they said.

They had barely gone when it began again. Thunder rolled in the hills and lightning flashed. All night we listened to heavy showers. The pattering of rain on tent canvas when one is warm and dry inside is the snuggest sound I know — provided I also know that I can stay inside till it stops. In the days which followed I began to dread that wet pattering.

Because we no longer dared to linger. If this was October, what would November be like? And though we could keep dry when camped and also when packed for travel, our kit-bags protected inside their French plastic fertiliser bags, we couldn't when pitching and unpitching. Later we overcame this problem by packing our bags in the shelter of the tent, collapsing the inner tent and packing that, then finally collapsing and folding the horrible soaking fly-sheet. After the day's walk we would make camp by the same method in reverse. That morning we were less experienced and began by waiting hopefully for the rain to stop, then lost patience, struck camp and got much of our equipment wet.

It continued to rain, less relentlessly than the day before at Ugliancaldo but steadily and wettingly, as we progressed slowly down the Serchio valley, keeping high above the river itself, making our way from village to village by dipping into the ravines between. For breakfast we found a little empty stone hut in one of these deep wooded gullies. "Are we camping here?" Jessica asked. "You've had worse ideas," Andrew said.

But a slight slackening in the rain tempted us on. Beyond the next hillside village of Casatico a spectacular view of the Serchio valley opened below us, with little villages and towns stretching all down the valley bottom towards Bagni di Lucca. Tall hills stood above them and beyond these something which really amazed us. High against the sky, the slopes and peaks of the Apennine Regio Emilia were thickly blanketed in snow.

Alarming as this was it was not till the next morning that we finally changed our plans. We had camped in a dank chestnut wood near Roccalberti. The late afternoon had grown drier and we had even lit a fire, but from midnight heavy rain had fallen without a break. It was still falling as we loaded next morning. Putting my weight on Hannibal to tighten the baggage cords, I was horrified to feel him collapse on to his knees. If our donkeys failed us we would really be stranded. We quickly unloaded him, gave him a huge feed of chestnuts and led him gently in circles, watching for returning strength. Long before it came back our decision was taken. The summer was over. We must go down into the valleys, march four or five stages a day and take the most direct route to our winter quarters.

Just as, in retrospect, the sun seemed to shine without a break all the days of our mountain passage to Fivizzano, so for the next seven days of our race for shelter the rain never seems to have ceased. Even the occasional newspaper placards telling of the deluges and floods which had struck the whole of Italy seemed eventually to grow bored with the story.

By the evening of October 13th we had climbed from Castelnuovo on to a spur of hills, short-circuiting a big loop in the Serchio. The rain was falling as heavily as ever and dusk was coming. Suddenly at a bend in the road we found a hill-top bar and dance arena, complete with rustic tables set among the trees, and loops of coloured bulbs suspended between their branches. It was firmly closed for winter so we helped ourselves, Jessica playing in the pebbles under the bar's plastic awning while Andrew and I made sallies from below the thatched roof of a picnic table to pitch the tent in lank, soaking grass. That night for the first time I didn't attempt a fire, but without one the problem of warming our sodden and icy feet was acute.

The only solution was to rough-dry them with a cloth then put them into our sleeping-bags. Here, after about half an hour, they grew surprisingly warm. That night I also took to bed my own socks, Jessica's socks and gloves, and a large face towel. Gradually during the night my body heat dried them. We had long given up using our space blankets, which kept in the heat but also prevented evaporation so that by morning the tops of our sleeping-bags were wet with our night-time moisture. Next night — beyond Bagni di Lucca near Benabbio — sitting writing my daily letter in the early hours of the morning while the rain once again beat steadily on the tent, I saw by the light of the candle that the far ends of all three of our sleeping-bags were an unusual dark blue. Wind-driven rain had soaked their bottoms for eighteen inches. We never again got them dry.

That day we came down into the Arno plain. At first a pleasant wooded road led us through the pass of Trebbio, but after our first break we saw far down the valley below us a weird complex of corrugated iron roofs. It was a paper recycling plant; and not just one but below it another, then another and another. All down the valley they continued, enormous piles of bales of shredded waste paper for pulping standing in their yards, the little mountain tributary of the Pescia growing greyer and more sud-covered as it descended from one to the next. Soon the valley began to have the unmistakable smell of rancid laundry water. For the whole of our crossing of the plains the same stench was with us, rising sometimes from the black mud of a plastic-bag-strewn canal, sometimes in fetid steam from a roadside drainage grille.

Near the foot of the valley of paper mills we came to Collodi, and here, at the centre of all this filth, we found a piazza set on three sides with gay souvenir stalls. How could anyone want a reminder of their visit to Collodi, I wondered, till I noticed that three-quarters of the garish toys for sale were long-nosed dolls. In wood, felt, plastic, aluminium, glass and ceramic, these hideous Pinocchios — that was what they were — commemorated the fact that Carlo Lorenzi, his nineteenth-century creator, lived and wrote at Collodi.

Finally we reached the plain itself and found an almost stranger landscape, where greenhouse followed greenhouse in huge sweeps of glass and plastic. The great majority were devoted entirely to carnations. Below transparent roofs they stood, supported in wire frames, for hectare after hectare. It seemed impossible that the whole world, let alone Italy, could use such a vast supply of this luxury. They created a camper's nightmare because they occupied every patch of this

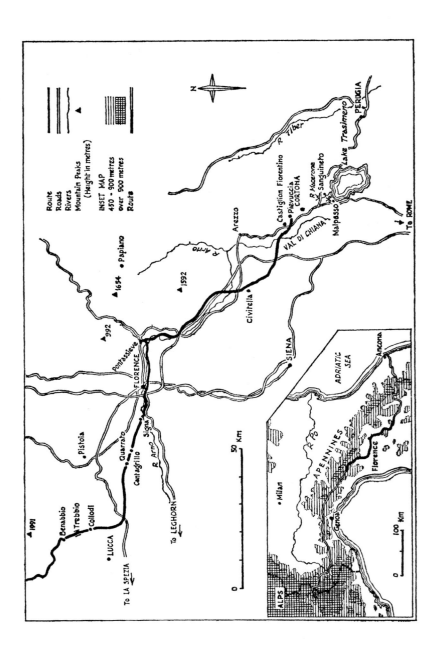

precious lowland soil. We camped at last in a tiny abandoned triangle
crushed between a concrete bridge and the rushing traffic of the Pisa–
Florence motorway.

At dawn next morning we were woken by a popping and banging
which reminded me of a misty November evening in England just
before Guy Fawkes day. In the plains the Italians apparently hunted
even more obsessively, though what they were firing at seemed an even
greater mystery. In the hills I had occasionally seen one with a little
bunch of tits and larks tied to his waist, or found some bright little
finch hopping along the track with only the bloody stump of one wing.
The only birds I ever saw in the Arno valley were about thirty thrushes
in the forecourt of a factory, each in its tiny square cage. Foul weather
never deters Italian hunters. It was raining again heavily as we packed
our bags and hurried on towards Florence.

At Quarrato that afternoon there was one of those Italian scenes
which cheered our gloomiest days. In the town's main square we asked
the way and in a couple of minutes seven or eight people collected,
all eager to give advice. At once they became involved in such a fierce
argument among themselves that we were left at its fringe, looking
on with detached amazement. "*Si, si,*" they cried, throwing out their
chests. "*No, no,*" they answered, turning way in disgust, or raising
their eyebrows to the sky that such madness could be left at large.
Secretly perhaps they knew that we were their audience for these fine
performances, but they hid it — till we moved on. Then several of
them in succession pursued us, each telling us urgently that *he* had
been right and the others were dangerous lunatics.

The dismal but fertile lowlands which we were crossing were the
marshes of Pistoia, now drained, where Hannibal, the year after the
crossing of the Alps and on the march which led him to Lake Trasimeno,
also suffered so badly. According to Livy, for four days his troops
walked in water. The only dry places they could find to sleep at night
were on their baggage or on mounds of dead pack-animals. Hannibal
himself caught an infection and permanently lost the sight of one eye.

By now we were averaging about twenty-eight kilometres a day, but
we had to do more next day or we should be pitching our tent exactly
on the steps of Florence's Duomo. That day's march began with the
heaviest rain yet. Hour after hour we plodded, hungry, cold and
miserable, along the side of a grey main road, the morning traffic
hissing past. By the time it lightened we were already in the traffic-
filled streets of Signa though still fifteen kilometres from Florence.

As we crossed the Arno we noticed that the southern floodbank
was topped by a grassy path. Nothing could be worse than Signa's
narrow streets, and so we decided to risk it and took the donkeys
down steps which would have tested a mountain goat. That path led

us right to the foot of Florence's first bridge. It also led us through a truly bizarre landscape. I have come to Florence in a number of different ways but never expect to arrive by a more peculiar one.

Perhaps five kilometres from the city centre where the first municipal flats of Florence's bee-hive zone rose to our right, we reached an area of refuse and filth which made all we had seen till now seem hygienic: not merely modern refuse dumps, with black-smoking bonfires of rubber tyres and fifty-metre craters bottomed with oily green lakes in which old refrigerators, drums and television sets lay in tight-packed masses, but ancient refuse pits twenty or thirty metres deep cross-sectioned by bulldozers which were grinding about making deep but apparently purposeless cuts in them. As if this were not enough, after half an hour we came to an area of motorway construction, a great unfinished bridge across the Arno, throbbing diesel air-compressors, churning cement plants and a service road so deep in liquid mud that the tyres of the lorries made bow waves of yellow sludge. Nothing seemed to have the remotest connection with Florence of the tourist posters, but there it was; for the whole of this amazing passage along the Arno's south bank we could see the peaceful and elegant green trees of some city arboretum running parallel along the north bank.

At last the familiar towers and spires came in sight, though against an unfamiliar dark grey sky. As we passed along the Arno's southern river front, a narrow alley suddenly brought us right to the foot of the Ponte Vecchio. There it stood, high above us, that strange structure with its rows of little shops, which always suggests a stage set rather than a real building, the only bridge spared by the Germans when they destroyed Florence's other six. Set theatrically above its farther end was the great dome of the Duomo. But the whole scene was so grey and overcast — by now it was four fifteen and raining again — that it suggested a mediaeval Leeds rather than Florence.

The rain grew heavy and we lunched among pigeon droppings under a gatehouse at the foot of the Boboli Gardens; dusk had come by the time we set out again, any open country where we could possibly camp still five or six kilometres away. But another area of *autostrada* construction saved us. As the rain fell steadily we slithered and tripped through the slimy mud of its excavations below looming concrete shapes to what seemed like an abandoned orchard.

All night the rain fell without a break, in a steady, unemphatic, thoroughly English way. By dawn, apart from a brief break while we were on the Arno's flood bank, it had rained without ceasing for thirty-six hours. "When we are finally rescued," Andrew said, "we shall be described as suffering from no serious injury, just shock and exposure."

Now we followed the upper Arno valley, using little roads which wound in and out of the *autostrada* and had often been half-abandoned, passing square brick farms, each with its square dovecot mounted centrally, and as big as a room so that at first I took them for lock-ups for the family lunatic. Two nights later we camped on a hilltop where a bright moon occasionally shone between heavy clouds, lighting one of the strangest scenes of the whole summer. Beyond two massive pylons the *autostrada* with its continuous rushing headlights reached as far as I could see to our right and left. Beyond again lay the old main road, bright from end to end with a string of villages, trains like little lit-up toys running in and out among them. Still further away the side of the valley rose steeply, dotted with the lights of isolated farms and villas. The vastness of this panorama, its weird mixture of the natural and the industrial, gave it a sinister beauty. By next morning all was hidden in thick mist from the Arno. As we slithered down the steep green side of the hill into this damp grey blanket we had no idea that we were leaving our last camp that year.

We still had forty kilometres to walk and the whole of the Val di Chiana to cross before reaching Castiglion Fiorentino and the primitive farmhouse on the mountainside in which we were to winter. Even six hours later at our lunch break, by which time we could see far ahead Cortona's jagged silhouette, the remaining twenty-four kilometres seemed too much to attempt. But at around four o'clock, when we set out again, we were saying, "In three more long stages we *could* be there." An hour later we were saying, "Let's try it." The rumbling thunder in the surrounding hills worried me, but it was more the prospect of once again pitching and unpitching our sodden tent that drove us to attempt this longest march of the whole summer.

Darkness was already falling at our next break where we sat by the roadside, Andrew in half-lotus position trying to read the map by the stub of a candle balanced on the toe of one boot. And without the moon I doubt if we should have found our final series of muddy tracks across the drainage canals of the valley bottom. Suddenly ahead of us we saw it, huge, round and red, centred exactly above an avenue of trees. All week we had known that it was waxing even when it was only a luminous glow above hurrying clouds. Now at last it was full.

We were lucky to find that these valley paths had changed less in the twenty-four years since our maps were revised than had those in the mountains. The drainage canals they led us across form one of Italy's oldest land reclamation systems. The Etruscans diverted the Chiana to flow north, instead of south into the Tiber, but by the Middle Ages this had produced a vast malarial swamp. Between the fourteenth century and the twentieth a succession of drainage schemes has turned this swamp into one of the country's most productive areas.

On and on we plodded in dumb and almost total exhaustion. The trouble was, Jessica said thoughtfully, that she didn't think she could ride any more, and Andrew had to be continually prepared to catch her if she fell asleep. Treading on the greasy side of a puddle, I lost my footing, fell into a ditch and lay there on my back, held down by my knapsack, wondering if I'd ever find the strength to get up.

At Castiglion Fiorentino there were lights, busy traffic and full Sunday-night cafés, but already a clock told us it was 9 p.m. and the little valley beyond became stiller and stiller as we went deeper into it. Not a light showed anywhere in the village of Pievuccia except above the new electric bell of the store. We pushed it, a tiny window opened above us and five minutes later we were being given the kind of welcome which makes me love Italians despite their many maddening and childish ways. The shop was opened, wine served, bread and milk provided.

A final testing moment remained. Three kilometres up the mountainside we stood at the house's front door in the brilliant light of the full moon, now high above us. Far below in the plains it also lit the surface of our summer's goal, the lake of Trasimeno, scene of Hannibal's great defeat of the Romans in 217 B.C. Bending, I poked the key into the door lock. It wouldn't go.

I peered and poked again. Some of the door's woodwork had been broken away and presently I realised that thin splinters had been forced into the Yale's keyhole. At the last moment we were going to be forced to camp again. For a quarter of an hour I picked at the lock with a darning needle. At last the key went in. Terrified that there were still particles of wood inside which would jam the mechanism, I turned it, pressed harder — and felt the latch go back.

Without even unbarring the windows we extracted the three beds from their winter pile, brushed away the inevitable mouse's nest, laid out our bags and for fifteen hours slept in the dreamy comfort of spring and mattress.

Four

ITALY — THE APENNINES

"Yes," I said, "I'm crazy enough to believe that the happiest man on earth is the man with fewest needs."

Henry Miller, *The Colossus of Maroussi*

CHAPTER 39

Winter quarters

Anyone passing through the station buffet at Arezzo railway station at six o'clock on the evening of November 17th, 1975, would have seen a strange sight. At a table in a corner a middle-aged English woman, somewhat crumpled after a twenty-four-hour journey from London, was crying loudly and so, more understandably, was a freckle-faced girl of eight who carried her left arm in a sling. A bearded man, evidently the husband of one and the father of the other, looked on with embarrassment while, at a half-circle of nearby tables, numerous Italians stared with steady amazement.

The explanation for this scene is that the man, who was, of course, none other than Thomas, had just announced that, three days earlier, Hamilcar had bolted down the side of a hill, throwing Jessica off and breaking her left arm. A couple of moments later he had added the news of the loss of Iago in the Alps, of which till then Miranda and I had known nothing. I'm ashamed to say that it was the latter news that released our deluge of tears. All through her painful recovery Miranda had been thinking of her reunion with Iago. When she went into Truro hospital to have her steel pin removed under a general anaesthetic (Mr. Robbins, the orthopaedic surgeon there, declaring it a most dangerous device that could lead to infection of the joint) it was of Iago she talked. As she practised the montonous exercises that would bring back movement and sensation to the fingers of her left hand I reminded her that every day she performed them was a day closer to Iago. And now Iago was gone and we would never see him again. "One thing is certain," said Thomas, when he could make himself heard above the lamentations, "there'll be no more donkey riding on this journey. The children must walk to Smyrna."

The story of Jessica's accident can be quickly told. She and Thomas were living alone at La Ripa, the mountain shack they had reached six weeks earlier, when it happened, for Andrew was picking grapes with my sister Lyndall's peasants. Every third day they made the six-kilometre journey down the mountain and back for food, Jessica riding Hamilcar and Thomas leading her. On this occasion Thomas left Hannibal tethered on a terrace above the path. On hearing his friend departing, he made one of his frantic lunges to the top of the terrace wall, so terrifying Hamilcar that he in turn took off at a gallop along the downhill path. Thomas had a firm grip of his leading-rope but was pulled off his feet and dragged ten metres along the ground before the rope was pulled from his grip. Meanwhile Jessica had somersaulted into the chestnut scrub.

She complained that her arm hurt but agreed to remount the donkey and continue the journey to the store at Pievuccia. She was to ride that mountain track twice more, once up and once down, before her constant plea of "Oh, it does hurt", convinced Thomas that the arm might be broken. Down at the store again on the following morning he telephoned Lyndall, who drove over at once and took Jessica to the casualty department at Arezzo hospital. A break between the shoulder and elbow was diagnosed.

Jessica's troubles were not over. After a three-hour wait that Saturday morning (during which she, with all the other patients, was served a pre-lunch quarter litre of red wine, off a trolley), a message from the orthopaedic surgeon announced that he was off for the weekend and Jessica must return to have her arm set on Monday. She was sent home without even a sling. Only frantic representations from medical friends of my sister finally persuaded the surgeon to return and do the job on Sunday afternoon. Perhaps it was to get his own back that he did it the way he did.

Certainly I have seldom seen a stranger little creature than that which confronted me at the door of Lyndall's converted mill on the night of my return. The head with the black fringe and the large wondering eyes was recognisably that of my youngest daughter, but it appeared to surmount a piece of Henry Moore sculpture. Not only the left arm but also the whole torso down to the waist were encased in plaster. The arm had been set in the position usually adopted for stopping a bus at a request stop and, to facilitate breathing, a large hole had been cut with the plasterer's knife in the region of the stomach. Within twelve hours Thomas and Jessica were on their way to Cornwall, to amaze Mr. Robbins at Truro hospital with another sample of continental medical practice.

"Was that put on for travelling?" he asked.

No one had said so, Thomas told him.

Pressed for his opinion Mr. Robbins eventually muttered, "A trifle over-medicated, I'd say." In his report on Jessica he added, "It might be advisable for these children to be given some riding-lessons."

Like Miranda, Jessica spent her month of convalescence with my father and stepmother in their farmhouse in Cornwall. It was as well she was in comfortable surroundings because, for several days, she was very ill. A cold turned into something close to pneumonia, as a result of the plaster round her chest which prevented her from coughing effectively, and for two nights she lay on the sofa in front of the fire, delirious.

That autumn in Italy, as Miranda continued her finger exercises, and mists blanketed the Val di Chiana and Lake Trasimeno in white cotton wool, it seemed to me unlikely that we could start our journey again in the spring. Constantly Thomas's words, "They must *walk* to Smyrna", echoed through my head. It was impossible. Lyndall agreed. But she was more resourceful than I. There was a pig dealer in the Val di Chiana, she said, who sometimes had carts for sale. Why not buy a donkey cart and carry the children to Smyrna that way? In high spirits we set off one morning for Dario's establishment on the plain. He had not only a dilapidated gig for sale but also a set of driving harness with brass mountings. Better still, he was prepared to let us have the lot for less than £60. My task was now to break Hamilcar to harness and teach him to pull the gig before Thomas returned. He was much more likely to agree to a working proposition.

Amazingly, Hamilcar proved a willing pupil. As I walked behind him each day, driving him to the shop and back in long reins, I began to suspect he had been driven before. When, very nervously, with Lyndall's help, I put him between the shafts of the gig for the first time, he threw his weight into the collar like an old-timer and pattered merrily along the level stretch of road that led to the village, while I sat, proud as a charioteer, in the rattling, floating contrivance.

Thomas and Jessica returned in time for Christmas. Jessica's arm was quite recovered, but we agreed that neither child was fit for the rigours of a winter at La Ripa. Instead we moved into a converted barn called the Cucculaia, or cuckoo's nest, at Ossaia, kindly lent us by John Enos, the friend who had spent ten days that summer pursuing us across the south of France but never quite catching us.

Ossaia was a village on the edge of the Chiana valley, even closer to Lake Trasimeno than was La Ripa. Indeed, it used to be claimed that it was called Ossaia after the bones of the Romans slaughtered by Hannibal at the lake, and that the battle also accounted for the name Sepoltaglia given to the hill above the village where a cypress-lined avenue leads to a church.

The Cucculaia stood in an abandoned olive orchard on the slopes of Sepoltaglia. It was built of stone with an enormous fireplace where we burned four-foot logs day and night for the next four months and where on Christmas Day we roasted a chicken on an improvised spit. The winter was not a severe one. As often as not the sun shone all day and in February, when the almond tree outside the front door blossomed, we photographed the children bathing naked in a plastic tub under the olives. There was always ample grass for the donkeys and we only once had to put them in the stable and feed them hay.

After a month of idleness Hannibal and Hamilcar became changed characters. Not only did they grow long woolly coats but they also became as playful as colts and, if let loose, would indulge in endless horseplay, chasing each other in and out among the olives. On flat ground in front of the house they would indulge in bouts of wrestling. These Hamilcar, who was both cunning and nimble, invariably won. Taking a firm grip of Hannibal's head-collar in his teeth he would whirl the larger donkey round in circles until he was dizzy, then dash round behind him and bite him in the hamstring. This would cause the instant collapse of the rear half of Hannibal, who would sit on his rump, his vast furry belly spread on the ground, looking exceedingly foolish.

The human members of the expedition were not idle in winter quarters. Miranda, dressed in a black pinafore with a white collar and a pink bow, attended the tiny village school at Ossaia. There she became deeply involved with a prize-winning operetta version of I Promessi Sposi, and fell under the spell of the villain, Don Rodrigo. Don Rodrigo was the ten-year-old son of a peasant living on the farm below ours, and certainly looked fetching in his feathered hat and curling moustache. There were only ten children in Miranda's class and, with their maestra, they took their lessons sitting in a circle round a large wood stove. Miranda found the Italian children good-natured and friendly and soon picked up a working knowledge of the language.

Thomas spent many hours a day rebuilding our little gig, and made frequent visits to Cortona, our local town, on its behalf. Unlike most of the Englishmen who climbed the stone-paved streets of the little Etruscan city that straggles so picturesquely down the slopes of Monte San Egidio, he was in search not of pre-Roman lamps or of Fra Angelico 'Annunciations', but of screws, timber and cans of undercoating. It was only when he had finally painted the gig fire-engine red and strapped a black leatherette cushion to the seat that we discovered that, although Hamilcar could pull it on the level, he was quite incapable of dragging it up hills, and going downhill the cart simply took control and pushed him before it. Even if we kept exclusively to roads on our journey, we would not be able to avoid hills.

Secretly I was still convinced that, with proper handling and proper tack, Hamilcar could be a safe ride for one child although I was now sure that two on a donkey was risky. Our mistake had been to assume that a Spanish headcollar with a running-chain noseband would be sufficient to control him. Wearing his driving bridle with a snaffle bit in his mouth and carrying Hannibal's straw pack-saddle, he was more comfortable and more obedient, and I took to riding him about the local hills. Then Jessica started to take short rides on him. Provided I kept a firm grip on the leading-rein and walked at his shoulder in the approved Pony Club manner, I found that he remained well under control.

I now turned my attention to Hannibal. He had never liked being led, preferring to lean gently on his attendant, and he was hard to stop unless a particularly succulent clump of grass took his fancy, in which case he was equally hard to start. I tried him in Hamilcar's bridle but the bit seemed to make little impression on him. Then the old saddler at Castiglion Fiorentino told me about the *semiluna* or half moon, which he said was the only instrument suitable for the control of mules and donkeys. The *semiluna* is a piece of metal with a serrated edge which is placed not in the animal's mouth but over its nose. The old man produced one attached to an antiquated Tuscan mule bridle. "In the old days my father used to sell three of these a week," he said sadly.

To the *semiluna*, clasped firmly over Hannibal's muzzle, we attached long reins. Round his mouth we fixed a plastic mesh muzzle, intended for the calves of white Tuscan oxen, to discourage his wayside feeding habit. We were now left only with the problem of a suitable pack-saddle for him. We needed something similar to those solid wooden *basti* which Thomas and Andrew had seen on the logging mules in the mountains of Liguria. But we were now far from Liguria.

A long and complicated search led us at length to a mountainous area know as the Casentino where the Arno has its source.

With David and Periwinkle Unwin, who had driven out from England to stay with us, we made the sixty-kilometre journey to Papiano, taking a chance on finding Signor Poppi at home. Not only was he at home but also, at the back of the stable where he kept his own pair of bony mules, he had a spare pack-saddle, made for a donkey which had taken one look at it and died. I sympathised with the donkey. The saddle seemed massive, supported on hoops of solid wood, grossly stuffed and covered with the furry hide of a brown pony. Metal rings and chains dangled from every part of it, and a mouse had raised a family in one corner. It was ours for 50,000 lire (£30). The price seemed high, but with no alternative in sight, we paid up and got, in addition, two sheepskin tubes that would soften the two girths which would encircle Hannibal and his new saddle.

To complete our preparations we decided that we must copy Italian *Alpini* practice and reduce our baggages to two, instead of four, kit-bags, even if they had to be larger and heavier. With the upper two bags eliminated, the centre of gravity of Hannibal's load would be much lowered and we hoped to avoid one of the more regular and ex-hausting mishaps of the previous year, when the whole erection used to tip from his back to hang under his belly. Reducing our baggage further was no easy matter, but somehow we managed it, in particular deciding that we could do without our bulky padded anoraks and keep ourselves warm by wearing sweaters under our light waterproofs.

In April, when the terraces round the Cucculaia were starred with little mauve anemones, grape hyacinths and yellow orchids, we made a trial journey to test our new arrangements and Miranda's walking powers. In several ways the trial was a success. Hannibal's new pack-saddle, now well weighted down with our two enormous kit-bags, settled firmly and immovably on to his broad hairy back, and in long reins he not only carried his burden boldly forward, but also stopped the instant he felt the pressure of the *semiluna* on his nose. At first when he tried to graze off tempting wayside shrubs and discovered that his bullock's muzzle made this impossible, he would give us an aggrieved stare, as if he could not quite believe we would do such a thing to him, but he soon learned to stand with patience till unharnessed.

Historically, too, the trip was fascinating. Climbing from Ossaia, passing over the shoulder of Sepoltaglia, we crossed two deep valleys before reaching the hills which look down directly on the broad smooth waters of Trasimeno. Between us and the lake lay the horse-shoe valley of the Macerone where the battle was fought. Passing the monument at Sanguineto (bloodily named after the battle) we camped near the Gorghe di Annibale, from which the general had an almost aerial view of his triumph.

Most battlefields are, to me, a confusion, and I listen uncomprehendingly to friends who try to describe the manœuvres of the opposing armies. The field of Trasimeno is an exception and beautifully clear. Below to our right we could see the Malpasso, a narrow way between the lake and hills through which Flaminius had led his Romans into Hannibal's trap. Ahead of them, on the hills at the inner end of the horse-shoe close below our camp, they saw the main body of Carthaginians and at once advanced to attack them. Too late they discovered that other Carthaginian troops were hidden on the sides of the horse-shoe, and found themselves attacked on both flanks and in the rear. Fifteen thousand Romans are said to have been slaughtered, for the loss of one thousand eight hundred Carthaginians.

In one respect, however, our trial was not a success. After an early burst of enthusiasm Miranda flagged and long before the first day was half finished, jealousy raised its head and she was having to be given alternate rides on Hamilcar while Jessica walked. The result was slow progress indeed and we returned to the Cucculaia realising that we still had a serious problem.

It was at breakfast next day that Andrew said, "I wonder how far we'll get before we buy the third beast."

Andrew had an ability to face facts which Thomas and I lacked. I decided then and there that the third animal must be bought at once, for I was not going to risk buying from strangers again. I even had a pony in mind. He was a tiny dark bay Shetland-Sardinian cross, called Picchio (which means wood-pecker in Italian) belonging to the Pomeroys, the people who had encouraged us to follow Hannibal over the Alps.

The Pomeroys had bought him eight years before as an irresistible cuddly foal, who had been taken prematurely from his mother and still had to be bottle-fed. He was brought up with their youngest son, Ralph, and shared his predilection for sweets. Indeed, the crackle of a toffee paper would bring him from the far side of a croquet lawn at a full gallop. Unfortunately, he could never resist a nibble at the hand that fed him and this nibble gradually became a painful love-bite. On one occasion he actually savaged Ralph, rolling him over in the dust with his front hooves. After that Picchio had led a life of idleness in the Pomeroys' orchard. For £140 he was ours, complete with a smart pigskin saddle and bridle.

CHAPTER 40

Abandoned Umbria

In the spring of 1976 Easter fell in mid-April and Thomas decided we should start the second half of our journey that weekend. Certainly it seemed appropriate, for it is on Easter Monday that travelling circuses traditionally hit the road. Our aim was to go straight over the Roman Apennines to the Adriatic and take a boat for Greece from Ancona. We hoped to find one that would take us (and our animals) to Igoumenitsa, an Adriatic port close to the Greek/Albanian frontier, so that we could join the route of the Italian contingent of the First Crusade across northern Greece and into Turkey.

But for that second year of our journey we had other plans besides geographical ones. We meant to enjoy ourselves. In the first year we had been obliged to cover too great a distance. The result had all too often been exhaustion for us and sore backs for the donkeys. Now we were convinced that travelling cheerfully was better than arriving, and we felt no urgent determination to reach Smyrna. With cheerful travelling in mind I drew up a Pilgrim Charter to which, somewhat unwillingly, Thomas and Andrew agreed. It went as follows:

H

No more than 4½ hours' walking a day.
Every third day a day of rest.
No working with raw patches.
No walking in steep or precipitous places.
No walking during periods of rain.
Susan to be mistress of the donkeys and to give advice which would, if possible, be taken.

The morning of our departure from the Cucculaia was not a propitious one, for it was pouring with rain. However, since we had spent the last forty-eight hours spring-cleaning the house, suspending the mattresses by wires from the ceiling and spreading mouse poison, we would rather have faced tornadoes and hurricanes than spend another night there.

Picchio accounted for our slow progress. He virtually needed rebreaking. For the first hour of the journey, which took us on tracks through our neighbours' olive orchards and farmyards, I rode him, my feet almost touching the ground on either side, in an attempt to calm him, for, unlike Hamilcar, he would rather trot than walk, and rather canter than do either. Miranda, meanwhile, walked wet and tearful with Thomas and Hannibal, clothed in waterproof blue nylon from head to toe. When we reached the main road even I had to dismount, for it became obvious that Picchio had forgotten all about cars. Every time a miniature Fiat hissed past on its way to Gubbio, he shot forward; a tractor caused him to make a violent sideways leap into a vineyard, and a loaded lorry coming towards us provoked a pirouette and a half, so that we ended facing the surprised Hannibal who was following behind. I began to doubt whether we would even reach the Province of Perugia a kilometre down the road, let alone Turkey. For the first time since we lost Iago I was grateful for his absence — with three pack animals to control we could never have managed a dog as well.

At last we turned on to the dirt road that leads up the Valecchi valley, a place full of memories, for one summer Lyndall had lent us a farmhouse at the wild and remote end of the valley, called Pianello, where we had survived an alarming forest fire. Emboldened by the absence of traffic I once more mounted Picchio but quickly regretted it. A car, turning off the main road, came up rapidly behind us and Picchio launched into a full gallop. The driver appeared to think I was putting on the performance for his benefit, for he accelerated in order to keep up with us. It was hard to suggest to him, as I sat astride the little beast's neck less than a metre from the ground, that if he stopped Picchio might do the same. The drama was brought to an abrupt close when a farm dog leapt to the full extent of its chain and so startled Picchio that he collapsed on to his knees and rolled both of us into

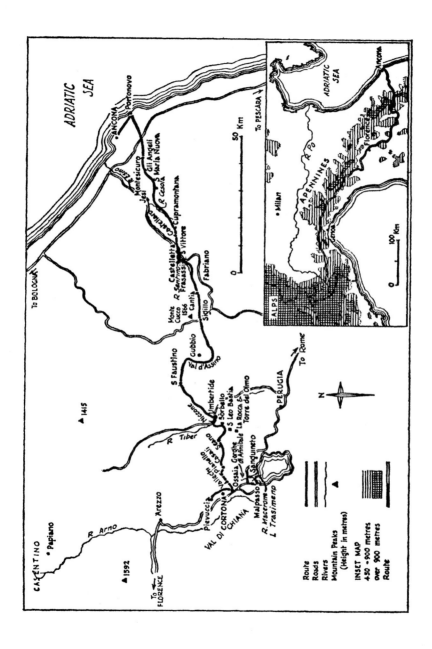

the ditch. The clot at the wheel of the car had the decency to get out at this point and enquire innocently if it was the car that had frightened the horse.

My little accident took place next to the mediaeval tower half-way up the Valecchi valley and this tower reminded us of Cuthie's house, on a steep track opposite. Cuthie lived in Rome and had spent weekends with us during the winter. This weekend her half-converted farmhouse would be empty and, provided the builders had not put in the doors and windows, accessible. The gods favoured us. The house was complete in most other respects. It had floors and windows, and water even came out of the taps, but it still lacked a front door. We settled in as uninvited guests for the night, and hid tiny chocolate eggs in the garden for the children to find at dawn next day.

These Easter eggs had been brought out from England, at my request, by the Unwins. I had little guessed how superfluous they would prove. Once the carnival season was over the Italian cafés and bars had started to fill with chocolate eggs that ranged from the minute to the monstrous. Jessica particularly admired the monstrous, which were half a metre high and clasped in the arms of furry bunnies as tall as herself.

As a result of the egg hunt we started late on the morning of Easter Sunday. It was mid-morning by the time we reached Pianello itself, the scene of our forest fire, now owned by Germaine Greer and regrettably surrounded by a high garden wall, no doubt a necessity for a celebrity who values her privacy. We thought it would be uncivil to pass without dingling the little bell that dangled by the gate. We were glad we did, for Germaine was welcoming, although she was in the middle of bedding out her geraniums, and was due to lunch in the Chianti in an hour's time. I had always seen her in the summer in Italy, superbly bronzed, wearing a bikini and speaking enviably colloquial Italian. After a winter in London she was pale as death and dressed like a rag doll in an old woollen dress, striped stockings and clogs. We sat on the sunlit terrace and drank fizzy white wine from her own vines. She claimed it was the first alcohol she had touched that year, because alcoholics were such a bore, and reformed ones even worse. "I feel like telling them for God's sake go and drink yourself to death and stop asking for sympathy." Perhaps out of consideration for Miranda and Jessica (who took to her at once) her conversation was remarkably pure and she only mentioned her vagina once.

All the peasants we knew at Valecchi had assured us that there was a footpath up the steep head of the valley behind Pianello, although when we had stayed there we had never found it. Now, anxious to reach Gubbio by the most direct cross-country route, we forced our way into the undergrowth where the path ought to have begun, while

Germaine watched us, her hands on her hips and legs apart, shaking her head in wonder at the idiocy, not only of this attempt but of the whole expedition. To Lyndall she later confided, "If they want to go to Turkey, why don't they just *go*?" Yet sure enough we did find the footpath, a sort of rock staircase overgrown with broom and exposed to the now hot spring sun. We had not taken long to break the clause in our charter which barred steep and precipitous paths. Poor Miranda, now stripped to T-shirt and jeans, was once more in tears, but as the slope became less extreme and Picchio tired she was able to ride him for the first time, and her tears were staunched until we reached the top. Then there was a fresh outburst for another reason: a sudden turn in the road along the ridge hid forever the view of Sepoltaglia.

That hilltop with its evenly spaced cypresses against the sky had remained in sight for the first two days of our journey, just as the Osborne bull had followed us for the first two days of our journey from Santiago. For Miranda the chapel among the trees on the summit of Sepoltaglia had become a symbol of all the people she had come to love during the winter, not least Don Rodrigo.

Now we turned into a new landscape of wooded hills, and somewhere amid these lived Jane Attwood. We had met Jane at the Pomeroys, where she coached Ralph in English twice a week, but my connection with her went back much further. Eighteen years earlier, when she had been a schoolgirl in Kenya, I had exercised her pony Tuoma for her and spent many happy hours pursuing herds of zebra and giraffe across the lower slopes of the Ngong Hills. Jane and her brother were now living near a hamlet called Casali where they were rehabilitating, single-handed, a derelict farm. It was a great stone villa with cultivated terraces descending steeply to a wooded valley. When we arrived she was down at the bottom of the farm clearing bush, and it was an effort not to imagine that we were back in Africa. Even the name of the place, if written Kasali, could have been a Kikuyu name.

Jane was a small fair girl with hands horny from hard labour. She lived in comfortable squalor in an upstairs room brown with the smoke of generations. Three collapsing chintz-covered sofas (also strongly suggesting the Lake Hotel, Naivasha) were pulled round a log fire and two uncontrollable yellow labradors dozed in front of it. While she stewed us a delicious mess of kidneys with red wine, oil and onions she told us how they had come to live on the farm. A second brother had bought it on an impulse and then not known what to do with it. Jane had thrown up her teaching job in England and moved in without experience or capital. Within a month she was down to her last 200 lire, the price of a loaf of bread. It was then that she started taking tutoring jobs, and her brother began to work intermittently as a bricklayer. So far the chief produce of the farm was an exceptional light red wine which we drank appreciatively.

The next morning Jane accompanied us for the first ten minutes up the hill at the back of her house, as she had to take a doe to be mated by the buck on an Italian neighbour's farm. She carried it in a sack over her shoulder, and the holes in the groin of her jeans were startling. I wondered what the local peasants made of her.

The mule-track over the mountains was easy to follow and led us down into a green flat-bottomed valley called Seano, where pigs, mares and foals grazed under the eyes of various ancient crones. By a pebbly brook we found an abandoned watermill and so, for the third night, I was able to sleep under a roof (at Jane's I had sneaked out of the tent into her spare room). Under the new regime we were due for a day of rest, and the children insisted that, as they had acted *Cinderella* for us at Cuthie's house, it was our turn to perform for them.

It was not difficult to decide on a play. Like so many Umbrian farmers, the owner of our mill house had kept his livestock on the ground floor and lived on the first floor which was approached by an outside stone staircase. At the top of this staircase was a balcony that might have been designed for Juliet's illicit meeting with Romeo. I was Juliet, draped in a donkey blanket, Thomas was Romeo with my denim sun hat pulled down dashingly over one eye, and Andrew played the parts of Mercutio, the nurse and the friar. He was particularly successful as the shrill, scolding, snoring nurse. Our audience of two squatted entranced at the base of an ivy-covered oak. As the light faded an owl rose softly from the branches above their heads and glided off in search of prey.

Many famous rivers are disappointing in their upper reaches. Not so the Tiber. It was wide and fast where we reached it next day at Niccone near the town of Umbertide, running between frog-filled gravel pits. At the place where we camped there was, according to our map, a ford. We had hoped to use this and so avoid the town bridge at Umbertide, but when Andrew waded in he was up to his thighs after three or four steps and hardly able to keep his footing against the current. That evening, when a farmer brought his tractor down for a load of gravel, we finally decided not to attempt the crossing. He told us that bulldozers had dug pits in the river-bed and any forder would soon disappear into them.

The rain which had greeted us on the first day of our journey now returned reinforced. Faithful to the Pilgrim Charter, we sat for two days by the Tiber while the frogs croaked cheerfully and the ground round our tent turned into a sticky morass over which we had to spread branches in the Galician manner. Miranda periodically visited the Tiber and recited an incantation largely cribbed from *Horatius*:

Oh Tiber, Father Tiber
To whom the Romans pray
We ask you not to burst your banks
Until we're on our way.

Father Tiber obliged. When all other distractions failed, Thomas read *Watership Down* to us. Crouched round the candle in the tent we ourselves looked like a meeting of the rabbits' 'ausla' in their underground council chamber.

When we finally set off, after two days' idleness, Picchio was as unmanageable as he had been at the beginning. Once more I had to ride him, and we had an embarrassing altercation about whether he would cross the Tiber at Umbertide. For some reason we had all decided, including evidently Picchio, that Umbertide would be boring, but in fact the old part down by the river was charming, with two connected squares flanked by Renaissance palaces, a circular castle and a moat. The famous Signorelli 'Deposition' however was no longer in the abandoned church of Santa Croce, and we were directed to the hospital. As this was on our way and, as Luca Signorelli was a native of Cortona, we allowed ourselves the rare pleasure of looking at a picture while travelling. "Of *course* we saw the 'Deposition' at Umbertide," we would be able for once to tell cultured friends.

Leaving the donkeys grazing on the hospital lawns we averted our eyes from the all-too-recently familiar sights and smells of the casualty department and made for the reception desk. There a bored man pressed a buzzer for a hospital porter while we eagerly watched trolleys laden with steaming spaghetti Bolognese disappearing into private rooms where, no doubt, fat yellow Italian gentlemen suffering from the national complaint of *mal di fegato* waited to give further work to their damaged livers.

The porter was an obliging little man and hurried us past various huts to a larger one, fitted out as a lecture theatre. The famous wooden altarpiece was modestly curtained behind the rostrum but a twitch of a cord and a flick of a spotlight switch revealed it. To me the figures were at the same time wooden and theatrical, their draperies stiff and their white up-turned eyeballs sentimental. No doubt they would have looked better in the dim religious light of a church.

The stretch between Umbertide and Gubbio, which we did largely by footpaths thanks to Andrew, who had pioneered the route with a girl friend during the winter, could have been one of the best in Italy. Rounded green hills, barely inhabited, stretched out of sight in all directions. Many were surmounted by abandoned farmhouses of amazing beauty, often with a foam of cherry blossom round their walls. Lush green clover grew near them, and into this the donkeys eagerly pushed their muzzles. At St. Faustino there was a whole deserted hamlet complete with church and church bell. It was near St. Faustino that a solitary woodcutter of rare beauty told us that the countryside had been reduced to this idyllic (for us) state by the nefarious *mezzadria* system, by which the peasant, in lieu of rent, surrenders half his produce to the landlord.

Only the weather marred our enjoyment of this solitude. As we started to climb into the green hills of Umbria the rain came again, now ice-cold and accompanied by wind. By the time we reached our first abandoned farm the rain had turned to snow and we were driven into a draughty ox-stall by a veritable blizzard which made our cheeks sting and our ears ache. We soon transferred our quarters to a pigsty lined with clean straw where we were more comfortable.

At our next abandoned farm the weather was only minimally kinder (sleet rather than snow) and there was a herd of sheep in the room next door to ours. We had to beat our way through brambles to our calf-shed and then work for forty minutes with broom branches to clear dried dung from the floor. At the bottom we came upon a flattened and mummified rat with skin like parchment and hollow eye sockets. The children were enchanted and even I rejoiced, for I felt it augured a dry night.

All through that afternoon the sleet descended and at three o'clock we heard distant lowing. Along the narrow path on the far hillside a string of white cattle, like pearls on a necklace, was moving towards us. In half an hour they were grazing round us. Soon their attendants arrived, a mentally defective youth, a friendly middle-aged matron (who quickly engaged Miranda in conversation) and a very old woman. The old woman amazed us most, as she sat on a rock clasping an old paint tin filled with red embers. We knew that the nearest inhabited house in that direction was eight kilometres away along deep muddy paths. She told us that her husband had died two months ago and life held little more for her. I could not help comparing her lot with that of our own pensioners, who, although they must sometimes choose between food and heat, can at least stay indoors during the winter weather. But perhaps she preferred to have work to do and still to feel she was some use.

In the Umbrian hills we had reached a truly feudal part of Italy. The old lady with the embers told us she could not give us permission to camp for she was only a *contadina* and the *padrone* was in New York. Woodcutters' mules, wearing *basti* identical to Hannibal's, were working on the wooded slopes towards Gubbio, and in the fertile foothills we saw farms where pairs of white oxen were harnessed to hand-hewn wooden sledges. Steady work in quiet hilly country had greatly improved Picchio's manners and Miranda was now riding him continuously, but the sight of a cart without wheels *did* nearly cause a spill.

By the time we reached the Val d'Assino icy rain was falling once more. We could not believe our luck when we found an abandoned ox-stall on the tractor-cultivated floor of the valley, only a few kilometres from Gubbio. Such luxuries were normally confined to the hills. It even held a pile of corn husks which proved infinitely preferable to the relentless chill of concrete. The bedraggled children's spirits soared as soon as they were tucked up in their warm sleeping-bags and so, after a liberal nip of *grappa*, did ours. While oilskins dripped from every peg we sang all the verses of 'The Mermaid', giving the chorus about 'the raging seas' everything we had.

Gubbio perches on the far side of the Val d'Assino where it has stood since Roman times. It is best seen from a distance, for then the mediaeval houses appear to stand on top of each other's tiled roofs, surmounted by the great Palazzo dei Consoli supported on its enormous arches. Inside, the palace is disappointing, for the entrance hall is as high and bare as a railway station, and an upper room decorated with inlaid panels has been exported to the United States.

Thomas and I walked the eight kilometres into Gubbio in the true Franciscan manner (a suitable pilgrimage on the 750th anniversary of the saint) but, apart from a small fresco in a corner of the palace, we could find little record of the famous story of his taming of the wolf. Searching eagerly for a postcard of *il lupo* in the numerous souvenir shops, we found only a sickly Victorian print which showed the palace (built 100 years later) in the background. At the Tourist Information Office they handed us a brochure advertising an expensive restaurant called Taverna del Lupo. This leaflet claimed that St. Francis had lived 250 years earlier than he did. We were more successful in our search for the famous keyhole-shaped doorways, now frequently blocked, through which the inhabitants of mediaeval Gubbio insisted that their dead must pass from their houses. More prosaically, we ran to earth a pair of wellingtons for Miranda, whose expensive new Italian walking-boots leaked. I bought them from a man with a stall in the market and succeeded in knocking 650 lire off the price. "*Povera Italia!*" he said cheerfully as he handed them over. The value of the lira was plunging sensationally that week.

One more range of hills lay between us and the Apennine watershed. Once more we took to footpaths but this time we got well and truly lost for Andrew had not pioneered beyond Gubbio. At dawn on the second day we were on an open hilly pasture beside a pink tower. Ahead of us was the little town of Sigillo.

"That," said Thomas, pointing to Sigillo, "is where we'll have a slap-up breakfast." He had not reckoned with an awesome gorge that lay between us and it. Three hours later, having been chased by a loose herd of woodcutters' mules through deep mud, we were back at the pink tower. Eventually an old shepherd abandoned his flock to show us the way into Sigillo by Torra dell' Olmo and the famous Roman Via Flaminia, after first ascertaining that we were respectable (*gente brava* was his word for it). The young man in black velvet who ran the Fenice Bar in Sigillo was not so sure. We had just settled down, mud-spattered and soaked, to coffee and fresh cream cakes, when a pair of gun-carrying *carabinieri* drew up with a flourish in a blue police Land Rover, a red light flashing. Luckily a lengthy inspection of our passports satisfied them.

In defence of the inhabitants of Sigillo, the last town of Umbria, I must record two acts of kindness. At a chemist's shop, prettily fres-coed and decorated with majolica jars as only Italian chemists' shops can be, the woman sold me Mogadon, my favourite sleep-inducer, with-out a moment's hesitation. "You know it became illegal without a pre-scription last week," she said cheerfully as she handed over the daintily wrapped package. At the stationer's opposite, which was also a barber's (the proprietor periodically running from his victim's foaming chin to serve notepaper and comics), four well-bristled men held a solemn dis-cussion about the best way for me to procure stiff cardboard on which to rest the exercise book in which I wrote my camp diary. Eventually one of them, a fearsome creature with a damp moustache and a squint, came in waving a piece of three-ply wood about the size of a large magazine which he had begged from the carpenter next door. It was my constant companion ever afterwards and the reverse side made an ex-cellent meat-chopping board.

CHAPTER 41

The great divide

We crossed the Apennines, the backbone of Italy, on May 1st, by a small road leading from Sigillo to Fabriano. It was far worse than we had expected. We zigzagged interminably up the face of the mountains in the teeth of a north wind known as the *tramontana*. It was the coldest, hardest wind I had ever encountered. We had to stop and pull the drawstrings of the children's anoraks close round their faces and tie handkerchiefs over their mouths till only their eyes were visible.

The air was so cold I could hardly catch my breath and I thought I would suffocate. The animals plodded on steadily and the gallant Picchio even broke into an occasional trot, but when the road went over a causeway the side wind was so strong that the donkeys were pushed across the road. Much of the time it was unsafe for Jessica to ride Hamilcar, and for long stretches Thomas carried her under one arm while driving Hannibal with the other.

When we finally reached the top we breakfasted in a large concrete drain to keep out the wind, and drank, children as well as adults, large mugs of milk laced with brandy.

May 1st is a public holiday in Italy, and at the pass we found eight carloads of young Italians on their way to the caves at Monte Cucco. They had stopped for a snowball fight at a large patch of sunlit snow beside the road. Such folly, we decided, was only possible for those who could retire to a heated car. Luckily the climate changed the moment we began to descend into the province of Italy named the Marches. The wind ceased and the sky became hazy as the road dropped sharply towards a land of lush green valleys. In the distance we soon saw the mediaeval town of Fabriano.

Apart from a fleeting visit to Ancona soon after the war, we had never been in the Marches. We did, however, know two facts about them, told us by Joan Martini, a Welsh friend in Arezzo who was married to Paolo, a native of the area. Until 1860 they were numbered among the Papal States, many popes being drawn from the noble families of the area, and one of these had been an ancestor of Paolo Martini's. He had perished slowly and horribly at the hands of poisoners. By the time he died, Joan told us with relish, his body was already green and putrefying, and it fell apart as they laid him out. We also knew that the people of the Marches eat a great deal of *pollenta*, a dish of ground maize similar to semolina. In Paolo's family the tradition was to pour the whole pan of bubbling goo on to a scrubbed wooden table, top it with sauce and then attack it from all sides, a procedure which led to much bonhomous horseplay.

The following day we skirted Fabriano on gravel roads to the north and passed through villages even more primitive than those of Umbria. At Cantia grotesque Brueghel-like peasants called each other into the street to watch us pass. In field after field of green corn stood bamboo crosses two metres high with sprigs of olive poked into the tops and cross pieces, unmistakable fertility charms.

As we walked along the green ridges the early summer flowers amazed us and reminded us of Spain at the same time the year before. The children gathered bright bunches of poppies, elderflowers, gladiolus, wild roses and honeysuckle. They stuck them in the donkeys' bridles and carried posies of them, like May queens. White poplar down was everywhere, getting up our noses and making us sneeze when we tried to talk to the people in the fields. It blew across the valleys below us, sometimes hard to distinguish from more distant flights of white farm pigeons.

On our third day in the Marches we found ourselves in a wide green valley with a great cliff rising at the far side. It was the opening of the Frasassi Gorge where, in 1971, one of the finest caves in Europe had been discovered. The gorge was impressive. High rock walls, noisy with jackdaws, rose close on either side and below was the rushing torrent of the Sentino. It was a shock after three kilometres of solitary walking to round a bend and see a queue of a hundred school children standing on a concrete ramp awaiting admission to the caves.

On the other side of the road eight charabancs with Turin and Florence number-plates were lined up in a car park and here we unloaded and tethered our beasts. It turned out that we had an hour to wait until the next conducted tour, and so we settled down to eat hot lasagna from a stall. The donkeys were less fortunate. They had not a blade of grass between them and their nerves were sorely frayed by herds of noisy children playing football with Coca-Cola tins. To soothe them I fed them peppermints, tranquillisers which were only too familiar to the spoilt Picchio, but they were new to Hannibal. His great velvet lips flapped and dribbled saliva for ten minutes after he had munched up his first.

Despite their noisiness, these Italian children were remarkably good-humoured. We never once heard one cry or whine. Miranda was amazed to see eight little girls of her age give their 100-lire pieces to a minute child who went and bought ice-creams for the party without any arguments developing. When the same group lined up for a photograph there were none of the cries of "We don't want *you*" that would have been heard in an English playground.

The caves were worth the wait. We entered them through a long tunnel with sliding metal doors opening and closing automatically at intervals. One guide went ahead and another brought along the stragglers (the children and myself). The last metal door slid open to reveal a fairy palace large enough, according to the guide, to contain Milan cathedral. Stalagmites like ornate candles rose many metres from the floor, their colours ranging from glistening white to chestnut brown. Stalactites, some resembling sheets on a washing line, hung from the roof and walls. In places there were pools of blue water with crystals floating on them like ice. The catwalk from which we viewed these wonders measured a kilometre in length, we were told, and there were thirteen kilometres more of caves still remaining in primaeval darkness. Indeed, the whole mountain is riddled with caves, like a giant Gruyère cheese. On the way out, the guide pointed to the fissure 200 metres above, through which the climbers had first entered. They had felt a draught coming through a hole, enlarged it, and crawled along eighty metres of tunnel before reaching a drop. How long a drop they realised when they threw a stone down.

Not far beyond the caves the gorge opened into a pretty village with a spa called Terme St. Vittore, where a Romanesque church stood on a green mound, and an old stone bridge crossed the river Sentino, Alas, the third feature of the village was a hideous modern hotel, built criminally close to the church. We little guessed how soon we would be grateful for it. That night, camped in a riverside poplar grove, Miranda paid the price of our bitter crossing of the Apennines three days before. She was drowsy, would not eat and complained of a sore throat. The next morning a doctor diagnosed a bronchial murmur. He prescribed antibiotics in double the quantities the instructions on our packets had recommended, and five days under a roof. I required little persuasion to move into the Albergo Terme St. Vittore with her.

The rates of the hotel, even out of season, were high, and since we doubted whether Lloyds would pay the bill, we avoided the dining-room. In the evenings Thomas would arrive with a cooked meal, tasting deliciously of woodsmoke, in his knapsack and share it with us in our bedroom. It was a strange experience to see the Italian bourgeoisie taking its annual cure. Water therapy went out of favour in England before the First World War, but the faith of the Italians in spa water has remained unshaken since Roman times, as Miranda and I discovered early on our first morning when we took the lift down to the basement where the mineral spring was housed. Even the lift-shaft smelt of bad eggs and when we reached the marble hall where the patients, wrapped in towelling robes, awaited treatment, it became overpowering. Above their heads a notice promised cures for arthritis, diseases of the kidney and liver, female disorders, deafness and many other complaints. The fee for a sulphur bath was 1,500 lire (about £1). For a mud bath you paid much more.

Once they had made their morning sacrifice to the god of health, our fellow-guests were free to spend their days as they liked, and usually started by making a rush for the bar, where they consumed large quantities of liver-enlarging coffee. Diet seemed to play no part in their treatment and five-course meals with free wine were served twice daily. In the evening the bar filled with cheerful family groups playing cards and drinking liqueurs. They were a friendly lot, mostly small shop-keepers from Ancona, and Miranda soon got to know several balding gentlemen who enquired after the health of 'Annibale' each morning and bought her ice-creams. The gentle Hannibal had now filled the gap in her affections left by Iago and she was missing him badly.

Our third evening at the hotel was one we shall not forget. Things started to take an unfamiliar turn at half-past seven, the hour when dinner was normally served. It was Miranda's habit to look out of our bedroom window at that time and watch the hotel guests sitting on the terrace, eagerly awaiting the summons to eat. As the clock struck the half hour a waiter would emerge, clap his hands and shout 'Cena, signori', causing a stampede for the dining-room.

"Mummy," called Miranda from the window that evening. "They're all looking at the sky." Sure enough the hotel guests were in a row along the terrace, chattering and pointing at something high above the building. Soon all the waiters joined them and, unable to contain my curiosity, I also went down, to discover that two village youths were stranded high on the rocky face of the gorge, unable either to go up or come down. They were just visible as pinpoints of white against the orange precipice. Darkness had fallen by the time Thomas brought dinner and both Miranda and I were in a somewhat nervous state when, at exactly five minutes past nine, the room shook. For several seconds not only did the windows rattle but also the bed on which I was lying shuddered. Miranda rushed into Thomas's arms, but he insisted that it was only a lorry passing and that the light would sway if it was an earth tremor. For Miranda's sake I refrained from pointing out that the light *was* swaying. The next morning we discovered that the terrible earthquake at Friuli had occurred at five-past nine the previous evening. We did not realise till later that we had done the right thing. Apparently in urban earthquakes the casualties among the young are much higher than among the old, because they are spry enough to run into the streets where they are hit by falling masonry.

It was not easy to settle down to camp life after the luxury of the hotel. The tent seemed stuffy and overcrowded and the sleeping-bags smelt decidedly overripe. It rained in the night and as we packed in the morning everything we touched was wet. Andrew and Picchio, however, had pioneered a path over the hills to Jesi and soon we were so high above St. Vittore that it seemed no more than a scatter of toy houses at the mouth of the gorge. As we descended the hill on the far side we passed several fine donkeys carrying pack-saddles and accompanied by cheerful women. Soon we were in the village of Castelletta, a strange place indeed, as we were to learn from an old man in the valley below. In the past Castelletta had been run by women, for the men went to earn their living in Rome. These stalwart women kept the home fires burning by bringing down loads of firewood from the hills on donkeys. Every family had two animals and there had been about 300 in the village.

A gentle, smiling landscape of green hills now lay before us, many of the hills surmounted by small towns known as the *castelli di Jesi*, for at one time they all acknowledged the supremacy of Jesi, the walled city in their midst. We camped below Cupramontana, one of the *castelli*, beside a river where men were breaking stones for cobbles. It was here that we first met the famous white *verdicchio*, produced at Cupramontana and said to have a strength of fourteen degrees. After three glasses under a waxing moon I could well believe it. Meanwhile Andrew was meeting the local girls, five of them. They worked in the slipper factory at Castellaro, not on the land like their parents, as they were quick to inform us. They bore him off to a discotheque from which he did not return till the early hours. Next day he declared that the girls of the Marches were bolder and brighter than the girls of Tuscany and less inclined to sit in corners and giggle.

The land round Jesi was intensively cultivated in vast holdings, and bulldozers had ravaged the margins of the poplar-shaded river Cesola where we wanted to camp, preparing a motorway designed to connect Ancona with Rome. There was half an acre of waste land on the far side of the river before the plough started again, but the only way to reach it was by a narrow concrete footbridge suspended high above the water.

Hamilcar was the first to attempt the crossing. Andrew managed to persuade him to put all four feet on to the bridge but there was no railing for the first three metres and suddenly his back legs went over the side, followed shortly by the rest of him, which landed in an un-dignified heap two metres below. The children sat on the bank, their arms round each other, howling, and we all waited anxiously to see if he would get up. He did, but by then he was stuck under the bridge because his saddle was too high. After Andrew had undone the girths he struggled out, leaving his somewhat scarred saddle behind him. He seemed none the worse and was not even shaking, but I was, for I had never seen a horse fall so far.

In the end we got the animals across the river by taking them down the bank at a place where it was not too steep, and wading down-stream with them till we reached another easy point. Picchio revelled in the aquatic exercise, riffling his nose through the water and pawing at it as he went. Later he crossed several times by the bridge, com-pletely unconcerned, his short ears pricked eagerly in the hope of better grass on the other side.

CHAPTER 42

Speed bonnie boat

Jesi is only twenty-five kilometres from Ancona, and, with the sea so
near, the practical problems of getting the donkeys and Picchio across
it began to loom large. As our plan to stand on the quayside at
Ancona and arouse the pity of a departing captain was a last resort
we hoped to avoid, it seemed that the sooner we booked a proper
passage the better. I took the bus into Jesi with two ambitions in
mind, a bath and a boat.

Jesi, like Umbertide, was nicer than I had expected. A town whose
main claim to fame was that, in 1194, the mother of Frederick II had
had the misfortune to give birth to him in a tent in the main square,
did not sound promising. In fact it had an interesting 'monumental
zone' surrounded by a city wall built on Roman foundations. The
present walls date from the fifteenth century and are made of brick
with decorative castellations and rounded corner towers. A connected
series of *piazze* boast, respectively, the twelfth-century cathedral,
the fifteenth-century town hall and the eighteenth-century Pergolesi
theatre. From the square where the theatre is sited, to Arco St. Clem-
entino, the westerly town gate, runs a busy shopping-street which is
almost the best feature of all, for it is closed to traffic at midday and
during the evening, when half the population saunters up and down it
in the traditional *passeggiata*.

I found the Albergo Italia, my kind of fourth-category hotel (key
for the bathroom on application at the desk), down by the station
and, bathed and refreshed, began my search for someone who knew
about shipping lines. It was about six o'clock in the evening and I
found a great many people, but their thoughts were not on ships. The
wolves I had sought at Gubbio were all at Jesi. I was still descending
from the station bus when an undernourished young man suggested he
should accompany me to the *corso* and then to bed. In the steep
cobbled side-streets of the old town the nuisance was just as bad and
I had to threaten one insistent Sicilian with the police before I could
shake him off. The suggestion that a furiously jealous husband and
three noisy children were waiting for me round the corner left him
unmoved. It was years since I had been bothered to this extent and I

could only assume that the pall of boredom which hangs so heavily over Italian provincial towns hung especially heavily over Jesi.

Eventually I plunged into an unattractive *tavola calda* and found I had jumped out of the frying-pan into the fire, for at the counter next to me was an obsequious, shifty little man, his chin covered with white bristles. He claimed to be the last Fascist living under house arrest in Italy. As he pawed my arm he told me he had held high office under Mussolini and was proud to be a martyr for the cause. I would have sworn he had been drinking, if the carafe wine had not so obviously been watered. When I asked for *pollenta* (which was advertised in the window) they said it was a winter dish and immediately removed the notice with a pair of tongs. As I left, a girl at the cold-meats counter cut deeply into her thumb with a salami slicer and had to be removed to hospital.

Next morning my luck was in. At the station bar, where I break-fasted, I read a newspaper advertisement for a firm called Cargo, which claimed that it would transport 'Anything to Anywhere'. How could I doubt that we were the very customers they had been waiting for? The offices of Cargo were above a Fiat showroom in a busy thorough-fare outside the city walls. A smart secretary let me in and, to my surprise, said that I could see Signor Palman at once. He was a dapper young man, somewhat dwarfed by the magnificence of his office furni-ture. He sat at a desk made of black glass and about the size of a barn door. Three grossly stuffed and buttoned leather armchairs jostled for the remaining floor-space and over the door was a spoof cheque a metre high, made out to S. Palman to the value of a thousand million lire.

I mustered my forces for a tricky interview. "Signor Palman," I commenced, with a fulsome smile, "they tell me in the town that you can do the impossible."

"The difficult I can do at once," said Signor Palman spryly. "The impossible takes a little longer." I didn't know that one had reached Italy.

"Can you transport two donkeys and a pony to Greece?"

"Of course," said Signor Palman, without hesitation. "Come back at three." It was as easy as that. I almost danced out of the office, eager to boast of my success to Thomas whom I was meeting at the post office at ten.

With five hours to fill, Thomas and I visited the famous thirteenth-century Gothic church of St. Marco. It is now in the possession of en-closed Carmelite nuns, and to obtain the key you must pass through a courtyard planted with pansies, ring a bell and wait till a faint female voice answers from behind a wooden screen. After a further wait the voice says that you will now find the main door of the church unlocked. We felt like Beauty visiting the palace of the Beast as we entered the church. Everything happened by itself. Doors clicked shut behind us, spotlights illuminated frescoes. There was a high wooden screen across the church, hiding the choir, but a little door had been left open at the left-hand end. We assumed that this had been done intentionally, as it was in the north side-chapel that, according to the guide book, the famous Nolfi tomb was situated. Great was our consternation to find half the community deep in silent prayer beside the tomb.

When Cargo reopened at three fifteen there was no sign of Signor Palman, but his rather plain younger sister informed us that no ships sailing from Ancona would accept donkeys and they must go by train through Venice and Yugoslavia.

By the following morning Signorina Palman had discovered that there were no trains going through Jugoslavia because of the Friuli earthquake. She refused to be defeated, however, and asked us to return the next day. When we did so we found her thick glasses flashing with triumph. The *Atalante*, a ship of the Med. Sun line, was willing to take our donkeys to Patras provided they embarked in a covered lorry and remained in their lorry during the crossing. It would be necessary for a driver to travel with the lorry but she knew of both a lorry and a driver. The cost would not be more than 300,000 lire (about £200). The only drawback was that the *Atalante* did not sail till June 5th, which left us three weeks to wait.

We returned to camp that day to find Andrew and the children in a state of dejection. The whispering poplars on the far side of the river, which had shaded us from the midday sun, had all been felled by a fat man with a mechanical saw. With the poplars gone and most of our grazing eaten, it was evidently time to move on. Why not fill the next three weeks with a camp on the shores of the Adriatic, I suggested. Instantly Miranda stopped crying. Would there be boats? Could she go in one?

Our rather fanciful tourist map of the coastline near Ancona showed a tempting mountain called Conero rising out of the sea about seven kilometres south of Ancona. Since a farmer had also assured us that the dark red wine of Monte Conero was exceptional, we set out in that general direction. At St. Maria Nuova we provoked a minor accident: the leading Fiat 500 in a wedding procession braked suddenly to look at us and caused the two behind to collide. But the incident rumpled none of the twelve occupants' good humour nor their trouser creases. "An Italian male in his best makes even a tailor's dummy look shabby," Andrew said enviously. At Montesicuro we had our first sight of the Adriatic. Segments of deep blue showed between broom-covered hills. Just beyond Gli Angeli, a fat peasant with the improbable name of Italo Pollenta said that Portonovo was the place for a seaside camp: so to Portonovo we went.

Or to be exact, to a small cove between Portonovo and Trave (a natural rock mole). Here a steep path led down to the beach where, to Miranda's delight, the first thing we saw was a plastic beer crate with Greek characters painted on it. Andrew had taught her the Greek alphabet and shown her how to read simple Greek sentences. "It's floated across the sea from Greece," she cried. We did not disillusion her.

Our cove was edged by a shanty town which would never have been permitted under British Town and Country Planning laws and which, as we later discovered, was due for destruction on orders from the Italian government since it was in a 'green zone'. It consisted of a row of ramshackle chalets made from asbestos and corrugated iron. Makeshift hoses and poles brought water and electricity, and upended boats were stored on verandas. Yet, since this was Italy, these shacks were not as ugly as you might expect. Oleanders and climbing plants veiled many of their worst features, and there was also a beach bar, although it consisted only of a few kitchen tables under a vine awning. And since this was Italy, at either end of the beach *new* shacks were being built in the confident expectation that procrastination or corruption would long delay any action by the Italian government.

Fortunately for us, most of the sheds would remain closed until the school term ended in mid-June. Only here and there a man in rolled-up trousers replaced a plank in a fence or added a coat of paint to a boat. At the south end of the beach we found two square metres of flat land between the cliff and the sand with a fresh-water tap nearby. Here we put up the tent while the children set about avidly beach-combing. Certainly that beach was a beachcomber's paradise, if plastic bottles happened to be your speciality. Sun-tan oil bottles, detergent bottles, bleach bottles and mineral-water bottles were piled in ridges along the shore.

The sun rose red out of a pearl grey sky the next morning and looked straight into our tent. Foaming waves had roared up the beach all night, urged on by a strong wind, and I had been afraid they might reach our ledge. Now the gale had dropped and five burly men, who must have arrived at a neighbouring hut during the night, were pushing a clinker-built rowing-boat with an outboard engine down to the sea. After a good deal of toing and froing, the one who gave the orders and was, presumably, the owner, embarked with one of the others and puttered off towards the mole. When they returned there was a mountain of something black in the bows. Thomas sent Miranda to buy some of whatever it was. She came back with a plastic bag of large knobbly black mussels so heavy she could hardly carry it. The skipper had refused payment, for he only caught them, he said, for sport.

We could only conclude that the Italian idea of sport was closer to our idea of work. Four times that day the boat returned from the mole heavy with mussels clawed from the rocks with a rake-like instrument. Three men were fully employed from dawn till dusk cleaning a small mountain of them. The sea was like glass now and all that night we could see the lights of the professional fishermen from Ancona moving along the coast. Apparently this stretch was a famous fishing ground. Our own quintet was back at work by 4.30 a.m.

After a week at the cove we had cooked mussels in every way we could devise: the French manner (*moules marinières*), the Italian manner (chopped in a tomato sauce and tipped over spaghetti), and the Greek manner (fried in batter). We had also feasted on a sardine-sized fish with a large head called a *guatto* and on squid cooked in wine with wild garlic.

But although good food for us was abundant, food for the animals was less so. Their only source of grass was beside the steep path leading to the top of the cliff, and each day Andrew had to take them higher in search of fresh grazing. As they had to come down for water three times a day this was a laborious business. He found it ·simplest to release them, clap his hands, yell " 'Ware donkeys! " and wait for the ensuing stampede. The three animals, led by Picchio, would then gallop down the precipitous path, snorting and whisking their tails, and plunge joyfully on to the beach in a spurt of sand. All three luxuriated in the sandy beach which they regarded as one enormous rolling area.

It was Mafalda who suggested a new camping ground. Mafalda was a motherly woman who ran a restaurant at Poggio, on the top of the cliff. She had a son, a daughter and a husband. The son was her despair. He was sixteen and knew that he looked like Paul McCartney. He refused to attend the maritime school at Ancona, preferring to dance, dress and rev up his motor-bike engine. The daughter was older and more serious. She had trained as a teacher but, posts in schools being short, worked at a bank in Ancona. The husband was an ineffectual little man who claimed that he longed to travel and give up 'all this', making an expansive gesture which appeared to include Mafalda, rolling out *pasta* on one of the restaurant tables.

Mafalda's solution for our foraging problem was Angiolotti's place, a farmhouse standing in several hectares of overgrown pasture just above Portonovo. The only difficulty was that it belonged to the Commendatore Mandolesi, the owner of three oil tankers, who was awaiting permission to transform it into a caravan park. It was rumoured that he might be found at the Sporting Hotel, just beyond Ancona, which he also owned. Thither, by bus, I set out with some trepidation.

The Sporting Hotel was a new building of unbelievable vulgarity, reminding me of a stranded ocean liner that had been sprayed with orange pebble dash. I was not permitted to penetrate beyond the reception desk, but fortunately the Commendatore was at lunch in the dining-room and sent back a note to say that the family called Chitty could camp in the house called Angiolotti's till June 5th.

Angiolotti had abandoned his house after a series of earthquakes in 1973, which has left many buildings in Ancona still supported by wooden buttresses. It was a large, solidly built farmhouse, but seared with gaping cracks. We were soon comfortably installed in the ox-stall, although most of our days were spent in what had once been the garden. Andrew occupied an upstairs room, after sweeping the floor clear of broken glass with a broom of branches. He studied Greek up there, listening to Greek news bulletins on a minute transistor. In the evenings he lounged on the window-sill overlooking the sea and played the recorder. From this window-sill he could see the steamers coming and going to Greece.

At Angiolotti's house we had everything we needed. There were loose doors and shutters from which we could make benches and tables. The Portonovo water supply was sited at the top of our land. By removing a piece of twisted wire, we could release a jet which, if allowed to flow unchecked, would presumably have caused all the taps in Portonovo to run dry. Best of all, deep in the grass below the house was a tree bearing enough ripe cherries to supply a fruit stall for a week.

From this stronghold we were able to make the acquaintance of Portonovo, a charming little place where a vast quadrangular Napoleonic fort had been turned into a luxury hotel. At the remotest part of the peninsula stood a solitary eleventh-century church of sea-weathered stone. It was an immensely romantic place. Through every ill-fitting door came the regular roar of surf like a heart-beat. You could imagine a knight of olden time kneeling all night before the altar, vowing himself to some selfless and heroic deed. The church is said to be the one Dante had in mind when, in *Il Paradiso*, St. Damian speaks of *La Casa di Nostra Donna in sul lido Adriano*.

On June 1st Thomas and I took the bus to Jesi, since we had agreed to pay Cargo for our boat tickets that day and to make final arrangements about the lorry. It was as well we arrived when the office opened, for it soon became obvious that the friendly but froglike Signorina Palman had not concerned herself with our affairs since we were last there. Now, apologetically, she began a series of phone calls to discover the exact cost. We accepted a rise in the price of our own fares from 53,000 lire to 64,000 lire per adult (owing to a seasonal increase on June 1st) but the progressively rising price, with every phone call, of transporting the lorry and its driver to Greece *and* back was more and more alarming. In the end she informed us that the bill, including at least six different taxes and veterinary fees, came to the staggering total of 916,000 lire (about £600). As consolation she said that by chance she could introduce us to our lorry-driver, Erico, who happened to have just arrived a day late from Milan

Erico was in the next-door office, drinking coffee with the secretary. He was a beardless, devil-may-care stripling who did not look a day over seventeen. He wore spotless Oxford bags and a denim shirt so closely fitting that it was a wonder he could breathe. He promised to erect movable partitions across his lorry to keep the animals apart, and to bring eight bales of hay and straw from his father's farm. His brother, who was a carpenter, would make a ramp up which the animals could climb to enter the lorry.

Ancona was our next port of call, for the tickets had to be procured from a Greek called Cagidemetrio, the Ancona agent for Med. Sun lines. When we had last seen Ancona twenty-three years before, it had been largely in ruins as a result of German bombing. Now we found ourselves in a city of ornamental modern squares, in the corner of the largest of which were situated Cagidemetrio's glossy premises. He was a serious bald man, usually speaking on three phones at once. He accepted Cargo's receipt for the donkeys' fares without a smile and on request gave us a free tourist pamphlet entitled 'Ancona, pearl of the Adriatic'.

Our pamphlet advised us to start our tour of the old town at the southern end of the port where, surrounded by water, stands a fine pentagonal plague hospital built in the eighteenth century and called the Lazzaretto. We discovered that the Lazzaretto could not be visited now because it is a government-bonded warehouse for tobacco. At the northern end of the port we were directed to the Arch of Trajan, built in A.D. 115. We found it surrounded by weeds and sadly dwarfed by the metal wall of an oil-tanker under construction a few metres away. High above us on Monte Guasco, the cathedral, built on the site of a Greek temple, still looked unspoiled. After climbing many hundreds of steps we discovered that it had been closed since the earthquake of 1973. So also had been the archaeological museum. We deposited our pamphlet in the nearest litter bin and returned to camp.

The auguries were not good on the morning of embarkation day. The sun, which had shone consistently for the last twenty days, had disappeared, and a thin cold rain was beginning to fall. We had arranged to meet Erico and his lorry at the half-built Hotel Emilia on the cliff top at eleven o'clock. By the time we reached the Emilia the rain had become heavy and a gale was rising fast which hurled it in bucketfuls against our faces. While Thomas and Andrew baled up the saddlery for transport and kept a watch for the lorry, the children and I retreated to the Emilia through a sea of yellow mud and asked the site foreman's permission to shelter for ten minutes.

It was a long ten minutes. Half an hour, an hour, an hour and a half went by and still Erico did not come. The place where we were sheltering would one day be the hotel dining-room but at present its windows gaped to the elements. Six of them, although unglazed, had been fitted with white venetian blinds which clattered and flapped at every squall. In the region of these we made our playground. We played Grandmothers' Footsteps, we danced the sailor's hornpipe and we played Pig-in-the-Middle with a screwed-up cement bag. Nevertheless, Jessica's cheeks turned relentlessly from white to mottled red and from red to mauve. At one o'clock Thomas, muffled in a wind-tormented anorak, fought his way across the mud towards us, looking like an extra in an overdone film about a shipwreck in the North Atlantic. Although his fingers had turned white from the cold and his nails blue, he had brought bread and cheese and brandy for our comfort. He said Andrew would telephone Cargo as soon as he relieved him at his post by the donkeys.

In another hour Andrew returned from the telephone to report that the offices of Cargo had been shut, it being Saturday, but that the Jesi *carabinieri* had got through to Signor Palman's residence and he had assured them that Erico was coming. At half-past two he came. The storm had lashed itself to a crescendo as Erico, murmuring excuses about losing his way but surprisingly little abashed, descended from his cab. He wore only a tight-fitting pale-blue denim suit which instantly became dark-blue from the drenching to which it was exposed. Within five minutes his face, to my satisfaction, had turned the same colour.

The ramp that he had promised turned out to be more in the nature of a rickety ladder, but fortunately Thomas had found a steep bank against which the lorry could be backed for loading and the animals went in surprisingly easily. Andrew travelled with them to make sure the fodder did not collapse on top of Picchio, and the rest of us crawled into the driving-cab.

Erico, half drowned and shivering, was a changed character from the spry young man we had met flirting with the office secretary at Cargo. Like the gay grasshopper at the end of the summer, he had begun to see the reality of winter gaping before him. Would the ship be safe? he enquired. Would there be food on board? How would he get back? When we reached the main street of Ancona he asked us, unbelievably, the way to the port.

At the docks, the *Atalante* was moored right in front of us, her dark-blue plates rising like a castle wall from the quayside. "Isn't she *sweet*," said Jessica, stretching her arms towards the ship as Thomas lifted her down from the lorry. She had a special interest in her, for the next day was her fifth birthday and we had promised that she should celebrate it on board.

There was a maritime station on the quay which contained the customs hall, the offices of the various shipping companies, a restaurant and a bank. The time was half-past three, and embarkation procedure was not due to begin till half-past seven. At this point Erico's older brother arrived in a car and asked if he could take Erico home to do his packing and say goodbye to his mother. We suspected he was going to make his will at the same time, but agreed to his going provided he left the lorry, with our animals in it, on the quayside.

Confident that everything was at last under control, we went to the upstairs restaurant to feast on hot lasagna. During the rest of the afternoon the reception hall began to fill with the clean, neatly dressed middle-aged Germans who were to be our fellow-passengers. At half-past six Erico returned, now accompanied by his girl friend as well as his brother, and at half-past seven the brown dome of Cagidemetrio's head appeared gleaming at the Med. Sun desk. We hurried to the counter to collect Erico's ticket, not issued to us before in case there was a change of driver. "Passport?" he said. Erico had no passport. "Identity card?" Cagidemetrio said. Erico had no identity card. Well then, Erico could not travel, Cagidemetrio said.

It took some seconds for us to believe that this could really be true, but we were not allowed more than a few seconds. Hordes of passport-bearing Germans in straw hats were pressing forward behind us. There was nothing to do but retire to a corner and ponder our fate.

At eight fifteen most of the Germans had embarked, for the *Atalante* was due to sail at nine, and we once more approached Cagidemetrio. He looked at us as if he wished we would vanish with our donkeys through a hole in the ground, then hurried off to the *Atalante*'s loading gates where he entered into animated conversations with a succession of Greek seamen and officers before disappearing altogether into the ship. Fifteen minutes later he emerged, unsmiling but grimly successful. Erico could drive the lorry on to the boat, leave it there and collect it a week later here in Ancona when it had completed a cruise of the Greek islands. The animals could disembark at Patras on their own feet.

When Erico had agreed to this suggestion we stood on the quay in the gathering darkness, watching the last of the tourist cars drive on board, waiting for his lorry to arrive and follow them. At last Erico drove up, bumped his front wheels on to the loading-ramp — and stopped. It was obvious to all of us that the lorry could not possibly go through the port. Measurements were taken and it was found to be over a metre too high.

It was at this moment, while Jessica burst into tears at her lost birthday afloat and the rest of us broke into slightly hysterical laughter, that Cagidemetrio showed his true quality. Undismayed by the fact that the ship was due to sail in fifteen minutes, he began new and more dramatic negotiations with the crew, compared to which his earlier high-pitched arguments had been mere tea-table talk. In a couple of minutes all was agreed. The donkeys could walk *on* and *off* the ship.

Forbearing to mention that this was what we had originally asked for three weeks earlier, we ran the lorry up against the steps of the customs house, brought the animals stumbling down by improvised steps of hay bales and hurried them to the loading-ramp. Even at this last moment there seemed a chance that we would be frustrated. Hannibal set his front feet firmly on the clanging metal plates and wouldn't budge. But Greek sailors know about donkeys. Within seconds four of them had seized a vast hawser, run it round his rump and, two on each end, hauled him bodily aboard. A last wave to Erico was all we had time for as the port slammed shut. As for Cagidemetrio, he was nowhere to be seen, nor have we so far seen any refund on our unused return tickets for Erico and his lorry.

Five

GREECE

Existence, these glances say, is a torment, an enemy, an adventure
and a joke which we are in league to undergo, outwit and enjoy on
equal terms as accomplices, fellow-hedonists and fellow-victims. A
stranger begins to realise that the armour which has been irking
him and the arsenal he has been lugging around for half a lifetime
are no longer needed. Miraculous lightness takes their place.

Patrick Leigh Fermor, *Roumeli*

CHAPTER 43

Birthday afloat

Jessica celebrated her fifth birthday during the thirty-six-hour crossing. It was hard to believe she had only been three when our journey started. How would a year and a half of nomadic life affect her character, I wondered. Would she be left with a permanently unsatisfied restlessness or would she, in three months' time, slot easily back into the life of an English schoolgirl? On several occasions when tempers became frayed in camp, she had said, "I want to get back on my donkey." There, enthroned on her great saddle, she would rock along undisturbed, telling endless stories to herself. Perhaps in adult life she would never feel truly at peace except in the saddle.

The steep coast of Albania, mysterious under a roof of cloud, was on the port bow as we went down to the birthday dinner. Jessica was allotted the place of honour, and crowned with a headdress of coloured feathers. She opened the presents that we had smuggled on board ready wrapped, pausing politely to accept friendly tickles from passing stewards. A German woman came over from another table with a tiny yellow corduroy rabbit which has been a close companion ever since. As the stewards were distributing the dessert, the head waiter bore down on us with a silver dish held high above his head. He placed it in front of Jessica. On it was a birthday cake composed of rich layers of cream and nuts. It even had 'Happy Birthday' written on it in white icing, and a white candle in the middle. A card informed us that it was a gift from the head purser, a nice man whose wife came from Carlisle.

During dinner Thomas had been systematically dropping rolls down the front of his shirt, as the ship's breakfasts were expensive and inadequate. As he led the way from the dining-room in a dignified patriarchal manner he looked pregnant, not only in front but also behind. We all insisted that three bread rolls should be earmarked for the donkeys. To reach them we had to walk along miles of corridor, down carpeted stairs and then down flights of metal steps. From below came the throb of the ship's screws and a smell of engine oil. But half-way down the fifth ladder we suddenly caught the aroma of new-mown hay. We were there.

Hannibal, Hamilcar and Picchio were at the far end of a cavernous hold, in the angle of the stern. They stood in deep straw, the two donkeys tethered side by side and Picchio, looking unusually demure, a few paces behind. A bare bulb shed a yellow light from above, giving the whole scene the air of a Morland painting of a rustic stable. The animals seemed quite unperturbed by the throbbing of the screw, which can only have been separated from them by a steel plate. While we watched, Hannibal stretched out a hind leg until it was absolutely straight and parallel to the floor. No doubt he was feeling the need of exercise.

We arrived at Patras at ten o'clock the following morning, three hours behind schedule. The town, although the third largest in Greece, looked mercifully small, its expansion inland being prevented by steep hills. After what looked like some fairly inept manœuvring with a tug, the ship was brought alongside the wharf, and the drawbridge for the cars was lowered from the stern garage. We hurried below to see to the donkeys. Fortunately they were as anxious to disembark as we. With enormous relief we tied the three animals to the dockyard railings, near the exit. I stood guard with the children while Thomas and Andrew brought out baggage in relays. At the last minute I suggested Andrew should bring the final bale of straw ashore (the four bales of hay were all gone). Perhaps I had some inkling of impending disaster.

The dockyard railings seemed a quiet place to leave the animals while we changed money and did some essential shopping, and we took it in turns to make forays into Patras. My acquaintance with Greece was limited to a lunch in Salonica fifteen years before. The first thing that struck me about Patras, and indeed about all Greece, was its scruffiness, far more reminiscent of Turkey than of anything I had seen in Europe. Gone were the glossy glass and aluminium bars that faced the port at Ancona. In their place was a row of ramshackle cafés and restaurants with flaking wooden fronts and pavement tables covered with greasy oilcloth. I sat the children at one of these and somewhat nervously ordered three pasties which I saw displayed in a small glass case resembling an aquarium. They turned out to be stuffed with the white ewe's milk cheese known as *feta* and we munched them happily while we watched a procession of incredibly battered lorries with gaily decorated cabs going by. At first we thought they belonged to some decayed circus but we eventually realised they were the normal means of transport in Greece.

Soon wet squalls swept under the rusty tin awning of our café and drove us inside. The interior was even grizzlier than the exterior. It appeared to be filled with a job lot of furniture picked up at an auction sale, any unwanted pieces being piled to gather dust in a corner. A bulky Greek sailor with one eye sat with his back to us at the next table. For the children's sake, I hoped he would stay that way. Greek curiosity soon overcame him, however, and he turned to put us through what we were to learn was the usual catechism. As luck would have it, his good ear was on the side of his bad eye, so this grizzly socket was turned relentlessly towards us and provoked many anxious whispers from Jessica, until she was suddenly visited by an imperious call of nature. The lavatory was a sort of cupboard behind the counter. When Jessica saw it, and worse, smelt it, she started back like a frightened horse. The woman who owned the café shook a bottle of the Greek equivalent of Harpic in the air, assuring me it was clean, and finally Jessica agreed to enter on condition I held the door open. Later we discovered we could buy perfumed paper handkerchiefs for her to hold over her nose on entering these places.

When Thomas returned from the shops he was carrying a well-filled knapsack and a couple of plastic shopping-bags besides. He stopped to drink an aniseed-flavoured *ouzo* from a miniature glass beer tankard and then we set off to rejoin Andrew and the baggage, picking our way between puddles in the badly broken pavement. It was midday before we had the donkeys saddled and loaded and were lined up in front of the dockyard gate ready to go on. But this was as far as we got. A weasel-faced man in uniform, who had watched the whole laborious process from his kiosk, now stepped forward and said *"Oxi!"* (the 'x' being pronounced as the 'ch' in 'loch'). He accompanied the word with the oriental jerk of the head backwards which adds such a terrible finality to the Greek negative.

"Why can we not pass through the gate?" enquired Andrew, in what sounded like passable Greek.

"Because you have not seen the port police."

"Where are the port police?" The man pointed to the far end of the quay and Andrew and Thomas set off in that direction.

They found a policeman and showed him our Italian veterinary papers. It was not his business, it seemed, but nor was it his companion's, when he returned half an hour later. They must go to the office of the port authority. Once more they set off along the harbour front and presently found a white-uniformed officer in an upper room. With much difficulty Thomas explained to him that we did not want permission to embark our donkeys for Italy, but just to pass the dock gate into Greece. At last an English-speaking civilian arrived. Everyone had a good laugh at the misunderstanding and the port authority promised to phone at once to the gate police.

Thomas and Andrew returned with the good news, but no phone call had reached the gate police; in fact their hut seemed to have no phone. A new and more officious official now arrived and we gradually made out that there was no possibility of leaving till we had passed customs. The customs officers had gone off duty at twelve o'clock and would not be back until six.

The prospect was a dismal one. My knowledge of Mediterranean habits told me a six-hour wait would probably prove to be an eight-hour one, and eight hours is a long time to keep two small children amused. There was nothing for the donkeys to eat except the bale of bedding we had brought ashore with us, and once we were out of the dock gate there would still be a long walk ahead of us before we could get clear of the town and find grazing and somewhere to camp. I did not fancy doing this walk after dark on a busy main road. The time had obviously come for one of my scenes. Making scenes does not come easily to the English, but amateur dramatics do, and I launched myself into the role of one of the heroines of Greek tragedy I had sometimes portrayed on the stage of the Old Barn Theatre, West Hoathly. Medea, abandoned with her children by the faithless Jason, seemed a good model. I gathered the children to me and yelled (in English) that they would be mown down by a lorry in the dark if we were detained a moment longer. Striding over to the unoffending bale of straw and throwing handfuls of it on the ground, I yelled that our animals would die of starvation before nightfall, a suggestion which caused Miranda to burst into loud tears but had no effect on the gate policeman who was now in the process of locking the dock gates.

There was nothing for it but to practise oriental resignation. We divided the straw between the three animals, and the treacherous Picchio began eating his at once, with evident relish, right under the eyes of the official. Soon another squally thunder shower drove us into the vast deserted customs shed, where even the bar was closed. Two clapped-out hippies and a Greek dock-worker lay asleep on the leatherette benches and only a limping souvenir-seller stayed at his post. He gave Miranda and Jessica postcards of a defunct cruise liner at intervals during the afternoon. Thomas faithfully handed out sandwiches and finally curled up to sleep.

At six o'clock heads began to move behind the plate-glass windows of the offices. Presently the customs officer himself appeared, a heavy man, also limping, and after a decent interval we approached him in his office, displaying our now damp and stained veterinary certificate from Ancona. "Yes, yes," he said. "But the donkeys must see a doctor." Unfortunately the doctor could not be found. In half an hour he would telephone again.

After an hour it seemed the vet still could not be found, so, in desperation, for evening was coming on, we all five took up positions on the sofa in the customs officer's office, determined not to leave until we had obtained our release. Gradually we thought we were getting

Arctic conditions at the summit of the Apennines, near Monte Cucco.

The Adriatic at last. Portonovo, south of Ancona.

Miranda suffering from food poisoning north of Thermon in the Aetolian Mountains of Greece.

A Greek donkey carries a mobile haystack, near Karpenision.

his attention. There were always at least four other Greeks in the room, all talking, or rather shouting, almost the whole time, but now we had the impression it was our problem that they were shouting about. Sometimes the customs officer would rise from his desk and limp over to a pay telephone at the other side of the room to continue the animated discussion into it, while the others stood round, shouting advice and encouragement. The phone required a one-drachma coin to work it, and every so often there would be no one-drachmas left in any of their pockets. Then an astonished pause would follow, as if God had somehow intervened and there was no point in resisting further. For about five minutes no one would even try to fetch a coin.

The scene finally seemed to reach a climax of excitement, a summit over which it was necessary to pass. The actual sign that we were beyond it was when the customs officer pulled out a bunch of keys and sent someone somewhere to fetch something. Several minutes later a block of forms, numerous sheets of carbon paper, and even a woman who could have been a secretary appeared. Very slowly, with long pauses for further animated discussions, though always in a *diminuendo*, he began to fill the form out, or rather, compose it, for at the end he added several paragraphs in laboured longhand. Even then our troubles were not quite over. "Tsitty!" he cried, on seeing Thomas's passport. For some totally obscure reason it caused him a new thought. Several phone calls followed in the middle of one of which Thomas was put on to the line. An English-speaking Greek woman was at the other end. He had no idea who she was, or what he was meant to ask her, and she seemed equally in the dark. Gradually he gathered that she was the Patras agent for the *Atalante* and wanted to know whether he had a ticket for the donkeys. As the only ticket he had was for the lorry and driver, now clearly marked in English "Lorry and driver did not embark", he was not a little worried, but succeeded in creating confusion until the phone was taken from him. A long Greek conversation ensued and all seemed well.

The form was about three-quarters completed when the vet arrived. He was a dapper little man in a chocolate-coloured suit and spoke fluent Italian. He carefully read the Italian form, made out by the provincial vet at Ancona, and handed it back to me. He pointed out that, although the form declared that there had been no case of *morbo* (African horse sickness) in Ancona for six months, it omitted actually to mention that the animals had been inoculated against it. It was a new experience to have lies fed to me so straightforwardly to tell. "What an oversight!" I cried. "Of course the provincial vet should have given me a written record of the injections." Honour was satisfied and we led the vet out to examine the animals.

I

This was the fourth veterinary examination Hannibal and Hamilcar had undergone since they had come into our possession. The vet at Santiago had not seen them at all but had signed the form in his office; the Anglo-Italian vet at Arezzo had looked up their noses until Hamilcar tried to kick him, and then escaped down the terrace with rather undignified haste; the provincial vet at Ancona had merely whistled at them. Our Greek vet seemed solely anxious to ascertain that they were truly without testicles. Once he had reassured himself on this point, all was well. Handshaking and general bonhomie followed. It was as if we had taken part in a slightly exhausting dramatic performance and could now relax in the happy knowledge that we had all played our parts well.

CHAPTER 44

A night of horror

It was eight thirty at night by the time we were released into Patras, and we made all haste to get out of it, following the main road along the waterfront. Our laden beasts caused some good-humoured merriment among the idlers by the railway line, and there were cries of 'Bravo!' as we passed.

Once we were clear of the town we began to see the mountains of Aetolia on the other side of the Gulf of Corinth. They were etched in purple against a fiery sunset and seemed so close that we could almost touch them across the slate-coloured sea. But in fact the narrowest point of the straits was at Rion, a few kilometres west, where there was a ferry. Opposite the newly built Hotel Delphini we found a patch of grass inhabited only by the wooden skeletons of a pair of half-built rowing boats. Here we tethered the donkeys to fluorescent lamp standards, or rather Thomas and Andrew did. Eight hours in the customs shed had left me fit to do nothing but creep on to the rocks and make severe inroads on a bottle of *retsina*. The sea boomed and splashed in the rock crevices under my feet and a blazing tower of light in the middle of the bay was the *Atalante* moving out to sea again. A dark mound against the western sky hid Missolonghi, the dusty garrison town where Byron died. But our way lay over the mountains to the north.

Our plan now was to cross the country diagonally, from Patras in

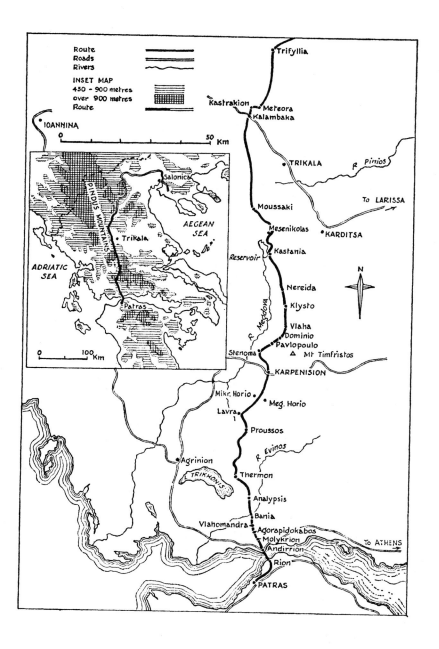

the south-west to the extreme north-east, following in the footsteps
of Edward Lear. Our enforced landing at Patras (instead of at Igoumenitsa) had set us way off the crusader route we had hoped to follow. Lear in any case seemed an appropriate companion on a journey
which we planned to make more lighthearted than the previous summer's. We had enjoyed his *Journals of a Landscape Painter in Greece
and Albania* during the winter and felt we could have no better companion. He was dear to all of us, for Miranda frequently recited his
'Self Portrait' which consists of eight verses, of which the second is
typical:

> His mind is concrete and fastidious
> His nose is remarkably big
> His visage is more or less hideous
> His beard it resembles a wig

Lear's route in 1848 and 1849 touched our own at many points,
notably Trikala, Meteora, Edessa and Salonica, and we felt even
closer to him in spirit since he, too, frequently travelled on foot (to
avoid the discomfort of a Turkish saddle). He also had trouble with
his pack, which often parted company with the sumpter mule, until he
hit upon the idea of "two brobdignagian saddle bags . . . united by a
cord". Like us, he gathered food at the wayside, and once grazed on
watercress. The amazed natives, assuming him to be omnivorous, brought
him thistles and grasshoppers to see what he would do with *them*.

Unlike us, however, Lear always carried a large supply of quinine
pills — "rather leave all behind than this" — for he suffered from
bouts of malaria. His heroism in travelling ten hours a day under constant threat of fever, passes belief. Added to this he rose daily at five
o'clock to sketch, and started work again with his pencil as soon as he
reached his destination. Relentlessly in pursuit of the picturesque,
he was amassing material for the twenty lithographs that eventually
illustrated his book.

It was Byzantine rather than Classical Greece that attracted Lear,
and not a single ruined temple or amphitheatre appears in these lithographs. Instead, they portray walled and towered towns perched
dizzily on cliff tops or reflected in mountain lakes. We also were in
flight from classical ruins, now seriously affected by what our guide-
book described as 'tourist blight'. Classical Greece ended at Naupaktos, according to the geographer Pausanias, and Naupaktos, we were
satisfied to discover, lay well to the east of our intended route. Darkness had fallen on the Gulf of Corinth by the time Thomas shouted
from the camp-fire that supper was ready. I went to collect the children
who were playing Swallows and Amazons in an abandoned fishing
boat, and together we watched the receding pinpoint of light which the

Atalante had now become. Suddenly the light went out. She was over the horizon.

"Goodbye, sweet *Atalante*," called Jessica.

"Take my love to Don Rodrigo," whispered Miranda.

The following morning Thomas and I took the bus back to Patras. Our experience in the customs shed had seriously alarmed me. I had visions of hours of our time in Greece being spent in interrogations by uniformed men whose language we spoke inadequately. Lear had carried a *boyourldi* from the sultan, although, most of the guards being illiterate, he found that "a bill from Mrs. Dunsford's hotel at Malta" often did as well. Our *boyourldi*, I decided, must be an interview in the local paper, which would explain, in Greek, who we were and what we were doing.

Our first move on arriving in Patras was to buy a copy of the local *ephemera* (newspaper), which was called *Peloponnese* and had its address conveniently printed at the top of the front page. Armed with this, we accosted a series of passers-by, pointed to the address, and followed their directions. The offices of *Peloponnese* were in an obscure part of the town, and our journey took us at one stage through the city's shambles. In 1848, when Lear had encountered one of these quarters devoted to butchery, he had found "dogs, blood and carcasses filling up the whole street . . . rather revolting". The modern shambles were not much better. Whole carcasses hung from the ceilings of the stalls and their blood-smeared owners chopped at them on circular chopping blocks. The stench was appalling but Thomas bravely enquired the price of a sheep's liver which was dangling from its owner's rib cage. When the butcher said we could only have the liver if we took portions of lungs, windpipe, kidney and spleen as well, even Thomas retired defeated. This odd method of selling offal turned out to be universal in Greece.

At last we reached a small house in a back street from which the clatter of printing-presses was coming. Convinced that someone working on *Peloponnese* would speak English, I strode boldly in, only to discover that no one did. The nervous young man in the downstairs office eventually got the impression that I was trying to *sell* him two donkeys. Fortunately at this moment the editor himself appeared, a lively old man who spoke French, and suddenly we were wafted to an upper room and plied with coffee and iced water brought in on a hanging brass tray. Evidently George Soutsos considered us a scoop, and grew increasingly excited as he dictated our story, in Greek, to a secretary, through the clatter of the press across the landing. When I suggested that Mr. Soutsos might like to take a photograph he looked slightly shaken, but quickly recovered himself, and rang the local studio, demanding "a very fine picture at two o'clock". It was only when we looked inside our copy of *Peloponnese* on leaving the building that we discovered there was not a single photograph in it.

In spite of a rainstorm, a smartly dressed photographer arrived at our camp at two o'clock precisely, and three days later not one but two pictures of us and our menagerie appeared in *Peloponnese*.

As soon as the photographer was gone we took down the tent and set off for the ferry at Rion, which involved an unpleasant walk along the main road, one of very few such walks during the whole of our time in Greece. Poor Miranda had to go on foot, as we still did not trust Picchio in heavy traffic. We would have followed the quiet track beside the railway line had not the crossing-keeper's wife intervened with a broom.

Rion consisted mostly of acres of parking space, but was redeemed by the ruins of the fifteenth-century Castle of Morea built by Sultan Bayazit. The fort at Andirrion on the other side, known as the Castle of Roumeli, was its twin. The rest of our journey would lie in Roumeli. There was little delay at Rion, for three ex-landing craft plied continuously, charging seven drachmas a trip. The donkeys went on board without hesitation and when Picchio demurred a sailor grabbed his tail and pulled him on board crabwise, his hooves slipping alarmingly on the metal plates of the deck. The crossing was all too short, for 'the little Dardanelles' are less than two kilometres across. Ahead of us we could see the massive bulk of an extinct volcano which is said now to erupt under the sea. We sniffed eagerly for sulphur and wished we could put our hands into the water to detect the warm patch reported by fishermen. More of our time, however, was devoted to eating nougat sandwiched between ice-cream wafers, and making use of the ship's conveniences.

There was another unpleasant stretch of main road on the Andirrion side, but after a couple of kilometres Miranda ran a splinter under her toe nail, and, although she bore the pain heroically, we had to stop. Through the olive trees, we could see a half-built concrete factory (we discovered later that it was destined for the manufacture of stockings). Here we camped, comforting ourselves with the reflection that at least the piles of sand would provide entertainment for the children. We had hardly tethered the donkeys before a furious old woman, swathed head and all in black, rushed cackling from the undergrowth and started untying Picchio and dragging him away. It seemed he was tied too close to her barley, although there was in fact what in Greece passes for a fence between. Once Picchio had been moved her mood changed and she even showed us how to draw water from the well. We found this approach quite common among Greeks — initial (and understandable) fury followed by kindness.

Our troubles, however, were not over. We had just finished supper when ten centimetres of rain fell with such violence that Thomas, who was in the factory at the time, was stranded there for half an hour. By the time it eased off it had deposited an ankle-deep puddle at the door of our tent. It was unfortunate that the summer, which was to beat all British records for heat, should also break Greek records for wetness. Unable to face the lake at the door of the tent, I spent a frightening night alone in the factory where a deafening waterfall was descending from the upper storey and forming a lake on the concrete floor which I hoped would not reach my sleeping-bag. Even Lear, in the rotting Khan at Tirana (where a whirling dervish whirled all night in the room next door) could not have been more uncomfortable, I reflected, as a Mogadon tablet carried me away on waves of artificially induced unconsciousness.

CHAPTER 45

How Hamilcar fell in love at Analypsis

On June 9th we discovered that Greece was our Nirvana. Nowhere in Europe had we found a country so perfectly adapted to travelling on foot, or peasants so welcoming to the wayfarer. As soon as we turned inland from the stocking factory and took the dirt road leading to Agorapidokabos, we were in donkey land. Mounted shepherds passed us sitting sideways on diminutive beasts. Hannibal, carried away with emotion at the sight of creatures so like himself, made a blundering lunge towards a little grey jackass which hopped sideways to avoid him. The patriarch aloft seemed quite unperturbed by these manœuvres. He sat on the universal Greek wooden saddle which reached halfway up his animal's neck, and guided it only with a halter rope and a shepherd's crook.

Our road climbed steadily through a wilderness of dark arbutus bushes. As we left the first green range behind, the grey hump of the volcano began to peer over its top at us, as if curious to know where we were going. Miranda, now riding Picchio who was at his best going uphill on a quiet country road, suddenly turned in the saddle. "Oh, look!" she cried. "The sea!" Sure enough, inverted triangles of deep blue were appearing between the hills behind us. As we rose higher we could see the white dots on the margin of the bay that were Patras. Then we sank into the next valley and it disappeared. We were not to see blue water again until the end of our journey. We were locked in the mountains of Roumeli which were to hold us imprisoned for many weeks.

On the outskirts of Molykrion was a shrine marking the confines of the village. There are literally thousands of these in Greece, and we later learned that those in open country have been put there by motorists who have survived accidents at these points. The shrine at Molykrion consisted of a glass case supported by a frame of blue-painted metal. Crowded inside it were three ikons, one representing the Virgin, one St. George, and the third a grey-bearded Elijah. Jessica wanted to know why this holy trio had been supplied with fizzy drinks, but in fact the Coca-Cola bottles that cluttered the shrine held oil for the lamps, lit every evening by a pious village crone.

Molykrion, like so many Greek villages, seemed to consist of a dusty open space where three cafés, selling an identical collection of groceries and hardware, competed amicably for trade. Already, at half-past eight in the morning, men in black hats were sitting outside these at wooden tables, and a friendly woman who, like many younger Greeks, had worked in Germany, came out with rush-seated chairs for us. We found that a breakfast of Greek coffee, hard-boiled eggs and bread was well within our means.

We had been warned that Agorapidokabos, the village where we planned to spend the night, was half-abandoned, and we soon discovered that the road was in a similar condition. Winter rains had taken deep bites out of it, leaving barely space for a car to pass. Soon we were walking along the side of a deep and beautiful gorge, the stream at the bottom hidden by giant plane trees. The sides of the gorge were covered with the universal arbutus, but every now and again a pink oleander bush burst into flames among them.

After a stiff climb we reached a ford where the road definitely ceased to be carriageable. A blue car, the only car of the day, was parked under the trees beside it, and beyond was the stony track to Agorapidokabos. Halfway up it Hannibal shied at what he took to be a moving stone. It was an enormous Greek tortoise (*Testudo Graeca*), with a beautifully marked shell the colour of honey and plain chocolate. Miranda was off Picchio before I could stop him, lifting the massive object with cries of joy. Jessica was soon by her side, peering raptly into its black and beady eye.

"Oh, please let us keep him!" they begged in chorus. Thomas agreed that it should be theirs for the night and Rodrigo (for such was his name) found a slippery purchase on Hannibal's ridged saddle, between the saddlebags.

Agorapidokabos had no village street or shop, and its eight square stone houses stood in an orchard. They had rickety wooden balconies and lace curtains at the windows. Normally during the day even the inhabited ones were empty, for the women went out with the sheep at dawn and did not come back until sunset. We were lucky, however, and found one old woman directing the picking of cherries. She was swathed in black like the married peasant women of all ages. Eventually two young men jumped from the tree, loaded with plastic bags. They looked incongruous in their tight city trousers and printed T-shirts. They were evidently the owners of the solitary blue car and were probably combining a visit to *Mama* with a raid on her fruit trees. They cut a branch red with cherries for each of the children, and gave us permission to camp near the stream, where there was good grazing.

It would be impossible to describe all our beautiful camp sites in Greece, but the one at Agorapidokabos was surely among the loveliest. It was at a point where the stream, shaded with plane trees, took a sharp bend, exposing a wide gravel beach. Here the children built a harbour representing Ancona, from which Rodrigo in one of our green washing-up bowls embarked on a hazardous voyage to Patras. Patras was a crevice in the rock opposite, from which a spring emerged. Wild white roses cascaded in profusion down the face of the rock.

We were to see many such streams in Greece, but perhaps this one made the deepest impression because, after Italy, we were so amazed to find a river-bed unscarred by a single piece of rubbish. The variety of unknown birds, too, was wonderful after Italy, and for the first time in my life I actually saw, and not merely heard, frogs croaking. I was on my way to water the donkeys when a harsh rattling sound began in the middle of the stream. A bright green frog was sitting on a stone, and every time he rattled, a pair of white balloons the size of peas appeared at the sides of his head. He was answered by another frog on a stone across the stream and, at an unseen signal, both frogs plunged into the water and clasped each other in a tight embrace, the one underneath occasionally giving a violent heave which turned their white bellies upwards.

That evening a shepherd visited our camp. We were embarrassed to discover that it was on his land we were camping, but he took it in good part. Greeks, we discovered, had a habit of giving us permission to camp on their neighbour's land. Later he returned with a bottle of resinated wine the colour of sherry. It was the strongest and fruitiest we had ever drunk. He told us that the region was fast becoming depopulated and people were going to Athens. "Life is too hard here," he said. "Too much work, too little money."

Very little of this conversation would have been comprehensible to us but for the invaluable Andrew, our dragoman. Without him we might, like the unfortunate Lear, have been reduced to imitating steamers and railway engines for the benefit of our hosts. "For my sins," Lear wrote, "this imitation became fearfully popular, and I had to repeat 'Squish-squash, tik-tok' till I was heartily tired." Andrew's Greek — originally ingested subliminally from a tape while he meditated — had made amazing progress during the few days we had been in Greece. His method now was to jot down unknown words on the palm of his hand as they occurred in conversation and to look them up in a dictionary when we reached camp.

On the morning of our departure there was a scream of excitement from Miranda. Rodrigo had had a ten-centimetre-long baby (introduced secretly into his washing-up bowl by Thomas). Later, when Miranda found white eggshells beside a small scrape in a bank, she realised that tortoises lay eggs, and that Thomas had been deceiving her, but she forgave him, as she forgives him everything. There was a tearful parting with the tortoise as we forded the stream once more, and Rodrigo had his shell kissed warmly.

Our way lay back along the path we had taken, for Agorapidokabos was a dead end. After a kilometre we came upon a sign which read *pros ote*. This, rather worryingly, meant 'towards sometimes' in Andrew's lexicon. Trying to persuade ourselves that it was the equivalent of the French *Toutes Directions*, we started to climb, glad of the shade the mountains cast between us and the rising sun, and enjoying the view of the green chequered plateau of Agorapidokabos below us. After an hour we were overtaken by a man riding a motorbike with a zeppelin-shaped sidecar from the 1920s. There was a sleek black-and-tan hunting dog in the sidecar, and the whole contraption was not going much faster than we were. Half an hour later we reached a post-office radio tower and the end of the road. We realised that OTE is the Greek equivalent of GPO, and that the man on the motorbike was the post-office employee in charge of the installation.

This was not the only time that our lack of maps caused us to stray. Large-scale maps (1/200,000) are not available to the public in Greece. The two maps we had bought in Patras seldom agreed about the exact location of any village. In the end we found it best to ask at one village for the next, and to keep asking all the way. Signposts to the larger places were both in Latin and Greek script, in obedience to a government decree, but those to smaller ones, where they existed, ignored the decree.

After another two hours of scrambling up rough roads we came upon several large white tents looking like pre-war government issue and reminding us of those used by District Officers in Africa on tours of inspection. Beyond them was Vlahomandra, a strange village where a mere half-dozen houses seemed to be scattered over a wide plateau. We asked a sad-faced woman at a half-built house if there was a shop, for we were out of food. There was none. We asked the way to Bania. She did not know it, and called to an old man who was building a chicken house in the garden. When he approached us we saw that he was a little smiling priest, with a long grey beard and a ragged cassock of blue cotton. He did not come much above Andrew's waist. He told us that every house in the village had been destroyed by terrible earthquakes in the previous summer. Before that there had been 200 inhabitants. He insisted on bringing three glasses of *ouzo* out for us on a tray before leading us to the outskirts of the village, and would not let us go till Andrew had promised to write to him.

As we rounded the corner by the rebuilt church we saw, far below, the River Evinos winding its way towards the Gulf of Corinth through its wide stony bed. "Bania is down by the bridge," said the old priest. It looked a long way, but we would get nothing to eat until we reached it.

On the way down the hill we passed several ruined houses, but more often the debris had been removed and the tiles neatly stacked to await rebuilding. An old woman sat at the door of a tent, a cloud of wool held on a wooden trident above her head and a wooden spindle, on to which the coarse thread was wound, spinning at her knee. Inside the tent we caught a glimpse of a bed with a brightly patterned blanket and a rush-seated chair.

It was two o'clock by the time we reached Bania, and there was little enough left of it when we got there: just three shops and three tents clustered at the approach to a temporary wooden bridge. We could tell that one of the shops was owned by a butcher, for a reversed kidskin was hanging on a frame outside. Passing under this, we subsided, hot and weary, at a table. As we sucked ice-cold lemonade through straws, our eyes travelled along the shelves of ancient fly-blown goods. Rows of large brightly-coloured plastic bottles stood on a high shelf, from which they looked as if they would never descend, and a bunch of the plastic shoes worn by peasant women hung from a hook, thickly coated in dust. In the end, surprisingly, we found all that we needed, with the exception of candles, which seemed to be unobtainable in Greece. They only had the orange tapers which are burned by the sack-load before ikons in the churches.

We were still gathering strength when the shopkeeper's three daughters, in sugar-bag-blue pinafores and white collars, returned from school. They immediately went up to their father and kissed his hand. Miranda's eyes widened as she sucked a spoonful of *vanili* (a sticky nougat served in a glass of water). "I'd like to kiss Daddy's hand," she said.

"I wouldn't," said Jessica. "It smells of onions and donkey."

The school girls were closely followed by an elderly man with broken glasses and a three days' growth of grey bristles, who drank several *ouzos* in quick succession. He turned out to be the *proithero*, or head man of the village, and, after directing us to a camp-site by the river, he suggested we should return in the evening to drink with him. That night as we sat at one of the three lighted cafés, with children and fireflies hovering in the dark street, it was hard to believe that we were surrounded by vast tracts of empty countryside. Two saddled donkeys stood under a plane tree, a woman lit the lamp in the shrine, and a giant toad hopped up the gutter as we sipped our *ouzos* and the *proithero* told us his sad tale. He and his fellow-villagers had lived in tents for almost a year now, ignored by the government. "They gave us tents, and then they forgot about us." We promised to put his case to someone in authority, although there seemed little chance that we could.

The next morning our way lay across the bridge. There was another range to climb before we reached the fabled lake of Trikhonis with its pelicans, but from Analypsis, where we camped, we had a superb view of it far below, lit by a molten sun and flanked by mountains turning purple before a thunderstorm.

It was against this romantic backdrop that Hamilcar fell in love. We had never thought of Hamilcar as a lover. Picchio, yes, with his assertive nature, even Hannibal with his youth and impetuousness, but not the elderly Hamilcar, the uncomplaining drudge for so many years of a gypsy caravan. Yet even he was not proof against the charms of a minuscule jenny tethered 100 metres from our tent. She bore a marked resemblance to himself, and we immediately named her Minerva. Hungry though he was, Hamilcar could not touch his food for looking at her. As the thunderstorm broke he lifted his muzzle to the sky and gave vent to the saddest of all his many melancholy brays.

There was also a human thunderstorm to be weathered at Analypsis (which means Ascension in Greek). We had just tethered the donkeys on the verge when a furious and filthy old woman with plaits tied round her black headscarf arrived and started scolding as only Greek peasant women can scold, insisting that our *zoa* were eating her grass. She shooed me and the offending beasts further up the path to eat somebody else's. We didn't recognise her when she came back an hour later with a bag of cherries for the children.

The Greek determination to give reached a high point at Ascension. Our track was on the donkey highway back to the village from the fields, and a constant succession of giggling milkmaids went by on donkeys. One poured milk from her flat-sided churn into our saucepan, another gave us half a loaf of bread left over from her lunch, two more gave us nearly a kilo of *feta* cheese. The men would accept cigarettes, but the only recompense we could think of for the women was to take their photographs, a process which sent them into peals of delighted laughter.

"I wish *we* could give things to people," said Miranda. "But there aren't any gypsies in England." I attempted a little sermon about charity to one's neighbour, but her real longing, I knew, was to rush out of Bow Cottage, her arms filled with good things for tattered wayfarers passing down North Lane, West Hoathly.

CHAPTER 46

Food poisoning

We were never to reach the fabled lake of Trikhonis with its flotillas of white pelicans, for our map had once more misled us. Thermon turned out not to be on the lake, but ten kilometres from it. Here we visited the only classical ruin of the whole trip, ancient Thermon, which lies some distance from the modern town. It was once the religious and administrative capital of Aetolia, a federation of mountain tribes. Assemblies of all the citizens gathered there periodically to make laws, stayed a few days, sacrificing to Apollo, and then returned to their mountain fastnesses, whose walls and towers still top many Aetolian peaks. The ruins of Thermon are flat and unimpressive on the dusty unshaded plain. Most important is the base of the temple of Apollo, unusually long and narrow, with five columns along the front and fifteen down each side. The city was sacked in 218 B.C. by Philip II of Macedonia, who gathered and destroyed there 2,000 works of sculpture.

Once more camping near a town proved unsatisfactory. There was a patch of flat ground behind Thermon's hill-top church, but we were by no means the first to discover it. Depressed donkeys picked at the shaven grass and flies from an adjacent dump descended in their legions. We were consoled by three young sisters we met when taking the donkeys down to the town for water. They helped us to recover Picchio, who had suddenly bolted down the main road, nearly upending a priest with flowing black beard and robes; then they insisted on taking us to their spotless bungalow to meet their mother, who sat us down with much ceremony in the front parlour. The room was sparsely furnished, but a low coffee table in the centre made up for all other deficiencies. There was not a square centimetre of its surface that was not covered with lace mats, flower-painted ash trays, iridescent vases and strings of giant wooden beads with tassels hanging from them. The Greeks have a passion for knick-knacks. Soon two plates of sticky cakes arrived from the kitchen, together with several little dishes of lumpy marmalade to be eaten with spoons, and a saucer each of Turkish Delight, which the Greeks call *loukoum*. Jessica confessed afterwards that she thought it tasted of lipstick, but we found it much superior to English imitations, for under the coating of white powder was a crystalline crust which you bit through before reaching the sticky pink interior.

From Thermon we walked ten kilometres north along the side of a steep gorge following a road which was, unbelievably, a bus route. It was made of soft red earth with piles of gravel which forced pedestrians close to the outside edge. To keep Miranda's mind off the precipice, I elaborated on one of her favourite themes, the siege of West Penwith. In this fantasy, revolution has broken out in London and all our relations have migrated to her grandfather's farm in Cornwall and set about fortifying it in the intervals of weaving cloth and raising rabbits. During the second summer of our journey both children were obsessed with the idea of getting all the family together in one place. They would also listen endlessly to forecast descriptions of Jessica's first day at school, dwelling lovingly on every detail of her new uniform, and the names of her imaginary classmates.

Where the road descended to a bridge, we saw one of the prettiest sights imaginable. A young woman in black with three children was hanging up handwoven blankets under plane trees by a waterfall. The blankets were of brilliant colours, pink, purple, orange, red and green. In the background was an old stone watermill. Our children were soon knee deep in the swift mountain river. The woman told us she combined the professions of washerwoman and miller. If she diverted the water one way it fell into a tub of churning water in which she rinsed the blankets; if she diverted it the other way, it turned a mill wheel. Inside the shed she tipped maize into a wooden hopper and it trickled out from beneath a revolving stone to form a pyramid of golden dust. The bread made from this flour was yellow and crumbled like cake.

The mill seemed a perfect place for a three-day stay while I took the bus into Athens. There were three reasons for my visit: I had maps to search for, a tooth to be filled and a promise to keep. The promise I had made to Helen Vlakos eight years earlier in London. At that time Mrs. Vlakos, the editor of the Greek newspaper *Kathemerini*, was in exile. I had been impressed by her personality at a lecture and had vowed to her that I would not visit Greece till democracy was restored, and that when I did I would also visit her.

That evening things started to go wrong. Miranda, who had eaten little lunch, refused *halva* at teatime, which was most unusual. *Halva* is a sweet compounded of crushed sesame seeds and honey, and is both delicious and sustaining. Thomas was lining us up for photographs for Helen Vlakos's paper when Miranda complained of pain in her stomach. By the time he had taken six shots she was doubled up, her face so pale that every freckle showed in 3-D. As Thomas took the last exposure she made a dash for the tent and curled up moaning. Five minutes later she was violently sick all over her sleeping-bag.

"I can't believe it's really happening," said Jessica, watching her with wide dark eyes. Half an hour later her turn came. Her cheeks turned the colour of *feta* and her eyes receded into caves in her face. Soon there did not seem to be a clean rag left in the whole camp and I longed for home, an airing cupboard full of towels, and a washing-machine. At this stage the miller's wife came to our rescue, insisting that the children should be laid on two of her tufted rugs and covered by a third. Deeply cocooned in scarlet wool they looked up at her, smiling wanly. She bent over them tenderly, apologising for not having a lemon, a sovereign remedy it seemed against queasiness. In ten minutes they were asleep.

But it was an uneasy night. The woman had said the children could sleep on an iron bed in the watermill, but in the end I slept, or rather lay there, leaving them the tent, with Thomas lying across the foot in case of emergencies. At the end of my shed the mill-stream roared and, as the night passed, moonlight crept over my face. My thoughts ran to and fro inside my head like a squirrel in a cage. Supposing the children were taken violently ill in the night? There was no way to get a doctor in a place without a telephone or passing traffic. People could die of food poisoning.

In the morning the children were far from dead and the only disaster was that I nearly missed my bus, which arrived early. Andrew had to sprint ahead and hold it for me while I stuffed a few essentials into a knapsack. A ride in a Greek country bus is a perfect antidote to worry, for the heat and excitement drive all other thoughts from one's head. Above the incessant chatter of fellow-passengers, music streams continuously from a pair of loudspeakers on either side of the driver's head.

Greek bus drivers decorate their cabs just as they decorate their horses, and indeed the brightly coloured baubles that dangle above their heads are bought from saddlers' shops. Holy pictures, bathing beauties, cut-out butterflies and family groups are pasted above the windscreen and every time the bus takes a corner twenty silk tassels sway in unison from the roof. These corners also have unfortunate effects on the peasant women's stomachs. The old lady next to me was of a pious turn of mind and crossed herself continuously (from right to left, in the Orthodox manner) whenever we passed a church. After the twentieth bend, however, her head disappeared into a plastic bag (supplied by the conductor) and churches passed unheeded until she got off at Agrinion, on the lake. Her place was taken by a little white-haired man who droned oriental folk-songs to himself

The petrol stations and hamburger joints at the approach to Athens were depressingly reminiscent of Indianapolis, and the city itself seemed to be a modern metropolis into which the Parthenon, on the raft of the Acropolis, had drifted by mistake. But Helen Vlakos did not disappoint me. Her palatial office was on the fifth floor of the *Kathemerini* building, filled with antique furniture and lined with books and photographs of herself shaking hands with the famous. She sat serenely at a mahogany desk, elegant and aquiline in a black-and-white silk dress, her dark eyes watchful behind thick lenses, reminding me of the benevolent principal of a woman's college. Between constant phone calls I had to prove myself worthy of admission. I must have gained at least a minor exhibition for, before she swept out for a conference with her editorial staff (six heavy men in suits) she commissioned an article about our journey. "I want 2,000 words by tomorrow," she said. "And don't pull any punches. This is a serious political paper." I hurried off, proud to be no longer one of the tourist herd, but working for a Greek newspaper, and a famous one. It was Mrs. Vlakos's father, a former editor, who printed the historic letter of defiance against the Nazis in 1940.

I wrote half the night, completed the piece early in the morning, and typed it on an office typewriter before lunch. That evening I presented myself before Mrs. Vlakos once more to hear her comments. She had not had time to read the piece and was engaged in entertaining an elderly English woman, Miss T., who had just flown in from London to do a job for her. Miss T. was being allowed her ritual ten minutes of editorial time and in this I was allowed to share. I remarked on a photograph of cats on the desk and Mrs. Vlakos said, with an expansive gesture, "I adore all animals, even elephants." Her personal assistant was sent to fetch a new batch of kittens from the caretaker's flat, and with these she toyed for a few minutes until the six men once again arrived to claim her. Our time was up, and we were bowed from the presence. But Mrs. Vlakos treated me honourably, printing my article in full. I was particularly pleased about this, as it contained a plea for the earthquake victims of Vlahomandra and Bania.

The bus back only went as far as Thermon, and there I set about spending my journalistic earnings on good things for my nomadic family. In this I was assisted by the resident 'American'. Almost every Greek village has an 'American', for such is the poverty of the country that there are as many Greeks living abroad as at home. Kostas Stoumbas had driven a taxi in New York for twenty-eight years and he looked like one of those bleached and wrinkled senior citizens in panama hats one can see on any park bench in the United States. Now he had come home to pass his last days in the cafés of his home town. What was sad about him and about so many of his kind was his small knowledge of English, which did not extend beyond a few dozen set phrases and routine wisecracks. For half a lifetime he must have lived in a tightly sealed ghetto, only emerging to earn his living.

While I bought food for the family and *loukoum* for the washerwoman's children, Kostas engaged a taxi and went to forage for hay. I knew grazing must be growing scarce after a three-day camp. As the taxi turned off the bridge at the bottom of our gorge the children ran barefoot from the river to meet me. "I've made a new friend!" shouted Miranda. "She's called Aglaia and she dances all the time." "And I helped the lady to do the washing in the river," Jessica called breathlessly, as she caught up. "Please let's stay here," they pleaded.

CHAPTER 47

Holy water and a tartan rug

There was a steep drag uphill next morning to the timber-line, and even then the road continued to climb under tall pine trees, where bare rocky peaks towered above us. The sun was reaching its zenith when the way ahead appeared to be blocked by a high bank of earth. A soldier mounted on a clattering bulldozer (roadwork in Greece seems to be largely undertaken by the army) was shouting something at us, but Thomas relentlessly drove Hannibal ahead, sinking up to the knees in loose red soil, and was soon out of sight. Almost at the same moment, we rounded a bend and came upon an improbable café under the pine trees, apparently in imminent danger of being scooped up by several road-making monsters that circled in front of it. Thankfully I sank on to a rush-bottomed chair and gasped for *limonada poli krio*. An hour later we came upon Thomas, sitting at the top of the pass, smiling peacefully at the view, the tent already erected. It was a view worth smiling at. The land fell away dramatically on either side only to rise equally steeply across the valley. In a natural amphitheatre a few green terraces had been carved out and the stone houses of the men who farmed them clung perilously to the hillside. As the sun set, several herds of goats passed through our camp on their way back to the village. They paused to stand on their hind legs and nibble at the tops of bushes.

The next day we were rewarded with an easy walk downhill all the way to Proussos. Our map marked a monastery there and we decided to rely on monastic charity for a camp-site, for we were once more above a deep gorge without level ground. Sure enough, just beyond the village, a steeply descending side-road revealed a barrack-like building crouching on a narrow shelf, its back pushed up against a wall of rock, its skirts drawn up to avoid a sickening precipice beneath. Far below, shrouded in trees, ran the Proussiotikos stream. It was a place of supreme beauty where one could imagine a pagan temple might once have stood.

Our thoughts, however, were centred on flat land for our tent and grazing for our donkeys. A shady terrace half-way to the monastery seemed to offer both. Andrew volunteered to go to the monks to ask permission to camp there and I accompanied him to add the respectability of age to the mission. I need not have bothered. I was promptly requested to leave as I was wearing trousers. There was no lack of warmth in the welcome the guest-master accorded to Andrew, however. He not only gave him permission to camp but also later paid us a visit. He was a slender young man wearing the beard, black soutane and tall round hat of an orthodox priest. It appeared that we had blundered upon one of the main centres of pilgrimage in Greece. In the church was preserved a miraculous ikon of the Virgin supposed to have been painted by St. Luke.

The next day was Sunday and a strange sound like African tom-toms came from the direction of the monastery. A monk was beating a long wooden stick, known as a *semantron*, with a hammer, to summon people to Divine Liturgy. Peasants in their best clothes were hurrying up the rock path below our camp.

"I wish I could go," I said.

"Wrap a rug round yourself," said Thomas. "I'll come."

Our tartan travelling rug had spent a year under Hannibal's saddle and was now not only dirty but full of holes. On the other hand our appearance must already be so strange to the natives that a slight additional eccentricity would hardly make much difference. Andrew and Thomas arranged the thing round me with the aid of some giant nappy pins.

"Don't worry, Mummy," said Miranda. "I'll stand in front if anyone looks at you." She had changed into her flounced tartan pinafore and looked as demure as a child out of an E. Nesbit book.

By the time our little procession reached the church, there was no room inside, for this was not the main church of the monastery but a small domed chapel on a promontory opposite. We could hear the priest intoning within and after half an hour an acolyte, carrying an ikon wreathed in flowers, came and stood at the door. As the congregation of old women filed out, each bowed three times in front of it, touching the ground with her fingertips, and kissed the hands of the Virgin and Child. At the other side of the door stood another acolyte holding a great bowl of what looked like stewed white currants which he was spooning into the cupped hands of the congregation. A friendly woman pushed the three of us forward, indicating that we should have our share. It turned out to be a delicious concoction of boiled wheat, black currants, pomegranate seeds and cinnamon.

"Poor Jessie," said Miranda triumphantly, as she buried her nose in it. "What she's missing!" We later learnt that we had been eating a traditional dish known as *kolyva*, offered us by a man, who had died forty days earlier, in the hope that we would forgive him any grudges we bore him.

Already a baptism party was pushing its way into the chapel. A baby called Basil had been brought overnight in a hired coach, together with a complete christening party of relations, and his godmother, who spoke English, invited us to attend. We followed her into the chapel which was not much larger than a jewel casket and densely painted with bloodthirsty murals in red and gold. Friends and relations were pressed up against these richly frescoed walls, hardly leaving room for the ancient priest, whose bare head was decorated with a neatly pinned bun at the back. He was intoning prayers beside a font that resembled a giant copper chalice. Basil entered in the arms of his godmother, crying lustily. He was a sturdy boy of ten months with golden curls, and his baptism had, perhaps mistakenly, been delayed because the monastery is inaccessible in the winter.

With the aid of a candle which he held in one hand, the priest read from a small book whose pages were translucent with the wax of previous baptisms. The godmother, struggling to restrain her godson, made promises on his behalf and blew into the air three times, symbolically spitting in the face of the devil. Meanwhile saucepans of hot water were being tipped into the font, alternating with yellow plastic jerricans of cold. The old priest rolled up the sleeves of his black soutane, placed his spectacles on a window ledge, and tied a plastic shower curtain decorated with goldfish round his waist. He began to stir the water in the font vigorously and Basil suddenly appeared stark naked, looking like a cherub from a Raphael nativity. Miranda's green eyes grew round under her cap of golden hair.

"I think they're going to put him in!" she whispered. The same idea had occurred to Basil. For a moment his crying ceased. Some faint memory of bath-time stirred at the back of his mind and he stretched out his arms to the steaming font. But only for a moment. In his heart he knew that, for the first time in his life, his comfort and convenience were not even secondary considerations. How right he was! While the priest held him, a half-litre bottle of olive oil was poured into his godmother's cupped hands and promptly tipped over his head. Oil streamed over his eyes, down his nose and into his mouth. He turned purple with rage and I thought he would choke. Everyone was talking now and the priest was shouting instructions while keeping a firm grip on Basil, whom he proceeded to drive up to his neck into the water. Basil's screams rose to a high-pitched screech as he attempted to claw his way out, but to no avail. He was destined for two more dowsings before the priest raised him triumphantly above his head to face the altar. It was an impressive moment. Streaming with oil and water, and yelling as if his lungs must burst, the naked baby was declared born again, this time into an Eternal Kingdom. On the way out everyone was given a bag of sugared almonds, a plaster of Paris statuette and a cake. Basil, however, clothed in white, was past caring.

The road to Karpenision ran high along the sides of the gorge of the Proussiotikos. It had been built only a few years earlier, and was almost immediately destroyed by a landslide which buried the village of Mikro Khorio. Before the road was built, Karpenision could only be reached by a mule-track that took the route of the present road for some kilometres and then plunged into the depths of the gorge. We were not the first English people to tramp this gorge. Every inch of it was known to the British officers who were parachuted into Greece in 1943 to assist the Greek resistance fighters. One of these, whom I met later, Michael Ward, now British consul in Salonica, remembered with nostalgia the point where the old track passed under a high rock archway. The archway was supposed to have been miraculously created by St. Luke's ikon on its flight to Proussos. Ikons have a habit of deciding where they wish to reside and devising their own means of transport thither.

The new road descends at a point further on, where the Proussiotikos joins the Karpenisiotis. We had left Proussos in the cool of a mountain morning but by eleven o'clock the sun had burnt away the smell of new-mown hay and honeysuckle. Even down by the river, where a solitary old man was making fishing-nets and baskets, it was hot, for it was June 21st, Midsummer Day. To salute the occasion, I unzipped my trouser-legs for the first time that year. It was a gesture I was to regret, for groups of painted beehives were everywhere and, as we passed a metropolis of blue ones, an angry worker drove his drill into my naked thigh so that I let go of Picchio and danced about screaming. The pony remained quite unmoved and was thereupon elevated by Miranda to the position of Archimandrite Wumblechook, abbot of a monastery and the possessor of a long grey tail plaited daily by a faithful acolyte.

We camped under trees by the river Karpenisiotis at Lavra, below Mega Horio on one side and Mikro Horio on the other, each perched on rocky slopes. The children had waded naked into the fast-flowing stream before we had even unloaded the donkeys, Miranda up to her waist, Jessica only to just above her ankles. Neither of them guessed that this water had run with blood in 1823. It was from Mikro Horio that Marco Botzaris, a hero of the Greek war of liberation, descended by night upon the Turks with his band of wild Suliot warriors. The reinforcements he was expecting from Mega Horio never came and he perished with a Turkish bullet through his head, mourned by the whole nation.

Karpenision clung to the lower slopes of Mount Timfristos. Although it had only 4,000 inhabitants it was the largest town in Evritania, the most sparsely populated nome in Greece. Here we discovered ewe's milk yoghurt, richer and sweeter than that made with cow's or goat's milk and sold in generously wide plastic containers with a creamy crust on it. We also discovered a saddler at work. He was sitting cross-legged on a platform, whittling away at part of the wooden frame of a pack-saddle. Bundles of leather for making saddles lay on shelves, and tall reeds for stuffing them were stacked in a corner. His window was a gay network of horse ornaments. I bought the children each a set of worry beads, those circles of beads on a thong with which Greek men continually play, often incorrectly thought to be a form of rosary.

We camped amid piles of stones and stunted plane trees above the town. Perhaps I should say 'they camped', for in fact I slunk back into Karpenision in search of an overdue bath. I found it at an overpriced hotel frequented, presumably, by skiers in winter, for the walls were covered with photos of pine trees under tons of snow. To compensate for the expense of the hotel I ate *souvlakia* off a paper napkin at a crowded café. *Souvlakia* are lumps of lamb threaded on to a wooden skewer and cooked over charcoal. They cost six or seven drachmas each, which is about the price of a cup of Turkish coffee. I was not allowed to sit alone long. A stout and grizzled tailor from

Williamsburg, Virginia, was celebrating the last night of his holiday with seven cronies at the next table. He sent two *souvlakia* and a glass of wine over to me by way of an invitation, which I found hard to refuse.

"Did you know ten people a day died of starvation here in 1943?" he said, demolishing most of a *souvlakia* at a mouthful "Then the Germans made a big fire. They burned all Karpenision. And then in 1949 we had the Communists. Eighteen days they occupied the town."

It was still dark when I woke next morning and lay luxuriating in the soft mattress and smooth sheets of my hotel bed. Cocks, dogs and donkeys were all making their appointed noises outside and at five o'clock a tinkling herd of goats passed under my window. I found it hard to imagine the horrors of war in that peaceful market town.

CHAPTER 48

How Hannibal saved the supper in Evritania

Between Karpenision and Karditsa lies one of the most isolated stretches of mountain country in all Greece. Not a single main road crosses it. It is, however, conveniently intersected by the gorge of the River Megdova, running from south to north, and into this, after some preliminary flounderings, we now dropped. We reached the river at Stenoma, where a crowd of friendly children showed us a camp-site on the far side of the stony riverbed. It should have been a perfect place to spend the day of rest that was due to us. It consisted of a little triangular meadow with steep slopes opposite, where the movement of goats would cause the stones to rattle for minutes on end. Yet everything was just wrong. The grass looked good but the donkeys paced in restless arcs at the ends of their ropes. There seemed to be shade, but in fact it was soon limited to one corner where we all crouched uncomfortably below a sparsely-leaved walnut on a pile of boulders. And the place was infested with insects. At lunch we continually fished sugar-ants out of our wine, our siesta was interrupted by flies, and at dusk mosquitoes took over. The one consolation was a little old man of eighty-two who came to tell us he had been a waiter in Buffalo in 1914 and sang 'God Save the King' in a tremulous voice to prove it. Of the ninety families in Stenoma, sixty were receiving money from relatives abroad, he told us.

In this part of Greece we were often struck by the contrast between one village and another. Each seemed a world of its own with a marked character and strong local patriotism. The following day, at Pavlopoulo, we met with our warmest welcome so far. Pavlopoulo was perched on a hillside. Its steep lanes looked like the boulder-strewn beds of mountain streams, and the only level place was a little concrete square, edged with benches and shaded by a plane tree. Before we had tied up the donkeys somebody had brought hay for them and we soon found ourselves at a table spread with a breakfast of coffee, cheese and sardines, while eleven men sat in a circle round us, leaning on their crooks and watching us eat. The village schoolmaster, who was also the *proithero*, conducted the interrogation, which followed the familiar pattern. They wanted to know what we had paid for the donkeys, how we earned our living, and why Andrew wasn't in the army. In Greece twenty-eight months' military service is compulsory.

It was to spare Andrew further questioning that I produced the newspaper article I had written for Helen Vlakos. (A copy had reached us at Karpenision.) I had not expected the *proithero* to read it aloud in its entirety to the nodding circle of Greeks, but this was what he proceeded to do. As we prepared to leave, Thomas approached the counter to pay. It was impossible. Our whole breakfast, including items we had asked to be fetched from nearby farms, had already been paid for.

By contrast, Dominio, another mountainous village, was not unfriendly but indifferent. The streets were so steep that water in the stone gutters beside them was a rushing torrent. It was evidently the chief amusement of the village boys to throw into these drains tiles which rattled loudly as they careered downhill. The effect of this on Hannibal must have been highly satisfactory to them. He bucked violently. Miranda, pink with fury, ran back up the hill towards the boys, shouting. She was met by several flying stones, but when I turned in pursuit the row of heads above us vanished.

At the bottom of the gorge we found a river and shade for our deferred day off. We thought we would be solitary here, little guessing that the villagers of Dominio had hayfields on the far side of the river. A steady stream of donkeys passed through our camp, though we could hardly recognise them as donkeys. They looked more like walking haystacks. All that was visible of them was their heads, which occasionally swung to one side to snatch a mouthful from their burden.

It was at the Dominio camp that the children informed Andrew that they wanted a proper school, not just lessons sitting in his lap. I had brought them turquoise head scarves sewn with gold sequins from Athens and these they tied round their waists as school uniform. Thomas was requested to supply school lunch in the form of packets of sandwiches. A distant 'ding-dong' from the headmaster was the signal for them to troop off to their lessons. On this occasion Andrew had found a perfect place for the school, where there was a circle of flat-topped stones for seats. Unfortunately a goat-herd had also found the flat-topped stones useful. He had spread a mixture of salt and bran on them for his goats, who shortly joined the school. As the herd moved on, it was discovered that the children's sandwiches had gone with them. Two mornings later we prepared to take the footpath to Vlaha.

As we packed, we discovered that a vital piece of equipment was missing. It was one of the two square washing-up bowls that Hamilcar carried inside his saddlebags and which made such convenient containers for our multitude of plastic bottles. Andrew had used it to water the donkeys, but now there was no sign of it. Somewhat disconsolately we set off to ford the river. Thomas, bootless, led Hamilcar across and Picchio followed alone, the water swirling round the tops of his diminutive legs. Last came Hannibal, also unaccompanied. He wandered out into the middle and then, typically, stopped. Slowly he revolved until his drooping head faced downstream. There he stood, motionless, allowing the water to ripple through his green plastic muzzle, until Thomas came to his rescue.

On the sheep-path on the other side we met a plump woman in a green suit carrying a bag full of hard green plums. She offered us some, and they proved sweeter than they looked. She talked continuously and largely incomprehensibly but it seemed that we would find the washing-up bowl further up the hill. Surprisingly enough we did. A less pleasant surprise awaited us round the next bend. At least, it was a surprise to me. Thomas, who had reconnoitred the path the day before, even had the photographic angles worked out. The hillside here formed an amphitheatre of almost sheer red shale. Across this, at a giddy height, travelled the footpath, a narrow strip of trodden earth set at only slightly less of an angle than the slope itself. Incredibly, the lady in green was already on the far side, and had settled on a rock to see what would become of us. I walked the 200 metres swiftly, being careful not to look down and keeping my thoughts on the green lady. "If she can do it, I can," I kept saying to myself. The children followed on foot, Miranda pale behind her freckles. Then came the donkeys. Hannibal's off hind foot slipped once but he had the advantage of three others to steady him.

After the amphitheatre came an ancient track of tightly packed boulders, washed away in many places, leaving loose stones and exposed tree roots. I was amazed at Hannibal's skill as he laboured upwards, digging the tips of his hooves into the cracks between the stones. Sometimes pebbles flew from under them like gunshot. After an hour we reached a wide upland valley where the grass was lush and water fell from a stone spout into a great trough. Here the path to Vlaha gave out. Above us was a boulder-strewn hillside and up this we painfully made our way, the children once more on foot. After another hour we knew we were lost. There was the sound of goat bells far below us, and while Andrew went in search of the herd the children made the acquaintance of some remarkable fauna.

This lonely hillside appeared to be the home of a race of titanic insects. Miranda gave a cry of delight when she found a black stag beetle sitting on a rock. His body was three inches long and he raised formidable antlers towards her. She was dissuaded with difficulty from imprisoning him in our butter box. "He would make such a lovely pet," she said sadly. At the mouth of a mouse-hole under the beetle's rock crouched an even more extraordinary creature, a hairy spider with legs as thick as Jessica's fingers. Fortunately even Miranda saw no possibility of friendship there.

By now Andrew was labouring up the hill towards us. The goatherd had proved unusually suspicious. He had wanted to see Andrew's identity card before giving him directions and when he gave them they proved vague. At midday we were winding our way between the moss-covered trunks of a grove of oaks. The trees were slender and graceful — Miranda thought they looked like frozen dancers — and tiny green moths fluttered round their leaves, though Hannibal and his burden sometimes became wedged between two of them. When we reached the edge of the wood a lovely sight met our eyes. The land dropped away sharply on our left and on the far side of the valley was Timfristos, its northern face capped with snow. At the foot of the mountain nestled three villages, one of them, presumably, Vlaha.

It would have been a perfect camp-site if we had had food, but it was three days since we had shopped, and supplies were low. As we chewed the last of our dry bread and hard-boiled eggs we gazed longingly at Vlaha, no doubt well stocked with fresh bread, cheese, *halva* and *retsina*. After a brief period of mosquito-haunted unconsciousness under the oak trees, Andrew volunteered to ride Hannibal there.

Andrew and Hannibal were away for a very long time. Four hours went by and still there was no sign of them. From time to time Hamilcar bellowed forlornly. A shepherd came and went and the light began to fade. There was nothing for it but to make a meal out of what we had left. Thomas lit a fire and concocted a soup out of a tin of tomato purée and three potatoes. The lights of Vlaha were beginning to appear when we heard someone whistling 'The Maid of York' among the trees. Presently a lean figure in a cowboy hat rode out of the gloom on a stalwart donkey. It was Andrew. From the bulging red saddlebags came cheese, *halva*, peanuts and *ouzo*. While Andrew crouched over the fire, eating his soup, he told us of the heroic exploits of Hannibal, who had carried him eight kilometres to the village and eight back. On the return journey Andrew nearly missed the fork to the footpath that led to our camp. It was Hannibal who recognised a roadside shrine and insisted on turning. Without doubt he had saved the supper.

CHAPTER 49

Exotic breakfasts in Thessaly

In Greece the best grazing for donkeys was always to be found high on the mountains. That was why we ended up on the following day camping far from any village, on a remote pass whose name we never discovered. We would have liked to stop near Klysto, a friendly place where we bought food. Within moments of our arrival there Andrew, who had been left holding the animals, was surrounded. He made all the standard answers while at the same time trying to prevent the incorrigible Picchio from chewing the village priest, a splendid-looking man with a black beard. Women with golden eye-teeth ran up to the children and stroked their cheeks while Thomas and I, at the shop, were plied with free *ouzos*. We had finally disengaged ourselves and were leaving the village when the keeper of a rival shop at the other end of the street ambushed us, running bottle in hand into the street and forcing several more *ouzos* on us.

Exhilarated if a little dizzy, we now passed through a landscape where haymaking was in full swing. Bales suitable for loading on to donkeys were being made by forcing hay into topless oblong boxes and then binding it. Further up the road we passed a young woman carrying one of these boxes on her back along with a pitchfork. Her husband walked unencumbered. The family donkey, who wandered ahead unattended, carried a large assortment of objects, including several dried kidskins stretched on sticks. Perched among these objects was a grubby flaxen-haired boy of about two whose head nodded with every step of his mount.

At this stage we ourselves formed an impressive procession, for we were followed by an old woman with a sheep, a lamb and a goat. Thomas was telling Jessica the story of Jack and the Beanstalk and when he came to the 'Fee-fi-fo-fums' the crone's mouth dropped open in amazement. After following us for an hour under a pitiless sun she turned off, assuring us that we would soon reach the church and a spring at the pass. At last, at 3 p.m., after seven hours of walking, we saw the sky through the trees. At the top was a crossroads, a small chapel and a chalet with the words 'House of the Wayfarer' written across it invitingly. Water fell into a stone basin below a terrace where two woodcutters were drinking coffee. From them we learnt that this was a forestry hostel, that it was the only house for many kilometres in any direction, and that, throughout the winter, the pass was a metre deep in snow.

We found a mossy clearing for our tent a short way into the forest. I have seldom been so hungry. No sooner had a slice of bread and corned beef gone down than I was frantic for a hard-boiled egg, and then another, and then a slice of bread and cheese. Thomas became understandably aggrieved, since he had not yet had time to peel his own first egg. Quite suddenly, and to my immense relief, my hunger was appeased. How awful, I thought, to have a hunger that could not be appeased.

There were to be many rest days under the new regime, but few were pleasanter than that one at the pass. A domestic day in the woods is a leisurely affair compared to one at home. After breakfast I wandered to the spring for water and heated it over a wood fire. When I had poured it over the clothes and added detergent powder the children played the Irish Washerwoman game, stamping up and down in the water. In this way they washed their feet and my clothes at the same time. All the time the sunbeams slanted down through the trees and the birds sang. Thomas was boiling soup for lunch when an old women arrived with a bag of dried haricot beans for sale. After hearing the story of Jack and the Beanstalk three times in three days we were all half-inclined to believe they might be magic.

Nereida, where we breakfasted the next day, was built down the side of a gorge which we crossed in order to follow the road along the other side. It was on this road that we encountered our angriest farmer. A kilometre beyond the most primitive village we had yet seen, a smooth green saddle of land beckoned to us and we were foolish enough to ignore a strand of barbed wire half-way across a path and a haphazard patch or two of wheat. During the afternoon we were un-molested except by a thunderstorm which began with a clap of thunder that sounded like a cannon going off above our heads and made both the children cry. In the evening Andrew offered to ride Hannibal back to the village for donkey water and that was our undoing. A series of ear-splitting brays from Hamilcar alternating with shrill whinnies from Picchio advertised our presence to everyone within a two-kilometre radius of the camp.

Darkness was falling as the farmer arrived, and the children and I had already taken off our trousers and crept into our sleeping-bags. It is difficult to face an angry farmer when you are trouserless, and I left Thomas to cope, well knowing his command of Greek was even feebler than my own.

"Daddy looks so sweet and pathetic," said Miranda, who had crept out of the tent to see what was going on. "Nobody could be cross with him." But the farmer *was* cross. He demanded not only that the donkeys should be removed from his sheep pasture but also that we should pay 100 drachmas for what they had already eaten. Nor was I to escape. After ten minutes of angry expostulation a beady black eye appeared at the tent opening. "*Kalispera sas*", I said as politely as I could from my sleeping-bag. I had the impression there was more than a hint of sarcasm in the unintelligible reply.

It was quite dark when Thomas left with Hamilcar and Picchio to find new grazing. The children and I lay in the tent, listening anxiously for his return. After half an hour we heard the heavy tramp of boots approaching the back of the tent. It was the angry farmer. I held my breath while he strode on down the hill. Next morning we had our revenge. As we looked down at dawn for the last time on those four dismal hovels, no one was stirring. One or two polite shouts were all we considered necessary for someone so rude, and when no answer came we set off to the north, retaining our 100 drachmas.

A steep mountain pass led us to Kastania, where there was a café among tall pine trees and an open-air dance floor where the children played circuses. The proprietor served us with a breakfast of cold potatoes, tomatoes, hard-boiled eggs, *feta* and, best of all, a leg of sucking kid, a delicacy indistinguishable from lamb. Afterwards he showed us the school reports of his three daughters, who all seemed to have got full marks for everything at the local *gymnasio*.

Soon after leaving Kastania we had our first view of Thessaly. The land suddenly dropped away on our right and there, below us, infinite as the sea, stretched the great plain in hazy sunshine. It was the first piece of really flat land we had seen since leaving the Val di Chiana in Italy. Greece had proved to be, as Jessica pointed out, 'mostly bumps'. Below us, on the other side, the river Megdova was once more visible, a green snake winding towards the lake where we planned to camp.

We reached the lake after little more than an hour. It was the colour of *eau de nil* and looked temptingly cool, but they told us at the café that we would find a better camp-site at the monastery further on. Believing them, we did not fill our water-bottles. It was a decision we were to regret. The sun beat down on us and the road was a monotonous one, passing through an endless forest of scrub oak that reminded us of the wilderness of Northern Rhodesia. At points we glimpsed the lake, with cattle standing knee deep to keep cool. After an hour our tongues were parched and our shirts were sticking to our backs. Even the stoical Jessica began to cry. Thomas took off her red shirt, soaked it in a muddy puddle, and put it back on her. It was dry again in ten minutes. Unwilling though we were to stop, it was becoming obvious that we would have to cool the children in the lake.

The lake of Megdova was a newly created one, formed by damming the river and causing its waters to spread over the plateau. At the lakeside everyone stripped and dashed into the wide bright mirror, fragmenting its surface; everyone that is except me. An unfortunate experience in southern Turkey fifteen years earlier had taught me that one is never alone in a Mediterranean country, however desolate the landscape.

During the last war the plateau, now covered by the Megdova reservoir, was used as a secret landing-strip by the British when, two years after abandoning Greece to German occupation, they began to send help to the Greek guerillas. Michael Ward, whose wartime memories of the road to Proussos I have already mentioned, was one of them. He told me of a dramatic occasion on which a troop-carrying plane became bogged down on this strip. After a frantic night, spent alternately covering it with branches and scouring the local farms for ropes and tackle, it eventually took off twenty minutes before the first Nazi reconnaissance plane arrived at dawn.

Another half hour on the road brought us to a paradise created by a woman called Seraphino. There were tables under an awning of vines, and Seraphino herself pumped water for us from a well round which roses grew on poles. Her son brought down cherries from the tree and spread them before us. He was a bearded young man who turned out to be in love with one of the three learned daughters of the café-owner at Kastania. He offered to show us a place by the lake where we could put up our tent.

That camp was worth the twenty-four-kilometre walk we had made to reach it. The lake lay at the tent mouth, with oak-covered hills forming a backdrop behind it. To the right were the jagged peaks of the Pindus Mountains. And we had it all to ourselves. During the afternoon a tremendous storm broke once more, but when the sky cleared the tent made a perfect bird-watcher's hide. For twenty minutes

we watched a pair of white fish-hawks, circling and diving. A great
heron flapped to and fro along the opposite shore, occasionally station-
ing himself like a white pole at the lake edge.

The lake did not appeal to the donkeys, however. Only Hannibal had
the courage to make the attempt to drink from it, and even he stood
on one front leg as far from the lake as possible. Picchio, with his
faith in people, was prepared to put both front feet in the water provided I waded in ahead of him, but not to drink. He merely played
water games, pawing the water and stretching his upper lip in the air.
He later made friends with a magnificent black horse that could have
starred as Black Beauty in any television version. The horse belonged
to Seraphino's husband, a shepherd, and wandered loose round the
lake, a foretaste of the fine Thessalian horses we were soon to see. As
Picchio reached up to nibble its withers he seemed to be saying, "Nice
to meet someone of one's own sort occasionally."

When we left, Seraphino's husband led us to Mesenikolas by a footpath that bordered the lake and then climbed through oak scrub. Although barely a foot wide, it was clearly a donkey highway, for we
passed three men sitting sideways on their beasts before we reached
an open hillside where sheep were being milked inside a stockade.
Mesenikolas was loud with buses, for it stood at the edge of the plain,
and to the plain we must descend if we wished to reach the rock monasteries of Meteora. By mid-morning the following day we were in the
thick of Moussaki, a bustling market town.

Moussaki was the nearest thing to an oriental bazaar I have seen
outside the Orient. Andrew said it could have been India if you'd
doubled the number of people, but then you could not have moved at
all. Groups of old women squatted at the curbside beside chickens
and sacks of potatoes, men crowded the café tables, and battered
country buses swarmed like bees. Our animals remained heroically
calm as we piloted them through this hubbub. Even a man rolling a
barrel under their noses and a woman carrying a squealing pig by one
leg did not unnerve them. At last we found a patch of waste ground
near the flour-mill where we could tether them while Thomas and
Andrew bought food.

The flour-mill was a fascinating place for the children. Four-wheeled
wagons loaded with sacks were constantly being driven up to it, pulled
by solid Thessalian horses. In ancient times the Plain of Thessaly was
famous for the breeding of horses. These were the first horse-drawn
vehicles we had seen in Greece, for in the mountains carts were not
used.

Walking on the plain was even hotter than walking in the mountains,
and we looked longingly at the vast rampart of the Pindus Mountains
on our left which, because it was roadless, excluded us. We passed

through villages where storks clacked on the telegraph poles, turkeys gobbled in vast herds, and whole orchestras of cicadas performed in the trees. It was July now and the summer heat was upon us. Three hours after leaving Moussaki we were still searching for a river marked on our map. It turned out that all its water had been diverted by skilful irrigators to make the farms of the plain grow tobacco and maize. For half an hour we struggled across the vast boulders of the dry river-bed, dazzled by their whiteness. At last we reached the far side and a plane tree under which we subsided.

At this camp we met the earless donkey. It was owned by a frail old man who had come for a load of leaves to feed his goats. When we asked him why his donkey had only the stumps of ears he told us that she had strayed into a neighbour's field, and this had been the neighbour's revenge. Then and there I vowed that never would I allow our donkeys to fall into the hands of Greek peasants.

It was the next morning that we had water-melons for breakfast. On either side of the red dirt-road, rows of low green plants stretched towards the horizon. Large green footballs looking curiously independent protruded between them, and these were water-melons. When we came upon four young men lying on beds under a rough shelter, apparently guarding the melons, we asked if we could buy one. The youngest, who looked like a student on vacation, went and cut three monsters and presented them to us. They must have weighed five kilos each. We could barely stagger under their weight to the next bank behind which, decently concealed, we ate them.

Perhaps three water-melons between five people seems excessive, but we had Hannibal to help. He was passionately addicted to their rinds. As he pulverised them with his rotating lower jaw the juice cascaded over his grey velvet lips. Picchio stood watching him with ears pricked and eyes bright. A crescent of melon rind lay at his feet. From time to time he would blow it and lip it, but by no stretch of the imagination could he persuade himself it was edible. Then he would lift his head and stare again at Hannibal in a puzzled manner. Meanwhile, wet from earhole to earhole, but with surprisingly little other inconvenience, we had consumed between a dozen and fifteen slices each.

CHAPTER 50

Pneumatic Monks

We had read about the rock monasteries of Meteora in Patrick Leigh Fermor's *Roumeli*, and for two more days we tramped across the oven-like plain, scanning the horizon for a sight of them. Half-way through the third morning we saw a black rampart of cliffs shimmering in the heat ahead of us. As we approached, we realised that it was in fact a series of giant pillars, over a thousand of them, we later learnt. We strained our eyes to pick out monasteries said to be perched on these pillars, but we had almost reached Kalambaka, at the foot of the cliff, before we saw St. Stephen, perched vertically above the town.

Beyond the town there was a short cut to the village of Kastrakion, and suddenly we were alone in the valley of the rocks. Fantastic shapes loomed above us, smooth as concrete and pockmarked with caves. It was in these caves that the first hermits had taken up residence. We looked up at them with longing, for it was way past our usual camping time, but, lacking rope ladders, we could not reach them. We wondered what agile housewife had hung a line of washing up there and later learnt that a boy took it up once a year in honour of a local saint.

It was five o'clock in the afternoon before we found a place where we could stop. A footpath signposted to the monastery of St. Nicholas tempted us up a deeply-cut creek, and below the path we saw a triangle of green beside a stream. It was fenced with a few branches of thorn but the people at the last farm (at work in a shed full of drying goat-skins) had assured us we could camp anywhere. We sank on to the soft grass.

That night, for the first time ever, I slept under the sky. At the last camp I had almost stifled in the tent inside my sleeping-bag, yet if I ventured out of the bag I was immediately attacked by midges, which were far more trying than mosquitoes. Since then I had bought a sheet and sewn its sides together to form a tube. Now, cool and midge-free, I lay and watched the waxing moon through a net of almond branches.

It was only when we sat up in our sleeping-bags the next morning that we appreciated the full beauty of the place we had found. Towers of rock were on three sides of us. Opposite, rising from the vineyards across the stream, was a pinnacle as riddled with caverns as a Gruyère

Andrew and the priest of Klysto.

Camp barber at work. Miranda sits on Hannibal's new Italian pack saddle.

In the village of Kastrakion, below the pinnacles of Meteora.

Water melon feast in the plain of Thessaly.

cheese. As the dawn sun gilded its smooth top, a pair of white eagles with black-tipped wings began to circle it. Behind us rose a formidable black precipice, smooth and sheer, while to our right lay a whole range of pinnacles, several crowned with monasteries. The closest was St. Nicholas, whose holy musak (we called it 'hosak') we had heard when we arrived. The most spectacular was Rousanou, which stood on its rock pillar like a mushroom head on a stalk.

At one time there were over thirty monasteries or religious settlements at Meteora. Comparatively few survive, but we could not hope to visit them all, even though we had allowed ourselves two days off in their honour. St. Nicholas, on our doorstep, was the obvious one to start with, and Thomas and I conceived a romantic desire to go up there before they switched on the 'hosak' at eight o'clock. It meant that we would not be able to go inside and see the fresco of Adam naming the animals, but we were willing to miss this to see the monastery as it had been before the tourists came. There was a notice at the foot of the steps requesting ladies to wear skirts but I imagined that Father Pandeleimon, the solitary monk in charge of the souvenirs, would not be there so early. I was wrong. At a turn in the steps we came upon a black-clad figure filling a fridge with the day's supply of Coca-Cola. Father Pandeleimon was there before us. I retired down the steps as fast as my shamelessly trousered legs would carry me. Until recently no female creature of any sort was allowed to enter the monasteries, not even a cow or a hen.

For my next assault on a monastery I went better prepared. In the heat of July a tartan rug was not an appealing prospect, but my new cotton sleeping tube, doubled and safety-pinned, made a cooler alternative. My plan was to take the bus to Kalambaka, secure a taxi and a bale of hay for the donkeys, return to pick up the children, and proceed on wheels up the valley to Barlaam and Great Meteora, the two most famous monasteries. I was particularly anxious to see Barlaam because Lear had drawn it. Lear detested monks whom he described as "Merriment-marring, monitoring, mocking, mournful, minced fish and marmalade masticating Monx". But monasteries provided just his brand of the picturesque. He sketched Barlaam at six o'clock one spring morning in 1849, enchanted to see "the detached and massive pillars of stone . . . rise perpendicularly from the sea of foliage, which at this early hour . . . is wrapped in the deepest shade, while the bright eastern light strikes the upper part of the magic height with brilliant force".

The taxi ride was not a success. The driver agreed to do the round trip, allowing us time to collect hay and visit two monasteries, for 200 drachmas, but he soon made it clear that he considered carrying hay beneath his dignity. He stood and looked on with disgust while

K

two girls from a farm struggled up the lane with my bale, and he would not even open the boot of the car for them to put it in. His temper was not improved by a further delay while I went to fetch the children from the camp, for it took me some time to persuade them to leave an island garden they were constructing for a tiny tortoise called Microlina. Only angry honks from the horn finally detached them. By the time we clambered into the plushy back seat our driver was in a raging temper and whirled us up the winding road to Great Meteora at breakneck speed, while the children moaned that they were going to be sick. It turned out to be early closing day at Great Meteora, but at Barlaam, on the neighbouring cliff, we got out, dazed but grateful to be free.

As we climbed the 192 steps to the monastery, and crossed the iron footbridge at a giddy height above the gorge, we realised why the *pneumatikos* (as the monks were called) chose to live between earth and heaven. Up here the growls of the angry taxi driver could no longer reach us. The steps to Barlaam were only cut in the 1920s to facilitate the pastoral visits of the Bishop of Trikala. Before that the monks were hauled up several hundred feet in nets, a terrifying experience, according to H. Holland who did it in 1815. "As we began to ascend, our weight drew close the upper aperture of the net, and we lay crouching together, scarcely able, and little willing, to stir either hand or foot . . . The ascent had something in it that was formidable . . . for our only support was the thin cordage of a net . . . and we were even ignorant of the machinery . . . which was thus drawing us rapidly upwards."[*] Holland was hardly consoled by the abbot's assurance that the rope was always replaced with a new one when it broke.

The final approach to the monastery is now through a stone tunnel guarded by a dragon who hands out pale-blue cardigans to bare-armed ladies. The monastery, with its church, its refectory (now a museum), and its rows of empty cells seemed spacious. There was even room for a tiny garden, but I preferred not to look over the edge. The sixteenth-century frescoes in the church are considered the finest in any of the monasteries. Rows of emaciated saints, among them St. Nektarios clad only in his floor-length hair, were surmounted by vivid scenes from their lives. German tourists smiled indulgently as Miranda explained the upper frescoes to Jessica. They little guessed that she was describing in lurid detail the method by which the skin of a saint was removed intact while he hung from a tree by his heels.

A pale young monk in the souvenir shop took an interest in our journey and only interrupted a lengthy inquisition in French to answer a distant phone, black skirts flapping. He told us there were four monks left at Barlaam now, just enough to keep the place open. There were

[*] H. Holland. *Travels in the Ionian Isles etc.* London, 1815.

forty-one monks altogether in the monasteries, including the sixteen nuns at St. Stephen. The monasteries at Meteora were mostly built in the sixteenth century. They were an expression of a spiritual renaissance which, strangely enough, coincided with the final political decline of Byzantium in the face of the invading Turks. During the years of Muslim domination they became a stronghold of Christianity, but it was not for that reason that they were built between earth and heaven. Since the early days of the desert hermits of Alexandria, the tendency of Eastern monasticism had been towards solitary contemplation, far from the distractions of the world. It was only for practical reasons that the original hermits of Meteora gathered together in communities.

Solitary contemplation, explained our young monk, is known as Hesychasm in the Eastern Church, and, under the inspiration of Arsenios of Crete, there was a great revival of Hesychasm in the fourteenth century. The posture and exercises recommended by Arsenios bear a remarkable resemblance to Yoga. The meditator is recommended to adopt an attitude known as *omphaloskepsis*, chin on breast and eyes on navel. While regulating his breathing he repeats "Jesus Christ, Son of God, have mercy on me" for many hours on end. This exercise produces a spiritual vacuum for the divine light to enter. The devout Hesychast then becomes transfigured, as Christ was transfigured. It was the revival of Hesychasm that drew the first hermits to Meteora, and the largest of the monasteries, Grand Meteora, is dedicated to *Metamorphosis*, the Greek word for the Transfiguration.

Before we were halfway down the 192 steps from Barlaam, the shouts and gestures of our taxi driver brought us back to another world. "I wish I could go home on Hamilcar," said Jessica sadly. Only by paying the man an extra 100 drachmas could I persuade him to go sufficiently slowly to prevent the children being sick. By the time we reached the camp-site his mutterings were continuous and alarming. He hurled our bale of hay to the ground and set about ostentatiously spring-cleaning his boot, throwing out rubber mats and jacks with imprecations. We parted without the normal *Adios*, for, in spite of the array of holy medals on his dashboard, neither party was in a godly state of mind.

When I returned to camp Andrew told me I should have visited Barlaam by donkey. He had just travelled to St. Stephen and Rousanou in this manner. With Hannibal as a mount he was able to use the footpaths that had provided the only access to the monasteries before the construction of a motor road. He wrote me the following account of his journey:

Hannibal makes a fine method of transport provided you're not in a hurry. His natural walking pace with me on his back is considerably slower than mine on foot, and I've long given up trying to urge him out of it as this uses up more energy than would going alone on foot. At a stately 2 mph climbing the rocky footpath I had all the time in the world to admire the fantastic rock pinnacles on either side of me, many of them like massive pieces of modern sculpture. Within an hour we had wound our way out of the valley and round to the monastery of St. Stephen, which we had first seen from the plain. The monastery was ugly but the view more than compensated. Kalambaka lay almost vertically below, and the plain stretched dead flat away from it, yellow with ripe cornfields and dotted with tiny trees, until it was lost to sight in the heat haze. My contemplation of all this was only interrupted by a German tourist who pulled up his Mercedes in front of me and, without saying a word, lined up his two women beside me for a photograph.

St. Stephen is used as an orphanage, and the only part open to the public is a small and overstocked museum and souvenir shop. I had just given my five postcards to the nun behind the counter for wrapping when we were interrupted by the entrance of three black-robed priests. The nun became highly confused as protocol demanded that she kneel, touch the floor and kiss the hand of each in turn while muttering some formula that I was unable to catch. This exercise was by no means easy to perform in the confined space of the shop, and the desolate braying of the abandoned Hannibal 100 metres down the road only added to the chaos. The whole interlude left her so flustered that I had to wait around for several minutes pretending to be unconcerned while she recovered her composure sufficiently to accept my 15 drachmas. Then I mounted Hannibal and slowly wound my way down the track to Rousanou.

Rousanou looked plain stupid up there on its 200-foot pinnacle, as if an overimaginative child had got loose with a magic lamp and wished a London tenement house up there, or a gang of students had moved it there brick by brick as a prank. From below it seemed utterly derelict, ready to be blown off its perch by the next storm. When I got inside, I discovered a couple of workmen stripping the place down and rebuilding it. It was as open to the elements as a bird cage and the empty space below the duck boarding was enough to make you giddy. While one of the workmen went to look at the monastery clock the other warned me that I must adjust the time by one hour, as they kept sun time up there.

The superiority of Andrew's mode of transport was brought home to me more strongly than ever on the morning of our departure, for I woke with a severe sore throat, obviously the result of a curse put on me by the taxi driver. I confessed that the management of the bouncy

Picchio was beyond me, and handed him over to Andrew. Thomas took charge of Hamilcar with Jessica and I found myself where I had secretly longed to be, trundling along in the rear with Hannibal.

Soon we were in gently rolling hills with good pasture, looking back on the oceanic plain of Thessaly. Up here there were herds of grey, newly-shorn goats guarded by massive black and white sheepdogs with hideously scarred faces and slavering jowls. They were not so fierce as they looked. When we threw stones at those that came barking after us, they turned and ran to fetch them, like spaniels after rubber bones.

I enjoyed driving Hannibal from behind with the long reins. It was relaxing not having continually to invent stories for Miranda, and the sight of his massive haunches, swinging along under their load, was mesmeric. Another advantage of being at the back with Hannibal was that, for the first time, I was able to see how Miranda looked on Picchio. It was a charming sight. The tiny pony, as brown and shiny as a conker, stepped along gaily with his long tail swinging and his ears pricked. Even Miranda, in her straw hat and Edwardian dress, looked large for him. She rode with her back straight and was unworried when he broke into a brisk trot as he did every few minutes. Jessica, by comparison, in her red shirt and trousers, looked not much bigger than a red dot on Hamilcar. She was dwarfed by the giant saddlebags that bulged below her and the massive saddle, padded like a sofa with all our spare blankets. As I watched she appeared to be performing a silent opera to herself with many gestures of her hands.

At breakfast a gentle rain began to fall, making the dry sand of the road smell of cornflakes with milk freshly poured on them. It was a relief to be cool again, and to think of the grass that would grow for the donkeys. As we started to walk once more a white mist rose from the plain behind us, drawing a final curtain across the improbable theatricality of Meteora.

CHAPTER 51

Curiouser and curiouser

Thomas continues: My part of the story of our second year's walk begins at Trifyllia. We were now two days' march north of Meteora

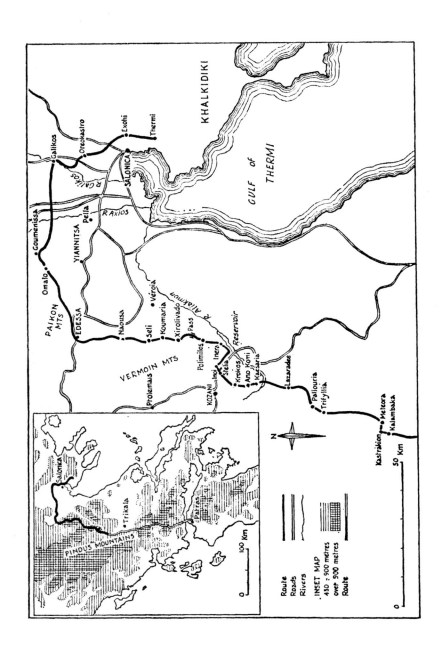

and Susan was still with us but from Trifyllia onwards she felt too unwell to write the diary — odd that my most vivid memory of her doing this daily duty is in fact at Trifyllia.

Glancing towards the grassy spot where she was sitting propped against Hannibal's saddle, a glass of brandy and water to hand, I saw that the children of the village had moved from the river edge, where they had been watching Andrew conducting Miranda's and Jessica's school, and that fifteen or twenty of them were now grouped in a thick crescent around her. Here they stood, their eyes following every tiny wriggle of her pen with a deep visual thirst, all shifting together to watch her hand move to the brandy glass, lift it to her lips, then set it back in the grass. As they noticed me crouch to photograph them I sensed their distress. Should they watch me or Susan? Suddenly life was offering them too much satisfaction.

We were not the first to be troubled by Greek curiosity. Lear found it a continuous impediment to his drawing. "The curiosity of half the people of Vodhena," he writes, "obliged me to stand on a stone in the midst of the kennel to draw. Their shouts of laughter as I represented the houses were electrifying: 'Scroo! scroo! scroo!' (He writes it down! he writes! he writes!) they shouted."

Old men and women would crouch by our camp fire, questioning us for hours till they had got exactly straight who we were, what we were doing and how we were all related to each other. On good days I was taken for Andrew's brother but on days when I hadn't shaved, for Miranda and Jessica's grandfather. The fact that Susan was Andrew's mother always provoked stares of disbelief.

As for Greek children, they would have stayed around our camp for ever if we had let them, watching every act from the first pitching of our tent to our night-time teeth-cleaning. Crouching half-undressed in the tent one hot afternoon, to apply ointment to a particularly private part of my person, I suddenly saw, silhouetted in the tent mouth, six little short-haired heads peering in at me with steady amazement.

Greeks seem to have little idea of the meaning of the word privacy — or if they do know its meaning to be unable to conceive that it is anything which anyone can possibly want. It never occurred to them to ask our permission to come and sit with us. Instead of questioning us they would sometimes just stay, content to wait and see what happened. They made the instant assumption that we were friends, and that we would accept them as the same.

I cannot remember a more disturbed night than the one we spent at Trifyllia. Our camp was in a low green triangle of ground, one side of which consisted of the river bed, the other two of tall grass banks three or four metres high. As soon as darkness fell the local sheepdogs came roaming out to the tops of these banks to bark at us.

Never have I heard such loud and persistent barking. Hour after hour they kept it up. By about two in the morning it seemed inconceivable that their larynxes were not shredded raw. Four hours later I was beyond wonder. Sometimes I could see their great silhouettes, black against the moonlit sky, bounding and yelping along the bank top; sometimes they came in a rushing pack through the camp itself, rooting for scraps in the ashes of the fire, snapping at our cans of food, hurtling through the bushes beside my sleeping-bag. I have rarely been more glad to see dawn in the sky.

When we had camped at Trifyllia we had been barely up to schedule. For the first time that summer we had a date to keep: our rendezvous with Cordelia at Kozani, and we were feeling the unaccustomed strain. Perhaps it was this which caused the morning's first accident.

The route we were now taking led us down the upper reaches of a tributary of the Aliakmon river, and though the road was only sketchily shown on one of our maps and not at all on the other we were dismayed to find it leading us to a ford when it should have stayed on one side. The river here ran down the centre of a typical Greek river-bed, if this term can be applied to something so unlike my previous conception of a river-bed. Not less than 500 metres wide, it consisted entirely of a flat expanse of grey sand and grey rock from which thousands of healthy young plane trees were growing. I had not expected the plane trees to be such a feature of the Greek landscape, and wondered how they could remain so green and healthy in a country where every other tree looks grey and parched, or has been nibbled to shrub size. Perhaps their leaves taste so foul that even goats won't eat them. At camp after camp they provided us with two of our principal needs: shade and firewood.

After occasional storms the river perhaps fills that vast bed, but now it consisted only of a couple of three-metre streams near the centre. These, however, were more than boot-deep and we forded them laboriously, riding Picchio in turn to keep as many feet dry as possible. We were just safely over the second when I noticed that our tent was missing.

Tent and fly-sheet travelled in separate bundles, wedged between Hannibal's pack-saddle and kit-bags, one on each side. Now the fly-sheet was in place, but there was only an empty space to balance it. We had lost many things before, but never something so vital, which could bring the whole expedition to a halt. Gloomily I set off to walk the five kilometres back to camp, peering right and left into the scrub but picturing our tent bobbing down the Aliakmon on its way to the Aegean. I was still just within hearing when loud cries called me back to the river. The tent had been found behind the trunk of a plane tree.

I would have been better pleased if, while I was away, Hannibal had not come nosing for good things around my knapsack and put a heavy muddy foot on my camera bag. Impossible to tell whether the camera was damaged or not. There followed one of those periods of general crossness with each other which surely disturb the peace of the most orderly expeditions. I accused Susan of failing to protect my camera and she accused me of implying distrust of her care of the tent by going back to hunt for it. Five minutes later as we again pursued our track it led us back to the river and another ford. We realised that if we had followed the river-bed we need never have crossed in the first place.

That day's culminating misfortune crept up on us more slowly. By mid-morning we had reached the village of Paliouria where we ignored an offer to exchange Hannibal for a good-looking grey mare about twice Picchio's size, and politely rejected the invitation of a combine-harvester team to stay and camp with them. These teams, with their vast red or yellow machines, and tents of transparent plastic sheeting, were a feature of this part of Greece. They so often pressed us to camp with them that we decided they must feel outsiders in the villages they visit and be desperate for company.

By this time we had completed all but a few kilometres of our planned walk for the day and meant to go only far enough out of Paliouria to find a less public camp than at Trifyllia. We had reckoned without the Aliakmon valley. The guide-book said that this narrowed, but had not told us that the earth track rose higher and higher up the valley side. Still worse, the sun was at its hottest, the scrubby terrain was entirely tilted at thirty degrees to the horizontal, and there was no sign of trees for shade or water for the donkeys.

After two more hours a spectacular monastery appeared, perched high on a rock top, but it was on the far side of the river and no help to us. We learned later that it was the monastery of St. Nicolas, still rich from surrounding estates but occupied only by two old monks. At last we began to see goat droppings and finally a bungalow-style building roofed with corrugated iron, from which a woman shouted to us that there was water soon and big trees. The single gnarled and nibbled oak which we eventually found was welcome enough, though it didn't exactly match the picture of bosky shade which she had suggested.

By then it was four o'clock, but at least we were in wild country and would have peace for our day off, not to mention a splendid view across the valley where the bell tower of the monastery still peeped above a rocky skyline. Half an hour later five or six small figures appeared among the scrub, staring goggle-eyed at everything we were doing. Presently they began a cautious approach, pushing each other forward and then scrambling back as if playing Grandmother's Footsteps.

CHAPTER 52

Water, water, everywhere

Dawn and dusk of our day of rest were announced by the departure for the mountains and return home of vast herds of goats and sheep. Sweeping past us, they set us scuttling round the camp, putting into shelter anything likely to be nibbled, which with goats meant everything. Between these events Susan and I rested, finding, as so often, that it was more effort to walk fifty metres on a day off than ten kilometres on a travelling day. The solitary oak was our only source of shade, and during the day we revolved slowly round it like the hands of a clock.

Miranda and Jessica were happy. The goat-trough at the top of the hill was ten metres long and they spent contented hours clambering naked between its various sections among its more usual population of frogs, toads and tadpoles.

Far below us, but out of sight in its deep valley, lay the Aliakmon. At this point it seemed a formidable defensive barrier, and that was the way in which the British hoped to use it in 1941 at the time of the German invasion. The plan disintegrated in misunderstanding. General Papagos, Greek commander on the Albanian front, failed to withdraw and join the British on the Aliakmon, continuing till too late to hope that Yugoslavia would resist the Germans and that a line could be established which would include Salonica.

I had just lit the fire to cook supper when a young shepherd called Dmitri arrived on a wiry pony whose bridle was decorated with a fringe of badger fur. Dmitri squatted by the fire in oriental manner. He did not look Greek, but was fair and had the long melancholy face of a Hapsburg. He told us that he was a Vlach.

This race of shepherds is to be found all over the Balkans, driving their flocks up into the mountains for the summer and then returning to the shelter of some village in a valley for winter. Their language is unlike Greek or any other Balkan language but so similar to Roumanian that some scholars consider the two to be dialects of each other. This might suggest that the Vlachs came from Roumania, but another theory is that they get their language direct from the Roman garrisons which were isolated at the time of the collapse of the Empire.

After supper Susan, who had lain inert all day nursing her sore throat, said she felt strong enough to help Andrew water the donkeys. She told me afterwards that the ride up the hill to the trough was a fitting climax to a journey that, for her, was soon to end. She rode Picchio at a brisk trot, Andrew following on Hannibal, Hamilcar bringing up the rear on his own. Darkness had fallen by the time they started, but the moon was bright. From the hills on either side came the wild whoops and whistles of unseen Vlachs, moving their flocks uphill towards the trough. The whole landscape was alive with them, like crickets. At the spring there was a silent multitude of sheep, and a dark figure stood in their midst. They recognised Dmitri's pale strip of face as he saluted and cleared a path between his beasts. As they rode back to the tent, fresh flocks were moving towards them in the dark.

At around ten o'clock, when we were all undressing on various sides of our shade tree, we had the day's final visit. In the moonlight we made out two shepherds approaching purposefully up the field, dragging what turned out to be a donkey no bigger than a decent-sized Great Dane. When Andrew in his long underpants arrived to interpret we discovered that they wanted to exchange this pea-sized creature for the massive Hannibal, on the grounds that it would need less water in the mountains.

But our donkeys were our friends, Andrew said, and repeated the tale of our walk, which, even in Greek, we now all knew by heart. Taking this merely for a bargaining ploy, the shepherds modified their terms to an exchange with Hamilcar. It took us a quarter of an hour to convince them that we were happy with our own donkeys. We then all shook hands and parted with polite good wishes.

Despite the admiration our animals clearly aroused, I slept peacefully that night. Before we had set out I had thought that the further east we went the more worried I should be that they might be stolen, but in Greece, on the contrary, I never felt that they were in the smallest danger, at least from human predators. Moving as we did among shepherds and peasants, it was hard to imagine how the Greeks had got their reputation for dishonesty, unless urban life transforms them.

At dawn next morning we were on our way. There, on a far hillside, across a deep tributary valley, lay a little village of white houses which must be Lazarades, the next on our route, though as so often it seemed to lie in a wrong direction. The moment we began to walk it disappeared from view and it was a long hot descent and an even hotter ascent before we saw it again. We breakfasted at a little café where a vast-bellied Greek in navy-blue T-shirt addressed his table of friends for half an hour on end, actually rising to his feet to make space for his gestures at the more impassioned moments of his monologue. Andrew meanwhile brought from the local shop a large supply of *loukoum*, still Jessica's passion.

Our long waterless trek on our last walking day should have enabled us to avoid at least this mistake in future, yet now we somehow succeeded in leaving our final village without even our normal six litres of drinking-water. Enough for the donkeys we could never carry, but they could often be watered in streams and ponds which we wouldn't risk ourselves.

Always before we had eventually found goat-troughs, fed by cool fresh springs. Greek water was one of the delights of the summer and we even developed a Greek sophistication about the quality of different sources. In many places we saw people carrying heavy jugs from springs several hundred metres outside their village when there were taps of apparently perfectly drinkable water right in the main street. This day we were in no doubt about the quality of the water we found: two goat-troughs full of murky green sludge with nothing flowing from their feed pipes.

On and on we went in the scorching sun, across corn land and scrub with nowhere a sign of a spring or even a shepherd to ask. Suddenly, over a small rise we saw again the Aliakmon valley far below us. It was an astonishing sight, much of it flat tableland, but everywhere so deeply cut by V-shaped valleys that it had more than a slight resemblance to the Grand Canyon. Even more amazing, a few hundred metres further along our track we saw that the main valley was no longer threaded by a modest river but occupied by a vast reservoir. Neither of our maps had hinted at such a thing.

So we began to descend, directed by some road-makers to a new source of water, "exactly on our route". Either they were wrong or we misunderstood them. It was an odd experience to see that huge sheet of water far below us but to be able to find not a drop of moisture anywhere that we could actually touch.

A further worry was that an earth-track beyond a deep side-valley was becoming more and more insistent and looking more and more as if it, and not the road we were on, led to the now obvious and only bridge across the reservoir.

The day's climax followed: first, another talk with the road-men who agreed that they had misdirected us, then the crossing of that deep side-valley. Any goat-track which may once have connected its two sides had been obliterated by a twenty-metre avalanche of loose bulldozed earth which now formed a steep and very unstable bank. The children dismounted, Andrew took Picchio down, up to his knees in loose earth, and I was following with Hamilcar, planning to return to unload Hannibal for such an appalling descent, when he set off on his own and virtually skied down. For thirty seconds I didn't dare look back, expecting at any moment to hear a thudding fall or the snapping of one of his leg bones. Unbelievably, he reached the bottom safely. He was certainly carrying no less than 150 kilos.

Much later we finally arrived close to the reservoir, where Andrew galloped on Picchio to the nearby village for drinking-water while I pitched the tent in another dry river-bed of sand, grey rocks and shady plane trees. Our modest one-hour final stage had become four hours and we needed four litres of diluted *retsina* to make us feel human again.

CHAPTER 53

The weed

Next day we crossed the long modern bridge we had seen from high above, looking left to mud flats and right to that huge artificial lake stretching away out of sight between grey hills. Some people like reservoirs, but for me their prettiness at a distance is undermined by the thought of those invariable zones of mud and rotting vegetation round their shores. I was glad when this one finally fell below the skyline.

An earth-road now led us across a new landscape. Rolling and arable, its principal crop was tobacco. On each side were large fields of this robust, knee-high, thick, green plant. Spread about the fields, parties of women with handkerchiefs over their heads were stooping to pick the lower leaves. Nearby stood donkeys saddled with pairs of deep wicker panniers to carry their gatherings home.

In the villages we saw the next stages of the process of turning the green leaves into their lethal final form. On porches and verandahs old women sat threading them on to wires. Sometimes these wires were strung across open frames and stood in the sun, but more often they were suspended inside low structures, rather like dwarfs' greenhouses, roofed with transparent sheet plastic. I found it difficult to connect hospital wards of lung-cancer patients with these healthy, busy, prosperous Greek peasants.

Prosperous, tobacco has certainly made them. Kaesaria where we breakfasted, had once been a small dusty village but it was growing into a town. Everywhere new houses were being built, and instead of the usual single café-shop, we seemed to have a choice of seven or eight. We were mistaken. All were closed, their owners in the fields picking tobacco before the sun became too hot. It took us half an hour to find an ancient granny who would open her shabby glass doors and serve us mountain tea, made from wild herbs.

Greek cafés like hers — it was typical of three-quarters of those we saw — would be dreary places if it wasn't for the friendliness of their owners. They consist of nothing but a square concrete shell, sided with metal-framed plate glass and painted in flaking pale-blue distemper. The tables and chairs would suit a pre-war village hall. In the mornings we would often find the owner and his wife seated at one of these in a small cloud of flies, facing a huge pile of chunks of raw flesh and offal which they were threading on to wooden skewers for the evening's *souvlakia* orgy. No doubt they washed their hands before they served our coffee, but somehow this was not the impression they left.

But every one of them was welcoming and alert with lively interest: typically, the old woman at Kaesaria sent us away with half a bottle of her home-distilled *chiporo*, a fiery spirit akin to Italian *grappa*, preferable to the usual *ouzo* which is aniseed flavoured and too sweet.

Our two unintended marathon walks had at last put us ahead of schedule, but though we camped early that day, finding a site in this cultivated countryside was difficult. In the end we made do with an unsavoury grove of poplars beside an apparently abandoned chapel at the village of Ano Komi. Though we were later told that it was one of twelve which served a village of 800 people, the chapel was *not* abandoned. Throughout the afternoon women and children came to light candles or perform other rituals inside. They showed not the slightest annoyance at finding us camped right outside their chapel. Some brought us tomatoes, and one ancient peasant woman produced five eggs for the children out of her black skirt. I tried to imagine the sort of welcome a family of Greeks would have if they pitched their tent in front of the porch of our village church in Sussex.

But it was another disturbed night. For the first time we were seriously troubled by midges. Susan claimed that they, and her sore throat, prevented her sleeping at all, and though the children slept, their faces in the morning were pitted and hillocked like those of the victims of some mediaeval plague. Andrew and I slept with shirts round our faces, leaving only tiny breathing holes, but by the morning I had been bitten all around the nose and mouth and it was anyway most uncomfortably hot.

At Ano Komi we had been even nearer to Kozani than we had realised. An hour's walk brought us to Krokos, so called because its principal crop used to be saffron, produced from the stamen of crocus flowers. Krokos was only five kilometres from Kozani. A familiar problem now faced us: finding a camp close enough to the town to be able to visit it but far enough away to be rural and peaceful. This time we needed a better site than usual because it would be Miranda's birthday camp. Surely no birthday has ever been looked forward to so passionately.

For a month she had carried a birthday chart, each day to be crossed off in a different colour, each of us allowed to perform the daily ritual in turn in our chosen colours — but frequently having the privilege withdrawn so that she could have the pleasure of re-allocating it. She also had a list of presents beginning "A puppy and a new dress", though what she really wanted was far simpler. "Just anything from a stationery shop," she said, her eyes shining at the idea of all those empty notebooks, pencils, pens, rubbers and pencil cases. How well I recognised her feelings!

But the land around Krokos was flat and cultivated and I was not optimistic. Corn stubble and tobacco stretched away in every direction. So when, less than a kilometre beyond the village, we saw what seemed to be a number of largish groves of young oaks standing among the yellow stubble it seemed too much good luck. Surely they must contain municipal rubbish tips or sewage farms. Not so. We needed to go no further than the first to find pretty, open glades and short grassy turf. As we entered, a long black snake slithered off the path and a hare bounded away among the trees. Best of all, Miranda quickly found several good-sized tortoises and at once established a birthday tortoise corral.

CHAPTER 54

Bell, book and candle

Susan collapsed into the first Kozani hotel we found, named inevitably The Aliakmon, and called a doctor. Her throat was ulcerated and when a swab came back from the laboratory she was found to have a streptococci infection known in the Greek medical profession as 'German Tourist Throat', a punishment perhaps for the number of times since arriving in Greece that we had indignantly denied that we were Germans. For proper treatment she should go to Salonica, where a

German doctor with a grant from the University of Bonn was making a special study of this disease, and two days later that was what she did.

Meanwhile it was my duty to visit a stationery shop, and also to buy such awkward items as yoghurt, iced birthday cake, *halva*, *loukoum*, water melon, *vanili*, and a dripping-hot barbecued chicken, and take them home by bus to Krokos for the birthday feast. Fortunately I had two days for the job.

Kozani is a noisy, scruffy but characterful town. Before the motorway took traffic far to the east, it lay on the main route connecting Athens with the rest of Europe. In its back streets there are still old Turkish houses with typical overhanging wooden balconies. As for its shops, I goggled at these in my usual state of wonder after periods in the wilds. The choice was baffling and the sheer quantity seemed unbelievable. How could so much of everything, from food and drink to shoes, clothes, pots and pans, ever be consumed? In particular, how could a town like Kozani support no less than six — I counted — shops entirely devoted to materials for home embroidery? While I toured the streets, Jessica spent two happy hours wallowing in the footbath of Susan's hotel shower.

I ended that day watching a sight which must be familiar to all dwellers in Greek provincial towns: the evening parade of the entire population up and down the main street. It began at eight o'clock when the babies were brought out to enjoy the cooling air in their prams and pushchairs, accompanied by little sisters precariously sucking ice-creams in their immaculate white dresses. It swelled as it was joined by young girls, linked arm in arm, and national-service men walking five abreast, and reached its climax at ten, when the whole street was a solid shouting mass of people who, in any other country, could only have been taking part in a revolution or a coronation. The stately *passeggiatas* of Italy seemed decorous by comparison.

The next day I had Cordelia's help. There she was, sitting writing postcards in the post office twenty minutes ahead of time, despite the fact that the driver of the bus which had brought her from London for £24 had been found, at the Yugoslav frontier to have no passport, with the result that she had had to spend a night in a Yugoslav public park.

By the evening of that day all was finally assembled in the wood at Krokos. Miranda had established a birthday enclosure by stringing the donkeys' reins between tree trunks and suspending from them all twenty-seven of the coloured plastic bags we had accumulated. And the feast was a success, though it could not quite compare with our great joint birthday at Moissac the year before, where eleven assorted family and friends had gathered. Miranda loved her capacious leather pencil case and I hid my concern at the extra half kilo it would add to Hannibal's load.

Only the midges mar the memory of our camp at Krokos. For many hours on the first two nights I lay awake, listening to the weird calls of two birds which answered each other in single bell-like notes, each on a slightly different pitch. Were they the famous little owls which appear on one-drachma coins? Each time I dozed off fresh hordes of little creatures began hopping about my cheeks and eyelids. By the third day I had had enough and, after saying goodbye to Susan, I brought home from Kozani twelve metres of cheese-cloth, which Cordelia and I sewed into two individual tentlets and one big sheet to cover the tent mouth. The result was an improvement though not perfect.

Amusing as it was, the city of Kozani was no place for donkeys. We were told that we could by-pass it to the east by taking earth-tracks in the direction of the airport. If this airport exists, its traffic must be minimal for we had heard no low-flying plane during our whole stay and we certainly never found it. What we did find was more extraordinary.

As we advanced steadily along bushy lanes, strange skeletal towers, clearly religious in character but with an oriental flavour, began to appear ahead of us. Suddenly we came face to face with the most astonishing erection. Perhaps a hectare in extent, it consisted of vast and entirely windowless concrete ramparts, rising fifteen or twenty metres from the ground and suggesting the massive foundations of a mediaeval town wall. Behind it, the oriental towers were now out of sight, as was everything except a battlemented gate tower — so battlemented and freshly cream-painted that it looked like part of the stage-set for a Walt Disney tale of fairyland. Above this hung a big blue banner with white lettering. Though Andrew copied the words into his notebook and worked at them in camp, he could only suggest that they *might* mean 'Those who Mother Church rejects'.

The tale was completed some weeks later by Susan in Salonica. Here, pursuing her researches into Orthodox Church ritual, she met Richard Oakes, thirty years old, born in Surrey, now an Orthodox priest complete with long brown beard and black pill-box hat. He invited her to one of his services, which concluded with the reading of a black-edged leaflet. Several times she heard the word "anathema". Afterwards he told her that it was the first official excommunication performed by the Church since the war. The victim was the Abbess Magdalini who, among other things, had deeply offended the Church by claiming that the twentieth-century St. Nektarios, a much-loved Greek saint, was a phoney. Furthermore, she had barricaded herself and her nuns inside their well-endowed convent where she kept herself incommunicado. The convent lay just outside the town of Kozani.

Between Kozani and Edessa, where we hoped to arrive in about a week's time so that Susan could rejoin us by bus from Salonica, lay the Vermoin Mountains. Our maps showed tracks leading up either side of the Vermoin range, but all seemed dead-ends, none actually making the crossing. Thinking we knew better, we were groping for a path just beyond the little village of Stelia when we met Pavlo. Pavlo dominated the next twelve hours — indeed in a sense the next three days.

What he was doing wandering about the stubble fields of Stelia we never discovered, because he instantly offered to escort us to his home village of Inoi. This, he assured us, lay on the best route to Edessa. The mountains were fit only for goats. Looking twenty (though in fact thirty-two), slim and dark, strolling beside us, he began to tell us his history, including the fact that he was a professional footballer but had been so badly kicked on the head three years ago that he hadn't played since. All the rest of the time he was with us Jessica kept peering intently at different sides of his skull in an effort to detect the scar or crater.

We had only gone a few hundred metres when we had our first encounter with the Greek police. Two of them, crammed dangerously on to a small motor scooter, spent twenty minutes trying to identify the place-of-entry stamps in our passports, before shrugging their shoulders and becoming involved with Pavlo in a long argument about the best route to Edessa. While I was trying to follow this, an ancient peasant, one of a small crowd which had gathered, produced a beautiful white root of garlic and, with a conspiratorial grin and many eating gestures, poked it into the breast pocket of my shirt.

Pavlo was a healthy corrective to romantics like myself, who look with regret at the disappearing village life of primitive countries like Greece. For Pavlo the village was a prison to which only his accident had brought him back. All the people of his age felt the same and most of them had left. Every Saturday night there used to be dancing in the café, he told us. Not any more. "Look at me," he said, sipping his first small glass of *ouzo*. "When I had friends here I could drink a litre at a sitting."

Late that afternoon, when he had found us a poplar grove to camp in, Pavlo led us to the local archaeological site, dating, he assured us, from Alexander's time. After a long climb up a typical Macedonian hillside of desiccated grey grass and white rocks, dotted with little clumps of juniper, dwarf holly and the occasional stunted crab tree, we eventually reached what was certainly an early hilltop settlement. Inside a collapsed circular rampart of mortarless stone there were many heaps of similar stones which must have been dwellings. But no explanatory notices told us what we were looking at; indeed we could have been the first foreign visitors for a year or a hundred years.

Bounding about the rocks, Pavlo at last found what he wanted: a deep rocky hole about four metres deep. Into this he climbed and threw stones down narrow crevices at its bottom which echoed in hollow chambers beyond. But whether these were natural or artificial he had no idea. When we climbed down and crouched near the crevices we could feel a steady wind being sucked past us into them.

Whatever the site had been, it had a splendid position. To our left and right we looked across range after range of similar grey hills; far away behind and below us we looked down on our poplar grove with its little orange tent; ahead, in a shallow valley which stretched out of sight in both directions, lay a more familiar sight: the Aliakmon reservoir.

CHAPTER 55

Wolves and Many Potatoes

Pavlo drew us a map. From Inoi (which meant 'Of wine') the route was simple. First came 'Tobacco Village' and then Polimilos ('Many Potatoes'), so-called because it grew such good ones: they would keep for three winters, Pavlo told us. We would be there in a couple of hours and then could take the old track across the shoulder of the Vermoin watershed. Like most Greeks, Pavlo measured distances in hours of walking-time rather than kilometres, but perhaps car travel during his urban, footballing period had distorted his judgment. They were a long two hours.

Almost at once a thunderstorm began to follow us. For much of the morning, as we wound along sandy tracks into hillier and even more desolate country, it kept wetting us with showers but never quite breaking. Perhaps we were distracted by it, but I suspect that Pavlo's map had omitted some vital turning. Whatever the cause, it was with profound irritation that, topping a rise, we saw quite close below us that reservoir again. We had spent the morning walking south-east instead of north-east.

Exhausted, we trudged above the reservoir for half an hour looking for something larger than a juniper bush to camp below, but nothing of the sort existed, and so eventually we settled for a piece of barren shore, and pitched the fly-sheet only, giving ourselves at least the benefit of a strong cooling wind. Under a grey sky, that wind and the surrounding desolation made the camp memorable if not beautiful. The wind grew stronger and stronger, raising white-topped waves on the reservoir. Some curious open concrete boxes half-buried in the scrub around us added to the sinister flavour of the place by suggesting that we might be camped on top of an old graveyard. Later I discovered from Susan that this was the afternoon when Salonica had one of the worst thunderstorms ever known.

Looking down from her hotel balcony, she told me, she saw that all the streets below her were not merely knee-deep in brown water but that this water was travelling at the speed of a mountain river in spate. The pavements had disappeared and water rushed along the walls of shops and hotels. Plastic bags and wooden fruit-boxes were being carried past at speed, and at the doorway of the nearest restaurant a group of waiters with white shirts plastered to their pink torsos were trying to repel the water with an upturned table. At the nearest street intersection a tidal wave was being created by the convergence of two streams. Where the water was opposed by the wheels of parked cars it rose in angry crests half a metre high. Susan discovered later that fifty cars and nine people had been washed out to sea.

By dawn next day every cloud had gone and we climbed in warm, still sunlight to the little village of Inera. Like so many villages, Inera's character seemed instantly established. Smiling tobacco-picking families waved to us, and the lady of the café, emerging in her pyjamas, first sold us half of one of last night's barbecued chickens for breakfast, then brought the other half to us as a gift. Even the noseless peasant woman on the café verandah, making it necessary to explain to Miranda the three stages of syphilis, didn't spoil our breakfast.

The day's most serious business followed. As we had approached Inera Cordelia, who now replaced Susan as Hannibal's driver, reported that his off-front shoe had split — not before it was due. Those Italian shoes were the best we had during the whole trip, but they had now lasted three and a half months; in Spain and France one month had been usual.

Fortunately the Italian smith had provided us with what he called a spare set of tyres. They saved us, because the smith at Inera had ceased to practise and had none. While he sharpened his rusty tools he told us how he had sheltered two British airmen during the war. An hour later the job was done and we left him with a bottle of *retsina* (he would take no payment) which he instantly opened and began to drink.

As we set out again the line-up against the shop front from left to right was: the one-armed local Communist Party secretary, the syphilitic granny, an idiot girl with a squint, and our smith squatting on his hunkers with the *retsina* bottle to his mouth. All waved cheerily and Cordelia confided to me, to my surprise, that she thought Greek villages like Inera would be good places to retire to.

Up and up we went. Although this was not the main range of the Vermoin but only a promontory which stuck out to the south, the climb was one of our stiffest. The surrounding bushes became a little taller, but there was no sign of water and we passed the ruins of a village, perhaps abandoned for this reason. At last, far ahead, though still only half-way up the mountain side, we saw a single tall poplar tree. At least it would make a target to aim for — I had been too often disappointed to hope for more.

This time there was no disappointment and we found not only ample grazing, a level space and a big patch of shade below the poplar itself but also a goat-trough filled by a cool spring. One and all we stripped and got straight into it. There was, besides all this, a sensational view back and down on the now blue and hazy Aliakmon reservoir. Beyond rose black mountain sides which that night became dotted with the lights of little villages. Perhaps it was our most perfect camp.

Late in the evening a mounted shepherd came winding up the track and stopped to water his horse at the trough. Were we planning to stay the night here with our animals, he asked, because they would certainly be eaten by *liki* (wolves).

Ever since we had arrived in Macedonia we had listened to warnings about wolves. That shepherd finally convinced us, because he had personally lost a donkey two weeks before, though it was tethered at the centre of a circle of shepherds' huts, each with dogs. Wolves, he told us, had a special liking for donkey flesh.

Our only hope was to sleep right beside our donkeys and whenever we woke to flash a light and shout loudly. So we laid out our bags along the earth-track, Cordelia, Miranda and Jessica at one end, myself at the other, Andrew on the grassy bank above, and tethered the animals between us. Periodically in the night I flashed my torch at their shining eyes and gave threatening yells into the surrounding blackness. It was a considerable relief to see their grey shapes emerging, all limbs complete, from the dawn twilight.

By sunrise we were at the summit, and found our shepherd again, with four or five companions. All around us they were emerging in braces and trousers from little tin-roofed sheds while dogs were barking, herds of goats and sheep were hurrying here and there, and the morning milk train of three horses, each with a pair of metal milk churns, was setting out down the further mountain side. It was a scene of astonishing activity up on this utterly remote pass. Exactly as we crossed over, walking on grassy turf as short and green as an English lawn, the sun topped the mountains and a herd of three or four hundred goats, horns erect, was silhouetted on the dazzling skyline.

Three hours later at the bottom of a descent as steep as the day before's climb, and beyond a second spur of hills, we at last reached our breakfast village — Polimilos, 'Many Potatoes'.

CHAPTER 56

A Macedonia of peaches

The chief problem of buying supplies at Polimilos was to find potatoes. Neither the fruit-van nor the first shop could provide any and, judging by the time it took, the second shop had to have them dug from the ground, while the owner fed us on black olives and *ouzo*. So we set out at last for the pass, crossing the new main road with its many smoothly tarmacked hairpin bends and climbing towards the old stone road — almost certainly the one which Philip of Macedonia had used 2,300 years before, when he brought his armies south to impose his rule on the rest of Greece.

We still had not reached it when two roadmen, abandoning their bitumenising machine, came hurrying up the hillside to intercept us. As soon as they discovered that we were of interest, one of them laid himself full length on his elbow on the grass. "Sit down and let's talk," he invited us. Alas, we had just spent two hours breakfasting at Polimilos, we explained, and hoped to reach the pass that day. But I was sad to find that we were still so conditioned by our achievement-orientated society.

The pass seemed important because we needed a *taverna* at which we could celebrate Cordelia's twenty-first birthday next day, as well as a bus stop for my trip to Salonica. Pavlo's map and our three-day detour had put Edessa far out of reach. So we climbed again, the old road becoming more and more impressive as a deep valley opened below to our right, and range after range of mountains, including (though unidentifiable) Mount Olympus, appeared beyond.

Close to the summit, level ground and shade again became a problem, and so we made for some huts in a wooded area which we were told was an empty scout camp. At first it seemed a disaster when we found the gate locked, but immediately outside stood another fine poplar, and a grassy hillside fell away below, decorated with thyme, wild hollyhocks and clumps of yellow-green spurge. Here we settled. Within an hour the camp's caretaker had appeared with apologies that he wasn't allowed to let us in and cooked *souvlakia* for the children. He was quickly followed by an ancient cow-woman who shrieked at her cows like a maniac. Later that night we saw her, silhouetted against the skyline on a rocky peak, bleating loudly at some sheep and sounding exactly like one.

It was dusk the following evening by the time we climbed to the little group of cafés at the pass itself and approached the scruffiest of them, which we had been told was the best. Every forecourt table was full of eating families. But our caretaker friend was there too, and he soon created space for us at his table, where he and his friend became a part of our party.

They could hardly have been in greater contrast. The caretaker, a broad balding fifty, never stopped talking the whole evening. The friend, with long lugubrious face and drooping moustache under his forestry guard's uniform cap, never spoke a word except when he occasionally raised his beer glass and murmured '*Yassou*' as he clinked it with us.

We ordered *ouzo* for ourselves and *souvlakia* and Coca-Cola for the children. Then came *retsina* and various types of meaty stew, followed by Greek rice pudding, a far more delicious cinnamon-flavoured goo than the English variety. When it grew late we moved into the lamp-lit interior (no electricity) where the children at one end of the table did a complete performance of the opera version of *I Promessi Sposi*, the characters represented by *souvlakia* sticks stuck into salt and pepper pots. At the other end, Andrew reported that the caretaker's Greek was becoming harder and harder to understand, while the forestry guard had begun to look about him from under his cap with a wild-eyed animation as if at any moment he might actually break into speech.

It was midnight before we finally stumbled down the hillside and climbed into our bags. We needed them. At 1,500 metres the night was cold but wonderfully insect-free.

At dawn next day I caught the bus into Salonica. The first hour of the ride was through the sort of mountainous country we had been walking across and I felt a certain satisfaction that we had actually been struggling on foot up and down such almost vertical-sided valleys through such dense scrub. Across this appalling country it was hard to believe that paths even existed.

But beyond Véroia the road ran on the hot dreary plain and I realised how wise we were to stay in the mountains. I found Sue perspiring gently on a comfortable bed in the Hotel Delta. Her news was not what I had hoped for. Despite the Herr Doktor's penicillin injections her throat was still infected. There was nothing to do but leave her to submit to another course of the same painful treatment and return to camp.

So, next morning, we set off again, this time hoping that we really would reach Edessa for my next bus ride. We hadn't even climbed to the pass before we were ambushed by the screeching cow-woman. She had brought a litre of milk, a kilo of soft white cheese (both slightly dust-speckled) and ten eggs. Fifty metres higher up she again intercepted us, this time with a large jar of honey.

Almost at once we found the potatoes. In a high lonely valley, fields of them stretched away on either side, rising gently to more familiar goat-nibbled Macedonian mountain slopes. Suddenly and unexpectedly in this empty landscape we saw a tiny procession approaching down the track ahead. Slowly it came nearer, suggesting as Cordelia said, a shot from a Bunuel film. First two women in trousers, then five peasant men all in their best black suits and clean white tieless shirts. The oldest rode a tiny donkey. They came from a shepherd settlement in the mountains and were making their weekly visit to town to buy provisions.

Two or three kilometres on we found their settlement and amazing it was, the houses — if that is the right word — consisting entirely of leafy brushwood, interwoven with tattered sheet plastic. Round the corners of these, groups of little children peered at us, while older women with headscarfs stood spinning wool on hand distaffs. The whole was perched on a little round-topped hill.

Xirolivado, which we reached an hour later, after a stop for a thorough boiling of our speckled milk, was a complete contrast. In an airless upland basin under a threatening thunder-cloud, it consisted of little square concrete buildings with red roofs. Like so many, it was a village of resettled Asian Greeks established after the population exchange which followed the Greco-Turkish war of 1922–3. At its centre lay a brown stagnant lake around which huge herds of cows, goats and sheep moved. Drinking-water came from wells (one inside the café) but our animals seemed to share our feelings and refused it.

As soon as we moved on, the basin turned into a steep ravine. Jessica, dismounted and stumbling down behind us, was delayed by beds of wild strawberries under the beech trees, but our real undoing was four fantastic horned caterpillars. All on one plant, yellow, green, black and blue, they suggested monstrous armoured trains rather than insects. The five minutes we spent staring at them gave the storm time to catch us and for half an hour we stood miserably under a thick beech tree which would have deflected any normal rain but instantly became a sieve. The storm passed and round the next bend in the track we found the piece of level ground we had been looking for, where we camped on a bed of fragrant mint.

Next day we reached our highest point in the Vermoin mountains — we were now travelling north along their eastern slopes. This was the holiday village of Seli, almost the only place in Greece where I saw a river-bed filled with garbage on an Italian scale. As we breakfasted here a steady stream of Sunday lunches in big open pans were being brought to the window of the baker next door, for him to put in his oven and roast. It seemed a sensible system.

From Seli we descended sharply and, resting on a dramatic promontory, saw far below us our target for the day: the little town of Naousa. Astonishingly compact, it seemed to have no straggling outskirts in any direction. We later discovered the reason: though it appeared to lie on the plain it is in fact set on a plateau, tightly compressed between mountains to the west and a steep precipice to the east.

The surprising feature of that resting-place only gradually dawned on us. It was covered in lank and, by Greek standards, lush grass. Soon, as we continued to descend, we realised that the countryside we were passing through had also changed dramatically. We were walking between a dense mass of every kind of deciduous tree, from beech and oak to ash and acacia. The total absence of animal droppings confirmed our guess. We were in a goat-prohibited area.

The mass of impenetrable forest, an even six or seven metres high, presumably represented the growth since the regulation was enforced. It seemed conclusive evidence of the damage goats do. Earlier in the summer I had seen them actually climbing about in the branches of sloping trees. Their eating pattern is equally alarming. They go at it with a ravenous nibbling intensity, their heads darting here and there about the ground, quite unlike the placid pulling and ruminative chewing of, say, a cow. It was an odd thought that these impenetrable forested hillsides must be more like the landscape of classical Greece than the bare eroded and picturesque country we see today.

Near Naousa we began to pass trees of another kind: extensive orchards of peaches, their branches dangling with succulent red and yellow fruit. We asked a youth who was filling crates if we could buy some and he disappeared into a thatched, half-subterranean shelter below the road where his parents soon called us down. When we produced a plastic bag they tipped it full from a bucket, and, as we moved away protesting that we had enough, the youth came running after us with another enormous bucketful, insisting on topping up our knapsacks and saddle-bags till we could barely stagger. The question of payment was waved aside as if it didn't merit an answer.

Our semi-aerial view of Naousa had shown me a little hill nearby, topped with what I had guessed was the villa of some shipping magnate. Instead, it turned out to be a pretty white chapel, set among shady acacias with fine views over the town. Though this was far below us, it was conveniently close. It needed to be, because we now had to take the shoeing problem seriously. On our way up to Seli, Picchio had also cast a shoe, and at Koumaria the farrier had been far from professional.

Before the job was done, no less than three locals had literally had a bash, each in turn hammering home a nail or two while Picchio heaved, reared and backed away with so much power that he would have uprooted anything less sturdy than the telegraph pole to which he was tied, meanwhile eating his way through a loaf and a half of supposedly calming bread. The shoe they finally fitted in a botched way was of the solid-plate type worn by most Greek donkeys — the Greek word for horseshoe also means 'petal', which is what these horseshoes look like. They prevent stones entering and becoming wedged, but give a less good grip and, I'm told, jar the feet because they impede the natural cushioning spread each time the hoof takes weight. Picchio was now unevenly, as well as poorly, shod, which I felt sure was a grave offence against the rules of pony management.

The blacksmith at Naousa was built like a bull. Many Greeks are broad, but he was a giant in height as well. Andrew had become skilful at holding up hooves, but when Picchio began to kick, the smith called to his aid an equally massive brother who, apart from being enormously strong, wrapped Picchio's long black tail round his rear hoof so that each time he kicked he gave it a violent jolt at its root. Among all this muscle it was touching to see, below a swallow's nest on the beams of the smithy, a little plywood tray, suspended there to catch any young which might topple out.

The smith's charge for two and half animals (ten English-style shoes) was 270 drachmas (about £4). We also got a discount to take back to camp in the form of an enormous plastic bag of peaches. I began to understand why the Italian word for a fruit salad is a 'Macedonia'.

CHAPTER 57

The uses of garlic

Two days later we reached Edessa, the historic burial place of the kings of Macedonia. By tradition disaster would follow if any were buried elsewhere, a forecast which was amply fulfilled when Alexander the Great was buried in Asia Minor in 323 B.C. and the empire he had created, reaching from Greece to India and Egypt, disintegrated in civil war between his generals.

Like Naousa, Edessa is set on a plateau, with mountains behind and a sheer drop to the plain of Salonica to the east, down which tumble the famous cascades. Despite its compactness, we were less lucky with a camp-site, and finally settled for a dank cherry orchard immediately outside the barbed wire of a military-lorry park.

In 1848 Lear had approached Vodhena — as Edessa was then called — from the plain. "A more beautifully situated place can hardly be imagined," he wrote. "It stands on a long ridge of wooded cliff, with mosques sparkling above and waterfalls glittering down the hillside, the whole screen of rock seeming to close up the valley as a natural wall."

Approaching from above, Cordelia and I discovered one surviving mosque, and a broad stream flowing through the town which disappeared into a hissing hollow near the edge of the precipice, but a vast metal pipe snaking across the plain below suggested that hydroelectric engineers had been at work on the cascades. So we consoled ourselves with yoghurt, the best yet, made in big earthenware bowls and thickly coated with crusted cream, in a shop entirely devoted to yoghurt.

Returning at five, we noticed that the military-lorry park had begun to wake up and one or two sentries were repainting the wayside shrine at its entrance. Beside our donkeys stood a youthful soldier, watching them thoughtfully. He'd been there for an hour, Andrew said. Were they reminding him of his home in some remote Peloponnesian village?

Just before supper, as thunder rumbled and the sky darkened, a party of one civilian and two soldiers approached us up the orchard. The taller soldier addressed us in slow but excellent English. Unfortunately there was a 'leetle beet of trouble'. It was not possible to camp so close to a military establishment. Were we the family he had read about in the newspapers? He had been most interested in our story. There were many beautiful places near Edessa which were more than 500 metres from a military establishment. He was sorry, but orders were orders. Incidentally, there were many poisonous snakes in this orch₂.⁻d.

Not too reluctantly we agreed to move next morning. An hour later two more soldiers arrived and told us more abruptly that we must be gone by 6 a.m. It was already half-dark when a final pair ∼rrived and asked us whether we were quite comfortable and had everything we needed. Yes, indeed there were snakes here but they could be repelled with garlic. Taking our root and a knife, one of them went carefully round the tent, cutting up the cloves and scattering the bits in the grass. Otherwise the snakes were likely to creep into our tent for warmth. If we had been drinking milk we should rub our mouths with garlic. Snakes had a passion for milk and one had recently been discovered with its head half-way down the throat of a child who had been drinking it.

A week later I discovered that our night beside the Edessa barracks had been the one on which Greece and Turkey almost went to war about underwater oil rights in the Aegean. I was more than ever impressed by Greek hospitality and restraint, though I realised sadly that these might not be the qualities which win wars.

We reached Edessa next morning in time for a sumptuous yoghurt breakfast. It was market day and all around us peasants from the stalls were also breakfasting. The standard fare was a large bowl of yoghurt served with a slice of plain bread, but for those with a bigger appetite there was also a dark-grey watery soup to which a ladle of much-boiled meat was added.

While Cordelia made plans to start a yoghurt restaurant in Bristol, supplied by a herd of Greek sheep which the family would keep in the Welsh mountains, I bought Jessica new sandals. The day before, one of the pair with which she had travelled since Mende last summer had been washed away down a fast-flowing irrigation ditch and though Andrew had chased it for 200 metres it had finally disappeared into a gaping concrete mouth.

Edessa provided one more diversion: the surviving cascade. Lear's lithograph shows six. We found it on our way out and tethered our animals in the empty tourist park above, then walked about among the vast hurtling bodies of water which disappeared over the cliff edge a few metres beyond. For no apparent reason the chief item for sale at the stalls above were rows of stuffed animals. Nor can I explain why the art of taxidermy in Greece is so atrocious. The birds were all in moult, the wolf clearly had rickets and the other mammals were at best shrunken and aged. Most dismaying, the rabbits, perched on their hind feet, each carried in their mouths what I took to be little rolled red umbrellas, though the children later assured me that they had been carrots.

There were still three days before my next date with Susan in Salonica, and so we now set off in a north-easterly direction, aiming for the small town of Goumenissa. That morning there occurred a tiny episode which for me symbolised all the generosity we had been shown in Greece. Walking down a sandy track we met a young man strolling out from his village, a luscious yellow pear in his hand, into which he was about to bite. As he came level with us he handed it to Cordelia. He waited for no thanks, asked us no questions, just strolled on past us, occasionally turning to smile back at us.

That night we camped in an arid stretch of hilly country beside a trickling stream among clusters of the thistle-like plant we had often seen that summer, which has the most delicate blue foliage but is apparently so sharp that even goats won't eat it. We were back in goat country, all right, and realised how we had missed, not the goats themselves, but their herds. We met two here, the first decanting a large saucepan of milk for us from his pannier churns, the second providing us with something which turned out to be more valuable: a dozen big wooden tent pegs which he cut from the plane trees of the stream bed.

All afternoon a strong wind blew, bringing spitting rain from a grey sky. That night it grew to a gale, and by dawn every one of our light-weight pegs had been flapped out of the ground, leaving only his more substantial ones to keep the tent and fly-sheet standing. This was our first experience of the Varvari, a northerly wind which tears down the valley of the Varvari (as the Axios is called in Yugoslavia), a valley which runs due south from the Yugoslavian mountains to the sea at Salonica. In winter it brings ice and blizzards.

All next day it continued, but the grey clouds had gone and we walked through a sunny gale which would have blown our hats into the distance if it hadn't been for their chinstraps. I was reminded of that violent mistral we had walked through when we crossed the Rhône valley. We were now following the foothills of the Paikon Mountains, but lower down than I would have liked, and when the time came to camp the only shade-tree stood above a dismal sandy gully. So we set off across another six kilometres of flat country towards the next spur of hills. As we came near, a group of ecclesiastical buildings appeared on the hillside, and beside them a single huge oak set at the centre of what looked like corn stubble. When we eventually arrived there we found the monastery deserted.

It was a perfect place, with an extensive view over the hazy plain of Salonica, good shade, a nearby goat-trough and a continuous stream of shepherds to interest us, driving huge flocks of sheep, goats, cows and even donkeys across the stubble. The moment we arrived a splendid black jack ass provided the children with a live biology lesson.

The monastery had only four rooms, all now with open sagging doors and broken floors. Recently a group of farmers had bought its land. The church itself, however, remained intact and was a pretty Romanesque building, full of colourful neo-Byzantine paintings. Like all the remote chapels we found in Greece, it was visited by women and little girls who tended the lamps. On August 15th there would be a vast assembly here to celebrate the greatest feast-day of the Orthodox Church.

Of the shepherds we met, Nikolaou was our favourite. He was a gentle, sad man in a big straw hat and smart green shirt, who wore a black armband which we thought might be in memory of his wife but in fact was for his mother. He brought us his home-grown, home-baked bread and home-made cheese, and told us about the economics of herding. Sheep's milk was the most valuable, goats' next, then cows'. He measured the production of his animals in litres per year. Ninety for a goat. Not much by the standards of an English goat.

Nikolaou had no children and his fellow shepherds sympathised. "What has he to celebrate?" one of them asked. But he had a dog who for two days displaced even Hannibal in Miranda's affections. It was the normal sturdy grey-black Greek sheep dog in all but one feature: its ears. One of these was long and floppy, the other cut into a little upright triangle.

Why had he cut his dog's ear, we asked Nikolaou. So that he could hear wolves better, Nikolaou said. Then why not cut both, we asked. "Ah," said Nikolaou, pausing and staring at us as if wondering whether he should disclose this valuable secret, "then when he is in the mountains and it rains he can sleep with his short ear to the ground and his long ear upwards to keep the water out."

CHAPTER 58

Last days in the mountains

This time my bus-ride to Salonica took me through Yiannitsa where a monument celebrates the victory of the Greeks over the Turks in the

Balkan War of 1912–13, as a result of which Greece regained the sections of Macedonia and Thrace which she still holds. Andrew had already noticed that the local shepherds referred to the rest of the country as Old Greece. The battle of Yiannitsa was in fact fought outside the town at the crossing of the river Balitsa, a line which the Turks defended fiercely.

Again I found Susan on her comfortable bed at the Delta, but in still lower spirits than before. Her throat was still infected in spite of her second course of penicillin injections and now her German doctor wanted to test an experimental drug on her. When she had refused he had become extremely angry, no doubt at the loss of an interesting paragraph of his research report. In about five minutes our minds were made up. She must go home and be treated in England.

Her better news was that she had found a home for our animals. My original plan had been to sell them to some Greek peasant, but even I had begun to doubt whether this would be possible when I thought of Hannibal's big furry neck clutched in Miranda's arms, a look of adoring love in her eyes as she laid her cheek alongside his benign if slightly dopey face. Now Michael Ward had discovered an Anglo-American-Greek farm near Thermi on the Khalkidiki Peninsula which would be glad to give all three animals a home. Susan wanted to have them transported there instantly by lorry but I was determined to finish on our own feet, and persuaded her that we would manage, even when Cordelia left us, as she must in a few days' time.

We spent a hectic morning buying tickets and running from bank to bank, in an attempt to get Italian and French currency for her journey before they closed, but ended it peacefully with an excellent meal at a small restaurant near the flower market. Here we had one of those uniquely Greek dishes of baked aubergine topped with a cheesy crust, containing at its centre great hunks of tender beef, and washed it down with a bottle of the apparently much valued red wine of Naousa.

Hurrying about the busy, colourful and brightly sunlit streets of modern Salonica, I found it difficult to connect the place with the one described by Lear — gloomy, shut-up and deserted, in the grip of a cholera epidemic. "Multitudes of the inhabitants of the suburbs and adjacent villages had fled to the plains", but "the surrounding villages had taken alarm and had drawn a strict *cordon sanitaire* between themselves and the enemy."

The day after his arrival he walked about "its narrow, ill-paved streets . . . the very few people I met in them carefully avoiding contact; the closed houses; the ominous silence; the sultry, oppressive heat of the day; all contributed to impress the mind with a feeling of heavy melancholy. A few Jews in dark dresses and turbans; Jewesses, their hair tied up in long, caterpillar-like green silk bags, three feet in length; Greek porters, aged blacks, of whom — freed slaves from Stamboul — there are many in Salonica; these were the only human beings I encountered in threading a labyrinth of lanes in the lower town."

Those Jews were descendants of the 20,000 who, driven out of Spain by Ferdinand and Isabella, settled here in 1492. Their language, Ladino, must have been one of the oddest mongrels ever devised: a Catalan dialect which they wrote in a Hebrew script. They remained a substantial part of the population of Salonica till the Second World War, when the Germans deported 60,000 of them to Poland from which country they never returned.

I was a lot less sure than I had pretended that Andrew and I could manage the two children and three animals. Next day we arranged a rehearsal: Cordelia would walk beside us but take no part in animal control. It was a testing day for this experiment.

All went well at first. Andrew as usual led Miranda on Picchio, while I led Jessica on Hamilcar. Hannibal followed on his own. But as we approached our first village I remembered to turn and look for him. He had totally disappeared. A second later I saw him, 500 metres back, plodding stolidly across country at right angles to our track, aiming for a local friend he had discovered. There was something touching about the sight of our plump and furry eunuch setting off on this love-making mission, still loaded down with his heavy pack-saddle and two huge kit-bags.

After that we positioned him between us, so that I wouldn't forget him, and could grab his reins in an emergency. At the entrances to villages Miranda and Jessica dismounted; Miranda led Hamilcar and I drove Hannibal.

The morning ended with a descent into a deeply eroded valley, through thick scrub and bush. Its sides were so steep that it was hard for the animals to keep their footing or find their way, and a succession of half-hearted goat tracks were little help. But now Hannibal behaved with astonishing good sense, plunging steadily downhill through growth which was often above his ears. When at last we reached the bottom we were rewarded by a pleasant stream and a water-meadow which might have been English in its green softness. Our attempts to catch rainwater from a shower failed and for almost the first time we were forced to drink boiled and sterilised stream water.

Next day was the last on which Cordelia would walk with us. Goumenissa was still our target — a small town about which our guide-book said not a single word. But it was a point on the road some kilometres short of it which for me marked the end of this part of our journey. Suddenly, as we descended round a bend in the hilly road I saw ahead the vast flat river basin which runs north from Salonica towards the Yugoslavian border. And there at its centre, a dull silver snake stretching from as far right to as far left as I could see, was the river Axios.

Across this flat river basin we would be walking on our next and final stage. Now, at Goumenissa, we would leave the mountains in which we had travelled for so many weeks, with their rugged stony tracks, goats, goat-herds and the agricultural practices of another century.

It was an appropriate good-bye. When we disturbed the shepherd, who lay asleep in his socks in the glade where we wanted to camp, we were rushed at by no fewer than ten dogs, all nearly identical and all large and fierce. Giorgiou, their owner, called them off before they could savage us, and showed us a spring of fresh cold water which bubbled up beside the stream bed. Squatting by our camp fire, he begged us to take him to England. It was his Mecca, and though he listened politely to Andrew's vivid comparison of his happy pastoral life with the dismal time he would have washing dishes in a Soho restaurant, I could tell that he wasn't believing a word of it.

Presently Andrew walked to town to arrange a farewell supper for Cordelia. When I went there next day I found that in the space of a couple of hours, half the town had become his friends. Wherever I went I was asked about 'Andrea' and complimented on his idiomatic Greek. He was eventually brought back by car, carrying a fine hunk of pork which he had had roasted in the baker's oven.

Late that evening, where the nearest bridge crossed our stream, a couple of hundred soldiers were suddenly decanted from lorries and began to roam about the hillside, eating supper out of square billy-cans. A little hazy with the good red wine of Goumenissa, I went to sleep to the sound of volleys of blank cartridge as their night exercise spread over the surrounding hills. By morning not a sign of them was to be seen, but they had increased my feeling that Greece's northern provinces are a kind of military bastion against her four hostile neighbours: Albania, Yugoslavia, Bulgaria and Turkey.

L

CHAPTER 59

Bridges, fords and ferries

The basin of the river Axios, and of the Galikos, which runs parallel
but twenty kilometres further east, is less flat than our first view had
suggested. All morning we walked across rolling cornland with contours which suggested the Wiltshire Downs. Presently corn gave way
to tobacco and here we met the first people we had seen all day in
this empty landscape. They were peasant families picking tobacco and
loading the leaves into horse-drawn wagons. Looking across the
countryside to a parallel track, I saw one of these wagons being driven
home at full gallop, the driver standing, whip circling above his
head. A race to get to his village to catch some tobacco merchant?
Or just an inherited behaviour pattern from his Macedonian charioteer
ancestors of 2,000 years ago? This second tobacco-growing area we
were crossing, which stretches east into Thrace, was the chief source
of the famous Balkan Sobranie tobacco, and made its special contribution to the history of the last war by delaying any possible alliance
against Germany till too late. Germany was the chief buyer of the
crop which was a vital part of the Greek economy.

Another tobacco-picking family gave us reassuring directions. The
point on the Axios we were aiming for was the best place to cross. We
would find something here called a *seli*, a word which Andrew's dictionary didn't give but which must surely mean a footbridge or at least
a ford. But when we eventually descended off the downland to the flat
river-beds, we were told that the river was quite impassable at this
point. The *seli* (ferry) had ceased to operate three years ago. We
camped nearby, among fields of flowering cotton, in a mosquito-in-
fested poplar wood, and spent one of the murkier nights of the summer.
Again the Varvari struck, this time preceded by a violent thunderstorm
which rolled and crashed around us most of the night. At dawn the
rain was still falling and the wind had risen to a gale. All that morning it blew us along the river's flood-bank, across a strange landscape,
half lowland meadows with white egrets standing up to their knees in
brown ponds, half fields of intensively cultivated maize, cotton and
tomatoes.

At last we reached a bridge and crossed the Axios, a modest river perhaps the size of the Thames at Oxford. As we looked back and down from a low hill, it was so brown with mud from the night's rain that it seemed more like a stretch of plough than water.

Forewarned, we turned north-east next day and aimed for Galikos, a village on the river of the same name, where we were assured there really was a bridge. For two long days we walked across dry flat land, broken only by occasional thorn trees among the stubble. The storks were the strangest feature of those days. Several times we met parties of eight or ten, spread across the country, poking about with their big beaks for dropped grain. One after another they would laboriously lift themselves into the air, their drooping necks and dangling legs forming a strange crescent as they finally became airborne. The swallows were equally interesting. As we crossed the big hedgeless fields, now often walking by compass and not troubling with tracks, flights of them would hover near us, frequently coming within a couple of metres, their little orange bibs brightly visible. Looking about, I would see none further away, as if all had congregated around us, genuinely curious about this odd party crossing their territory.

Two nights later we at last camped near Galikos and I walked ahead to find the river and bridge. Presently I came to a tiny trickle of clear running water, perhaps two paces across. A hundred metres further on I found another, similar but still smaller. I stepped across the Galikos without even getting the uppers of my boots wet.

Next day we descended the river's wide but almost dry bed. All through Greece we had seen birds, a contrast to Italy where the few which have not been blasted to pieces are so timid that they flit into cover when they are still in the middle distance. That morning in the bed of the Galikos the variety was amazing — storks, egrets, white and black herons, rollers, and even an eagle with thick feathery legs, to mention only the larger and more spectacular.

The river, which widened marginally as we descended it, was also full of fish. As we breakfasted beside it, the local rural guard — an official we had met before in Greece with roughly the position of the old English village policeman combined with the lesser authority of a traffic warden — gave us advice about the route. He carried a strange weapon: a stick as tall as a walking-stick ending in a mesh of wire about the size of a ping-pong bat. "For fishing," he told us, and demonstrated his method by raising it threateningly above his head.

Following his advice, we climbed steeply into hills once more. A couple of hours later, as we topped a pass, we saw the sea, and there beside it, a sprawling mess of houses, flats, factory chimneys and power-station cooling-towers, grey and dim in its heat haze, was the city of Salonica. It lay in a crescent on the shores of the Gulf of Salonica, a gulf so fouled by sewage that fishing is no longer allowed there. Somewhere in the distance beyond the hazy city lay Thermi and the Litsas Farm, our final destination.

Late the following night, camped on a carpet of pine needles above Oreokastro, we looked down on a prettier view of the city, lit from end to end in the pink dusk. But as we had found when we passed close to Florence the autumn before, the fall-out of even the most elegant modern cities can be horrific. Salonica specialised in stinking broiler houses, tiny factories with black-smoking chimneys which seemed to be processing mounds of ancient woollen underwear, and marble quarries.

For three days we circled it, using the steep hills which hem it in, frequently meeting such unpleasantnesses. At dawn we would be woken by violent explosions, and clouds of white dust would billow slowly above some pretty hillside, as if an artillery battery had arbitrarily decided to lay down a barrage there. These were the quarries blasting down the portions of hillside which enormous lorries would cart away during the day. But for hours at a time we would also cross country as empty and unspoiled as any we had seen.

On the first of these days, as we sat in utter exhaustion, drinking gassy lemonade at a chromium and rexine café — we were now finding such things in otherwise simple villages, as if the whirling city had flung them out and they had landed arbitrarily in quite inappropriate places — Andrew announced that we now had another problem. For the past forty-eight hours he had been suffering from sharp pains in the correct area for appendicitis.

All those days his pains came and went. Every few hours I asked about them. Salonica and its hospital were near, but a sudden flare-up could mean a journey over three or four kilometres of rugged hillside to reach a road, not to mention creating the problem of what to do with the children and animals if I had to go with him. "What shall we do," Jessica asked me anxiously. "If Andrew does have laminitis?"

Perhaps Andrew's pain disturbed his concentration. He understood the café owner at Exohi to say that above the village we would pass a resident English family. It would be interesting to meet them, I thought. They would know of the earth-track we were looking for. Uphill we went and just as we were losing momentum and wondering which way to go, we saw low grey walls surrounding a garden-like enclosure. A moment later we recognised it as a cemetery and at its gate read that it held the graves of 900 English dead from the First World War. "Private J. Lee," I read on the nearest concrete gravestone below the bugle badge of the Ox and Bucks Light Infantry. "Died 12 Oct 1918."

From a shack higher up the cemetery a complete Greek family now emerged, the mother carrying a child who timidly stroked the donkeys' noses. The father was proud of his graveyard, which was green and neatly mown, an odd rectangular oasis in the brown countryside. He was delighted to find that we were English. How different all those lonely military cemeteries of northern France would seem if each had its caretaker and family engaged in a kind of day-long picnic among the ranks of crosses!

Salonica receded, the blue mountains of the Khalkidiki Peninsula rose ahead and, early on the fourth day, we saw below us a little village which was surely Thermi. From above it looked hot and bare. We came down the hillside towards it with apprehension. What I feared was that Miranda would decide that it was no place for Hannibal to spend his retirement.

There was just one area of trees, lying on a rise above the village and exactly in our path. We would call there and ask directions. It was only when I saw among the shady pines a bright blue horse-jump of the sort which dot the roadside paddocks of the Home Counties that I dared to hope for anything better. Ten minutes later we were being welcomed by Fiona, who at the same time held Henrietta, the tame hen, under one arm and attempted to drive off a pack of unruly dogs with the other.

CHAPTER 60

The farm at Salonica

Little remains to be said. We spent four happy days at the Litsas Farm — for Miranda and Jessica, blissful would not be too strong a word, as they helped tend the three horses, four geese, Billy the mauled goat who had been rescued from wild dogs, the nameless white rabbit, and Mother, the farm bitch, who should have been in isolation because she was on heat — but rarely was. In those four days it became the children's home, showing how much they now needed a stopping-place. There were tears when we left.

On the second evening Fiona and Nic, an English-American boy who helped manage the animals, improvised a gymkhana, and Picchio, Hannibal and Hamilcar solemnly performed the rituals of a Surrey park: bending, egg and spoon race, sack race. They were certainly adaptable animals, though at show-jumping we drew the line. As for their future, Picchio was to give riding-lessons to rich little Greek girls, while Hannibal and Hamilcar were to wait on Thalis the stallion and Carmen the mare by pulling their dung cart.

Later we sat through half the warm night listening to Niko singing and playing on the bazouki the soft sad music of *rebetika*, music of Greece's urban proletariat of the twenties, trying to ignore the swarms of mosquitoes which fed busily on our ankles. Niko was the only Greek who lived on the farm, a charming and sympathetic person whose teddy-bear shape and manner hid considerable intelligence. He slept so much, he expained, to catch up with all that he had missed during his twenty-eight months of military service. While Niko slept, Barbara, his pretty American wife, played a responsible and rather anxious controlling role on the farm, separating Nic and Fiona when their water fights became too destructive, continuously listening for the yelps and howls which would mean that Mother's lovers had leapt the wire fence and got into her isolation pen again.

Finally there was Taki Litsas, the owner of the farm. When he had inherited it from his grandfather it had been a wilderness. About thirty, tall, thin and quiet, Taki was a romantic. For him the others were fulfilling a dream by bringing the farm to life again and as he sat silently at the succession of splendid meals they gave us I guessed that we and our donkeys had become a part of his dream.

But he was practical. We had been there less than an hour before he was driving Andrew to Salonica hospital. Here Andrew's appendix was given a full examination and found entirely healthy. Those pains remain a mystery.

One evening I asked Taki about the Vlachs. Certainly he knew about them because he was a Vlach. His family came from the Lake Ochrid part of Yugoslavia and his grandparents had spoken Vlach. But in nationality and customs they had always considered themselves Greek Vlachs.

His grandfather, apart from buying the farm at Thermi and planting its fine avenues of pines and orchards of almonds, had dealt in textiles. In this business he had spent the longest period of his life as a merchant in Smyrna. So, for those who like a tidy conclusion, a tiny connecting link had been established between ourselves and the destination we never reached. Taki's grandfather and Joseph Chitty, my great-great-great-great-grandfather had both been merchants in the city of Smyrna.

But, looking back on our journey, I see it more as an episode than as something complete in itself. Our previous life had led to it, and it in turn will lead us to a new life, not apparently very different, but in fact much changed because we can never again be the same.

The journey itself, the places seen, the distances marched, the people met are all important, but it is this change in ourselves which remains the essence of what we have brought back, though just how to define it I find difficult.

Certainly it consists in part in a sense of having more or less successfully passed through a prolonged physical endurance test. We all walked further and survived more heat, cold, wet and general hardship than we had ever believed we could. And in part it is the acquiring of a new sense of landscape; I shall never again travel about in the two-dimensional world of maps and road patterns. It has become automatic to lift my eyes to the hills and valleys beyond. More important, the generosity and kindness of the Greeks has given us a standard for human behaviour from which we shall never escape. The actual physical gifts they gave us were only outward signs of a broader and better view of life, which makes meanness not so much deplorable as absurd.

On a more public level, our relationships with each other were put under a considerable strain, which they have, I hope, survived. Weaknesses emerged. We were not always harmonious, though perhaps a little more often than we might have expected. In essence our disagreements mostly took the form of myself wanting to walk further and Susan wanting to stop, but the simple isolation of the issue gives little idea of the passions which were aroused.

Less tangibly, we were brought into a new relationship with decision-taking because the effects of a wrong decision could not be mitigated or postponed as they usually can be in easier circumstances, but were often immediate and very unpleasant. Each day's march contained several of these. It now seems to me that apparently quiet days at home may also contain significant decisions, though we conspire to pretend that they don't.

As for Miranda and Jessica, I know of no way to forecast what the experience may ultimately mean for them. Their broken arms have recovered. Their formal education, under Andrew's tuition, is ahead. They have fitted back with no apparent difficulty into the village school. So I hope that at least the journey has done them no harm. At best it may have given them a permanent awareness that England is not the centre of the world and English ways of behaving are not the only possible ones. Certainly they were as aware as the rest of us of the generous spirit of Greece.

They, Susan and I are back in Sussex, where, however changed in ourselves, we have nominally taken up the life we left eighteen months before. Andrew has not. For him the journey was more literally an episode. Three weeks after we reached England we heard that he and Fiona were setting out to walk up the Nile to Tanzania.

Index

EPILOGUE

THIRTY YEARS LATER

by Jessica Chitty

By all appearances the experience of my being taken across Europe on the back of a donkey at the age of 3 has very little effect on my life. My life is neither adventurous nor bohemian. After five dedicated years at various Art Colleges I am now a 34 year old Software Project Manager. I have a two year old daughter who goes to a very nice nursery and I live with my partner of 15 years in a Victorian terrace on the edge of London. I like buying clothes. I have perfume, and a handbag, and lately I have even started doing my grocery shopping online.

But that isn't to say it hasn't influenced me. As a child who returned home at the age of five puzzled by her total lack of recognition of this place called 'home' everyone was so excited to be in, I see the journey in a very romantic light.

I can imagine nothing more idyllic for a three year old than travelling all day with her parents and her older siblings. No 'Daddy will be home from the office soon, go and watch a video while I try and get the dinner on'. Imagine being three without the constraints of cream carpets, china plates and not-to-be-drawn-upon emulsion walls: nothing to break; everything to get messy and new experiences every day. I feel I was totally free.

Now I attempt to bring order to my life – and the lives of others. I'm a Project Manager for *gawd's* sake! But deep down I think those that know me best know lurks great chaos – and I hasten to add *enormous* c-r-e-a-t-i-v-t-y. I have no idea when to stop, I fall into bed, never put myself to bed, I dream up mad schemes, I try and cook three new evening meals while my daughter has her afternoon nap and even as I write this I very much doubt it'll be anywhere near legible when I attempt to type it in the morning.

I feel my freedom at that time has allowed me to be like this, to reject certain values and to see clearly the importance of family, humour, good food and - well play. Maybe I'm not hungry to travel but that isn't what The Donkey Walk was to me. Through my Vaselined spectacles it was a time when we were all together, we had friends all over the world (well Europe) and we had things to do.

I have never thought hard about how it was to anyone who had reached the age of responsibility or reasoned thought. I'm prepared to believe it must have all seemed a pretty bad idea at times! What I can't deny is that when we did come home those times were gone. Mum was very ill shortly afterwards. My next clear memory is of going into the bathroom one morning at the age of six to find these strange brown foamy spots around the basin: the residue of vomit after Mum had taken an overdose of aspirin. It was a way of life that it wasn't practical to continue forever but in retrospect coming home was the stark and early point where my adult life had to begin – and maybe why I am this strange combination of order and chaos.

I don't regret these negative aspects of the walk – they've made me what I am as much as the glorious aura of the journey – and I'm happy with that – and I'm now happy I can pass on the values that my early life gave me to my family. The Donkey Walk was significant. I'm impressed that my parents did it and I'm grateful to have been part of it. Maybe surprisingly, it has also eliminated any desire I have to embark upon a similar adventure. A camping holiday or a long distance train journey across Europe, maybe, but nothing more.

Abernathy, Miles, *Ride the Wind* – the amazing true story of the little Abernathy Boys, who made a series of astonishing journeys in the United States, starting in 1909 when they were aged five and nine!

Beard, John, *Saddles East* – John Beard determined as a child that he wanted to see the Wild West from the back of a horse after a visit to Cody's legendary Wild West show. Yet it was only in 1948 – more than sixty years after seeing the flamboyant American showman – that Beard and his wife Lulu finally set off to follow their dreams.

Beker, Ana, *The Courage to Ride* – Determined to out-do Tschiffely, Beker made a 17,000 mile mounted odyssey across the Americas in the late 1940s that would fix her place in the annals of equestrian travel history.

Bird, Isabella, *Among the Tibetans* – A rousing 1889 adventure, an enchanting travelogue, a forgotten peek at a mountain kingdom swept away by the waves of time.

Bird, Isabella, *On Horseback* in *Hawaii* – The Victorian explorer's first horseback journey, in which she learns to ride astride, in early 1873.

Bird, Isabella, *Journeys in Persia and Kurdistan, Volumes 1 and 2* – The intrepid Englishwoman undertakes another gruelling journey in 1890.

Bird, Isabella, *A Lady's Life in the Rocky Mountains* – The story of Isabella Bird's adventures during the winter of 1873 when she explored the magnificent unspoiled wilderness of Colorado. Truly a classic.

Bird, Isabella, *Unbeaten Tracks in Japan, Volumes One and Two* – A 600-mile solo ride through Japan undertaken by the intrepid British traveller in 1878.

Boniface, Lieutenant Jonathan, *The Cavalry Horse and his Pack* – Quite simply the most important book ever written in the English language by a military man on the subject of equestrian travel.

Bosanquet, Mary, *Saddlebags for Suitcases* – In 1939 Bosanquet set out to ride from Vancouver, Canada, to New York. Along the way she was wooed by love-struck cowboys, chased by a grizzly bear and even suspected of being a Nazi spy, scouting out Canada in preparation for a German invasion. A truly delightful book.

de Bourboulon, Catherine, *Shanghai à Moscou (French)* – the story of how a young Scottish woman and her aristocratic French husband travelled overland from Shanghai to Moscow in the late 19th Century.

Brown, Donald; *Journey from the Arctic* – A truly remarkable account of how Brown, his Danish companion and their two trusty horses attempt the impossible, to cross the silent Arctic plateaus, thread their way through the giant Swedish forests, and finally discover a passage around the treacherous Norwegian marshes.

Bruce, Clarence Dalrymple, *In the Hoofprints of Marco Polo* – The author made a dangerous journey from Srinagar to Peking in 1905, mounted on a trusty 13-hand Kashmiri pony, then wrote this wonderful book.

Burnaby, Frederick, *A Ride to Khiva* – Burnaby fills every page with a memorable cast of characters, including hard-riding Cossacks, nomadic Tartars, vodka-guzzling sleigh-drivers and a legion of peasant ruffians.

Burnaby, Frederick, *On Horseback through Asia Minor* – Armed with a rifle, a small stock of medicines, and a single faithful servant, the equestrian traveler rode through a hotbed of intrigue and high adventure in wild inhospitable country, encountering Kurds, Circassians, Armenians, and Persian pashas.

Carter, General William, *Horses, Saddles and Bridles* – This book covers a wide range of topics including basic training of the horse and care of its equipment. It also provides a fascinating look back into equestrian travel history.

Cayley, George, *Bridle Roads of Spain* – Truly one of the greatest equestrian travel accounts of the 19th Century.

Chase, J. Smeaton, *California Coast Trails* – This classic book describes the author's journey from Mexico to Oregon along the coast of California in the 1890s.

Chase, J. Smeaton, *California Desert Trails* – Famous British naturalist J. Smeaton Chase mounted up and rode into the Mojave Desert to undertake the longest equestrian study of its kind in modern history.

Clark, Leonard, *Marching Wind, The* - The panoramic story of a mounted exploration in the remote and savage heart of Asia, a place where adventure, danger, and intrigue were the daily backdrop to wild tribesman and equestrian exploits.

Cobbett, William, *Rural Rides, Volumes 1 and 2* – In the early 1820s Cobbett set out on horseback to make a series of personal tours through the English countryside. These books contain what many believe to be the best accounts of rural England ever written, and remain enduring classics.

Codman, John, *Winter Sketches from the Saddle* – This classic book was first published in 1888. It recommends riding for your health and describes the septuagenarian author's many equestrian journeys through New England during the winter of 1887 on his faithful mare, Fanny.

Cunninghame Graham, Jean, *Gaucho Laird* – A superbly readable biography of the author's famous great-uncle, Robert "Don Roberto" Cunninghame Graham.

Cunninghame Graham, Robert, *Horses of the Conquest* –The author uncovered manuscripts which had lain forgotten for centuries, and wrote this book, as he said, out of gratitude to the horses of Columbus and the Conquistadors who shaped history.

Cunninghame Graham, Robert, *Magreb-el-Acksa* – The thrilling tale of how "Don Roberto" was kidnapped in Morocco!

Cunninghame Graham, Robert, *Rodeo* – An omnibus of the finest work of the man they called "the uncrowned King of Scotland," edited by his friend Aimé Tschiffely.

Cunninghame Graham, Robert, *Tales of Horsemen* – Ten of the most beautifully-written equestrian stories ever set to paper.

Cunninghame Graham, Robert, *Vanished Arcadia* – This haunting story about the Jesuit missions in South America from 1550 to 1767 was the inspiration behind the best-selling film *The Mission*.

Daly, H.W., *Manual of Pack Transportation* – This book is the author's masterpiece. It contains a wealth of information on various pack saddles, ropes and equipment, how to secure every type of load imaginable and instructions on how to organize a pack train.

Dixie, Lady Florence, *Riding Across Patagonia* – When asked in 1879 why she wanted to travel to such an outlandish place as Patagonia, the author replied without hesitation that she was taking to the saddle in order to flee from the strict confines of polite Victorian society. This is the story of how the aristocrat successfully traded the perils of a London parlor for the wind-borne freedom of a wild Patagonian bronco.

Dodwell, Christina, *Travels with Fortune* – the truly amazing account of the courageous author's first journey – a three-year odyssey around Africa by Landrover, bus, lorry, horse, camel, and dugout canoe!

Dodwell, Christina, *A Traveller on Horseback* – Christina Dodwell rides through Eastern Turkey and Iran in the late 1980s. The Sunday Telegraph wrote of the author's "courage and insatiable wanderlust," and in this book she demonstrates her gift for communicating her zest for adventure.

Dodwell, Christina, *Travels in Papua New Guinea* – Christina Dodwell spends two years exploring an island little known to the outside world. She travelled by foot, horse and dugout canoe among the Stone-Age tribes.

Ehlers, Otto, *Im Sattel durch die Fürstenhöfe Indiens* – In June 1890 the young German adventurer, Ehlers, lay very ill. His doctor gave him a choice: either go home to Germany or travel to Kashmir. So of course the Long Rider chose the latter. This is a thrilling yet humorous book about the author's adventures.

Farson, Negley, *Caucasian Journey* – A thrilling account of a dangerous equestrian journey made in 1929, this is an amply illustrated adventure classic.

Fox, Ernest, *Travels in Afghanistan* – The thrilling tale of a 1937 journey through the mountains, valleys, and deserts of this forbidden realm, including visits to such fabled places as the medieval city of

Heart, the towering Hindu Kush mountains, and the legendary Khyber Pass.

Galton, Francis, *The Art of Travel* – Originally published in 1855, this book became an instant classic and was used by a host of now-famous explorers, including Sir Richard Francis Burton of Mecca fame. Readers can learn how to ride horses, handle elephants, avoid cobras, pull teeth, find water in a desert, and construct a sleeping bag out of fur.

Glazier, Willard, *Ocean to Ocean on Horseback* – This book about the author's journey from New York to the Pacific in 1875 contains every kind of mounted adventure imaginable. Amply illustrated with pen and ink drawings of the time, the book remains a timeless equestrian adventure classic.

Goodwin, Joseph, *Through Mexico on Horseback* – The author and his companion, Robert Horiguchi, the sophisticated, multi-lingual son of an imperial Japanese diplomat, set out in 1931 to cross Mexico. They were totally unprepared for the deserts, quicksand and brigands they were to encounter during their adventure.

Hanbury-Tenison, Marika, *For Better, For Worse* – The author, an excellent story-teller, writes about her adventures visiting and living among the Indians of Central Brazil.

Hanbury-Tenison, Marika, *A Slice of Spice* – The fresh and vivid account of the author's hazardous journey to the Indonesian Islands with her husband, Robin.

Hanbury-Tenison, Robin, *Chinese Adventure* – The story of a unique journey in which the explorer Robin Hanbury-Tenison and his wife Louella rode on horseback alongside the Great Wall of China in 1986.

Hanbury-Tenison, Robin, *Fragile Eden* – The wonderful story of Robin and Louella Hanbury-Tenison's exploration of New Zealand on horseback in 1988. They rode alone together through what they describe as 'some of the most dramatic and exciting country we have ever seen.'

Hanbury-Tenison, Robin, *Mulu: The Rainforest* – This was the first popular book to bring to the world's attention the significance of the rain forests to our fragile ecosystem. It is a timely reminder of our need to preserve them for the future.

Hanbury-Tenison, Robin, *A Pattern of Peoples* – The author and his wife, Marika, spent three months travelling through Indonesia's outer islands and writes with his usual flair and sensitivity about the tribes he found there.

Hanbury-Tenison, Robin, *A Question of Survival* – This superb book played a hugely significant role in bringing the plight of Brazil's Indians to the world's attention.

Hanbury-Tenison, Robin, *The Rough and the Smooth* – The incredible story of two journeys in South America. Neither had been attempted before, and both were considered impossible!

Hanbury-Tenison, Robin, *Spanish Pilgrimage* – Robin and Louella Hanbury-Tenison went to Santiago de Compostela in a traditional way – riding on white horses over long-forgotten tracks. In the process they discovered more about the people and the country than any conventional traveller would learn. Their adventures are vividly and entertainingly recounted in this delightful and highly readable book.

Hanbury-Tenison, Robin, *White Horses over France* – This enchanting book tells the story of a magical journey and how, in fulfilment of a personal dream, the first Camargue horses set foot on British soil in the late summer of 1984.

Hanbury-Tenison, Robin, *Worlds Apart – an Explorer's Life* – The author's battle to preserve the quality of life under threat from developers and machines infuses this autobiography with a passion and conviction which makes it impossible to put down.

Hanbury-Tenison, Robin, *Worlds Within – Reflections in the Sand* – This book is full of the adventure you would expect from a man of action like Robin Hanbury-Tenison. However, it is also filled with the type of rare knowledge that was revealed to other desert travellers like Lawrence, Doughty and Thesiger.

Haslund, Henning, *Mongolian Adventure* – An epic tale inhabited by a cast of characters no longer present in this lackluster world, shamans who set themselves on fire, rebel leaders who sacked towns, and wild horsemen whose ancestors conquered the world.

Heath, Frank, *Forty Million Hoofbeats* – Heath set out in 1925 to follow his dream of riding to all 48 of the Continental United States. The journey lasted more than two years, during which time Heath and his mare, Gypsy Queen, became inseparable companions.

Holt, William, *Ride a White Horse* – After rescuing a cart horse, Trigger, from slaughter and nursing him back to health, the 67-year-old Holt and his horse set out in 1964 on an incredible 9,000 mile, non-stop journey through western Europe.

Hopkins, Frank T., *Hidalgo and Other Stories* – For the first time in history, here are the collected writings of Frank T. Hopkins, the counterfeit cowboy whose endurance racing claims and Old West fantasies have polarized the equestrian world.

James, Jeremy, *Saddletramp* – The classic story of Jeremy James' journey from Turkey to Wales, on an unplanned route with an inaccurate compass, unreadable map and the unfailing aid of villagers who seemed to have as little sense of direction as he had.

James, Jeremy, *Vagabond* – The wonderful tale of the author's journey from Bulgaria to Berlin offers a refreshing, witty and often surprising view of Eastern Europe and the collapse of communism.

Jebb, Louisa, *By Desert Ways to Baghdad and Damascus* – From the pen of a gifted writer and intrepid traveller, this is one of the greatest equestrian travel books of all time.

Kluckhohn, Clyde, *To the Foot of the Rainbow* – This is not just a exciting true tale of equestrian adventure. It is a moving account of a young man's search for physical perfection in a desert world still untouched by the recently-born twentieth century.

Lambie, Thomas, *Boots and Saddles in Africa* – Lambie's story of his equestrian journeys is told with the grit and realism that marks a true classic.

Landor, Henry Savage, *In the Forbidden Land* – Illustrated with hundreds of photographs and drawings, this blood-chilling account of equestrian adventure makes for page-turning excitement.

Langlet, Valdemar, *Till Häst Genom Ryssland (Swedish)* – Denna reseskildring rymmer många ögonblicksbilder av möten med människor, från morgonbad med Lev Tolstoi till samtal med Tartarer och fotografering av fagra skördeflickor. Rikt illustrerad med foto och teckningar.

Leigh, Margaret, *My Kingdom for a Horse* – In the autumn of 1939 the author rode from Cornwall to Scotland, resulting in one of the most delightful equestrian journeys of the early twentieth century. This book is full of keen observations of a rural England that no longer exists.

Lester, Mary, *A Lady's Ride across Spanish Honduras in 1881* – This is a gem of a book, with a very entertaining account of Mary's vivid, day-to-day life in the saddle.

Maillart, Ella, *Turkestan Solo* – A vivid account of a 1930s journey through this wonderful, mysterious and dangerous portion of the world, complete with its Kirghiz eagle hunters, lurking Soviet secret police, and the timeless nomads that still inhabited the desolate steppes of Central Asia.

Marcy, Randolph, *The Prairie Traveler* – There were a lot of things you packed into your saddlebags or the wagon before setting off to cross the North American wilderness in the 1850s. A gun and an axe were obvious necessities. Yet many pioneers were just as adamant about placing a copy of Captain Randolph Marcy's classic book close at hand.

Marsden, Kate, *Riding through Siberia: A Mounted Medical Mission in 1891* - This immensely readable book is a mixture of adventure, extreme hardship and compassion as the author travels the Great Siberian Post Road.

Marsh, Hippisley Cunliffe, *A Ride Through Islam* – A British officer rides through Persia and Afghanistan to India in 1873. Full of adventures, and with observant remarks on the local Turkoman equestrian traditions.

MacCann, William, *Viaje a Caballo* – Spanish-language edition of the British author's equestrian journey around Argentina in 1848.

Meline, James, *Two Thousand Miles on Horseback: Kansas to Santa Fé in 1866* – A beautifully written, eye witness account of a United States that is no more.

Muir Watson, Sharon, *The Colour of Courage* – The remarkable true story of the epic horse trip made by the first people to travel Australia's then-unmarked Bicentennial National Trail. There are enough adventures here to satisfy even the most jaded reader.

Naysmith, Gordon, *The Will to Win* – This book recounts the only equestrian journey of its kind undertaken during the 20th century - a mounted trip stretching across 16 countries. Gordon Naysmith, a Scottish pentathlete and former military man, set out in 1970 to ride from the tip of the African continent to the 1972 Olympic Games in distant Germany.

O'Reilly, Basha, *Count Pompeii – Stallion of the Steppes* – the story of Basha's journey from Russia with her stallion, Count Pompeii, told for children. This is the first book in the *Little Long Rider* series.

O'Reilly, CuChullaine, (Editor) *The Horse Travel Handbook* – this accumulated knowledge of a million miles in the saddle tells you everything you need to know about travelling with your horse!

O'Reilly, CuChullaine, (Editor) *The Horse Travel Journal* – a unique book to take on your ride and record your experiences. Includes the world's first equestrian travel "pictionary" to help you in foreign countries.

O'Reilly, CuChullaine, *Khyber Knights* – Told with grit and realism by one of the world's foremost equestrian explorers, "Khyber Knights" has been penned the way lives are lived, not how books are written.

O'Reilly, CuChullaine, (Editor) *The Long Riders, Volume One* – The first of five unforgettable volumes of exhilarating travel tales.

Östrup, J, (*Swedish*), *Växlande Horisont* - The thrilling account of the author's journey to Central Asia from 1891 to 1893.

Patterson, George, *Gods and Guerrillas* – The true and gripping story of how the author went secretly into Tibet to film the Chinese invaders of his adopted country. Will make your heart pound with excitement!

Patterson, George, *Journey with Loshay: A Tibetan Odyssey* – This is an amazing book written by a truly remarkable man! Relying both on his companionship with God and on his own strength, he undertook a life few can have known, and a journey of emergency across the wildest parts of Tibet.

Pocock, Roger, *Following the Frontier* – Pocock was one of the nineteenth century's most influential equestrian travelers. Within the covers of this book is the detailed account of Pocock's horse ride along the infamous Outlaw Trail, a 3,000 mile solo journey that took the adventurer from Canada to Mexico City.

Pocock, Roger, *Horses* – Pocock set out to document the wisdom of the late 19th and early 20th Centuries into a book unique for its time. His concerns for attempting to preserve equestrian knowledge were based on cruel reality. More than 300,000 horses had been destroyed during the recent Boer War. Though Pocock enjoyed a reputation for dangerous living, his observations on horses were praised by the leading thinkers of his day.

Post, Charles Johnson, *Horse Packing* – Originally published in 1914, this book was an instant success, incorporating as it did the very essence of the science of packing horses and mules. It makes fascinating reading for students of the horse or history.

Ray, G. W., *Through Five Republics on Horseback* – In 1889 a British explorer - part-time missionary and full-time adventure junky – set out to find a lost tribe of sun-worshipping natives in the unexplored forests of Paraguay. The journey was so brutal that it defies belief.

Rink, Bjarke, *The Centaur Legacy* - This immensely entertaining and historically important book provides the first ever in-depth study into how man's partnership with his equine companion changed the course of history and accelerated human development.

Ross, Julian, *Travels in an Unknown Country* – A delightful book about modern horseback travel in an enchanting country, which once marked the eastern borders of the Roman Empire – Romania.

Ross, Martin and Somerville, E, *Beggars on Horseback* – The hilarious adventures of two aristocratic Irish cousins on an 1894 riding tour of Wales.

Ruxton, George, *Adventures in Mexico* – The story of a young British army officer who rode from Vera Cruz to Santa Fe, Mexico in 1847. At times the author exhibits a fearlessness which borders on insanity. He ignores dire warnings, rides through deadly deserts, and dares murderers to attack him. It is a delightful and invigorating tale of a time and place now long gone.

von Salzman, Erich, *Im Sattel durch Zentralasien* – The astonishing tale of the author's journey through China, Turkistan and back to his home in Germany – 6000 kilometres in 176 days!

Schwarz, Hans *(German), Vier Pferde, Ein Hund und Drei Soldaten* – In the early 1930s the author and his two companions rode through Liechtenstein, Austria, Romania, Albania, Yugoslavia, to Turkey, then rode back again!

Schwarz, Otto *(German), Reisen mit dem Pferd* – the Swiss Long Rider with more miles in the saddle than anyone else tells his wonderful story, and a long appendix tells the reader how to follow in his footsteps.

Scott, Robert, *Scott's Last Expedition* – Many people are unaware that Scott recruited Yakut ponies from Siberia for his doomed expedition to the South Pole in 1909. Here is the remarkable story of men and horses who all paid the ultimate sacrifice.

Skrede, Wilfred, *Across the Roof of the World* – This epic equestrian travel tale of a wartime journey across Russia, China, Turkestan and India is laced with unforgettable excitement.

Steele, Nick, *Take a Horse to the Wilderness* – Part history book, part adventure story, part equestrian travel textbook and all round great read, this is a timeless classic written by the foremost equestrian expert of his time, famed mounted game ranger Nick Steele.

Stevens, Thomas, *Through Russia on a Mustang* – Mounted on his faithful horse, Texas, Stevens crossed the Steppes in search of adventure. Cantering across the pages of this classic tale is a cast of nineteenth century Russian misfits, peasants, aristocrats—and even famed Cossack Long Rider Dmitri Peshkov.

Stevenson, Robert L., *Travels with a Donkey* – In 1878, the author set out to explore the remote Cevennes mountains of France. He travelled alone, unless you count his stubborn and manipulative pack-donkey, Modestine. This book is a true classic.

Strong, Anna Louise, *Road to the Grey Pamir* – With Stalin's encouragement, Strong rode into the seldom-seen Pamir mountains of faraway Tadjikistan. The political renegade turned equestrian explorer soon discovered more adventure than she had anticipated.

Sykes, Ella, *Through Persia on a Sidesaddle* – Ella Sykes rode side-saddle 2,000 miles across Persia, a country few European woman had ever visited. Mind you, she traveled in style, accompanied by her Swiss maid and 50 camels loaded with china, crystal, linens and fine wine.

Trinkler, Emile, *Through the Heart of Afghanistan* – In the early 1920s the author made a legendary trip across a country now recalled only in legends.

Tschiffely, Aimé, *Bohemia Junction* – "Forty years of adventurous living condensed into one book."

Tschiffely, Aimé, *Bridle Paths* – a final poetic look at a now-vanished Britain.

Tschiffely, Aimé, *Mancha y Gato Cuentan sus Aventuras* – The Spanish-language version of *The Tale of Two Horses* – the story of the author's famous journey as told by the horses.

Tschiffely, Aimé, *The Tale of Two Horses* – The story of Tschiffely's famous journey from Buenos Aires to Washington, DC, narrated by his two equine heroes, Mancha and Gato. Their unique point of view is guaranteed to delight children and adults alike.

Tschiffely, Aimé, *This Way Southward* – the most famous equestrian explorer of the twentieth century decides to make a perilous journey across the U-boat infested Atlantic.

Tschiffely, Aimé, *Tschiffely's Ride* – The true story of the most famous equestrian journey of the twentieth century – 10,000 miles with two Criollo geldings from Argentina to Washington, DC. A new edition is coming soon with a Foreword by his literary heir!

Tschiffely, Aimé, *Tschiffely's Ritt* – The German-language translation of *Tschiffely's Ride* – the most famous equestrian journey of its day.

Ure, John, *Cucumber Sandwiches in the Andes* – No-one who wasn't mad as a hatter would try to take a horse across the Andes by one of the highest passes between Chile and the Argentine. That was what John Ure was told on his way to the British Embassy in Santiago-so he set out to find a few certifiable kindred spirits. Fans of equestrian travel and of Latin America will be enchanted by this delightful book.

Warner, Charles Dudley, *On Horseback in Virginia* – A prolific author, and a great friend of Mark Twain, Warner made witty and perceptive contributions to the world of nineteenth century American literature. This book about the author's equestrian adventures is full of fascinating descriptions of nineteenth century America.

Weale, Magdalene, *Through the Highlands of Shropshire* – It was 1933 and Magdalene Weale was faced with a dilemma: how to best explore her beloved English countryside? By horse, of course! This enchanting book invokes a gentle, softer world inhabited by gracious country lairds, wise farmers, and jolly inn keepers.

Weeks, Edwin Lord, *Artist Explorer* – A young American artist and superb writer travels through Persia to India in 1892.

Wentworth Day, J., *Wartime Ride* – In 1939 the author decided the time was right for an extended horseback ride through England! While parts of his country were being ravaged by war, Wentworth Day discovered an inland oasis of mellow harvest fields, moated Tudor farmhouses, peaceful country halls, and fishing villages.

Von Westarp, Eberhard, *Unter Halbmond und Sonne* – (German) – Im Sattel durch die asiatische Türkei und Persien.

Wilkins, Messanie, *Last of the Saddle Tramps* – Told she had little time left to live, the author decided to ride from her native Maine to the Pacific. Accompanied by her faithful horse, Tarzan, Wilkins suffered through any number of obstacles, including blistering deserts and freezing snow storms – and defied the doctors by living for another 20 years!.

Wilson, Andrew, *The Abode of Snow* – One of the best accounts of overland equestrian travel ever written about the wild lands that lie between Tibet and Afghanistan.

de Windt, Harry, *A Ride to India* – Part science, all adventure, this book takes the reader for a thrilling canter across the Persian Empire of the 1890s.

Winthrop, Theodore, *Saddle and Canoe* – This book paints a vibrant picture of 1850s life in the Pacific Northwest and covers the author's travels along the Straits of Juan De Fuca, on Vancouver Island, across the Naches Pass, and on to The Dalles, in Oregon Territory. This is truly an historic travel account.

Younghusband, George, *Eighteen Hundred Miles on a Burmese Pony* – One of the funniest and most enchanting books about equestrian travel of the nineteenth century, featuring "Joe" the naughty Burmese pony!

We are constantly adding new titles to our collections, so please check our websites:

    www.horsetravelbooks.com and **www.classictravelbooks.com**

Printed in the United Kingdom
by Lightning Source UK Ltd.
117314UKS00001B/253-261